Lecture Notes in Computer Scie

T0238569

Commenced Publication in 1973
Founding and Former Series Editors:
Gerhard Goos, Juris Hartmanis, and Jan van Leeuwen

Anthony T.S. Ho   Yun Q. Shi   H.J. Kim
Mauro Barni (Eds.)

Digital Watermarking

8th International Workshop, IWDW 2009
Guildford, UK, August 24-26, 2009
Proceedings

 Springer

Volume Editors

Anthony T.S. Ho
University of Surrey
Faculty of Engineering and Physical Sciences
Department of Computing
Guildford, Surrey, GU2 7XH, UK
E-mail: a.ho@surrey.ac.uk

Yun Q. Shi
New Jersey Institute of Technology
University Heights, Newark, NJ, 07102-1982, USA
E-mail: shi@njit.edu

H.J. Kim
Korea University
Multimedia Security Lab
Science Campus, Seoul 136-701, Korea
E-mail: khj@korea.ac.kr

Mauro Barni
University of Siena
Department of Information Engineering
Via Roma 56, 53100 Siena, Italy
E-mail: barni@dii.unisi.it

Library of Congress Control Number: 2009932260

CR Subject Classification (1998): E.3, D.4.6, K.6.5, I.5.4, I.4.10, I.3

LNCS Sublibrary: SL 4 – Security and Cryptology

ISSN   0302-9743
ISBN-10   3-642-03687-2 Springer Berlin Heidelberg New York
ISBN-13   978-3-642-03687-3 Springer Berlin Heidelberg New York

springer.com

© Springer-Verlag Berlin Heidelberg 2009
Printed in Germany

Typesetting: Camera-ready by author, data conversion by Scientific Publishing Services, Chennai, India
Printed on acid-free paper   SPIN: 12736515   06/3180   5 4 3 2 1 0

Preface

The 8th International Workshop on Digital Watermarking (IWDW 2009) was hosted by the University of Surrey, Guildford, Surrey, UK, during August 24–26, 2009. As with previous workshops, IWDW 2009 aimed to provide a balanced program covering the latest state-of-the-art theoretical and practical developments in digital watermarking, steganography and steganalysis, and the emerging area of image forensics. The selection of the program was a challenging task for the Technical Programme Committee members and reviewers, who ensured the highest quality and reputation of the workshop.

From around 50 submissions received from authors in 14 countries, the committee selected 26 regular papers (22 oral and 4 poster presentations). In addition to the contributed papers, the workshop featured three keynote lectures on watermarking, cryptography and forensics kindly delivered by internationally renowned experts, Ingemar Cox, Fred Piper and Ed Delp, respectively. The regular papers and keynote lectures can be found in this proceedings volume.

First of all, we would like to thank all the authors, speakers, reviewers and participants for their significant contributions to the success of IWDW 2009. Our sincere gratitude goes to all the Technical Programme Committee, International Publicity Liaison and Local Committee Members for their enthusiasm, hard work and effort in the organization of this workshop. We greatly appreciate the generous support from all of our sponsors, particularly Korea Institute of Information Security and Cryptography (KIISC), MarkAny, DataMark Technologies, IET, Cyber Security KTN, and the University of Surrey. Finally, we hope that you will enjoy reading this volume and that it will provide inspiration and opportunities for your future research.

August 2009

Anthony T.S. Ho
Yun Q. Shi
H.J. Kim
Mauro Barni

Organization

IWDW 2009 was hosted by the University of Surrey and sponsored by Korea Institute of Information Security and Cryptography, MarkAny, DataMark Technologies, IET, and Cyber Security KTN.

General Chairs

Anthony T.S. Ho	University of Surrey, UK
Kwangjo Kim	Korea Institute of Information Security and Cryptology, Korea

Technical Programme Chairs

Yun-Qing Shi	New Jersey Institute of Technology, USA
Hyoung-Joong Shi	Korea University, Korea
Mauro Barni	University of Siena, Italy

Publicity Committee and Secretariat

Hans Georg Schaathun	University of Surrey, UK
Johann Briffa	University of Surrey, UK
Xi Zhao	University of Surrey, UK
Philip Bateman	University of Surrey, UK
Maggie Burton	University of Surrey, UK

Local Arrangements Committee

Helen Treharne	University of Surrey, UK

International Publicity Liasons

Chang-Tsun Li	Warwick University, UK
Andrew Ker	Oxford University, UK
Andreas Westfeld	University of Dresden, Germany
C.C. Chang	National Chung Cheng University, Taiwan
Alex Kot	Nanyang Technological University, Singapore
Nasir Memon	Polytechnic University, USA
Pierre Moulin	University of Illinois at Urbana-Champaign, USA

Technical Programme Committee

Charith Abhayaratne	University of Sheffield, UK
C. Barbier	DGA, France
Jeffrey Bloom	Thomson, USA
François Cayre	Institut Polytechnique de Grenoble, France
Wen Chen	Dialogic, USA
L.M. Cheng	City University of Hong Kong, China
Jana Dittman	University of Magdeburg, Germany
G. Doërr	University College London, UK
Jean-Luc Dugelay	Eurecom, France
Miroslav Goljan	State University of New York at Binghamton, USA
Byeungwoo Jeon	Sungkyunkwan University, Korea
Ton Kalker	HP, USA
Mohan Kankanhalli	National University of Singapore, Singapore
Andrew Ker	Oxford University, UK
Alex Kot	Nanyang Technological University, Singapore
C.C. Jay Kuo	University of Southern California, USA
Martin Kutter	AlpVision SA, Switzerland
Inald Lagendijk	Delft University of Technology, The Netherlands
Heung-Kyu Lee	Korea Advanced Institute of Science and Technology, Korea
C.T. Li	University of Warwick, UK
Zheming Lu	Sun Yat-sen University, China
K. Martin	Royal Holloway University of London, UK
Nasir Memon	Polytechnic University, USA
J. Sun Ni	Yat-sen University, China
Zhicheng Ni	LSI (formerly WorldGate Communications), USA
Jeng Shyang Pan	National Kaohsiung University of Applied Sciences
Fernando Perez-Gonzalez	University of Vigo, Spain
I. Pitas	University of Thessaloniki, Greece
A. Piva	University of Florence, Italy
Yong-Man Ro	Korea Advanced Institute of Science and Technology, Korea
Ahmad-Reza Sadeghi	University of Bochum, Germany
K. Sakurai	Kyushu University, Japan
Hans Georg Schaathun	University of Surrey, UK
Helen Treharne	University of Surrey, UK
Sviatoslav Voloshynovskiy	University of Geneva, Switzerland
Adrian Waller	Thales Research and Technology, UK

S. Wang   University of Shanghai, China
Shijun Xiang   Jinan University, China
Guorong Xuan   Tongji University, China
H. Zhang   Beijing University of Technology, China
Dekun Zou   Thomson, USA

Additional Reviewers

Chunhua Chen   Dialogic, USA
Chris Culnane   University of Surrey, UK
Bin Li   Sun Yet-sen University, China
Hongmei Liu   Sun Yet-sen University, China
Tian-Tsong Ng   I2R, Singapore
Vasiliy Sachnev   Korea University, Korea
Hao-Tian Wu   Eurecom, France
Weiqi Yan   Queen's University of Belfast, UK
Rui Yang   Sun Yet-sen University, China

Table of Contents

Session VI: Image Forensics and Authentication

Data Hiding and the Statistics of Images

Ingemar J. Cox

Department of Computer Science
University College London
Gower Street
London WC1E 6BT
UK

Abstract. The fields of digital watermarking, steganography and steganalysis, and content forensics are closely related. In all cases, there is a class of images that is considered "natural", i.e. images that do not contain watermarks, images that do not contain covert messages, or images that have not been tampered with. And, conversely, there is a class of images that is considered to be "unnatural", i.e. images that contain watermarks, images that contain covert messages, or images that have been tampered with.

Thus, at the simplest level, watermarking, steganalysis and content forensics reduce to a two-class classification problem. Specifically, the recognition of natural and unnatural images. A fundamental question is whether all natural images share some common statistical properties. And are these distinct from the statistical properties of unnatural images? These questions are key to understanding the limitations of data hiding technologies with respect to false alarm rates. In this paper we review work pertaining to these questions.

A.T.S. Ho et al. (Eds.): IWDW 2009, LNCS 5703, p. 1, 2009.
© Springer-Verlag Berlin Heidelberg 2009

The Changing Face of Cryptography

Fred Piper

Information Security Group
Royal Holloway, University of London,
Egham, Surrey, TW20 0EX, UK

Abstract. The last few decades have seen cryptography 'transform' from a black art - practised mainly by governments, the military and a few financial organisations - to a popular science that is widely taught as an academic subject and features in a number of popular novels and films.

At the same time, cryptographic services have become much more widely used and are now a central feature of many e-commerce and other business applications. In this talk we will look at how technological advances have led to improved algorithm design and how the concept of public key cryptography has dramatically increased the range of cryptographic services that are available.

A.T.S. Ho et al. (Eds.): IWDW 2009, LNCS 5703, p. 2, 2009.
© Springer-Verlag Berlin Heidelberg 2009

Forensic Techniques for Image Source Classification: A Comparative Study

Edward J. Delp

Purdue University
465 Northwestern Avenue, West Lafayette, IN 47907-2035, USA
ace@ecn.purdue.edu

Abstract. Digital images can be captured or generated by a variety of sources including digital cameras, scanners and computer graphics softwares. In many cases it is important to be able to determine the source of a digital image such as for criminal and forensic investigation. Based on their originating mechanism digital images can be classified into three classes: digital camera images, scanner generated images and computer-graphics generated images. Image source classification is helpful as a first step for identifying the unique device or system which produced the image. This paper presents a survey of different methods for solving image source classification problem, some improvements over them and compares their performance in a common framework. As expected with the advances in computer graphics techniques, artificial images are becoming closer and closer to the natural ones and harder to distinguish by human visual system. Hence, the methods based on characteristics of image generating process are more successful than those based on image content.

A.T.S. Ho et al. (Eds.): IWDW 2009, LNCS 5703, p. 3, 2009.
© Springer-Verlag Berlin Heidelberg 2009

Digital Watermarking Schemes Using Multi-resolution Curvelet and HVS Model

H.Y. Leung, L.M. Cheng, and L.L. Cheng

Department of Electronic Engineering, City University of Hong Kong,
Tat Chee Avenue, Kowloon, Hong Kong SAR
hyleung@cityu.edu.hk, itlcheng@cityu.edu.hk

Abstract. In this paper, a robust non-blind watermarking scheme based on Curvelet transform is proposed. This work extends the work proposed by Leung [1] to increase the quality of watermarked image. The proposed algorithm modifies the watermark extracting rule and adds a Human Visual System (HVS model). The experimental results demonstrate that the proposed algorithm can provide great robustness against most image processing methods.

Keywords: Watermarking; curvelet; HVS.

1 Introduction

Since the second half of the 1990's, digital data hiding has received increasing attention from the information technology community due to concerns about piracy of digital content [2-5]. Digital watermarking is a technology that embeds information, in machine-readable form, within the content of a digital media file. By extracting these secret messages, it can protect the copyright of and provide authentication to digital media.

A digital watermark should have two main properties, which are robustness and imperceptibility. Robustness means that the watermarked data can withstand different image processing attacks and imperceptibility means that the watermark should not introduce perceptible artifacts.

In the past two decades, many research papers are proposed to embed the watermark in different frequency domains. Recently, Candµes and Donoho [6] developed a new multiscale transform which is called the Curvelet transform. The transform can represent edges and other singularities along curves much more efficiently than traditional transforms. As stated in [7], Curvelet only uses $O(1/\sqrt{N})$ to represent an edge, while wavelet needs $O(1/N)$. It is proved that one can recover the object from noisy environment by simple Curvelet shrinkage better than other transform.

This work extends the watermarking method proposed by Leung [1] to increase the quality of watermarked image. Since the quality of watermarked image is not good enough, we consider adding a Human Visual System (HVS) to the original algorithm to provide better perceptibility of the watermarked image. Watermarking schemes combined with HVS have been receiving more and more attentions and many schemes related to HVS were proposed [8-12].

A.T.S. Ho et al. (Eds.): IWDW 2009, LNCS 5703, pp. 4–13, 2009.

Since the curvelet transform has the orientation parameter, it can naturally lead to add a human visual system easily. Several papers using HVS model based on the curvelet transform were also be proposed [13-14]. As curvelet Transform can decompose the image into several bands, we will make use of this property to embed the watermark within those bands.

The remainder paper is organized as follows: In section 2, we briefly introduce the Curvelet Transform. The HVS model is presented in section 3. The detail embedding and extracting approach are given in section 4. The experimental results are described in section 5. Finally, section 6 provides the conclusion.

2 Curvelet Transform

The curvelet transform is a multi-scale pyramid with many directions and positions at each length scale, and needle-shaped elements at fine scales. Its main idea is to compute the inner product between the signal and curvelet function to realize the sparse representation of the signal or function.

A curvelet coefficient $c(j,l,k)$ can be expressed as:

$$c(j,l,k) := \langle f, \varphi_{j,l,k} \rangle \tag{1}$$

where $j = 0, 1, 2, \ldots$ is a scale parameter; $l = 0, 1, 2, \ldots$ is an orientation parameter; and $k = (k_1, k_2), k_1, k_2 \in \mathfrak{I}$ is a translation parameter.

The $\varphi_j(x)$ is defined by mean of its Fourier transform $\varphi_j(w) = U_j(w)$, where U_j is frequency window defined in the polar coordinate system:

$$U_j(r,\theta) = 2^{-3j/4} W(2^{-j} r) V\left(\frac{2^{\lfloor j/2 \rfloor} \theta}{2\pi}\right) \tag{2}$$

W and V are radial and angular windows and will obey the admissibility conditions. Curvelet at scale 2^{-j}, orientation θ_l and position $x_k^{(j,l)} = R_{\theta_l}^{-1}(k_1 \cdot 2^{-j}, k_2 \cdot 2^{-j/2})$ can be expressed as:

$$\varphi_{j,l,k}(x) = \varphi(R_{\theta_l}(x - x_k^{(j,l)})) \tag{3}$$

where $\theta_l = 2\pi \cdot 2^{-\lfloor j/2 \rfloor} \cdot l$, with $l = 0, 1, \ldots$, $0 \le \theta_l < 2\pi$, R_{θ_l} is the rotation by θ_ℓ radians.

A curvelet coefficient is the inner product between an element $f \in L^2(R^2)$ and curvelet $\varphi_{j,l,k}$ is defined as:

$$c(j,l,k) := \frac{1}{(2\pi)^2} \int \hat{f}(w) U_j(R_{\theta_l} w) e^{i\langle x_k^{(j,l)}, w \rangle} dw \tag{4}$$

3 HVS Model Based on Curvelet Transform

It is well-known that the human eye is not equally sensitive to signals at all spatial frequencies and frequency orientations. Many psycho-visual models were built to determine the just noticeable difference thresholds. JND thresholds depend on the features of both the signal and the background pattern it is imposed on. To find out these thresholds, many psycho-visual measurements have been carried out using gratings [15]. In this paper, we choose the contrast sensitivity function proposed by Mannos and Sakrison [16] to estimate the JND threshold:

$$A(f_r) \approx 2.6 \, (0.0192 + 0.114 f_r) \exp(-(0.114 f_r)^{1.1}) \qquad (5)$$

where spatial frequency is $f_r = \sqrt{f_x^2 + f_y^2}$ (circle and degree), f_x and f_y are the horizontal frequency and vertical frequency, respectively. To normalize the CSF, we choose $f_r \, (circle/\deg) = f_N \, (circle/pixel) \cdot f_S \, (pixel/\deg)$, where the observed distance is $f_s = 65(pixel/\deg)$ and $f_N \in [0,1]$ is the normalized spatial frequency. By substituting the f_R in CSF, $A(f_R)$ can be calculated.

We modify the idea of [14] proposed by Xiao to develop the HVS model. First apply a **S** scale curvelet transform to a image **I**. and then divide the frequency axis to S + 1 intervals, $\{[0,1/2^s], [1/2^s, 1/2^{s-1}], \cdots, [1/2,1]\}$, and let w_s, s=0, 1 ... S denote the average of the value of normalized CSF in each interval, we get the frequency factor v :

$$v = \left\{ v_s \left| \frac{1}{\sqrt{w_s}}, \, s = 0,1,2,\cdots,S \right. \right\} \qquad (6)$$

Let an angular factor $\alpha(\theta)$ to approximate the theory in paper [17]:

$$\alpha(\theta) = \frac{c^{\frac{a_0}{\pi}(\theta - \frac{\pi}{4}(k + \mathrm{mod}(k,2)))}}{d} + a_0 \qquad (7)$$

where $k = \left\lfloor \frac{\theta}{\pi/4} \right\rfloor$, $0 \le \theta < 2\pi$, which θ stands for the angular direction and a_0, c and d are constants which are determined in the experiment.

Combine the above two factors, we define the HVS model as:

$$A(f_r) \approx 2.6 \, (0.0192 + 0.114 f_r) \exp(-(0.114 f_r)^{1.1}) \qquad (8)$$

4 Proposed Method

4.1 Watermark Embedding

The detailed watermark embedding steps are as follows:

1) Apply S scale curvelet transform to original image O, and obtain the coefficient matrices for different scale and orientation.
2) Add 7-4 Hamming code to the watermark sequence.

3) Repeat the code 11 times to form a new code to create the redundancy data.

4) Choose coefficients (absolute value closed to 1) which are between the specified ranges to embed watermark w.

5) For every selected coefficient C, compute $\xi(s,\theta)$ according to equation (8).

6) For a selected coefficient $C_{s,\theta}$ of scale s and orientation θ, coefficient modification is done as equation (9):

$$
\begin{aligned}
C'_{s,\theta} &= C_{s,\theta} \cdot \beta \cdot \xi(s,\theta) && if \quad w_i = 0 \ and \ C_{s,\theta} < 0 \\
C'_{s,\theta} &= -C_{s,\theta} \cdot \beta \cdot \xi(s,\theta) && if \quad w_i = 1 \ and \ C_{s,\theta} < 0 \\
C'_{s,\theta} &= -C_{s,\theta} \cdot \beta \cdot \xi(s,\theta) && if \quad w_i = 0 \ and \ C_{s,\theta} > 0 \\
C'_{s,\theta} &= C_{s,\theta} \cdot \beta \cdot \xi(s,\theta) && if \quad w_i = 1 \ and \ C_{s,\theta} > 0
\end{aligned}
\tag{9}
$$

where $\xi(s,\theta)$ denotes the HVS model parameter, $C_{s,\theta}$ denotes the selected coefficient, $C'_{s,\theta}$ denotes the modified coefficient, β denotes the embedding strength and w_i denotes the watermark bit

7) Apply the inverse curvelet transform to the modified coefficients matrices and form a watermarked image

4.2 Watermark Extracting

The detailed extracting processes are as follows:

1) Apply the curvelet transform to the original image O and the watermarked image I.

2) Compare the coefficients within the chosen embedded range and locate the watermark positions from original image.

3) Retrieve the watermark bits w_i with the following rule.

$$
w_i = \begin{cases} 1, & if \ O_{s,\theta}(i,j) \le I_{s,\theta}(i,j) \\ 0, & if \ O_{s,\theta}(i,j) > I_{s,\theta}(i,j) \end{cases}
\tag{10}
$$

4) Decode the watermark's data bits from w_i Hamming code.

5) Divide the watermarked bits into eleven individual codes and compare the number of bit 1 and bit 0 at the same position to recover the correct watermark bits.

5 Experimental Results

In this section, experimental result is provided. We used Lena image for the experiment. The host image size is 512×512 and the binary watermark size is 16×16. Peak signal-to-noise ratio (PSNR) and normalized correlation (NC) are employed to evaluate the watermarked image quality and robustness of the algorithms. For an $M_I \times N_I$ image, the peak signal to noise ratio and normalized correlation are defined as follows:

$$PSNR = 10\log[M_I N_I \frac{\max(I^2(m,n))}{\sum_m^{M_I}\sum_n^{N_I}(I(m,n)-I'(m,n))^2}] \tag{11}$$

$$NC = \frac{\sum_m^{M_W}\sum_n^{N_W}W(m,n)\cdot W'(m,n)}{\sqrt{\sum_m^{M_W}\sum_n^{N_W}[W(m,n)]^2}\sqrt{\sum_m^{M_W}\sum_n^{N_W}[W'(m,n)]^2}} \tag{12}$$

where M_W, N_W denote the dimensions of the watermarked image and I , I' denote the original and the watermarked images, W and W' denote the watermark and recovered watermark respectively.

The watermarked image, whose PSNR is 48dB, and the embedded watermark are shown in Figure 1(b) and 1 (c) respectively.

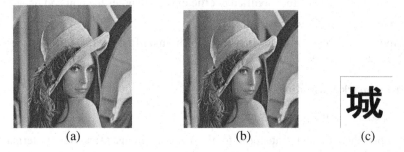

(a)   (b)   (c)

Fig. 1. (a) Original Image, (b) Watermarked Image, (c) Watermark

5.1 PSNR-Comparison of Two Schemes

We compute the PSNR values of different images for the proposed method with HVS model and the original scheme [1] to evaluate the quality of watermarked image. The results are shown as follows.

Table 1. PSNR values of our original scheme without HVS model

Images	Aerial	Frog	Lena	Sailboat	Goldhill	Pepper	Baboon
Scale-4 band	42.92	42.78	42.86	42.85	42.87	42.71	42.84
Scale-5 band	48.07	48.13	48.07	48.06	48.08	48.11	48.09
Scale-6 band	47.63	47.57	47.62	47.58	47.59	47.52	47.55

From tables 1 and 2, we can find that both schemes achieve high PSNR values. The PSNR of different images in table 2 is relatively higher than table 1. It means that when our HVS model is used, the PSNR of the watermarked image is higher.

Table 2. PSNR values of our proposed scheme

Images	Aerial	Frog	Lena	Sailboat	Goldhill	Pepper	Baboon
Scale-4 band	48.13	48.05	48.11	48.11	48.13	47.97	48.07
Scale-5 band	51.76	51.80	51.78	51.77	51.78	51.82	51.76
Scale-6 band	48.47	48.37	48.44	48.41	48.43	48.37	48.36

5.2 Robustness Tests

Since we decompose the original image into six bands using the curvelet transform, we choose fourth, fifth scale band and sixth scale band to carry out robustness tests individually. We perform several image processing attacks such as Gaussian low pass filtering, Gaussian additive noise, Laplacian image enhancement, JPEG compression, Salt and Pepper noise and use normalized correlation to evaluate the results. The simulation results are shown as following tables.

Table 3. NC value of our proposed scheme under Gaussian Noises attack

Standard Variance of Gaussian Noises	6	8	10	12	14	16	18	20	25	30
Scale-4 band	0.98	0.96	0.89	0.85	0.78	0.78	0.79	0.73	0.70	0.67
Scale-5 band	0.94	0.81	0.74	0.69	0.70	0.74	0.64	0.69	0.63	0.61
Scale-6 band	1.00	0.99	0.94	0.93	0.89	0.87	0.81	0.82	0.74	0.70

Table 4. NC value of our proposed scheme under Salt & Pepper noises

Density parameter	0.01	0.02	0.03	0.04	0.05	0.06	0.07	0.08	0.09	0.1
Scale-4 band	0.72	0.70	0.66	0.57	0.64	0.61	0.62	0.62	0.62	0.52
Scale-5 band	0.62	0.53	0.63	0.61	0.62	0.56	0.58	0.50	0.58	0.60
Scale-6 band	0.83	0.73	0.71	0.67	0.65	0.61	0.61	0.59	0.60	0.57

Table 5. NC value of our proposed scheme under Gaussian low pass filtering

Standard Variance(Window)	0.5(3)	1.5(3)	0.5(5)	1.5(5)	3(5)
Scale-4 band	1.00	1.00	1.00	0.99	0.97
Scale-5 band	1.00	0.96	1.00	0.61	0.50
Scale-6 band	1.00	0.49	1.00	0.49	0.49

It can be seen from table 3 that sixth scale band is more robust than the other two bands for the Gaussian Noises Attack. Most NC values of sixth scale band are nearly 0.8 to 1. For the Salt and Pepper noises, sixth scale band still performs better than other two bands as shown in table 4 because the mean of NC values of sixth scale band is larger than other two rows. However, table 5 shows that sixth scale band is poor to resist the Gaussian low pass filtering, while the fourth band is the best to resist as its NC values are much closed to 1. As shown in table 6, three bands can resist well under Laplacian filtering attacks, whose NC values are all near to 1. Under JPEG compression, the fourth scale band has better robustness, while the sixth scale band cannot withstand JPEG compression attack totally. According to the table 7, the NC values of sixth scale band are much lower than that of fourth and fifth scale bands.

Table 6. NC value of our proposed scheme under Laplacian sharpening

Laplacian parameter	0.01	0.02	0.03	0.04	0.05	0.06	0.07	0.08	0.09	0.1
Scale-4 band	1.00	1.00	0.99	1.00	1.00	1.00	1.00	1.00	0.99	0.99
Scale-5 band	1.00	1.00	1.00	1.00	1.00	1.00	1.00	1.00	1.00	1.00
Scale-6 band	1.00	1.00	1.00	1.00	1.00	1.00	1.00	1.00	1.00	1.00

Table 7. NC value of our proposed scheme under JPEG compression

Jpeg factor	100	80	60	45	40	30	25	20	15	5
Scale-4 band	1.00	1.00	0.99	0.98	0.90	0.94	0.80	0.75	0.65	0.56
Scale-5 band	1.00	0.84	0.73	0.60	0.62	0.81	0.54	0.56	0.61	0.58
Scale-6 band	0.61	0.53	0.54	0.53	0.54	0.59	0.50	0.50	0.50	0.48

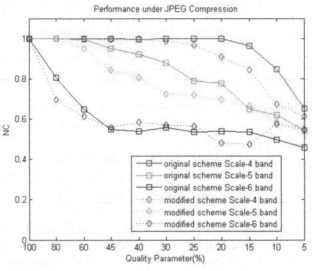

Fig. 2. NC values of two schemes under JPEG compression

5.3 NC-Values Comparison of Two Schemes

To compare the robustness of our proposed method with HVS model and the original scheme, we tested the robustness against standard noise attacks for both schemes i.e. JPEG compression, Salt and Pepper noises and Gaussian noises. Figures 2, 3 and 4 show that the NC values of our proposed method with HVS model are not as good as the original scheme under the JPEG compression, Salt and Pepper noises and Gaussian noises.

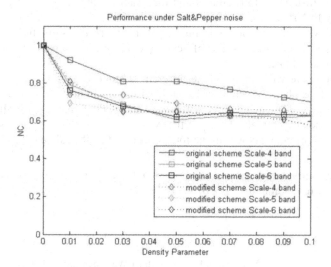

Fig. 3. NC values of two schemes under Salt and Pepper noises

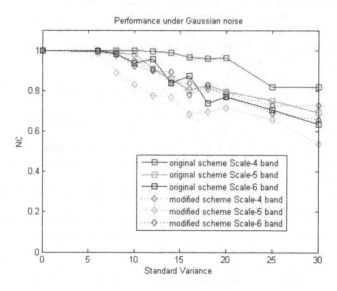

Fig. 4. NC values of two schemes under Gaussian noises

6 Conclusions

Our proposed method is the improved algorithm of paper [1]. In order to enhance the watermarked image quality of original algorithm, human visual system is added to the original algorithm to form the proposed method. In this paper, we have provided an intensive study on the robustness of watermarking using curvelet transform and HVS model based on various scale bands. Experimental results show that our proposed method can withstand various attacks and the watermarked image is of good quality by measuring PSNR values.

Compared with the original algorithm, experimental results show that the proposed method gives a watermarked image of better quality, but its robustness is not comparable to the original one.

In the future, we will employ three different strategies to study the robustness of watermark: (1) Embed the same watermark within the fourth, fifth and sixth scale band respectively, (2) Embed three different watermark within the fourth, fifth and sixth scale band respectively, (3) Split the watermark into three segments, and then embed these three segments within the fourth, fifth and sixth scale band respectively.

Acknowledgments. This work was supported by City University of Hong Kong Strategic Research Grant No. 7002018 and Applied Research Grant No. 9668006.

References

1. Leung, H.Y., Cheng, L.M., Cheng, L.L.: A Robust Watermarking Scheme using Selective Curvelet Coefficients. In: 2008 International Conference on Intelligent Information Hiding and Multimedia Signal Processing, Harbin, China, pp. 465–468 (2008)
2. Lutz, R.: Software Engineering for Safety: A Roadmap, in The Future of Software Engineering. In: Finkelstein, A. (ed.) ICSE 2000, pp. 213–224. ACM Press, New York (2000)
3. Sindre, G., Opdahl, A.L.: Eliciting security requirements by misuse cases. In: Proc. 37th Technology of Object-Oriented Languages and Systems (TOOLS-37 Pacific 2000), Sydney, Australia, pp. 120–131 (2000)
4. Hermann, D.S.: Software Safety and Reliability: Techniques, Approaches, and Standards of Key Industrial Sectors. Wiley-IEEE Computer Society Press (2000)
5. Fenton, N.E., Neil, M.: A strategy for improving safety related software engineering standards. IEEE Trans on Software Eng. 24, 1002–1013 (1998)
6. Candes, E.J., Donoho, D.L.: New tight frames of curvelets and optimal repesentations of objects with C2 singularities. Communications on Pure and Applied Mathematics 57, 219–266 (2004)
7. Candes, E.J., Donoho, D.L.: Fast Discrete Curvelet Transform. Applied and Computational Mathmatics, California Institute of Technology, 1–43 (2005)
8. He, K.-f., Gao, J., Hu, L.-m., Gao, H.-y.: Watermarking for images using the HVS and SVD in the wavelet domain. In: Proceedings of the 2006 IEEE International Conference on Mechatronics and Automation, pp. 2352–2356 (2006)
9. Maity, S.P., Kundu, M.K.: An ImageWatermarking Scheme using HVS Characteristics and Spread Transform. In: Proceedings of the 17th International Conference on Pattern Recognition, vol. 4, pp. 869–871 (2004)

10. Delaigle, J.F., Vleeschouwer, C.D., Macq, B.: Watermarking Algorithm Based on A Human Visual Model. Signal Processing 66, 319–335 (1998)
11. Podilchuk, C.I., Zeng, W.: Image-adaptive watermarking using visual models. IEEE Journal on Selected Areas in Communications 16, 525–538 (1998)
12. Hannigan, B.T., Reed, A., Bradley, B.: Digital Watermarking Using Improved Human Visual System Model. In: Proc. SPIE Electronic Image, Security and Watermarking of Multimedia Content, San Jose, CA, vol. 4314, pp. 468–474 (2001)
13. Taoa, P., Dexterb, S., Eskiciogluc, A.M.: Robust Digital Image Watermarking in Curvelet Domain. In: Proceedings of the SPIE, vol. 6819, pp. 68191B–68191B-12 (2008)
14. Xiao, Y., Cheng, L.M., Cheng, L.L.: A Robust Image Watermarking Scheme Based on A Novel HVS Model in Curvelet Domain. In: 2008 International Conference on Intelligent Information Hiding and Multimedia Signal Processing, Harbin, China, pp. 343–346 (2008)
15. Cornsweet, T.N.: Visual Perception, ch. 12, pp. 311–364. Academic press, London (1970)
16. Mannos, J.L., Sarkrison, D.J.: The Effects of a Visual Fidelity Criterion on the Encoding of Images. IEEE Transactions on Information Theory 20, 525–536 (1974)
17. Campbell, F.W., Kulikowski, J.J., Levinson, J.: Orientational Selectivity of The Human Visual System. The Journal of Physiology 187, 437–445 (1966)

Semi-blind Fingerprinting Utilizing Ordinary Existing Watermarking Techniques

Mitsuo Okada[1], Yasuo Okabe[2], and Tetsutaro Uehara[2]

[1] Graduate School of Informatics, Kyoto University
mitsuookada@net.ist.i.kyoto-u.ac.jp
[2] Academic Center for Computing and Media Studies, Kyoto University, Kyoto, Japan
{okabe,uehara}@media.kyoto-u.ac.jp

Abstract. We propose a concept of feasible blind fingerprinting called "semi-blind fingerprinting" which provides as secure content trading as conventional blind fingerprinting methods. In a basic model of conventional fingerprinting for content trading, user's security could be guaranteed only under the premise that a content provider is trustworthy. Such premise makes a scheme unpractical. To overcome this defect, various blind methods have been proposed in which cryptography is used in order to protect the information on a user. However, computation cost and robustness have not been well considered as a scheme should be feasible, though it provides high-level of protection. A semi-blind scheme fulfills a need for both feasibility and robustness. Under this scheme, feasibility can be achieved by applying newly proposed functions called "Image Division" instead of using cryptography. In order to gain robustness, a protocol for watermarking has been so designed that any well-developed existing watermarking technique can be applied with no restriction. We will not only propose the idea but also implement and evaluate several image division functions as well as an optimized embedding program in order to prove validity of the proposed method.

1 Introduction

We propose an idea of feasible blind fingerprinting called "semi-blind fingerprinting" which provides as secure content trading as conventional blind fingerprinting methods within feasible processing cost and sufficient robustness. We also present some implementation and evaluation results to show a validity of our concept. Before we get into the technical detail, we describe the background. Demand for a protection of intellectual property of digital content is increasing due to severe crime augmentation accompanying rapid development of information technology and its infrastructure. As a result, an enormous number of digital content might have been pirated for illegal use.

Digital fingerprinting [1] that uses watermarking technique is one of the technical approaches to protect one's intellectual property. In this scheme, a content provider (CP) embeds a purchaser ID into digital content before giving an image to a purchaser (user). When CP found a pirated image, extracts ID to identify an illegal user who illegally redistributes an image. However, this model only works under the assumption that CP is trustworthy. In other words, inappropriate trading might be easily carried out if CP is malicious since CP possesses an embedded image and user information.

A.T.S. Ho et al. (Eds.): IWDW 2009, LNCS 5703, pp. 14–28, 2009.

Conventional blind fingerprinting methods [2,3,4,5,6,7,8,9] have been proposed as a countermeasure to resolved the above defect. In general, blind methods use encryption to protect such information as user name, purchasing record, and so on. Therefore, a user can obtain an image without revealing the information. However, computation cost and sufficient robustness have been sacrificed for the high-level of security.

To overcome the defect of conventional blind fingerprinting techniques, we propose a semi-blind method that possesses blind properties at low processing cost with sufficient robustness. A semi-blind method allows replacing an encryption with proposed functions called "Image Division", and interposition of a trusted third party (TTP) for user verification and watermark embedding. Robustness is gained by designing a protocol for watermark that well-developed existing watermark technique can be applied with no restriction. The procedure is described below. Assume a user wants to purchase an image from CP. First, CP divides an image into two unrecognizable images, and then sends them to a user and TTP by different route. Second, TTP embeds a pseudonymous user ID issued by TTP into a received image, and then sends it to a user. Finally, user combines those images to obtain an embedded image.

A scheme provides following achievement; CP doesn't know who a user is, TTP has no clue as to what kind of image has been traded, and a user can obtain an image without revealing information to CP and TTP. CP can certainly identify an illegal user in cooperation with TTP when a pirated image has been found even though user information is not available to CP.

In section 2, we describe preliminaries including conventional and related techniques. In section 3, we describe a proposed concept. In section 4, we describe implementation. In section 5, we show evaluation results. In section 6, we conclude this paper.

2 Preliminaries

2.1 Basic Model of Fingerprinting

A fingerprinting method [1] based on a watermarking technique is one of the approaches to protect digital content from illegal use. In this scheme, as illustrated in Fig. 1, CP (Provider) embeds a unique user ID into an image. When a pirated image has been found, CP extracts ID to identify an illegal user (Purchaser). However, this model is valid only if CP is perfectly trusted. Otherwise, inappropriate trading can be easily carried out by CP since CP manages an embedded image and user information used at a verification process. Despite the fact that a pirated image has been found, it is not able to distinguish which party (CP or a user) is pirating an image since both CP and a user possess the same embedded image. Another problem is that malicious or untrustworthy CP may expose user's private information such as user name, purchasing record, and detail of purchased image.

2.2 Conventional Blind Fingerprinting

Various blind fingerprinting techniques [2,3,4] have been proposed to solve the problems of conventional methods. Each of their schemes varies in detail, but a basic idea of blind methods is applying encryption to protect information regarding to a user as illustrated in Fig. 2.

Assume, a user prepares a pair of public and secret keys. First, a user (Purchaser) encrypts user ID by the public key, and then sends an encrypted ID and the public key to CP. Second, CP (Provider) encrypts an original image using the public key and then embeds an encrypted ID into the encrypted image without any decryption. CP sends the image to a user. Third, user decrypts the encrypted embedded image by the secret key.

We focused on problems that most of them are somehow infeasible due to heavy processing cost and lack of robustness. We briefly overview conventional blind methods of which a list is summarized in Table.1.

Fig. 1. Basic Model of Fingerprinting   **Fig. 2.** Basic Model of Blind Fingerprinting

Blind Method Using Bit-Commitment. A bit-commitment technique is used in [2,3] for watermark extraction. However, computation and communication cost increases in proportion to a size of an image that makes a protocol inefficient. Moreover it is indicated in [10] that robustness is not sufficiently provided because XOR operation used for embedding can be easily removed by compression.

A Blind Method Using El Gamal and Paillier Encryption. Some asymmetric watermarking methods [7,8,9] are proposed that use a homomorphic public key encryption. In [7,8], information of modified pixels in I is encrypted. Watermark is extracted without decrypting an image so that extractor has no clue as to how or where watermark is embedded. However, the size of ciphertext, an extraction key increases in proportion to the size of an image.

Hence, embedding and extraction involving an encryption make a protocol infeasible. According to [7,8], if we apply 1024 bits El Gamal encryption to *Lenna* ($z = 256 \times 256$ pixels), ciphertext (extraction key) will be $2048 \times z$ bits. Note that two chipertexts are generated for El Gamal. Embedding time is approximately $0.1 \times z$ seconds where a single bit encryption is 0.1 seconds. Another example in [9] uses Paillier encryption. Assuming 1024 bits Paillier encryption is applied, the size of ciphertext will be $1024 \times z$ bits and encryption time will be approximately $3.3 \times z$ seconds. In addition to infeasible processing cost, watermark robustness is also sacrificed since applicability of embedding algorithms as well as embedding capability is very restricted due to encryption of property.

A Blind Method Using Okamoto-Uchiyama Encryption. An asymmetric watermark method [5,6] using Okamoto-Uchiyama encryption has been proposed. Message is embedded by modifying pixels using Quantization Index Modulation (QIM) and Okamoto-Uchiyama encryption in [5]. Encryption is carried out as follows.

Table 1. A List of Conventional Blind Fingerprinting

Methods	Technical Elements for Blinding
[2,3]	Bit-Commitment
[7,8]	El Gamal Encryption
[9]	Paillier Encryption
[5]	Okamoto-Uchiyama Encryption

Assume a pair of public key pk and secret key sk are provided by a user. For embedding, CP encrypts message ω and an original image I using pk, and then embeds an encrypted message without decrypting as $E_{pk}(I') = E_{pk}(I) \oplus E_{pk}(\omega)$ where $\oplus$ is an additive homomorphic calculation for embedding and $E(\cdot), D(\cdot)$ is homomorphic encryption and decryption respectively. A user obtains an embedded image I' by decrypting using sk as $I' = D_{sk}(E_{pk}(I'))$. A scheme in [6] has been developed based on the one in [5] that applies DC-QIM and RDM to emphasize watermark robustness. However, overhead in computation cost still needs to be considered.

3 A Concept of Semi-blind Method

Semi-Blind fingerprinting is an alternative method to conventional blind methods in consideration of feasible processing cost and robustness.

We have achieved by means of overcoming the defect of most conventional blind methods as well as satisfying requirements of blind methods, that is, providing secure image trading to both a user and CP by allowing an interposition of TTP for embedding and user verification. The detail is described below and illustrated in Fig. 3. Assume, a persuadenimous user ID is issued by TTP, and then a user is verified,

1. CP divides an image into two unrecognizable images, and then sends them to a user and TTP,
2. TTP embeds a pseudonymous user ID into an unrecognizable image by using a well-developed existing watermark algorithm,
3. a user restores divided images by putting them together to obtain an embedded image.

Following advantages are accrued by a secure image trading scheme,

– CP has no clue as to who a user is, because of a pseudonymous user ID,
– an illegal user is distinguishable either CP or a user since only a user has a complete embedded image,
– TTP has no clue what kind of image has been traded because of unrecognizable property of a received image,
– a user can obtain an image without exposing private information.

3.1 Problem Definition of Conventional Blind Methods

We focused on two infeasibility problems possessed by most conventional blind fingerprinting; that is, high computation cost of encryption and inadequate robustness due to embedding restriction. Embedding is restricted due to encryption properties that a watermark algorithm needs to satisfy several conditions under which a hybridization with encryption is made possible. Moreover, embedding capability tends to be decreased. The detail of encryption will not be discussed in this paper.

3.2   A Concept of a Proposed Method

Our goal is to provide a feasible blind fingerprinting scheme, "Semi-Blind Fingerprinting" with implementation and evaluation results. Unlike conventional blind methods, a proposed method allows utilizing any well-developed existing watermarking that allows inheriting robustness of existing watermarking techniques without restriction caused by encryption properties.

3.3   A Privacy-Secure Image Trading Scheme Based on a Semi-blind Method

We begin with describing a big picture of our scheme which is handled by three entities; Alice (a user), Bob (CP), and Catharine (TTP), a trusted third party for account of privacy protection of Alice. Assume core technique based on a proposed concept is adapted to a digital image trading scheme which provides Alice to trade an image without revealing privacy information to the opposite parties. The scheme is described below and illustrated in Fig. 4 which mainly composed of two phases, user verification and embedding.

Assume Alice purchases an image from Bob, but she doesn't want to expose her information to both Bob and Catharine.

A User Verification Scheme.   In prior to image trading, Alice completes user registration to obtain a verification ticket TID from Catharine. Next, Alice requests an image to Bob by using TID used as a pseudonymous user ID. Bob verifies TID in cooperation with Catharine. At this point, Catharine possesses a user name and a pseudonymous ID, whereas Bob only has a pseudonymous ID.

An Fingerprint Embedding Scheme.   We describe an embedding phase that contains mainly three steps carried out by Bob, Catharine, and Alice respectively corresponding to; offering an image, embedding message, and obtaining an embedded image.

1. The first step is carried out by Bob. Assume Alice is verified by Bob in cooperation with Catharine by verifying validity of TID. Bob puts an image I into an image dividing function $ImDiv(\cdot)$ to obtain two unrecognizable images as $(I_1, I_2) = ImDiv(I)$ which are sent to Alice and Catharine respectively. At this point, Bob has no information about Alice besides a pseudonymous user ID that implies one of the blindness properties.
2. The second step is carried out by Catharine who possesses a user name, TID, and I_2. Catharine embeds message $\omega = TID$ into I_2 by embedding function $Emb(\cdot)$ as $I_2' = I_2 \oplus \omega = Emb(I_2)$ where $\oplus$ represents embedding. I_2' is sent to Alice. Since I_2 should be unrecognizable to Catharine, she has no clue as to what kind of image Alice obtains which is another blindness property.
3. The final step is carried out by Alice who combines (I_1, I_2') to obtain an embedded image by an image restoring function as $I' = I_1 + I_2' = ImRst(I_1, I_2')$.

Fig. 3. Semi-Blind Fingerprinting

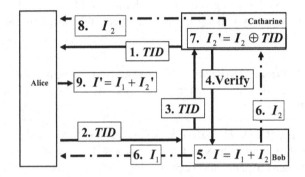

Fig. 4. A Protocol for an Example Scenario

Table 2. Properties of Entities

Entities	Properties	Unknown Information
Alice	user name, TID, I', I_1, I_2'	I, I_2
Bob	TID, I, I_1, I_2	user name, I_2', I'
Catharine	user name, TID, I_2, I_2'	I_1, I, I'

An Fingerprint Extraction Scheme. An extraction may be carried out by another third party regarding to Bob that enables identify an illegal user. For example, a web-crawler managed by Bob observes the website to find pirated images. When a pirated piece has been found, a crawler extracts an ID. A crawler asks Catharine to disclose user information to identify an illegal user.

4 Implementation

In this section, we describe our implementation results to examine various image dividing functions and a customized embedding program ($FQemb$).

4.1 A Naive Dividing Method

We briefly review [11,12] that shows several types of image dividing methods. An objective of these schemes is protecting privacy information of recorded subjects in an image. For example, Alice wants to purchase an image of private party last week from Bob, but she does not want to expose privacy information in purchased images since Bob may be able to profile Alice by gathering information of a user name, other recorded subjects, where she was, her friends appear in the image, and so on.

We have resolved this issue by adopting a proposed concept that results in enhancing privacy protection as indicated by following facts. Bob does not know who a purchaser is, and Catharine can hardly guess what she is purchasing. As a result, Alice can obtain an image without revealing privacy information. Hence, two important issues are the one not to give her user name to Bob by using a pseudonymous user ID and another not to give much clue to guess image detail to Catharine. In [11,12], we have pursued an unrecognizable property by making I_2 into unrecognizable image by various kinds of dividing methods as shown below.

Technical Detail of Image Divisions. We introduce some of the dividing methods from [11,12]. Following dividing functions are used as combination toward better unrecognizability.

Block Noise Division BND. $BND(\cdot)$ makes I into two random noise layers as $BND(I)$ and $\overline{BND}(I)$ as shown in Fig. 5. Note that noise is added by $n \times n$ blocks ($n = 4$ in this case). The two images are generated by computing random numbers as $BND(I) = rnd$ by a pseudo random number generator for the number of blocks in I and $\overline{BND}(I) = I - BND(I)$. Restoring process can be done by summing up the images as $I = BND(I) + \overline{BND}(I)$.

rnd is generated within a range given in Table 3, since random image should have maintained at least some detail of an image such as edge information for the sake of embedding room of watermark. Otherwise, watermark does not survive throughout a restoration process if a random image is completely random. rnd generator divides brightness of I into $lv = 4$ levels as shown in Table 3. Increment of lv indicates more image detail remains at higher recognizability that is able to preserve much room for watermark, whereas decrement indicates increasing unrecognizability at sacrifice of watermark strength.

Block Check Division BC. $BC(\cdot)$ divides I into two $M \times M$ block check images (M=64 in Fig 5), $BC(I)$ and $\overline{BC}(I)$. Restoring process is carried out by combining them as $I = BC(I) + \overline{BC}(I)$.

Combination of Face Clipping Division FC and BND. $FC(\cdot)$ divides I into a face part, $FC(I)$ and background part, $\overline{FC}(I)$ using face detection of OpenCV. This is developed by following two concepts that are protecting recorded subjects in an image and enhancing unrecognizability of an image by masking human face (or eyes).

$FC + BND$ is shown in Fig. 6. Watermark is successfully extracted from a restored image. We have applied this combination to a test image as shown in Fig. 7. In this test, face detection failed to detect a face in the image since it was too small to detect. However, a human face and license number, considered as privacy information, is well blinded. As a result, we found that block noise blinds up small faces even though face detection failed.

Table 3. A Range of Random Generation for 256 Brightness Levels

lv	Brightness of I	Range of rnd
1	255,…,192	192,…,128
2	191,…,128	127,…,64
3	127,…,64	63,…,0
4	63,…,0	0

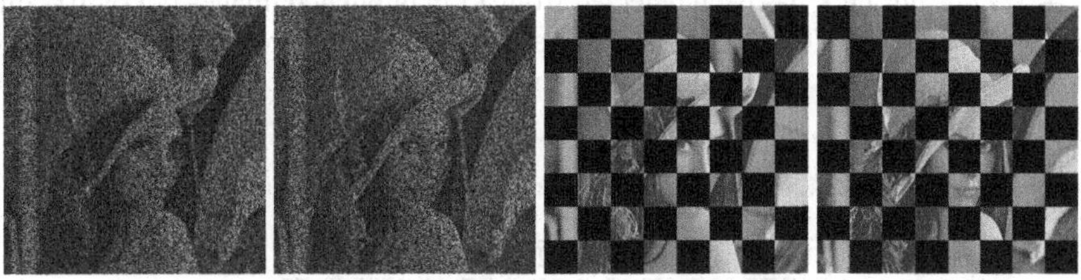

   $BND(I)$ $\overline{BND(I)}$ $BC(I)$ $\overline{BC(I)}$

Fig. 5. Block Noise Division (BND) and Block Check Division (BC)

Fig. 6. $FC + BND$ for *Lenna*

Fig. 7. An Original Image and ($FC + BND$) applied image

Robustness Evaluation Results. We show the robustness evaluation of combinations of various image division and Digimarc, a Plug-in of Adobe Photoshop CS2 which should have broad robustness against various types of manipulations. Robustness evaluation results are shown in Table 4 for the case of ND, FC, and $FC + ND$. Note that *NONE* denotes no division has been applied. In other words, *NONE* indicates radical strength of Digimarc. In this case, 108 total attacks (manipulations) at 15 different manipulations with several levels is applied by Stirmark[13].

Manipulations are; Affine transform, Conversion filter, Cropping, JPEG compression, Latest small random distortion, Median cut, Adding noise, Rescale, Remove lines, Rotation, Small random distortions, Rotation, Rotation cropping, Rotation scale, and Self similarities. For instance of JPEG compression, several compression levels from $10, 20, \ldots, 90\%$ is applied. For more detail about Stirmark, refer [13]. For a case of $FC + ND$, watermark has been detected from 73 manipulated images out of 108 images. It indicates that $FC + ND$ possesses approximately 84% of robustness compare to *None* where $100\% = 87$ images.

Table 4. Robustness of Dividing Functions with Digimarc

Division + Embedding Tool	Succeeded Cases
None+Digimarc	87/108
ND+Digimarc	74/108
BC+Digimarc	47/108
$FC + ND$ +Digimarc	73/108

4.2 Frequency Division and an Optimized Embedding Method

In this section, we describe new dividing and embedding functions with implementation results. A frequency division function, $FQ(\cdot)$ divides an image by frequency components. An optimized embedding program (*FQemb*) embeds watermark in frequency domain as described below.

Example Scenario for a Semi-Blind Method. Before we getting into detail, we describe an example scenario based on a semi-blind method. A protocol consists of mainly three phases; generating two non-recognizable images by Bob, embedding by Catharine, and restoring images to generate an embedded image by Alice. Assume Alice has been verified and purchasing an image *Lenna*.

1. Bob makes I into (I_1, I_2) by $FC + FQ$ and then sends I_1 to Alice and I_2 to Catharine.
2. Catharine embeds message by $I_2' = FQemb(I_2)$ and then sends it to Alice.
3. Alice combines images as $I' = (I_1 + I_2') = ImRst(I_1, I_2')$ to obtain an embedded image as shown in Fig. 9.

Technical Detail

Image Dividing by $FC + FQ$. The first step is carried out by Bob by dividing I into a face I_F and background I_B parts using $FC(\cdot)$ as $(I_F, I_B) = FC(I)$, and then divides I_B into $I_{B1} = FQ(I_B)$ and $I_{B2} = I_B - I_{B1}$ using $FQ(\cdot)$.

FQ divides I_B into $M \times M, M = 8$ blocks, and then extracts middle and high frequency component for a highpass filtered image $I_{B1} = FQ(I_B)$ as well as an image of $I_{B2} = I_B - I_{B1}$ as shown in Fig. 9. $I_1 = (I_{B1}, I_F)$ is sent to Alice and $I_2 = I_{B2}$ is sent to Catharine.

Coefficients Comparison Embedding (FQemb). The second step is carried out by Catharine who proceed with embedding as $I_2' = (I_2 \oplus \omega) = FQemb(I_2)$. The detail is described below and illustrated in Fig. 8

1. divides I_2 into small $M \times M$ blocks ($M = 8$ in this case) blocks.
2. selects high-complexity blocks by a block analysis function $BA(\cdot)$ which finds blocks containing complicated part in an image such as edge of objects, hair of human, and so on. Detail of $BA(\cdot)$ is described later on.
3. choose two coefficients (A, B) as $A = a_1, \ldots, a_\ell, B = b_1, \ldots, b_\ell$ from the selected blocks where ℓ is a number of pairs. (A, B) is required to satisfy large dst, distance between A, B for better detection accuracy. For example, if dst is small, even slight manipulation affects watermark. (A, B) are randomly selected within a range of low to middle frequency and middle to high frequency respectively in order to obtain as large dst as possible. Middle and high frequencies are represented as $MQ_j, HQ_j, (j = min, \ldots, max)$ where j is an index of zigzag ordered coefficient elements in blocks. In other words, coefficients $(a_i, b_i), i = 1, \ldots, k$ where k is the number of selected blocks are chosen within a range of $MQ_{min} \geq a_i \geq MQ_{max}$, and $HQ_{min} \geq b_i \geq HQ_{max}$ respectively.
4. (A, B) are modified as $A - \delta < B + \delta$ for $\omega = 0$ and $A + \delta \geq B - \delta$ for $\omega = 1$. where δ is a parameter to enlarge dst to enhance robustness.

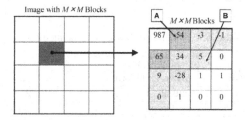

Fig. 8. Coefficients Selection in $M \times M$ blocks

A Highpass Filtered Image (I_{B1})   Embedded Image I'_{B1} Restored Embedded Image (I')

Fig. 9. Output Images of $FQemb$

5. continue the above process according to ecc and message length. For example, for the case of this implementation, 15 (length of ω)$\times$150(ecc) pairs of coefficients form the selected blocks are modified where ecc is Error Correcting Code.

Block Analysis BA. $BA(\cdot)$ is a function in embedding to enhance detection accuracy. $BA(\cdot)$ analysis all blocks to find blocks containing large standard deviation σ. Large σ indicates high-complexity part in an image where small modification is hardly notified by human eyes. Indeed, conventional watermarking embeds watermark into high-complexity part in an image. Blocks satisfying $\sigma \gg \tau$ are selected for embedding where τ is a threshold. Increment of τ indicates higher robustness at heavy image degeneration and vice versa. In other words, blocks possessing large σ provides better detection accuracy, whereas small σ indicates causing false detection.

5   Evaluation

Our implementation based on $(FC + FQ) + FQemb$ shows mainly two results, comparison with other watermark applications to figure out overall performance of our scheme, and examining $FQemb$ using various types of images. Following parameters, $\omega = 1, 0, 1, 0, 1, 0, 1, 0, ecc = 300$, and $\delta = 100$ and 512×512, 256 gray-scale images are used for this implementation. ecc (Error Correction Code) is a parameter that redundantly modifies 300 pairs of coefficients to represent 1 bit of watermark. Matlab2008b is used for Image division and OpenCV 1.0 is used for face detection. The environment is Core 2 Duo T7100 (1.80GHz), 2.5GB RAM, and Windows XP SP3. For robustness evaluation, we have used Stirmark Benchmark that applies various kinds of manipulations attacks as shown in Table 5.

Table 5. Parameters of Stirmark Benchmark 4.0

Attacks	Description	Levels
AFFINE	Affine Transform	$1, \ldots, 8$
CONV	Gaussian Filtering	$1, 2$
CROP [%]	Cropping	$25, 50, 75$
JPEG[%]	JPEG compression	$20, \ldots, 80$
MEDIAN[filter size]	Median cut	$3, 5, 7, 9$
NOISE[%]	Add noise	$10, \ldots, 80$
RESC [%]	Rescale	$50, 75, 90, 125, 150, 200$
RML [lines]	Remove lines	$10, 20, \ldots, 100$
ROTCROP	ROT+ CROP	$-2, -1, -0.5, 0.5, 1, 2$
ROTSCALE	ROT+RESC	$-2, -1, -0.5, 0.5, 1.2$
ROT[degrees]	Rotation	$-2, -1, 0.5, 1, 2, 5, 10, 25, 90$

5.1   Robustness against Restoring Using Various Watermark Applications

Our first evaluation is application comparison to find out overall performance of $FQemb$ and other existing embedding applications, selected from open source , Steghide and

Table 6. Failed Cases of Each Applications

Attacks	Failed Case of $FQemb$	Failed Case of Digimarc
AFFINE	1/8 (4 case is failed)	0/8(0 failed)
CONV	0/2(0 failed)	0/2(0 failed)
CROP	3/3 (All failed))	1/3 (25% case is failed)
JPEG	0/7(0 failed)	2/7 (20, 30% cases are failed)
MEDIAN	3/4 (5, 7, 9 cases are failed)	3/4 (5, 7, 9 cases are failed)
NOISE	1/8 (80% cases are failed)	8/8 (All failed)
RESC	0/6 (0 failed)	0/6 (0 failed)
RML	0/9(0 failed)	0/9 (0 failed)
ROTCROP	6/6(All failed)	0/6 (0 failed)
ROTSCALE	6/6(All failed)	0/6 (0 failed)
ROT	8/10 ($-2, -1, 1, 2, 5, 10, 25, 90$ cases are failed)	0/10 (0 failed)
Total	29/70 cases are failed	14/70 cases are failed

$(FC + FQ) + FQemb$ $(FC + FQ)+$ Digimarc

PSNR=61.98   PSNR=33.75

Fig. 10. Comparison of I'

Table 7. Parameters of Various Strength for Embedding

Label	Strength Level	Embedding Tool	Parameters	Failed Cases
Mid$FQemb$	Intermediate Level	$FQemb$	$ecc = 200, \delta = 75$	32/70
MidDigi	Intermediate Level	Digimarc	$strength= 3$	15/70
Low$FQemb$	Low Level	$FQemb$	$ecc = 100, \delta = 50$	50/70
LowDigi	Low Level	Digimarc	$strength= 2$	17/70

commercial one Digimarc, Watermarking Plug-in of Adobe Photoshop CS4. Throughout our scheme, we have two robustness examination points that are robustness against restoration process and image manipulations of I'. For the first point, after restoring process ($I' = I_1 + I'_2$), watermark embedded by Steghide didn't survive, while watermark embedded by $FQemb$ and Digimarc is successfully extracted.For the second point, robustness against various image manipulations, we applied Stirmark Benchmark which may be a stage that an illegal user tries to remove watermark. More detail is described below.

MidFQemb   MidDigi   LowFQemb   LowDigi

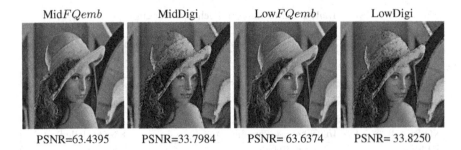

PSNR=63.4395   PSNR=33.7984   PSNR= 63.6374   PSNR= 33.8250

Fig. 11. I' of Lower Strength Embedding Levels

Table 8. Robustness Evaluation of Other Images

Attacks	Baboon	Peppers	Lexlex
AFFINE	5/8 (2, 4, 6, 7, 8 are failed)	3/8 (2, 4, 8 are failed)	1/8(4)
CONV	0/2(0 Failed)	0/2(0 Failed)	0/2(0 Failed)
CROP	3/3(All Failed)	1/3(25% is failed)	3/3(All Failed)
JPEG	0/7(0 Failed)	2/7(20, 30% are failed)	0/7(0 Failed)
MEDIAN	3/4(5, 7, 9)	3/4(5, 7, 9 are failed)	3/4 (5, 7, 9 are failed)
NOISE	2/8(50, 80% are failed)	1/8(70% is failed)	1/8(80% is failed)
RESC	0/6(0 Failed)	0/6(0 Failed)	0/6(0 Failed)
RML	0/9(0 Failed)	0/9(0 Failed)	0/9(0 Failed)
ROTCROP	6/6(All Failed)	6/6(All Failed)	6/6(All Failed)
ROTSCALE	6/6(All Failed)	6/6(All Failed)	6/6(All Failed)
ROT	10/10(All Failed)	10/10(All Failed)	10/10(All Failed)
Total failed cases	35/70	32/70	34/70

5.2 Robustness against Various Attacks

We have examined robustness of $(FC + FQ) + FQemb$ and $(FC + FQ)$+Digimarc. The parameters stated in the above is used for $FQemb$, and paremeters $strength= 4$ (the most robust), $\omega = 170$, and $\omega = 682$ are used for Digimarc where strength level ($strength = 1, \ldots, 4$) is provided. Note that, an embedding message in Digimarc is decimal representation, whereas the one in $FQemb$ is binary representation. Results are shown in Table 6.

For example of AFFINE transform, 8 levels of transforms are applied. As a result, watermark from one of 8 manipulated image is failed to detect by $FQemb$, while all manipulated images are successfully detected by Digimarc. Total performance of $FQemb$ and Digimarc is 41/70 and 56/70 which indicates watermark is successfully extracted from 41 attacked images out of 70 . From the above, it is inferred that $FQemb$ is lack of robustness against rotation manipulations. On the other hand, $FQemb$ is superior in (Add) NOISE and JPEG Compression to Digimarc. Embedded images and PSNR by $FQemb$ and Digimarc are shown in Fig. 10.

Evaluation on Various Strength Levels and Images. Embedded images that use various strength levels with the above parameters are shown in Fig. 11, and summary of

$$I \qquad\qquad I_2 \qquad\qquad I_2' \qquad\qquad I'$$

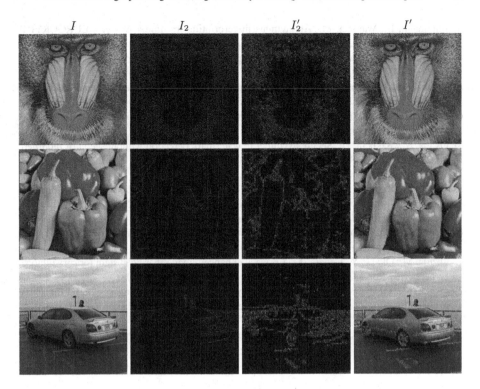

Fig. 12. Examination with various images

robustness and output images based on various kinds of images using $(FC + FQ) + FQemb$ are shown in Table 8 and Fig. 12.

6   Concluding Remarks

A concept of semi-blind fingerprinting has been materialized by means of overcoming difficulty in attaining feasibility and robustness which are lacking in conventional blind methods. Feasibility has been satisfied by replacing encryption with image dividing functions and an optimized embedding program. Moreover, implementation and evaluation results have convinced us validity of our concept. A semi-blind fingerprint protocol may be used for a privacy-secure digital image trading system under which user's privacy can be protected at feasible processing cost with sufficient robustness. Semi-blind fingerprinting is developing toward better performance. The latest information can be obtained from http://www.net.ist.i.kyoto-u.ac.jp/mitsuookada/.

References

1. Stefan Katzenbeisser, F.A.P.: Information Hiding Techniques for Steganography and Digital Watermarking. Artech House (2000)
2. Pfitzmann, B., Schunter, M.: Asymmetric fingerprinting. In: Maurer, U.M. (ed.) EURO-CRYPT 1996. LNCS, vol. 1070, pp. 84–95. Springer, Heidelberg (1996)

3. Pfitzmann, B., Waidner, M.: Anonymous fingerprinting. In: Fumy, W. (ed.) EUROCRYPT 1997. LNCS, vol. 1233, pp. 88–102. Springer, Heidelberg (1997)
4. Iwamura, K., Sakurai, K., Imai, H.: Blind fingerprinting. Technical report of IEICE. ISEC 97, 63–74 (1997)
5. Kuribayashi, M., Tanaka, H.: Fingerprinting protocol for images based on additive homomorphic property. IEEE Trans. Image Processing, 2129–2139 (2005)
6. Prins, J.P., Erkin, Z., Lagendijk, R.: Anonymous fingerprinting with robust qim watermarking techniques. European Journal of Information Systems 2007, 1–13 (2007)
7. Okada, M., Kikuchi, H.: Secure asymmetric watermark detection without secret of modified pixels. In: Song, J.-S., Kwon, T., Yung, M. (eds.) WISA 2005. LNCS, vol. 3786, pp. 165–178. Springer, Heidelberg (2006)
8. Okada, M., Kikuchi, H., Okabe, Y.: Multi-bit embedding in asymmetric digital watermarking without exposing secret information. IEICE E91-D(5), 1348–1358 (2008)
9. Furukawa, J.: Secure detection of watermarks. IEICE E87-A(1), 212–220 (2004)
10. Inaba, H., Yamamoto, Y.: Proposal on digital contents distribution system for protecting both privacy and copyrights. IEICE J89-D(12), 2536–2542 (2006)
11. Okada, M., Okabe, Y., Uehara, T.: A privacy enhanced image sharing system for surveillance cameras based on a fingerprinting technique. CSS 2008 (October 2008)
12. Okada, M., Okabe, Y., Uehara, T.: A privacy enhanced image sharing system on the sensing web based on a fingerprinting technique. In: International Workshop on Sensing Web (December 2008)
13. Petitcolas, F.A.P.: Watermarking schemes evaluation. IEEE Signal Processing 17(5), 58–64 (2000)

Robust AVS Audio Watermarking

Yong Wang and Jiwu Huang

Guangdong Key Lab. of Information Security Technology
Sun Yat-Sen University, Guangdong, China, 510275
`isshjw@mail.sysu.edu.cn`

Abstract. Part III of AVS(China Audio and Video Coding Standard) is the first standard for Hi-Fi audio proposed in China and is becoming more popular in some IT industries. For MP3 audio, some efforts have been made to solve the problems such as copyright pirating and malicious modifications by the way of watermarking. But till now little efforts have been made to solve the same problems for AVS audio. In this paper, we present a novel robust watermarking algorithm which can protect the AVS audio from the above problems. The watermark is embedded into the AVS compressed bit stream. At the extracting end, the watermark bits can be extracted from the compressed bit stream directly without any computation. This algorithm achieves robustness to decoding/recoding attacks, and low complexity of both embedding and extracting while preserves the quality of the audio signals.

Keywords: AVS Audio, Robust Watermarking.

1 Introduction

Audio Video Coding Standard Working Group of China (AVS Workgroup) was established on June 2002. The goal of the working group is to establish an integrated standard set for compression, decompression, manipulation and displaying of digital audio and video in multimedia systems[1]. The AVS standard is applied in many significant IT industries such as high definition TV, digital audio broadcast, high density laser-digital storage media, wireless broadband multimedia communication, and internet broadband stream media[2]. AV3, or AVS part III, is a high quality stereo coding standard for audio. It can be applied to those fields such as high density digital storage media, broad band audio service over internet, multimedia E-mail, multimedia services on packet networks, digital audio broadcasting, and ect. As its applications are becoming wider in China, the problems such as copyright pirating, illegal downloading and malicious modifications, will become urgent. Watermarking is a technique to solve these problems.

In recently years some efforts have been reported on the compressed domain video watermarking [3] [4] [5]. In the audio field, basically the equivalent efforts are focused on on the protection of MP3 music works by watermarking. [6] proposed MP3Stego, a tool to hide information into MP3 audio by assigning

A.T.S. Ho et al. (Eds.): IWDW 2009, LNCS 5703, pp. 29–38, 2009.

odd/even numbers of bits to represent "1" and "0" during the compression process. The hidden information is inaudible and the extracting is blind. However, it is not robust to the decoding/re-encoding attack, i.e., the hidden bits will be removed after the MP3 audio is decompressed and recompressed. The reason lies that when the audio is recompressed the numbers of bits assigned to the frequency lines will be changed and the watermark will be erased. In order to be robust to decoding/re-coding, Kim [7] used the "lin bits" characteristics of MP3 bit stream to embed the watermark into MP3 audio. The method is convenient. But the robustness is poor. In [8] the watermark bits are embedded into the scaling factors or samples but apparent noises are easy to be introduced and the detection is not blind. In [9], energy relation between two adjacent channels is used for watermark embedding which proves to be robust to decoding/re-encoding. In [8] and [9] the watermark bits are extracted by computation in the decoding end which may be not applicable in some real time applications.

On the other hand, watermarking schemes for AV3 have not been reported yet. The purpose of this paper is to design an applicable and robust watermarking scheme that can protect an AV3 clip. We exploit the technologies and features of the AV3 coding and decoding process and propose a watermarking algorithm which is combined with the coding/decoding process. The watermark is robust to decoding/recoding attacks and is inaudible within the audio. The watermark bits can be extracted directly from the compressed bit stream without decoding it, so the extracting speed is as fast as required in many applications.

The structure of this paper is as follows. We introduce coding/decoding process of AV3 in Section 2. The watermarking scheme will be illustrated in Section 3. Section 4 shows the experimental results. Finally we summarize the conclusions and the future work in Section 5.

2   AVS Audio Coding and Decoding

Since the watermark should be robust to decoding/recoding attacks we should examine the whole AV3 codec process to search the field that can robustly contain the watermark. We find that frame type, which is determined by the psychoacoustic model adopted in AV3, can be used to represent the watermark bits robustly. In this section we introduce the basic process of AV3 codec as well as the psychoacoustic model.

2.1   The Basic Process of AV3 Codec

The framework of AVS Audio codec is shown in Fig.1. In the coder, the input PCM signal is divided into frames of 1024 samples and the compression coding is performed on each frame. The frame is first analyzed by a psychoacoustic model to determine whether this frame is a stationary or transient signal. The long/short window switch decision is based on this analysis. IntMDCT is used to transform the signal from time domain to frequency domain. Long IntMDCT will be performed on a stationary frame and short IntMDCT will be on a transient

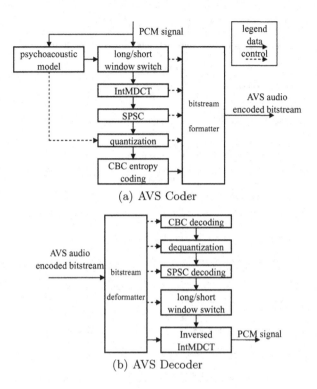

(a) AVS Coder

(b) AVS Decoder

Fig. 1. AVS Codec

frame. If the signal is stereo and the two channels are strongly correlated, SPSC will be done on the signal to reduce the correlation. The IntMDCT components will be quantized and CBC entropy coded. The coded data along with the side information will be grouped together to form the final AV3 audio bit stream. In the decoder the AV3 bit stream will be undergone a reversed process to obtain the PCM stream.

2.2 Frame Type Decision Based on the Psychoacoustic Model

In order to eliminate pre-echo artifacts introduced during the coding process and promote the coding efficiency, the audio should be classified as stationary or transient signal [10]. Transform of different lengths will be performed on different types of signals. In AV3 the audio is divided into frames, and the type of a frame is determined by a psychoacoustic model. Then long IntMDCT will be performed on a stationary frame and short IntMDCT will be on a transient frame.

In AV3 encoder, each current frame $X = \{X_0, X_1, \cdots, X_{1023}\}$ is partitioned into 16 subblock of 64 samples, as illustrated in Fig.2(a). The kth subblock can be denoted as $\overrightarrow{X}_k = \{X_{64k}, X_{64k+1}, X_{64k+63}\}|_{k=0,1,\cdots,15}$.

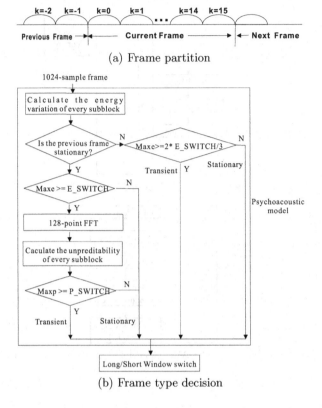

(a) Frame partition

(b) Frame type decision

Fig. 2. Long/Short Window Switch(Frame Type Decision) Based on the Psychoacoustic Model

Fig.2(b) shows the psychoacoustic model for the long/short window switching decision (frame type decision) as following:

1. Calculation of the Maxe of each frame: Firstly each subblock energy e_k is calculated as following:

$$e_k = \vec{X}_k \bullet \vec{X}_k \tag{1}$$

Then the two energy values of every adjacent subblock are added to obtain E_k:

$$E_k = e_k + e_{k-1} \tag{2}$$

The energy variation of the kth subblock is calculated as following:

$$\Delta E_k = \frac{|E_k - E_{k-1}|}{E_{k-1}} \qquad 0 \le k < 16 \tag{3}$$

Then the maximum energy variation of the current frame is:

$$Maxe = \max\{\Delta E_k | k = 0, 1, 2, \cdots, 15\} \tag{4}$$

2. Calculation of the Maxp of each frame:
   Firstly every 2 adjacent subblocks of the frame is weighted by a hanning window $\vec{H}$ and transformed to FFT spetral as following:

$$Y_k = \{Y_{k,0}, Y_{k,1}, \cdots, Y_{k,127}\} = FFT\{[\vec{X_k}, \vec{X}_{k+1}] \bullet \vec{H}\} \qquad (5)$$

Then the predicted spectral value is calculated as following:

$$Y^p_{k,i} = (2|Y_{k-1,i}| - |Y_{k-2,i}|)e^{j(2arg(Y_{k-1,i})-arg(Y_{k-2,i}))} \qquad 0 \le i < 64 \qquad (6)$$

The unpredictability of the ith spectral line of the kth subblock, $c_{k,i}$, is calculated as following:

$$c_{k,i} = \frac{|Y^p_{k,i} - Y_{k,i}|}{|Y^p_{k,i}| + |Y_{k,i}|} \qquad 0 \le i < 64 \qquad (7)$$

Then the unpredictability of the kth subblock is the weighted sum of $c_{k,i}$:

$$C_k = \sum_{i=0}^{63} \{|Y_{k,i}|c_{k,i}\} \qquad (8)$$

Finally the maximum unpredictability of the the current frame is:

$$Maxp = \max\{C_k|k = 0, 1, 2, \cdots, 15\} \qquad (9)$$

3   AV3 Watermarking Scheme

Our goal in this paper is to design a fast, robust and inaudible AV3 watermarking scheme based on AV3 codec processing. We hope that the watermark bits will be in the coded bit stream so that they can be extracted from the coded bit stream without any computation. Also we hope that the watermark is robust to decoding/recoding attack. And the modifications should as small as possible so that the watermark is inaudible. From Section 2.2 we know that since the frame type relies on its own samples' values and is independent of the quantization, it is a robust feature that can contain the watermark bits.

3.1   Watermarking Algorithm

In this paper we use the stationary/transient type of a frame to indicate a watermark bit:

stationary-1 transient-0

The core is to change $Maxe$ and $Maxp$ of a frame so that it becomes a desired type. The details are as following.

Suppose the watermark $\vec{W} = \{w_j|w_j \in \{0,1\}, 1 \le j \le L, L \in Z^+\}$. Choose L frames to be watermarked. Denote this set of frames as

$$F = \{F_j|F_j \text{ is the } j^{th} \text{ watermarked frame, } 1 \le j \le L, L \in Z^+\}$$

The embedding can be done according to the 2 different cases:

i) If frame F_j is transient and $w_j = 1$, modify the samples' values of frame F_j so that this frame becomes a stationary type. The algorithm of the modification is shown as following:

```
====================================================
     α₁ = β₁ * 2 * E_SWITCH/3    0 ≤ β₁ < 1
     for( k = 0; k < 16; k + + )
     {
          Denote the samples in the kth subblock as X_{k,i}|_{i=0,1,···,63}
          Calculate e_{k-2}, e_{k-1} and e_k according to Equ.(1).
          Calculate ΔE_k according to Equ.(2) and (3).
          if( ΔE_k >= 2 * E_SWITCH/3 )
          {
               e'_k = α₁ * (e_{k-2} + e_{k-1}) + e_{k-2}
               for( i = 0; i < 63; i + + )
                    X'_{k,i} = √(e'_k/e_k) * X_{k,i}
          }
     }
====================================================
```

$X'_{k,i}$ is the modified sample. According to Equ.(1-3) we have

$$\Delta E'_k = \frac{|E'_k - E_{k-1}|}{|E_{k-1}} = \frac{\sum_{i=0}^{63} |X'_{k,i}|^2 + e_{k-1} - (e_{k-1} + e_{k-2})|}{e_{k-1} + e_{k-2}}$$

$$= \frac{|\frac{e'_k}{e_k} \sum_{i=0}^{63} |X_{k,i}|^2 - e_{k-2}|}{e_{k-1} + e_{k-2}} = \frac{|e'_k - e_{k-2}|}{e_{k-1} + e_{k-2}} \qquad (10)$$

$$= \frac{|\alpha_1 * (e_{k-2} + e_{k-1}) + e_{k-2} - e_{k-2}|}{e_{k-1} + e_{k-2}}$$

$$= \alpha_1 < 2 * E\_SWITCH/3$$

From (10) and (4), it can be easily known that maximum energy variation of the watermarked frame, $Maxe'$, satisfies:

$$Maxe' = \max\{\Delta E'_k | k = 0, 1, 2, \cdots, 15\} < 2 * E\_SWITCH/3 \qquad (11)$$

which means that this frame has been changed from a transient type to a stationary type(see fig.2).

ii) If frame F_j is stationary and $w_j = 0$, modify the samples' values of frame F_j so that this frame becomes a transient type. The modification includes 2 steps:

```
====================================================
```
Step I: Modify the sample's values to obtain a new maximum energy variation, $Maxe'$, as following:

$\alpha_2 = \beta_2 * E\_SWITCH \quad \beta_2 > 1$

k_1 = the subscript of the subblock which has Maxe;

$$e'_{k_1} = \alpha_2 * (e_{k_1-2} + e_{k_1-1}) + e_{k_1-2}$$

for($i = 0; j < 63; j + +$)

$$X'_{k_1,i} = \sqrt{e'_{k_1}/e_{k_1}} * X_{k_1,i}$$

Step II: Modify the samples' values to obtain a new maximum unpredictability, Maxp', as following:

$k_2 =$ the subscript of a subblock that satisfies $|k_2 - k_1| >= 4$

$\alpha_3 = \beta_3 * P\_SWITCH \quad \beta_3 > 1$

for($i = 0; i < 63; i + +$)
{

$$X'_{k_2,i} = \frac{\alpha_3}{C_{k_2}} * X_{k_2,i}$$

$$X'_{k_2+1,i} = \frac{\alpha_3}{C_{k_2}} * X_{k_2+1,i}$$

$$X'_{k_2-1,i} = \frac{\alpha_3}{C_{k_2}} * X_{k_2-1,i}$$

$$X'_{k_2-2,i} = \frac{\alpha_3}{C_{k_2}} * X_{k_2-2,i}$$

}

==

Like the deduction in i) we can know that after step I the new maximum energy variation, $Maxe'$, satisfies

$$Maxe' >= E\_SWITCH \tag{12}$$

From Equ.(1-4) and by the restriction $|k_2 - k_1| >= 4$ we can know that the modification of step II will preserve the relationship of (12). From Equ.(5-7) we can also know that the unpredictability of each line in $k_2{}^{th}$ subblock, $c_{k_2,i}$, remains unchanged. From Equ.(8), the new unpredictability of this subblock is:

$$C'_{k_2} = \sum_{i=0}^{63}\{|Y'_{k_2,i}|c_{k_2,i}\} = \sum_{i=0}^{63}\{\frac{\alpha_3}{C_{k_2}}|Y_{k_2,i}|c_{k_2,i}\}$$
$$= \frac{\alpha_3}{C_{k_2}} * C_{k_2} = \alpha_3 > P\_SWITCH \tag{13}$$

From (13), it can be easily known that the new maximum unpredictability, $Maxp'$, is:

$$Maxp' = \max\{C'_k|k = 0, 1, 2, \cdots, 15\} > P\_SWITCH \tag{14}$$

After these two steps of modification, the new maximum energy variation and the new maximum unpredictability of this watermarked frame, $Maxe'$ and $Maxp'$, satisfy:

$$Maxe' >= E\_SWITCH \ \& \ Maxp' >= P\_SWITCH \tag{15}$$

which means that this frame has been changed from a stationary type to a transient type(see Fig.2).

During the AV3 coding processing, the type of each frame will be recorded as one bit in the side information of the coded bits stream. Therefore the watermark can be extracted from the coded bits stream directly.

3.2   Some Issues in Implementation

Firstly the frames for watermark bit embedding must be carefully chosen for in-audibility. If the frames are randomly chosen some abrupt noises will be introduced due to the modifications of the very stationary or very transient frames. In this algorithm we choose those 'intermediate' frames for embedding whose maximum energy variation and maximum unpredictability are near the thresholds, i.e. $|Maxe - \frac{2}{3}E\_SWITCH)| < \gamma_1$ (for embedding "1") and $|Maxe - E\_SWITCH| < \gamma_2$ & $|Maxp - P\_SWITCH| < \gamma_3$ (for embedding "0").

Secondly from Fig.2 we can see that the frame type depends on its own Maxe, Maxp and the type of the previous frame. During the research we find that the type of the previous frame may be changed due to the decoding/recoding. If that happens the decision making for the current watermarked frame will follow a different route and thus the watermark bit may be erased. In order to avoid this problem we adopt the modifications in section 3.1 by which the type decision of the watermarked frame is independent on the the type of the previous frame.

Thirdly the β_1, β_2, β_3 are the embedding strength. The smaller β_1 is and the larger β_2 and β_3 are, the higher robustness and less inaudibility will be. They must be carefully chosen for the balance of robustness and inaudibility. Here we adopted $\beta_1 = 0.9$, $\beta_2 = 1.1$, $\beta_3 = 1.1$.

4   Experiments

In the experiments,we tested 100 clips. They are divided into 10 groups: blues, classical, disco, country, hiphop, jazz, metal, pop, rock and speech. Each group consists of 10 clips. All of them are of wav format, 44.1k sampling rate, 16-bit quantization, mono, 30 seconds. The embedding is integrated into the compression processing. We embedded a watermark of 120 bits when the compression rate is 128kbps.

4.1   Distortions

The watermark must be inaudible so as not to affect the audio quality. Here we firstly tested the distortion by values of SNR. In the following tables and figures SNR1 refers to the distortions brought by compression, and SNR2 refers to the distortions brought by compression plus embedding. Table 1 shows the average SNR values of the ten groups. We can see that the average SNR drop of every group is around 1.5 db and the average drop of the ten group is 1.5896 db which means that the watermark is not audible. Fig.3 shows the SNR of the 100 clips.We can see that all SNR values of the compressed plus watermarked clips drop less than 2 db compared with the merely compressed ones and are still over 20 db meets the requirement of IFPI.

We also conducted a subjective test by 10 listeners and obtained the mean opinion score(MOS) which is proposed by ITU-T P.800. The average MOS of the 100 clips is 4.2 which means nearly perceptible but not annoying.

Table 1. Average SNR values(in db) of the ten groups

group	blues	classical	disco	country	hiphop	jazz	metal	pop	rock	speech
average SNR1	25.2950	24.8666	24.2929	25.3448	25.6647	25.3577	25.8506	25.0057	24.8626	24.0934
average SNR2	23.4546	23.0517	22.8702	23.5125	24.1335	23.6377	24.1946	23.6276	23.5870	22.5992
drop	1.8404	1.8149	1.4227	1.8323	1.5312	1.7200	1.6561	1.3780	1.2756	1.4941

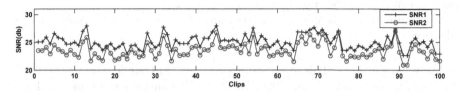

Fig. 3. SNR values of AV3 compression vs. compression plus embedding

4.2 Robustness

The extracted watermark $\overrightarrow{W'}$ is compared with the original watermark $\overrightarrow{W}$ by bit error rate(BER). From Fig.4(a) and (b), we can see that when the recoding rate is 128kbps or 32kbps, the lowest bit rate of AV3, the BER values are all zero, which means that the watermark is very robust to decoding/recoding(AV3 recoding) attacks. Since MP3 is the most popular compression standard we also tested the robustness of our algorithm to decoding(AV3 decoding)/recoding(MP3 recoding) attacks. From Fig.4(c) and (d) we can see that it is also robust to MP3 recoding even when the recoding rate is is 32kbps, the lowest bit rate of MP3.

Till now no efforts have been reported on the watermarking for AV3. We compare with the one in [9] which are of MP3. The watermark capacity of [9] is 17bps, and ours is 4bps. But in [9] error occurs when the recoding rate is changed to a lower coding rate. In ours even when the recoding rate drops to the lowest one, the watermark can still be completely recovered.

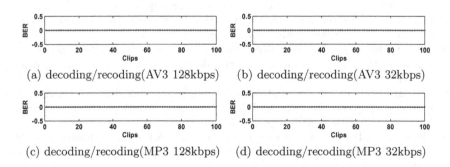

(a) decoding/recoding(AV3 128kbps)   (b) decoding/recoding(AV3 32kbps)

(c) decoding/recoding(MP3 128kbps)   (d) decoding/recoding(MP3 32kbps)

Fig. 4. Robustness to decoding/recoding attacks

5   Conclusions

In this paper we propose an AV3 watermarking algorithm which proves to be robust to decoding/recoding(AV3 recoding and MP3 recoding) attacks. It also achieves blind detection and inaudibility. The complexity is low since the embedding is done by modifying some small portions of the audio and the watermark can be extracted from the bit stream directly without any computation. This method can protect the copyright of an AV3 works.

The future work is the optimization of frame selection and embedding strength adaption.

Acknowledgements. This work is supported by NSFC under Grants 60633030 and 973 Program under Grant 2006CB303104. The authors would like to thank Dr. Fan Liang of Sun Yat-sen Univ. for providing us with the source code of AV3.

References

1. Ruimin, H., Shuixian, C., Haojun, A., Naixue, X.: AVS generic audio coding. In: 6th Int.Conf. on Parallel and Distributed Computing, Applications and Technologies, pp. 679–683 (2005)
2. MPEG, Information technology generic coding of moving pictures and associated audio, part 3: Audio, International Standard IS 13818C3, ISO/IEC JTC1/SC29 WG11 (1994)
3. Xingguang, S., Yuting, S., Yu, L., Zhong, J.: A video watermarking scheme for avs based on motion vectors. In: 11th IEEE Int. Conf. on Communication Technology, pp. 738–741 (2008)
4. Noorkami, M., Mersereau, R.M.: Digital video watermarking in p-frames with controlled video bit-rate increase. IEEE Trans. Information Forensic and Security 3, 441–455 (2008)
5. Jian, L., Hongmei, L., Jiwu, H.: A robust watermarking scheme for h. 264. In: IWDW 2008 (2008)
6. http://www.cl.cam.ac.uk/-fapp2/steganography/mp3stego/index.html
7. Kim, D.-h.y.: Additive data inserting into mp3 bitstream using linbits characteristics. In: Proc. on ICASSP 2004, vol. IV, pp. 181–184 (2004)
8. Qiao, L., Klara, N.: Non-invertible watermarking methods for mpeg encoded audio. In: SPIE Proceedings on Security and Watermarking of Multimedia Contents, vol. 3675, pp. 194–202 (1999)
9. Kuilong, Z., Limin, H.: A mp3 watermarking scheme based on the energy relation of two adjacent channels. In: IET Conference on Wireless, Mobile and Sensor Networks (CCWMSN 2007), pp. 717–720 (2007)
10. Shuixian, C., Haojun, A., Ruimin, H., Guiping, D.: A window switching algorithm for avs audio coding. In: Int. Conf. on Wireless Communications, Networking and Mobile Computing, pp. 2889–2892 (2007)

Comparative Study of Wavelet Based Lattice QIM Techniques and Robustness against AWGN and JPEG Attacks

Dieter Bardyn[1], Ann Dooms[1], Tim Dams[1,2], and Peter Schelkens[1]

[1] Dept. of Electronics and Informatics (ETRO),
Vrije Universiteit Brussel (VUB) -
Interdisciplinary Institute for Broadband Technology (IBBT),
Pleinlaan 2, B-1050 Brussels, Belgium
dieter.bardyn@vub.ac.be,
ann.dooms@vub.ac.be,
peter.schelkens@vub.ac.be
http://www.etro.vub.ac.be
[2] Dept. of Applied Engineering (electronica-ict),
Artesis University College of Antwerp
Paardenmarkt 92, B-2000 Antwerp, Belgium
tim.dams@artesis.be
http://www.artesis.be

Abstract. We study watermarking techniques based on Quantization Index Modulation for which sets of lattice quantizers Q_m are used (LQIM). A recipe for constructing such quantizers Q_m is proposed, where the size of these sets is variable, so that the payload is easily adaptable. We make a comparative study of 8 dimensional lattices with good quantizer properties, where the embedding is done in the wavelet domain. Along the way, the gap between the theoretical ideas behind QIM and practical systems using lattices is closed by extending techniques, such as dithered quantizers and distortion compensation, from the scalar case to LQIM.

Keywords: Digital Watermarking, Quantization Index Modulation, Lattice.

1 Origin of Quantization Index Modulation

In 1998, Chen and Wornell [2] introduced a new class of watermarking techniques called Quantization Index Modulation (*QIM*) which use the host signal at the encoder. In a second paper by Chen and Wornell [3] from 2001 these, as the name indicates, quantization based techniques were proven to be, in a information theoretical sense, a good class of watermarking techniques. In particular, they proposed a method using a set of scalar quantizers, which is called *scalar QIM*, that theoretically outperformed other watermarking techniques that were used until then (Least Significant Bit, Spread Spectrum). Scalar QIM is nowadays commonly found as the basis for a variety of watermarking techniques. One

A.T.S. Ho et al. (Eds.): IWDW 2009, LNCS 5703, pp. 39–53, 2009.

extension of this method, *sparse QIM* [3,12], groups samples together in a vector and projects this vector on a 1-dimensional subspace in which scalar QIM can be applied. Another extension is the use of lattice quantizers [3], referred to as Lattice QIM techniques (*LQIM*), which we study in this paper and compare to sparse QIM.

When developing a watermarking technique, three important properties need to be carefully balanced. The first property, *fidelity*, indicates the perceptual closeness of the watermarked *cover work* to the original cover work. Ideally, watermarked cover works are perceptually indistinguishable from their originals. A second property, *robustness*, measures how good the watermark can be detected after common signal processing operations (possibly under the form of an attack). Thirdly, *payload*, indicates how much bits can be embedded in the cover work.

In Sect. 2 we will take a closer look at LQIM techniques and propose some lattices that can be used. Along the way we extend the ideas of dithered quantizers and distortion compensation to LQIM. Next, we elaborate on a method to construct a set of quantizers from a coarse lattice quantizer and apply it on the proposed lattices in Sect. 3. Then, in Sect. 4 we propose a framework to test LQIM and compare it to sparse QIM. Section 5 contains the obtained results, which include robustness tests against addition of white Gaussian noise (*AWGN*) and JPEG compression for the different techniques.

2   A Closer Look at Lattice QIM

Lattice QIM is a technique similar to scalar QIM[1], but a set of lattice quantizers is used to embed information following the idea of binning as presented by Zamir et al. [17]. These lattice based techniques were proven to achieve *capacity* for AWGN channels by Erez and Zamir in 2004 [9]. Capacity, in the information theoretic sense, is the highest rate[2] that can be attained for a given set of encoders and a given class of attacks. The ideas behind LQIM were illustrated in the work of Balado and Pérez-González [1], and Zhang and Boston [18]. In 2005, Moulin and Koetter discussed theoretical performance aspects of LQIM techniques, and conceptual ideas were illustrated through some examples [12].

2.1   Lattices

First, recall that a lattice (in $\mathbb{R}^n$) is defined as a collection of vectors that are integral combinations of a set of basis vectors in $\mathbb{R}^n$. If G is such a set $\{g_1, \ldots, g_n\}$ of basis vectors, the associated n-dimensional lattice Γ is the set $\{\sum_{i=1}^{n} z_i g_i \mid \forall i \; z_i \in \mathbb{Z}\}$. Lattice QIM techniques present an approach that uses an n-dimensional lattice Γ_{F} for which a coarser sublattice Γ_{C} (i.e. $\Gamma_{\mathrm{C}} \subseteq \Gamma_{\mathrm{F}}$) is identified so that

$$\Gamma_{\mathrm{F}} = \bigcup_{m=1}^{M} \Gamma_{\mathrm{C}} + g_m$$

---

[1] Note that when talking about QIM we mean a method based on dithered quantizers.
[2] The rate is the number of information bits per encoded sample.

for some $g_m \in \mathbb{R}^n$. Note that, if $\Gamma_C \subseteq \Gamma_F$, there exist an $n \times n$ integer matrix J with determinant greater than one so that [17]

$$G_C = G_F J \ , \tag{1}$$

where G_C and G_F are the generator matrices[3] of the lattices Γ_C and Γ_F respectively. As lattices are (additive) groups, the number of bins M that can be created using Γ_C and Γ_F equals the number of cosets of Γ_C in Γ_F.

2.2 Lattice Quantizers

These cosets $\Gamma_m = \Gamma_C + g_m$, where g_m is a coset leader $(1 \leq m \leq M)$, are used to create a set of lattice quantizers Q_m to, as in the original QIM scheme, watermark the cover work c with message m using an embedding function E,

$$\begin{aligned} E\,(c, m) &= Q_m\,(c) \tag{2} \\ &= Q_{\Gamma_C}\,(c - g_m) + g_m \ , \end{aligned}$$

where Q_{Γ_C} is the quantizer associated with the coarse lattice Γ_C. We will propose a construction for finding these fine and coarse lattices together with coset leaders for some specific lattices in Sect. 3. The implementation of all considered coarse lattice quantizers is based on [4]. Note that in 1 dimension, LQIM is equivalent to scalar QIM.

The choice of lattices used in the binning scheme is important, as is indicated by Zamir et al. [17]. Since the coarse lattice is used as a quantizer, it should be an optimal quantizer in the sense that it has to minimize the mean squared error. To this end, the *Voronoi regions*[4] should be nearly spherical which rephrases to finding a lattice that is optimal for the sphere packing problem. As the finer lattice is in fact used to embed the messages it should be optimal relative to the source coding criterion. In the case of a uniform use of the messages, this is equivalent to finding lattices that are optimal for the covering problem.

The sphere packing and sphere covering problems have been intensively studied and an overview of the obtained results can be found in [5].

2.3 Dithered Quantizers and Distortion Compensation

One adaptation of the original QIM technique includes the application of *distortion compensation* [3]. This technique improves robustness for constant fidelity, by applying a small variation to the original QIM scheme (2). Distortion compensation combines an expansion of the Voronoi region of the coarse lattice with noise reduction. These effects cancel each other out, so that fidelity remains constant. Reduction of embedding noise is obtained through the use of a compensation factor α, which is known to embedder and detector. The adjusted scheme is the following

---

[3] A generator matrix has lattice basis vectors as it columns so that right multiplication with an $n \times 1$ vector with integer entries gives a new lattice element.

[4] The collection of points that are closer to the origin than to any other lattice point.

$$\mathrm{E_{DC}}\left(c, m\right) = \frac{1}{\alpha} Q_m \left(\alpha c\right) + (1 - \alpha) \left[c - \frac{1}{\alpha} Q_m \left(\alpha c\right)\right] . \qquad (3)$$

Optimization of the compensation factor α has been studied for scalar QIM techniques [8,13], but no studies on distortion compensation for LQIM techniques were found.

In order to optimally apply distortion compensation we need uniform distribution of the quantization noise in the Voronoi region. To realize this we apply a specific random dither sequence[5]. If we choose the dither sequence to be independent of the message and the cover work, and drawn from a uniform distribution on the Voronoi region of the coarse lattice on which the quantizer is based, then uniform distribution of the quantization noise in the Voronoi region follows [12]. The construction of such dithers is straightforward in the scalar QIM case, while for the LQIM-case we propose to use a result from Kirac and Vaidyanathan [10]. This result states that, for a lattice quantizer Q_Γ associated with the lattice Γ having generator matrix G, the quantization error is independent of the input, and uniformly distributed in the Voronoi region if the dither vector is chosen as follows:

1. generate a set of D independent random variables $Z_1, Z_2, \ldots, Z_D$ each of which is uniform in $[\frac{-1}{2}, \frac{1}{2}[$;
2. form a vector $z = (z_1, z_2, \ldots, z_D)$, where each z_i is a realization of the random variables Z_i;
3. dithering with the vector $v = Gz$ then assures independent, uniform quantization noise.

2.4 Some Examples

First, we introduce some lattices, that are known to have good results for the sphere packing and sphere covering problems (see Sect. 2.2).

A_n and the Hexagonal Lattice. In general, the n-dimensional lattice A_n is the subgroup of vectors of $\mathbb{Z}^{n+1}$ for which all coordinates sum to zero,

$$A_n = \left\{ (z_1, \ldots, z_{n+1}) \in \mathbb{Z}^{n+1} \mid \sum_{i=1}^{n+1} z_i = 0 \right\} .$$

We are particularly interested in the 2-dimensional case, since it has been shown that the lattice A_2 is optimal for both the sphere covering and the sphere packing problem in 2 dimensions, and as such we can consider A_2 as a candidate for LQIM. To create a lattice quantizer based on A_2 we use that A_2 is *congruent*, i.e. there exists an isometry, to the following lattice.

---

[5] This dithering is not to be confused with dithering for security reasons, but, when key depended, it can be used to achieve this goal [12].

Let $\omega = \frac{-1+i\sqrt{3}}{2}$ and let $\mathfrak{D}$ be the subring $\mathbb{Z}[\omega]$ of $\mathbb{C} \simeq \mathbb{R}^2$. An additive basis for $\mathfrak{D}$ in $\mathbb{R}^2$ is given by $(1,0)$ and $\left(\frac{1}{2}, \frac{\sqrt{3}}{2}\right)$, which can be used to generate an *hexagonal lattice* [11] which turns out to be congruent to A_2. An hexagonal lattice is a 2-dimensional lattice having a basis b_1, b_2 of vectors of equal minimal norm for which the inner product $\underline{x} \cdot \underline{y}$ equals half their norm.

As an isometry is by definition distance preserving, quantizing to A_2 or to this congruent hexagonal lattice is equivalent and hence, from here on, we will call A_2 the hexagonal lattice. A generator matrix G_C for A_2 is given by

$$G_C = \begin{pmatrix} 1 & \frac{1}{2} \\ 0 & \frac{\sqrt{3}}{2} \end{pmatrix} . \tag{4}$$

The Checkerboard Lattice D_2. The n-dimensional lattice D_n is the subgroup of vectors of $\mathbb{Z}^n$ for which the sum of all coordinates is even,

$$D_n = \left\{ (z_1, \ldots, z_n) \in \mathbb{Z}^n \mid \sum_{i=1}^n z_i \text{ is even} \right\} .$$

The *checkerboard* lattice D_2 is one of the most basic lattices and often used in QIM, hence we will compare LQIM based on D_2 to the other discussed LQIM techniques. For D_2, a generator matrix G_C is given by

$$G_C = \begin{pmatrix} 1 & 0 \\ 1 & 2 \end{pmatrix} .$$

The E_8 Lattice is a subgroup of vectors in $\mathbb{R}^8$ for which the coordinates are all in $\mathbb{Z}$ or all in $\mathbb{Z} + \frac{1}{2}$ and their sum is even,

$$E_8 = \left\{ (x_1, \ldots, x_8) \mid \forall x_i \in \mathbb{Z} \text{ or } \forall x_i \in \mathbb{Z} + \frac{1}{2}, \sum_{i=1}^8 x_i = 0 \mod 2 \right\} .$$

A generator matrix G_C for the E_8 lattice is given by,

$$G_C = \begin{pmatrix} 2 & 0 & 0 & 0 & 0 & 0 & 0 & 0 \\ -1 & 1 & 0 & 0 & 0 & 0 & 0 & 0 \\ 0 & -1 & 1 & 0 & 0 & 0 & 0 & 0 \\ 0 & 0 & -1 & 1 & 0 & 0 & 0 & 0 \\ 0 & 0 & 0 & -1 & 1 & 0 & 0 & 0 \\ 0 & 0 & 0 & 0 & -1 & 1 & 0 & 0 \\ 0 & 0 & 0 & 0 & 0 & -1 & 1 & 0 \\ \frac{1}{2} & \frac{1}{2} & \frac{1}{2} & \frac{1}{2} & \frac{1}{2} & \frac{1}{2} & \frac{1}{2} & \frac{1}{2} \end{pmatrix} .$$

The E_8 lattice is optimal for the sphere packing problem in 8 dimensions. The dual of the A_8 lattice is the best covering, but it is closely followed by E_8 and as we are looking for lattices that are good solutions to both problems we focus on the E_8 lattice.

3 Construction of Coding Bins

Lattice QIM techniques follow the idea of binning as presented by Zamir et al. [17]. In order to construct the bins, we start from a lattice Γ_C (which will play the role of the coarse lattice), construct a finer lattice Γ_F and identify the coset leaders, which are the elements of the quotient group Γ_F/Γ_C. In this way, we create a set of quantizers that allow a number of messages equal to (at most) the number of cosets to be embedded.

3.1 Similar Lattices

Our bin construction will be based on coarse sublattices that resemble the fine lattice. A linear map $\sigma : \mathbb{R}^n \to \mathbb{R}^n$ for which $\sigma(\underline{u}) \cdot \sigma(\underline{v}) = d(\underline{u} \cdot \underline{v})$, (for $\underline{u}, \underline{v} \in \mathbb{R}^n$ and $d \in \mathbb{R}$) is called a *similarity* of norm d. Two n-dimensional lattices $\Gamma_C \subseteq \Gamma_F$ are *d-similar* if their exist a similarity σ of norm d so that $\sigma(\Gamma_F) = \Gamma_C$ or $M_\sigma G_F = G_C$, where M_σ is the matrix associated with the linear map σ. Applying this to (1) gives

$$J = G_C^{-1} M_\sigma G_C , \tag{5}$$

where $J \in M_2(\mathbb{Z})$ and $\det J > 1$ determine conditions on M_σ.

Conway et al. studied the existence of d-similar sublattices [5,6] from which we deduce the following theorem.

Theorem 1. *Let σ be a similarity on $\mathbb{R}^n$ of norm d and $\sigma(\Gamma_F) = \Gamma_C$ d-similar lattices, then the number of messages that can be embedded using binning is $d^{n/2}$.*

3.2 Construction of a Similarity

An easy to prove result that will become useful in constructing similar lattices in 2 dimensions is the following.

Theorem 2. *In $\mathbb{R}^2$, any combination of rotation over an angle θ and scaling with factor h is a similarity of norm h^2.*

It follows from Theorem 1 and 2 that, in $\mathbb{R}^2$, a combination of a rotation R and a scaling S by a factor $\sqrt{M}$ results in a similarity of norm M which can be used to construct M-similar lattices to embed M messages.

3.3 Examples

As both the E_8 lattice and the hexagonal lattice A_2 are optimal for the sphere packing problem in the space on which they are defined, we will construct LQIM techniques based on these lattices. The A_2 lattice will prove not to be optimal for embedding binary messages.

Constructing Bins for the Hexagonal Lattice A_2. Can we find a lattice similar to A_2 that allows us to embed M messages for any $M \geq 2$? Applying (5) to the generator matrix G_C for A_2 (4) and M_σ as in Theorem (2) gives

$$J = \begin{pmatrix} h\cos\theta + \frac{\sqrt{3}}{3}h\sin\theta & \frac{-2\sqrt{3}}{3}h\sin\theta \\ \frac{2\sqrt{3}}{3}h\sin\theta & h\cos\theta - \frac{\sqrt{3}}{3}h\sin\theta \end{pmatrix} ,$$

with $h = \sqrt{M}$ and the angle θ to be determined. As J needs to have integer entries, we get that

$$z_1 = 2h\cos\theta \in \mathbb{Z} ,$$
$$z_2 = \frac{2\sqrt{3}}{3}h\sin\theta \in \mathbb{Z} .$$

From which it follows that,

$$z_1^2 + 3z_2^2 = 4M .$$

For i even and $M = 2^i 3^j$, solutions to this equation can be found, which on its turn implies that the angle of rotation is given by

$$\theta = \begin{cases} 0 & j \text{ even} , \\ \frac{\pi}{6} & j \text{ odd} . \end{cases}$$

Note that the condition on M is sufficient, but not necessary. All solutions for M can be found in [6], from which it also follows that $M = 2$ is impossible.

The Voronoi regions associated with the hexagonal lattice $\Gamma_C = A_2$ and Γ_F are illustrated in Fig. 1 for a different number of bins. To embed 3 messages using A_2 a combination of a rotation over an angle of $\frac{\pi}{6}$ and a scaling by $\sqrt{3}$ maps G_F onto G_C, such that Γ_C becomes a sublattice of index 3 in Γ_F defined by G_F. As no similarity of norm 2 exists we need a different approach to embed 2 messages using A_2. One can, for example, construct a similarity of norm 3 and not use the third coset. Our test results in Sect. 5.2 will show that even this gives far better performance than creating a coset of A_2 using a point of a scaled version of A_2 with Voronoi region half the size of the Voronoi region of A_2.

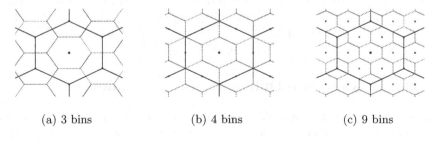

| (a) 3 bins | (b) 4 bins | (c) 9 bins |

Fig. 1. Voronoi regions for nested similar A_2 lattices

Constructing Bins for the Checkerboard Lattice D_2. Construction of the bins for the checkerboard lattice D_2 is straightforward using (5).

Constructing Bins for the E_8 Lattice. From [6] it follows that for E_8 there exist similar lattices for any norm d and hence any number of messages can be optimally embedded. However, the complexity of an 8-dimensional construction is evidently a lot higher than the 2-dimensional case. Describing the E_8 lattice as a *Hurwitzian lattice* [5] reduces the complexity. An n-dimensional Hurwitzian lattice is generated by taking linear combinations over the *Hurwitz quaternionic integers* $\mathbb{H}$ of n vectors that span $\mathbf{H}^n$. The field of quaternions $\mathbf{H}$ and the Hurwitz quaternionic integers $\mathbb{H}$ are defined as

$$\mathbf{H} = \{a + ib + jc + kd \mid a, b, c, d \in \mathbb{R}\} \ ,$$

$$\mathbb{H} = \left\{a + ib + jc + kd \mid a, b, c, d \in \mathbb{Z} \text{ or } a, b, c, d \in \mathbb{Z} + \frac{1}{2}\right\} \ ,$$

where $i^2 = j^2 = k^2 = -1$ and $ij = -ji = k$.

If $\Gamma_{\mathbb{H}}$ is a 2-dimensional Hurwitzian lattice then one can associate to it a lattice $\Gamma_{\mathbb{R}}$ in $\mathbb{R}^8$, by replacing in every vector in $\Gamma_{\mathbb{H}}$ the two components of the type $u + iv + jw + kx$ by $(u, v, w, x) \in \mathbb{R}^4$. Let $\omega = \frac{1}{2}(-1 + i + j + k)$, then a generator matrix for $\Gamma_{\mathbb{R}}$ is obtained from a generator matrix $G_{\mathbb{H}}^6$ of $\Gamma_{\mathbb{H}}$ by

$$G_{\mathbb{R}} = \begin{pmatrix} U' & V' & W' & X' \\ -V & U & -X & W \\ -W & X & U & -V \\ -X & -W & V & U \end{pmatrix} \ ,$$

where $\omega G_{\mathbb{H}} = U' + iV' + jW' + kX'$. For the Hurwitzian lattice $\Gamma_{\mathbb{H}}$ with generator matrix

$$G_{\mathbb{H}} = \begin{pmatrix} 1+i & 0 \\ 1 & 1 \end{pmatrix} \ ,$$

the obtained $\Gamma_{\mathbb{R}}$ is E_8. Now, multiplication in $\mathbb{H}^2$ by any quaternion $q = u_q + iv_q + jw_q + kx_q$ induces a similarity on $\mathbb{R}^8$ of norm $d = |q|^2 = u_q^2 + v_q^2 + w_q^2 + x_q^2$. Using Theorem 1, we see that, for example to embed $16 = 2^{8/2}$ messages using E_8-LQIM we need a similarity of norm at least 2. Now $q = (1 + i)$ induces a similarity of norm 2 on $\mathbb{R}^8$, which results in a matrix J with integer entries and $\det J > 1$ when applied as in (5) with $G_C = G_{\mathbb{R}}$. Thus multiplying $G_{\mathbb{H}}$ with q^{-1} gives a fine lattice 2-similar with E_8. We can identify 4 coset leaders for which bitwise combinations give 16 coset leaders of G_F/G_C allowing us to embed 4 bits.

4   How to Compare Different LQIM Techniques

In this section we give information about our test setup used in Sect. 5. First of all we need a common ground for our techniques to compare the performance of

---

[6] $G_{\mathbb{H}}$ can be decomposed as $U + iV + jW + kX$, where U, V, W, X are real matrices.

the different constructions. As there is a trade-off between fidelity, payload and robustness, we choose to control the first two properties for all techniques under inspection and investigate the robustness.

4.1   Matching Fidelity

For simplicity of calculations, the *peak signal to noise ratio* (*PSNR*) is used to measure fidelity, as this metric is commonly used to compare two images im_1 and im_2 with a resolution of n by m pixels. A formal definition is

$$\text{PSNR}(im_1, im_2) = 10 \log_{10} \frac{\text{MAX}^2}{\text{MSE}(im_1, im_2)} \quad [\text{dB}] \ ,$$

where MAX is the maximum signal value in the channel (for example, in an 8-bit grayscale image we have MAX$= 255$), while the mean squared error (*MSE*) is defined as

$$\text{MSE}(im_1, im_2) = \frac{1}{mn} \sum_{i=1}^{n} \sum_{j=1}^{m} |im_1(i,j) - im_2(i,j)|^2 \ .$$

For watermarking purposes, we need to match the fidelity of the different techniques. When embedding occurs in the spatial domain, controlling fidelity is obvious, though, when embedding in a transform domain this happens indirectly. The Stirmark benchmark [14,15] expresses the PSNR between the cover work and the watermarked cover work as a function of an embedding strength s

$$\text{PSNR}_{\text{Stirmark}}(s) = 60 - 20 \log_{10}(s) \ .$$

As the MSE depends on the lattice quantizer being used for embedding, the embedding strength s can be matched with a quantizer stepsize δ. This stepsize will be used to scale the lattice uniformly in all directions so that a constant fidelity, measured by the PSNR, can be assured when using the same strength for different techniques.

The use of dither sequences, as explained in Sect. 2.3, implies the quantization error to be independent of the host and uniformly distributed in the Voronoi region. Some results on the size of the Voronoi region for different lattices can be found in [5]. The uniform distribution allows us to calculate the distortion for each Voronoi region and the stepsize δ as a function of the embedding strength s in case embedding occurs in the spatial domain

$$\delta_{ScQ}(s) = \frac{255\sqrt{12}}{10^3} s \ , \qquad \delta_{A_2}(s) = \frac{153\sqrt{10}}{500} s \ ,$$

$$\delta_{D_2}(s) = \frac{51}{200}\sqrt{6}s \ , \qquad \delta_{E_8}(s) = \frac{459\sqrt{9290}}{46450} s \ ,$$

where *ScQ* stands for scalar QIM. In case embedding occurs using the wavelet coefficients of a (bi)orthogonal transform, the formulae approximately hold, as our experiments confirmed. Note that, regardless of the domain used for watermarking, these stepsizes should be scaled if not all coefficients are modified. Thus, to keep the fidelity constant throughout the different techniques, we need to embed the watermark with different stepsizes.

4.2   Matching Payload

Depending on the region being used for embedding, the total payload of an image can vary. In the region chosen we will embed at a rate of 0.5 bits per coefficient.

The information will be embedded in the wavelet coefficients of a 5-level biorthogonal wavelet decomposition of the images. We will not modify the LL coefficients as this has a noticeable impact on fidelity and also the first two levels of the decomposition are discarded as these contain high resolution information that is vulnerable to various attacks.

Since grouping of the coefficients has an impact on the robustness we will follow two techniques proposed by Cornelis et al. [7] that proved their efficiency; information is embedded using a tree-based and a block-based region.

The *tree-based* embedding region contains the first 8 coefficients of wavelet trees starting in the detail levels of the highest wavelet decomposition level. Our test only includes 512 by 512 images, so embedding information using the tree-based embedding region results in a total payload of $\left(3 \times \frac{512}{2^5} \times \frac{512}{2^5} \times 8\right) \frac{1}{2} =$ 3072 bits. As 1 coefficient comes from the 5th, or highest wavelet decomposition level, 4 from the 4th level and 3 from the 3th level, it is clear that the two first levels of the decomposition are not modified.

The *block-based* embedding region contains coefficients from all but the 2 or 3 lowest wavelet decomposition levels and excluding the LL band. Excluding the 2 lowest levels results in a total payload of $\left(\frac{512}{2^2} \times \frac{512}{2^2} - \frac{512}{2^5} \times \frac{512}{2^5}\right) \frac{1}{2} = 8064$ bits. Excluding the 3 lowest levels allows a total payload of $\left(\frac{512}{2^3} \times \frac{512}{2^3} - \frac{512}{2^5} \times \frac{512}{2^5}\right) \frac{1}{2}$ $= 1920$ bits.

4.3   Dimensionality

For the comparison of the different techniques we chose to study them in 8 dimensions. In this way we focus on finding gains resulting from shaping gains of the Voronoi region of the lattices under inspection. Practically this means that the techniques which are defined on two coefficients are extended by applying them 4 times on a tuple of 8 coefficients. Similarly, decoding is done by identifying in which of the 16 bins the received tuple of 8 coefficients is located and returning its label. As the binary labeling of the sixteen bins in an optimal way is not evident (cfr. Gray Code), we will use the symbol error rate *(SER)* instead of the common bit error rate *(BER)* to evaluate the proposed techniques.

5   Comparative Test Results

We now compare the proposed techniques (all applied in the same vector space) and see how they perform relative to sparse QIM. However, this section is not meant as an exhaustive comparison but is merely an illustration of the performance of some LQIM-techniques. The experiments were run using the Stirmark benchmark. The different techniques were tested on 8-bit grayscale images (Lena, Barbara, Boat and Pepper) with a resolution of 512 by 512 pixels. The presented results are those obtained for Lena as there were no noticeable differences between the test results of the different images.

5.1   Sparse QIM

The stepsize calculation for scalar QIM translates easily to that of sparse QIM by dividing the MSE for scalar QIM by the number of coefficients over which the information is spread.

   In order to get a rate of 0.5 bits per coefficient in the embedding region sparse QIM can be applied to 8 coefficients by projecting them on a 1-dimensional space and creating a set of 16 dithered scalar quantizers to embed 16 messages. Another solution is to combine 2 coefficients and embed 1 message per couple. The first technique, which we call *SpQ 8*, has the advantage that it spreads the information over more coefficients. However, the technique that combines 2 coefficients (*4 SpQ 2*) shows a clear performance benefit over *SpQ 8*. Figure 2(a) shows the resulting SER for the discussed techniques with fidelity 45.8 dB for the block-based embedding region (excluding 3 levels) after AWGN attack. The reason for this behavior can be found in the fact that although the information is spread over more coefficients using *SpQ 8* the bins are significantly smaller than using *4 SpQ 2*.

5.2   Lattice QIM

LQIM Based on the Hexagonal Lattice A_2. As mentioned before, the hexagonal lattice A_2 cannot be optimally used to embed 1 message in 2 coefficients. Creating 2 bins using the construction proposed in Sect. 3.3 results in suboptimal performance of the resulting watermarking technique. Figure 2(b) illustrates this problem by comparing the sparse QIM technique *4 SpQ 2* to *4 A_2 2 bins* after AWGN attack. We used the block-based embedding region (excluding 3 levels) with a fidelity of 45.8 dB. The SER is given for different levels of noise measured by the PSNR between watermarked cover work and received (noisy) watermarked work. The graph also shows results for *4 A_2 3 bins*, which is the proposed work-around to this problem; 3 bins are created but only 2 of them are being used.

LQIM Based on the Checkerboard Lattice D_2. The construction of bins for the checkerboard lattice gives us embedding of 1 message in 2 coefficients and is used as a basis for D_2-LQIM.

LQIM Based on the E_8 Lattice. The proposed construction gives us the possibility to embed 16 messages in 8 coefficients, attaining a rate of 0.5 bits per coefficient. JPEG compression is an image processing attack that is very common and thus cannot be neglected in estimating the robustness of any watermarking technique. We tested our techniques under a variety of quality settings and evaluated the decoding after JPEG compression. Figure 3(a) illustrates the impact of the use of different regions, for a fidelity of 45.8 dB, under the JPEG attack on the watermarking scheme based on the E_8 lattice. The regions are labeled by *tree* when tree-based, *block excl 2* when block based and excluding 2 levels and *block excl 3* for the one that excludes 3 levels. The results shown give the

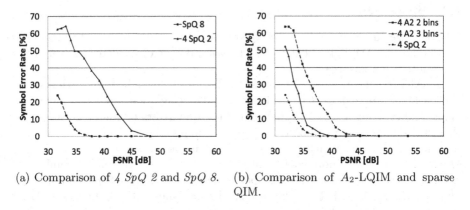

(a) Comparison of *4 SpQ 2* and *SpQ 8*.   (b) Comparison of A_2-LQIM and sparse QIM.

Fig. 2. Robustness results for sparse QIM and A_2-LQIM techniques after noise addition

SER for different quality parameters Q for JPEG compression. As *block excl 3* clearly outperforms[7] the other schemes, from now on we will use this scheme as a basis for our comparisons.

5.3 Embedding Effectiveness

Now we compare the *embedding effectiveness*; i.e. in the absence of noise, which embedding strength is necessary for correct decoding? Figure 3(b) shows the embedding effectiveness for sparse QIM and the proposed LQIM techniques. It shows that E_8 based techniques can achieve 100% embedding effectiveness for a fidelity of 54.6 dB, while sparse QIM, A_2 and D_2 based techniques achieve this for 53.7 dB. This is compliant to information theoretical results on this matter: techniques become capacity achieving for lattices that perform well on the sphere packing and covering problem. As the PSNR is not a reliable perceptual metric, we also computed the Structural Similarity metric [16], which was nearly constant for the different embedding techniques and always higher than 99 for our presented results. This assures us that embedding with the considered techniques induces hardly any perceptual distortion to the image structures.

5.4 Robustness

Comparison of robustness is based on *block excl 3* embedding scheme which we test under AWGN attack and JPEG compression.

If we want flawless decoding for a channel where the noise distortion is constraint to 35 dB, we require an embedding fidelity of 42.5 dB for the E_8 based technique (see Fig. 4(a)), but 42 dB for sparse QIM and D_2-LQIM. Lattice QIM based on A_2 does not achieve the same performance (fidelity needs to be 40.4 dB).

---

[7] Here, performance is penalized by a reduction in payload.

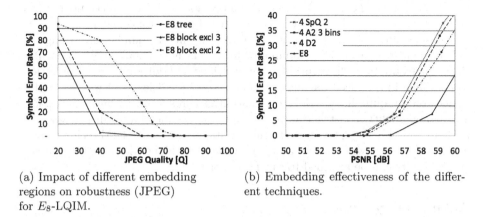

(a) Impact of different embedding regions on robustness (JPEG) for E_8-LQIM.

(b) Embedding effectiveness of the different techniques.

Fig. 3. Results for E_8-LQIM and embedding effectiveness

For decoding to be perfect after JPEG compression at quality 60, i.e. 35 dB distortion, embedding is done with fidelity of 45.9 dB for E_8, 45 dB for sparse QIM, 44.6 dB for D_2 and 43.6 dB for A_2-LQIM. Figure 4(b) gives the SER for different quality parameters Q for JPEG compression where the results are shown for a fidelity of 50.5 dB.

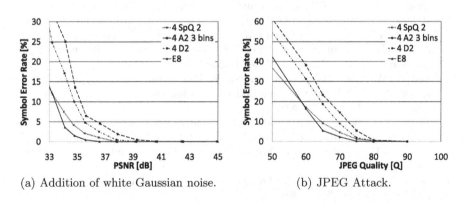

(a) Addition of white Gaussian noise.

(b) JPEG Attack.

Fig. 4. Robustness results for different techniques

6   Conclusion

Lattice QIM techniques have been proven to achieve capacity over the AWGN channel for high dimensions. Our comparison of E_8-LQIM with sparse QIM showed some improvements indicating that the use of higher dimensional lattices may return more noticeable differences. Compared to the other lattices, the impact of the shaping gain of E_8 was clearly visible. Overall, we have shown that LQIM techniques are a feasible alternative for sparse QIM and have illustrated how to implement the ideas of dithered quantization and distortion compensation behind QIM for LQIM. Moreover, the proposed geometric construction for the coding bins offers a flexible solution to embed a different number of messages.

Note that, the proposed techniques achieve relatively small payloads, insufficient, for example, in fingerprinting applications or additional error correction coding. The block-based technique where we exclude 3 levels of wavelet coefficients would require images of HD resolution to apply a fingerprinting code. For a constant fidelity, constructing more, and thus smaller bins will increase the payload but decrease robustness, as the results for the sparse QIM techniques illustrate. However, we believe that, again when using higher dimensional lattices, better results can be attained to tackle this problem.

Acknowledgements

This research was supported by the Fund for Scientific Research Flanders (project G.0206.08 and the postdoctoral fellowship of Peter Schelkens) and the DaVinci project of the Interdisciplinary Institute for Broadband Technology (IBBT).

References

1. Balado, F., Pérez-González, F.: Hexagonal quantizers are not optimal for 2-D data hiding. In: Proc. of SPIE Security and Watermarking of Multimedia Contents V, vol. 5020, pp. 623–631. Santa Clara (2003)
2. Chen, B., Wornell, G.W.: Digital watermarking and information embedding using dither modulation. In: Proc. of 1998 IEEE Second Workshop on Multimedia Signal Processing, pp. 273–278. IEEE Press, Redondo Beach (1998)
3. Chen, B., Wornell, G.W.: Quantization Index Modulation: A class of provably good methods for digital watermarking and information embedding. IEEE Trans. Inf. Theory 47(4), 1423–1443 (2001)
4. Conway, J.H., Sloane, N.J.A.: Fast Quantizing and Decoding Algorithms for Lattice Quantizers and Codes. IEEE Trans. Inf. Theory 28(2), 227–232 (1982)
5. Conway, J.H., Sloane, N.J.A.: Sphere Packings, Lattices and Groups. Springer, New York (1999)
6. Conway, J.H., Rains, S.N.J.A.: On the existence of similar sublattices. Canad. J. Math. 51(6), 1300–1306 (1999)
7. Cornelis, B., Barbarien, J., Dooms, A., Munteanu, A., Cornelis, J., Schelkens, P.: Design and evaluation of sparse quantization index modulation watermarking schemes. In: Proc. of SPIE Applications of Digital Image Processing XXXI, San Diego, vol. 7073 (2008)
8. Eggers, J.J., Bäuml, R., Tzschoppe, R., Girod, B.: Scalar Costa scheme for information embedding. IEEE Trans. Signal Process. 51(4), 1003–1019 (2003)
9. Erez, U., Zamir, R.: Achieving (1/2)log(1+SNR) on the AWGN channel with lattice encoding and decoding. IEEE Trans. Inf. Theory 50(10), 2293–2314 (2004)
10. Kirac, A., Vaidyanathan, P.P.: Dithering in lattice quantization. In: Conf. Rec. of the 29th Asilomar Conference on Signals, Systems and Computers, Pacific Grove, vol. 2, pp. 1066–1070 (1995)
11. Martinet, J.: Perfect Lattices in Euclidean Spaces. Springer, Berlin (2003)

12. Moulin, P., Koetter, P.: Data Hiding Codes (tutorial paper). Proceedings IEEE 93(12), 2083–2127 (2005)
13. Pérez-González, F.: The Importance of Aliasing in Structured Quantization Index Modulation Data Hiding. In: Kalker, T., Cox, I., Ro, Y.M. (eds.) IWDW 2003. LNCS, vol. 2939, pp. 1–17. Springer, Heidelberg (2004)
14. Petitcolas, F.A.P.: Watermarking schemes evaluation. IEEE Trans. Signal Process. 17(5), 58–64 (2000)
15. Petitcolas, F.A.P., Steinebach, M., Raynal, F., Dittmann, J., Fontaine, C., Fatès, N.: A public automated web-based evaluation service for watermarking schemes: StirMark Benchmark. In: Proc. of electronic imaging, security and watermarking of multimedia contents III, San Jose, vol. 4314, pp. 20–26 (2001)
16. Wang, Z., Bovik, A.C., Sheikh, H.R., Simoncelli, E.P.: Image quality assessment: From error visibility to structural similarity. IEEE Trans. on Image Process. 13(4), 600–612 (2004)
17. Zamir, R., Shamai, S., Erez, U.: Nested linear/lattice codes for structured multi-terminal binning. IEEE Trans. Inf. Theory 48(6), 1250–1276 (2002)
18. Zhang, Q., Boston, N.: Quantization Index Modulation using the E_8 lattice. In: Proc. of the 41th Annual Allerton Conference on Communication, Control and Computing (2003)

Watermark Embedding and Recovery in the Presence of C-LPCD De-synchronization Attacks

Andrea Abrardo, Mauro Barni, and Cesare Maria Carretti

Department of Information Engineering, University of Siena
via Roma 56, 53100, Siena, Italy
{abrardo,barni,carretti}@dii.unisi.it
http://www.dii.unisi.it

Abstract. The development of a watermarking system that is robust against de-synchronization attacks (DAs) is a major challenge. In this paper we make two steps towards the development of such a system by: i) proposing a fast algorithm for exhaustive watermark detection in the presence of C-LPCD DAs; ii) introducing a new watermarking system that by pre-distorting the watermark to be embedded greatly improves the performance of the exhaustive watermark detector. The validity of the proposed system is tested by means of Monte Carlo simulation on Gaussian white sequences. The results we obtained are rather promising thus suggesting to apply the newly proposed system to the watermarking of real audio sequences.

Keywords: watermarking, de-synchronization attacks.

1 Introduction

Despite more than a decade of intense research has passed since digital watermarking started raising the interest of the signal processing community, a few central problems still need to be solved, making digital watermarking a potentially useful, yet incomplete, tool in several multimedia security applications. Among the unsolved problems, robustness against de-synchronization attacks (DA) play a central role, since DAs provide an easy and perceptually friendly way of impeding watermark recovery. Even worse, de-synchronization of the decoder (detector) may be the consequence of common processing operators that are not necessarily applied with the explicit intention of hindering the extraction of the watermark.

De-synchronization attacks are a major threat in image watermarking, since they correspond to the application of a geometric transformation to the watermarked image, e.g. a rotation, a scaling or a translation, whose effect on the perceptual quality of the image is null, but whose effect on watermark decoding or detection is often dramatic. For this reason, several approaches have been proposed in the past to deal with RST (Rotation, Scaling and Translation) attacks, including exhaustive search [1,2], template-based re-synchronization [3,4,5],

A.T.S. Ho et al. (Eds.): IWDW 2009, LNCS 5703, pp. 54–68, 2009.

self-synchronizing watermarks [6,7] and watermarking in invariant domains [8]. A common assumption behind all the above methods is that the number of parameters specifying the DA is rather limited. For instance, it is the relatively low cardinality of the set of possible RST attacks that makes the estimation of the geometric transformation applied by the attacker via exhaustive search or template matching computationally feasible. This is not the case with local de-synchronization attacks, or local geometric transformations. As opposed to global transformations, local geometric distortions, refer to non-parametric transforms affecting in different ways the position of the pixels of the same image or affecting only part of the image. The random bending attack - RBA [9], contained in the Stirmark utility, is the most famous example of local DA. Other local DAs include the LPCD and MF attacks recently introduced in [10]. Attempts to survive the RBA attack have sometimes been reported, e.g. in [3], the RBA DA is modeled as the local application of space-varying RST distortions affecting only part of the image, however no theoretically-grounded method capable of dealing with a wide variety of DAs exist.

Though less studied, DAs, and in particular local DAs, are a threat also for watermarking of 1D signals, e.g. audio watermarking. Applying a simple time-varying pitch control is often enough to de-synchronize the watermark decoder (detector) thus preventing the correct extraction of the hidden message [11]. As for image watermarking, no general solution exists to cope with local DAs for 1D signals. Among the reasons for the difficulty of developing suitable remedies against DAs is the lack of an accurate mathematical model to define the class of perceptually admissible DAs. Should such a model be available, it would be possible to devise suitable countermeasures based on optimal watermark decoding and detection theory. In the case of 1-bit watermarking[1], for instance it could be possible to apply an exhaustive search (ES) strategy consisting in looking for the watermark by considering all the possible distortions that could have been applied to the watermarked signal. If the number of such distortions is not too high, e.g. it increases polynomially with the watermark length, it can be proven that ES watermark detection is asymptotically optimum [2,14]. Of course, a problem with ES detection is computational complexity since considering all possible distortions rapidly becomes unfeasible when the signal length n increases.

A flexible, yet simple, mathematical model for 1D DAs has been recently proposed in [10]. Given an original sequence $\mathbf{y} = \{y(1), y(2) \ldots y(n)\}$, the model proposed in [10], denoted with C-LPCD (Constrained Local Permutations with Cancellation and Duplication), describes the attacked sequence $\mathbf{z}$ by means of a sequence of displacement values that applied to the samples of $\mathbf{y}$ produce $\mathbf{z}$. In order to create a smooth (hence perceptually admissible) distortion, the displacement sequence is subject to some constraints and applied in a multi-resolution framework. In [10], an interpretation of the C-LPCD DAs in terms of markov chains theory is also given.

---

[1] In 1-bit watermarking the detector is only asked to verify the presence of a given watermark [12,13].

In the above framework, the purpose of this paper is twofold. First of all a computationally feasible algorithm for applying ES detection to 1D watermarked signals affected by C-LPCD distortions is proposed. By assuming a spread spectrum watermarking system and a correlation based detector [12,13], the fast ES algorithm we propose relies on Viterbi's optimization algorithm to perform an exhaustive search detection with a computational complexity that increases linearly with the sequence length n. By applying the proposed algorithm to synthetic Gaussian sequences, we show how the dimensionality of the DA class and the length of the host sequence influences the false alarm probability, resulting in a satisfactory detection accuracy only if the host sequence is long enough.

As a second contribution, we propose a new watermarking scheme that relies on the proposed fast ES detector to pre-distort the watermark sequence in such a way that the correlation with the host sequence is maximized. Watermark detection is obtained by applying the fast ES detector to the watermarked and possibly attacked sequence. By properly tuning the parameters of the fast ES used by the embedder and those used by the detector, we show how the ES applied by the detector is able, at the same time, to account for both the pre-distortion introduced by the embedder and the DA applied by the attacker.

We tested the validity of the proposed approach by applying the watermarking scheme to synthetic i.i.d. Gaussian sequences, and measuring, for various settings of the operational parameters, the performance in terms of false and missed detection probabilities. The results we obtained are very promising, thus opening the way towards the application of the new watermarking scheme to real audio sequences.

The rest of the paper is organized as follows: in section 2 we summarize the C-LPCD model for DA. In section we introduce the fast algorithm for ES watermark detection. In section 4 we describe the new watermarking algorithm, while in section 5 we evaluate its performance through Monte Carlo simulations. Finally in section 4 we draw some conclusions and present some ideas for future research.

2   The C-LPCD Model

In this section we describe the C-LPCD class of DAs.

For sake of simplicity, let us start with the non-constrained version of the model (plain LPCD). As said, let $\mathbf{y} = \{y(1), y(2) \ldots y(n)\}$ be a generic signal and let $z = \{z(1), z(2) \ldots z(n)\}$ be the distorted version of $\mathbf{y}$. The LPCD model states that $z(i) = y(i + \Delta_i)$ where $\boldsymbol{\Delta} = \{\Delta_1, \Delta_2 \ldots \Delta_n\}$ is a sequence of i.i.d random variables uniformly distributed in a predefined interval $I = [-\Delta, \Delta]$. For simplicity we assume that Δ_i can take only integer values in I. This way, the values assumed by the samples of $\mathbf{z}$ are chosen among those of $\mathbf{y}$. A limitation of the plain LPCD model is the lack of memory. As noted in [10], this is a problem from a perceptual point of view: with no constraint on the smoothness of the displacement field there is no guarantee that the set of LPCD distortions is perceptually admissible even by considering very small values of Δ.

With the C-LPCD model the above problem is solved by requiring that the sample order is preserved. In practice, the displacement of each element i of the distorted sequence $\mathbf{z}$ is conditioned to the displacement of the element $i-1$ of the same sequence. In formulas, $z(i) = y(i + \Delta_i)$ where Δ_i is a sequence of i.i.d integer random variables uniformly distributed in the interval

$$I = [\max(-\Delta, \Delta_{i-1} - 1), \Delta]. \tag{1}$$

The C-LPCD model can be mathematically described by resorting to the theory of Markov chains, where the chain states correspond to the displacements applied to the previous sample[2]. Specifically, the possible states are all the integers in the interval $-\Delta, \Delta$, and the transition matrix P of the Markov chain is:

$$P = \begin{bmatrix} \frac{1}{2\Delta+1} & \frac{1}{2\Delta+1} & \frac{1}{2\Delta+1} & \cdots & \cdots & \frac{1}{2\Delta+1} \\ \frac{1}{2\Delta+1} & \frac{1}{2\Delta+1} & \frac{1}{2\Delta+1} & \cdots & \cdots & \frac{1}{2\Delta+1} \\ 0 & \frac{1}{2\Delta} & \frac{1}{2\Delta} & \cdots & \cdots & \frac{1}{2\Delta} \\ 0 & \frac{1}{2\Delta-1} & \frac{1}{2\Delta-1} & \cdots & \cdots & \frac{1}{2\Delta-1} \\ \cdots & \cdots & \cdots & \cdots & \cdots & \cdots \\ 0 & 0 & 0 & \cdots & \frac{1}{2} & \frac{1}{2} \end{bmatrix} \tag{2}$$

where the element p_{11} gives the probability of going from state $-\Delta$ to state $-\Delta$, the element p_{12} the probability of going from state $-\Delta$ to state $-\Delta + 1$ and so on.

To make the distortion less perceptible, in [10] a multiresolution version of the C-LPCD model is also proposed (hereafter referred to as MC-LPCD), whereby the DA is applied at different resolutions to obtain the global displacement sequence: a low resolution displacement sequence is first generated, then a full size displacement is built by means of a given interpolation strategy, e.g. by means of linear or bicubic interpolation. The full resolution displacement is applied to the original sequence to produce the distorted signal.

More specifically, the multiresolution model consists of two steps. Let n be the length of the signal (for sake of simplicity we assume that n is a power of 2). To apply the C-LPCD model at the L-th level of resolution, a displacement sequence δ of size $\frac{n}{2^L}$ is generated. Then the full resolution sequence Δ is built by means of linear or bicubic interpolation. Note that, in this way non-integer displacement values are introduced[3]. The full resolution displacement sequence Δ is used to generate the attacked signal $\mathbf{z}$ as follows:

$$z(i) = y(i + \Delta_i). \tag{3}$$

---

[2] In [10] the number of states is reduced by considering as the current state the size of the interval in which the displacement may vary. Here we adopt a different approach that simplifies the derivation of the fast ES algorithm.

[3] It is still possible to obtain integer displacements by applying a nearest neighbor interpolation, of course at the expense of the smoothness of the displacement sequence.

As opposed to the full resolution version of C-LPCD, however, the presence of non-integer displacements is now possible due to interpolation. To account for this possibility, whenever the displacement vector points to non integer coordinates of the original sequence, the sample value of the attacked sequence $z(i)$ is computed by interpolating the original sample values.

2.1   Probabilistic Vs. Deterministic Interpretation

If we adopt the description given in [10] and summarized before, the C-LPCD model is seen as a probabilistic model (a Markov chain) whereby the displacement sequence is generated samplewise according to a probabilistic rule. A problem with this approach is that for a given Δ (and level of resolution) the displacement sequences defining the distortions belonging to the C-LPCD class do not have the same occurrence probability. As shown in [10], certain status of the Markov chain are more probable than others, hence resulting in a tendency to prefer displacements with positive Δ_is. The approach taken in [10] to solve this problem is to assign a non-uniform probability to the transitions from one state to the other, trying in this way to make all the displacement sequences equally probable. In this paper we adopt a different approach, i.e. we abandon the probabilistic interpretation of the LPCD model and simply consider all the displacement sequences for which the condition expressed in (1) holds as (equiprobable) admissible sequences. In this framework, we find it useful to define the set of all the admissible displacement sequences according to the MC-LPCD model with maximum displacement Δ and applied at resolution level L as $\mathcal{D}(\Delta, L)$

3   Exhaustive Watermark Detection through Viterbi's Algorithm

In this section we introduce the first contribution of our research. Given a sequence $\mathbf{y}$ and a watermark $\mathbf{w}$, we introduce an algorithm that permits to find the displacement field belonging to $\mathcal{D}(\Delta, L)$ that applied to $\mathbf{w}$ produces a distorted watermark $\mathbf{v}$ that maximizes the correlation between $\mathbf{v}$ and $\mathbf{y}$. In formulas, let $\mathcal{T}(\mathbf{w}, \boldsymbol{\Delta}) = \mathbf{v}$ be the operator that applies the displacement field $\boldsymbol{\Delta}$ to the sequence $\mathbf{w}$. We show how it is possible to solve in a very efficient way the following optimization problem:

$$\boldsymbol{\Delta}^* = \arg \max_{\boldsymbol{\Delta} \in \mathcal{D}(\Delta, L)} corr(\mathcal{T}(\mathbf{w}, \boldsymbol{\Delta}), \mathbf{y}). \qquad (4)$$

where $corr(\mathbf{v}, \mathbf{y})$ indicates the correlation between the sequences $\mathbf{v}$ and $\mathbf{y}$, namely

$$corr(\mathbf{v}, \mathbf{y}) = \sum_{i=1}^{n} v(i)y(i). \qquad (5)$$

Specifically, we propose a fast algorithm whose complexity grows only linearly with the length n of $\mathbf{w}$, while the cardinality of the set $\mathcal{D}$ grows exponentially with n (see [10]).

To elaborate, let us rewrite correlation (5) as:

$$corr(\mathbf{v}, \mathbf{y}) = \sum_{p=1}^{P} \sum_{l=1}^{2^L} v((p-1)2^L + l)y((p-1)2^L + l). \tag{6}$$

where $P = \frac{n}{2^L}$ is the length of the low resolution displacement sequence. The distorted watermark samples $v((p-1)2^L + l)$ are evaluated by applying the displacements $\Delta_{(p-1)2^L + l}$ $(p = 1 \ldots P, l = 1 \ldots 2^L)$ to $\mathbf{w}$, where, following the multiresolution C-LPCD model described in Section II, $\Delta_{(p-1)2^L + l}$ depends on a limited set of consecutive low resolution displacements of the sequence δ. The exact number of samples of δ that contribute to the computation of an element of Δ depends on the interpolation rule used to generate Δ from δ. As an example, by considering a linear interpolation, $\Delta_{(p-1)2^L + l}$ depends solely on the couple of adjacent low resolution displacements δ_p and δ_{p+1}. In this case, it is possible to rewrite (6) as:

$$corr(\mathbf{v}, \mathbf{y}) = \sum_{p=1}^{P} \rho_p(\delta_p, \delta_{p+1}). \tag{7}$$

where $\rho_p(\delta_p, \delta_{p+1})$ is the correlation evaluated in the interval $\left[(p-1)2^L + 1, \ldots, p2^L\right]$. For the sake of simplicity, throughout the paper we will refer to the case of linear interpolation, however the results we obtain are easily extended to higher order interpolation rules. Under this assumption, problem (4) may be expressed as:

$$\delta^* = \arg \max_{\delta \in \mathcal{D}(\Delta, 0)} \sum_{p=1}^{P} \rho_p(\delta_p, \delta_{p+1}). \tag{8}$$

By letting $N = 2\Delta + 1$, it is possible to associate with problem (8) a trellis $T(N, N)$ with N vertexes, N edges, and depth $P + 1$. Vertexes at epoch p represent all the possible values of δ_p while edges which originate from a vertex at epoch p represent all the admissible values of δ_{p+1}. In particular, edge $E_p(m, q)$, $m, q = \{-\Delta, \ldots, \Delta\}$, $p = \{1, 2, \ldots, P\}$ connects vertex $V(m, p)$ with vertex $V(q, p+1)$ only if the couple of low resolution displacements $\delta_p = m$, $\delta_{p+1} = q$ satisfy the C-LPCD constraint, i.e., if $m \geq q + 1$. Such a connection is associated with the correlation $\mu_p(m, q)$. Problem (4) can now be solved by applying the Viterbi algorithm over the trellis $T(N, N)$. As in traditional Viterbi algorithm, among all paths which converge in the same vertex, only the one which have accumulated the highest correlation survives. Since the watermark sequence $w(i)$ is defined for $i = 1, \ldots, n$, at the first step, i.e., for $p = 1$, only edges which originate from vertexes $m \geq 0$ are admitted while at the last step, i.e., for $p = P + 1$, only edges which terminate in vertexes $m \leq 0$ are admitted. In Fig. 1 we show an example of the trellis corresponding to problem (4) in the case of $\Delta = 1$, $P = 3$. In this case, we have a maximum of 3 transitions originating from each vertex corresponding to displacements $\{-1, 0, 1\}$. In the

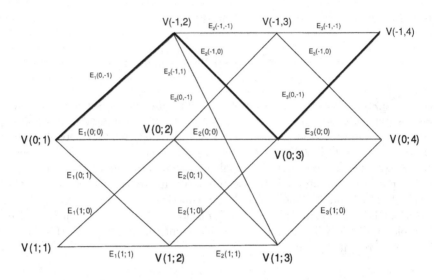

Fig. 1. Trellis representation of problem (8) for $\Delta = 1$, $P = 3$

considered illustrative example, the path which survives, i.e., the path which maximizes (7) is $\delta = (0, -1, 0, -1)$. Such a path is drawn as a tick line in Fig. 1. Regarding the complexity of solving (4) through the Viterbi algorithm, note that at each step N^2 correlations (at most) and N comparisons must be computed to get N survivors, and, hence, problem (4) can be solved in $O(PN^2)$ operations, i.e., the complexity increases linearly with P and hence with n. Of course, if the interpolation order increases, the correlation of the samples in the interval $[(p-1)2^L + 1, \ldots, p2^L]$ depends on more than two samples of the low resolution displacement sequence hence augmenting the memory of the system.

The existence of a fast algorithm for exhaustive watermark detection (within a given class $\mathcal{D}(\Delta, L)$ of DAs) opens the way towards a watermark detection scheme that is intrinsically robust against MC-LPCD DAs. More specifically, by assuming an additive spread spectrum watermarking system wherein the watermarked sequence $\mathbf{y}$ is built as:

$$y(i) = x(i) + \gamma w(i), \tag{9}$$

the watermark detector simply compares

$$\rho^* = \max_{\Delta \in \mathcal{D}(\Delta, L)} corr(\mathcal{T}(\mathbf{w}, \boldsymbol{\Delta}), \mathbf{y}), \tag{10}$$

against a detection threshold set by fixing the false detection probability.

3.1   False Alarm Probability

While it is obvious that any DA belonging to $\mathcal{D}(\Delta, L)$ will not have any impact on the probability of missing the watermark, problems may arise because of the false detection probability. In order to evaluate the discrimination capability of the detection statistic ρ^*, we must evaluate the pdf of ρ^* under the hypothesis H_0 that the sequence under analysis is not watermarked and under the hypothesis H_1 that the watermark $\mathbf{w}$ the detector is looking for is indeed present.

While a theoretical analysis of such a pdf is possible under some simplifying assumptions, for sake of brevity here we estimate the mean value and the variance of ρ^* be resorting to Monte Carlo simulations. We start by considering H_0, i.e. we evaluate $\mu_{\rho^*|0}$ and $\sigma^2_{\rho^*|0}$. In doing so, several parameters have to be taken into account, including the length n of the host sequence and the parameters of the class of DAs considered by the detector. In table 1 we report the values of $\mu_{\rho^*|0}$ and $\sigma^2_{\rho^*|0}$ that we estimated by generating 1000 i.i.d. Gaussian random sequences with variance $\sigma^2_x = 1000$, and by computing ρ^* by means of the Viterbi algorithm described before, looking for a randomly generated antipodal watermark taking values ± 1 with equal probabilities. As it can be seen the mean value of ρ^* does not depend on the length of the host sequence, and decreases when L increases. This is an expected result, since when the M-LPCD model is applied at a lower resolution level, the capability of generating a distortion that increases the correlation between the host sequence and the watermark decreases, due to the reduced dimensionality of the $\mathcal{D}(\Delta, L)$ class. The behavior of the variance of ρ^* is opposite to that of $\mu_{\rho^*|0}$, since it does not depend on L and decreases with n. This is very interesting result, showing that the watermark detection reliability can be improved by increasing the watermark length.

Table 1. Mean and variance of ρ^* under hypothesis H_0

		$\Delta = 1$					$\Delta = 2$				
		L=4	L=5	L=6	L=7	L=8	L=4	L=5	L=6	L=7	L=8
$n = 10000$	$\mu_{\rho^*|0}$	5.20	3.66	2.5	1.82	1.27	6.56	4.62	3.27	2.30	1.62
	$\sigma^2_{\rho^*|0}$	0.05	0.05	0.05	0.05	0.05	0.04	0.04	0.04	0.04	0.04
$n = 50000$	$\mu_{\rho^*|0}$	5.20	3.66	2.58	1.82	1.29	6.56	4.63	3.27	2.31	1.63
	$\sigma^2_{\rho^*|0}$	0.01	0.01	0.01	0.01	0.01	0.007	0.008	0.007	0.007	0.008
$n = 100000$	$\mu_{\rho^*|0}$	5.20	3.66	2.58	1.82	1.28	6.56	4.63	3.28	2.31	1.64
	$\sigma^2_{\rho^*|0}$	0.005	0.005	0.005	0.005	0.005	0.004	0.004	0.004	0.004	0.004
$n = 150000$	$\mu_{\rho^*|0}$	5.19	3.66	2.59	1.82	1.29	6.57	4.63	3.27	2.31	1.64
	$\sigma^2_{\rho^*|0}$	0.003	0.003	0.003	0.003	0.003	0.003	0.003	0.003	0.002	0.002

We then considered hypothesis H_1. To do so we generated again 1000 i.i.d. random sequences and added a binary random watermark generated according to an i.i.d. distribution with equiprobable symbols ($P(w(i) = 1) = P(w(i) = -1) = 0.5$). The watermark generated in this way was added to the sequence $\mathbf{x}$ as in equation 9. In particular we used $\gamma = 1$ thus obtaining a document to watermark ratio (DWR, see [12]) equal to 30dB. The mean value $\mu_{\rho^*|1}$ and the variance $\sigma^2_{\rho^*|1}$ obtained in this case are reported in table 2. Upon inspection of the table we see that the behavior of $\mu_{\rho^*|1}$ and $\sigma^2_{\rho^*|1}$ under H_1 is very similar to that we obtained for H_0. Interestingly, $\mu_{\rho^*|1} > \mu_{\rho^*|0}$ and for large values of

Table 2. Mean and variance of ρ^* under hypothesis H_1

		$\Delta = 1$					$\Delta = 2$				
		L=4	L=5	L=6	L=7	L=8	L=4	L=5	L=6	L=7	L=8
$n = 10000$	$\mu_{\rho^*\|1}$	5.63	4.09	3.02	2.29	1.76	6.84	4.90	3.56	2.62	1.97
	$\sigma^2_{\rho^*\|1}$	0.051	0.055	0.052	0.050	0.055	0.040	0.040	0.038	0.040	0.041
$n = 50000$	$\mu_{\rho^*\|1}$	5.62	4.09	3.02	2.28	1.77	6.84	4.92	3.56	2.62	1.97
	$\sigma^2_{\rho^*\|1}$	0.010	0.010	0.010	0.011	0.010	0.008	0.008	0.008	0.008	0.009
$n = 100000$	$\mu_{\rho^*\|1}$	5.62	4.09	3.03	2.28	1.77	6.84	4.92	3.57	2.62	1.97
	$\sigma^2_{\rho^*\|1}$	0.005	0.005	0.005	0.006	0.005	0.004	0.004	0.004	0.004	0.004
$n = 150000$	$\mu_{\rho^*\|1}$	5.62	4.09	3.03	2.28	1.77	6.84	4.9	3.57	2.62	1.97
	$\sigma^2_{\rho^*\|1}$	0.003	0.003	0.004	0.004	0.004	0.003	0.003	0.002	0.003	0.003

n such a distance is significantly larger than the standard deviation of ρ^* both under hypothesis 0 and 1.

To give a quantitative measure of the discriminative power of ρ^*, we can consider the quantity:

$$\sqrt{SNR} = \frac{|\mu_{\rho^*|1} - \mu_{\rho^*|0}|}{\sigma_{\rho^*|0}}, \tag{11}$$

it is such a quantity, in fact, that determines the performance of the watermark detector[4]. In the left part of figure 2 the SNR parameter is expressed as a function of n for $\Delta = 2$ and various values of L ($L = 4, 6, 8$). As it can be seen, the SNR increases significantly with n and, to a lesser extent, with L.

Passing from the SNR to the false and missed detection probabilities (respectively P_f and P_m), requires that the exact pdf of ρ^* under H_0 and H_1 is known. For instance, by assuming that ρ^* follows a normal distribution[5], we have

$$P_m = \frac{1}{2} \operatorname{erfc}\left(\sqrt{\frac{SNR}{2}} - \operatorname{erfc}^{-1}(2P_f)\right). \tag{12}$$

In this case, if we let $P_f = 10^{-6}$, we obtain the values of P_m reported in figure 2 (right). By inspecting the figure it is evident that though ρ^* permits to discriminate H_0 from H_1, the error probability tends to be rather high. For instance, by letting $P_f = 10^{-6}$, a value that is rather common in watermarking applications, we have $P_m = 10^{-2}$ (for $n = 150000$), which is a rather high value. All the more that the results in figure 2 refer to the case $L = 8$, that is to a class of MC-LPCD attack with a rather low cardinality.

Though not reported here for sake of brevity, the results we obtained do not change significantly in the presence of DAs belonging to the class of MC-LPCD attacks considered by the detector during its search. This is an expected result, since on one side the statistics of ρ^* under hypothesis H_0 are not affected by

---

[4] The definition in equation (11) is justified by the observation that $\sigma^2_{\rho^*|0} \simeq \sigma^2_{\rho^*|1}$.

[5] An assumption that could be justified by resorting to the central limit theorem for weakly depending random variables [15].

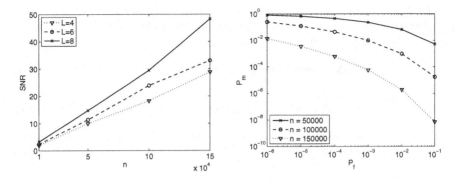

Fig. 2. SNR as a function of n for different values of L (left), and (right) P_m vs P_f for different values of n and $L = 8$ ($\Delta = 2$, DWR = 30dB)

DAs due to the independence of the host sequence samples[6], and on the other side, the exhaustive search carried out by the detector is able to nullify the de-synchronization effect of the attack.

4   A New Watermarking Algorithm

The results reported at the end of the previous section show that for reliable watermark detection the search space must not be too large, that is the displacement fields considered by the detector must be smooth enough and, most importantly, n must be very large. For instance, with $\Delta = 2$, and $L = 8$, $n = 150000$ may not be enough to ensure reliable watermark detection. With regard to L, it is worth observing that the characteristics of the class of distortions that the attacker will use to impede watermark detection is not under the detector's control. On the contrary such characteristics depend of the perceptual distortion introduced by the attack and the resulting quality of the watermarked content. Such an analysis, that would necessarily depend on the particular media being watermarked, is outside the scope of this paper, we only mention that some preliminary results carried out on audio signals shows that, for $\Delta \in [1,4]$ attacks are inaudible as long as $L \geq 6$ or $L \geq 7$ depending on the audio content. As to n, 150000 samples corresponds to about 3 seconds of an audio signal sampled at 44KHz, hence, even if it may be feasible to go beyond such a value, we can not expect n to grow much larger than this.

   In order to achieve a better separation between the statistics of ρ^* under hypothesis 0 and 1, we propose a new watermark embedding strategy. The main idea the new scheme relies on, is to geometrically pre-distort the watermark in such a way to maximize its correlation with the host sequence. To be specific, the new watermark embedding algorithm works as follows. We assume that the

---

[6] DAs applied at lower resolution levels may introduce a weak correlation between adjacent samples due to interpolation, however we verified experimentally that such an effect is negligible.

class $\mathcal{D}(\Delta_a, L)$ of de-synchronization attacks the adversary may use to attack the watermark is known. The embedder runs the exhaustive search algorithm on $\mathbf{x}$ and $\mathbf{w}$, obtaining a pre-distorted watermark $\mathbf{v}$:

$$\Delta^* = \arg \max_{\Delta \in \mathcal{D}(\Delta_a, L)} corr(\mathcal{T}(\mathbf{w}, \Delta), \mathbf{x}), \tag{13}$$

$$\mathbf{v} = \mathcal{T}(\mathbf{w}, \Delta^*). \tag{14}$$

Then, the embedder adds the pre-distorted watermark $\mathbf{v}$ to $\mathbf{x}$, generating the watermarked sequence $\mathbf{y}$:

$$y(i) = x(i) + \gamma v(i). \tag{15}$$

Given a possibly marked and attacked sequence $\mathbf{z}$, the detector performs an exhaustive search of $\mathbf{w}$ over $\mathbf{z}$. In this phase the detector has to take into account both the displacement sequence used by the embedder to pre-distort the watermark and the possible presence of a DA. To do so, it uses a search window Δ_d that is larger than Δ_a, say $\Delta_d = K\Delta_a$. The choice of the parameter K is a crucial one, since a large value of K would increase the false detection probability, whereas low values of K would augment the probability of missing the watermark. In the sequel, we will assume that $K = 2$, a set-up justified by the assumption that applying a DA with $\Delta_d = \Delta_e$ after watermark pre-distortion roughly correspond to an attack with a doubled Δ. In the next section we show how the pre-distortion of the watermark prior to its insertion within the host sequence permits to significantly improve the performance of the system presented in the previous section.

5   Experimental Results on Synthetic Sequences

The performance of the new watermarking system has been analyzed by means of Monte Carlo simulations. We started by considering the performance of the system in the absence of attacks. Throughout the experiments we let $K = 2$, $\Delta_e = \Delta_a = 1$. The statistics of ρ^* under H_0 coincides with those reported in the previous section (table 1, $\Delta = 2$). To obtain the statistics of ρ^* when H_1 holds, we generated 1000 watermarked sequences (with different embedded watermarks) by applying equations (13) through (15) with $\Delta_e = 1$. We then applied the watermark detector with $\Delta_d = 2$. The result we obtained for different values of L and n are summarized in table 3.

The dependence of $\mu_{\rho^*|1}$ and $\sigma^2_{\rho^*|1}$ upon L and n is similar to that obtained for standard watermarking scheme reported in the previous section, however the distance between $\mu_{\rho^*|1}$ and $\mu_{\rho^*|0}$ is now much larger (for a similar variance) yielding a much better SNR and hence much better performance as reported in figure 3, where the SNR as a function of n and the plot of P_f vs P_m (still under the normality assumption of ρ^*) are given. As it can be seen the introduction of a pre-distorted watermark greatly enhance the watermark detectability. A second difference with respect to the previous case that worths attention is the lower dependence of the SNR upon the resolution level L, as a matter of fact the right

Table 3. Mean and variance of ρ^* under hypothesis H_1 for the new watermarking scheme with pre-distorted watermark ($\Delta_e = \Delta_a = 1$, $\Delta_d = 2$)

		L=4	L=5	L=6	L=7	L=8
$n = 10000$	$\mu_{\rho^*\|1}$	7.170	5.227	3.891	2.953	2.302
	$\sigma^2_{\rho^*\|1}$	0.041	0.041	0.039	0.041	0.043
$n = 50000$	$\mu_{\rho^*\|1}$	7.166	5.244	3.891	2.959	2.308
	$\sigma^2_{\rho^*\|1}$	0.008	0.008	0.008	0.008	0.009
$n = 100000$	$\mu_{\rho^*\|1}$	7.167	5.240	3.899	2.953	2.311
	$\sigma^2_{\rho^*\|1}$	0.004	0.004	0.003	0.005	0.004
$n = 150000$	$\mu_{\rho^*\|1}$	7.171	5.241	3.898	2.957	2.311
	$\sigma^2_{\rho^*\|1}$	0.003	0.003	0.003	0.003	0.003

plot in figure 3 refers to the case $L = 8$, however almost identical results are obtained for $L = 4$ and $L = 6$.

A difference of the system based on watermark pre-distortion is that the answer of the detector in the presence of an MC-LPCD attack is not equal to the one obtained in the absence of attacks. The reason for the diminished value of ρ^* in the presence of DA, is that as a consequence of such an attack the host sequence $\mathbf{x}$ and the watermark suffers different distortions, the host sequence is distorted only by the attack, while the inserted watermark undergoes both the pre-distortion and the distortion due to the attack. The detector is not able to compensate for both the distortions, despite the use of a value of Δ_d that is larger than Δ_e and Δ_a, hence justifying a decrease of the performance. Once again we verified this phenomenon by means of Monte Carlo simulations. The watermarked sequences used to produce table 3 were attacked by an MC-LPCD characterized by $\Delta_a = 1$ and the detector run again. The new results we obtained are summarized in table 4.

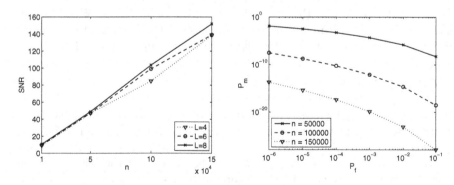

Fig. 3. Performance of the watermarking system based on watermark pre-distortion: (left) SNR as a function of n for different values of L, (right) P_m vs P_f for different values of n and $L = 8$. ($\Delta_e = 1, \Delta_d = 2$, DWR = 30dB).

Table 4. Mean and variance of ρ^* in the presence of DA. ($\Delta_e = \Delta_a = 1$, $\Delta_d = 2$, DWR $= 30$dB).

		L=4	L=5	L=6	L=7	L=8
$n = 10000$	$\mu_{\rho^*|1}$	6.950	5.021	3.705	2.790	2.139
	$\sigma^2_{\rho^*|1}$	0.0446	0.0472	0.046	0.049	0.047
$n = 50000$	$\mu_{\rho^*|1}$	6.944	5.043	3.708	2.790	2.140
	$\sigma^2_{\rho^*|1}$	0.009	0.009	0.009	0.009	0.010
$n = 100000$	$\mu_{\rho^*|1}$	6.945	5.041	3.716	2.783	2.146
	$\sigma^2_{\rho^*|1}$	0.005	0.005	0.004	0.005	0.005
$n = 150000$	$\mu_{\rho^*|1}$	6.948	5.041	3.715	2.786	2.143
	$\sigma^2_{\rho^*|1}$	0.003	0.003	0.003	0.003	0.003

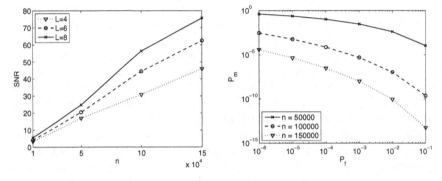

Fig. 4. Performance in the presence of DA: (left) SNR as a function of n for different values of L, (right) P_m vs P_f for different values of n and $L = 8$ ($\Delta_e = \Delta_a = 1, \Delta_d = 2$, DWR $= 30$dB)

The SNR as a function of n and the plot of P_f vs P_m (still under the normality assumption of ρ^*) are given in figure 4. Upon inspection of the results, we see that though lower than in the attack-free case, the performance of the system are still rather good (definitely better than those obtained without watermark pre-distortion), thus confirming the validity of the proposed approach.

6   Conclusions

In this paper we have introduced a fast watermark detector that implements an exhaustive search detector in the presence of de-synchronization attacks belonging to the class of MC-LPCD DAs. As expected the performance of the exhaustive search detector are rather poor due to the increase of the false detection probability typical of such systems. To cope with this problem, we introduced a new watermarking algorithm based on the pre-distortion of the watermark signal and the fast exhaustive search detector introduced previously. Results based on Monte Carlo simulations show the effectiveness of the new system to combat DAs belonging to the MC-LPCD family. This is an interesting result that opens the way toward the development of a watermarking system for audio signal that is robust to de-synchronization attacks. Before such a system is developed though, further research is needed, including the adaptation of the new watermarking system to low-pass signals, the incorporation of perceptual issues onto the system, the evaluation of the proposed mechanism in presence of DA attacks that do not belong to the MC-LPCD family, and finally the evaluation of the new scheme in the presence of other kinds of attacks, including noise addition, quantization, filtering.

Acknowledgments

This work was partially supported by the Italian Ministry of Research and Education under FIRB project no. RBIN04AC9W.

References

1. Lichtenauer, J., Setyawan, I., Kalker, T., Lagendijk, R.: Exhaustive geometrical search and the false positive watermark detection probability. In: Wong, P.W., Delp, E.J. (eds.) Security and Watermarking of Multimedia Contents V, Proc. SPIE, Santa Clara, CA, USA, January 2003, vol. 5020, pp. 203–214 (2003)
2. Barni, M.: Effectiveness of exhaustive search and template matching against watermark desynchronization. IEEE Signal Processing Letters 12(2), 158–161 (2005)
3. Voloshynovskiy, S., Deguillaume, F., Pun, T.: Multibit digital watermarking robust against local non linear geometrical distortions. In: Proc. 8th IEEE Int. Conf. on Image Processing, ICIP 2001, Barcelona, Spain, October 2001, vol. 3, pp. 999–1002 (2001)
4. Pereira, S., Pun, T.: Fast robust template matching for affine resistant image watermarking. In: Pfitzmann, A. (ed.) IH 1999. LNCS, vol. 1768, pp. 200–210. Springer, Heidelberg (2000)
5. Pereira, S., Ruanaidh, J., Deguillaume, F., Csurka, G., Pun, T.: Template based recovery of Fourier-based watermarks using log-polar and log-log maps. In: Proc. ICMS 1999, Int. Conf. on Multimedia Systems, Florence, Italy (June 1999)
6. Delannay, D., Macq, B.: Generalized 2D cyclic patterns for secret watermark generation. In: Proc. 7th IEEE Int. Conf. on Image Processing, ICIP 2000, Vancouver, Canada, September 2000, vol. 2, pp. 72–79 (2000)
7. Kutter, M.: Watermarking resisting to translation, rotation, and scaling. In: Proc. of SPIE, Int. Conf. on Multimedia Systems and Applications, vol. 3528, pp. 423–431 (1999)
8. Lin, C.Y., Wu, M., Bloom, J.A., Cox, I.J., Miller, M.L., Lui, Y.M.: Rotation, scale, and translation resilient watermarking for images. IEEE Trans. on Image Processing 10(5), 767–782 (2001)
9. Petitcolas, F.A.P., Anderson, R.J.: Evaluation of copyright marking systems. In: Proc. IEEE Int. Conf. on Multimedia Computing and Systems, ICMCS 1999, Florence, Italy, June 1999, vol. I, pp. 574–579 (1999)
10. D'Angelo, A., Barni, M., Merhav, N.: Stochastic image warping for improved watermark desynchronization. EURASIP Journal on Information Security, 1–14 (2008)

11. Arnold, M.: Attacks on digital audio watermarks and countermeasures. In: Proc. 3rd Int. Conf. WEB Delivering of Music, WEDELMUSIC 2003 (2003)
12. Barni, M., Bartolini, F.: Watermarking Systems Engineering: Enabling Digital Assets Security and Other Applications. Marcel Dekker, New York (2004)
13. Cox, I.J., Miller, M.L., Bloom, J.A.: Digital Watermarking. Morgan Kaufmann, San Francisco (2001)
14. Merhav, N.: An information-theoretic view of watermark embedding-detection and geometric attacks. In: First Wavila Challenge, WaCha 2005, Barcelona, Spain (June 2005)
15. Bakirov, N.K.: Central limit theorem for weakly dependent variables. Mathematical Notes 41(1), 63–67 (1987)

A Robust Watermarking for MPEG-2

Huang Li , Jian Li, and Hongmei Liu

School of Information Science and Technology
Sun Yat-sen University, Guangzhou, China, 510006
isslhm@mail.sysu.edu.cn

Abstract. Motion information is special to video. It provides enough space for watermark embedding. However, the watermark embedded in motion information is usually not robust. In this paper, a robust watermarking algorithm which embeds watermark in motion vectors of P frames is proposed. The reason why the watermark embedded in motion vector is not robust to recompression is that the watermarked motion vector will be changed when the video is recompressed. In order to improve the watermark robustness to recompression, we present to modify the pixel of the current block while embedding watermark bit in its motion vector. In order to minimize the perceptual degradation of video quality, we adopt our previously proposed geometrical method. The experimental results demonstrate the strong robustness of the scheme against common signal processing operations.

Keywords: Video Watermark, MPEG-2, Motion Vector.

1 Introduction

With the rapid development of Internet and multimedia technology, the requirement of copyright protection becomes more and more urgent. Watermarking technologies have been considered as one of the solutions for this problem. Video is usually stored and transmitted in compressed format, so it is more practical to embed the watermark in compression domain.

A variety of watermarking schemes have been proposed for MPEG-2 video watermark. Some schemes proposed to embed watermark by using motion vector which is one of the most important elements in video compression. In [1], Kutter first proposed the video watermark scheme in motion vector by slightly altering the motion vectors. However, it can not achieve good robustness. J.Zhang et al. [2] improved Kutter's scheme. They proposed an algorithm to choose the motion vector which had larger amplitude and small phase change. And it was robust against video content attacks. In literature [3], scrambling and permutation were performed before embedding the watermark. Then they embedded the watermark by modifying the value of motion vector slightly. In [4], the scheme proposed to alter the motion vectors according to the texture of the area, and prediction errors of the matched blocks were calculated again after changing the motion vectors. The above schemes above all embed the watermark into MV directly. But they are sensitive to the attacks such as recompression. There are

A.T.S. Ho et al. (Eds.): IWDW 2009, LNCS 5703, pp. 69–80, 2009.

other methods which embed the watermark into DCT coefficients [5][6][7],such as differential energy watermarking (DEW) scheme. And most of DCT schemes use I frames which are crucial for the video to embed watermark. If those schemes are extended to P frames, the performance is supposed to degrade. Because the P-frames and B-frames are highly compressed by using motion compensation, there is less capacity for embedding a watermark in them.

In this paper, we extend the watermarking scheme which is proposed for H.264 [9] to MPEG-2. According to the structure of MPEG-2 encoder, a novel algorithm is proposed to embed robust watermark into motion vectors (MV) in P-frames. When the MV isn't suitable for embedding, the current block will be modified to make the encoder choose the block whose MV fits the embedding condition. Moreover, we explore a modification algorithm to control PSNR, which will minimize the degradation of video quality. The experimental results show that the proposed algorithm works well and is robust to recompression.

The rest of the paper is arranged as follows. In section 2, our previous work for H.264 [9] is briefly described. Section 3 presents the extended watermarking scheme for MPEG-2. Section 4 shows the results and analysis. In section 5, the conclusion and some future direction are presented.

2   Our Previous Work for H.264

In [9] we proposed a robust watermark scheme for H.264. When encoding the video, the watermark was embedded into reference index, a new syntax element first proposed by H.264 standard. Because the value range of reference index was quite small, only the last bit of reference index was employed to carry watermark information. In some cases, we need alter the value of reference index to fit the embedded bit. However, it was observed that the altered reference indexes are naturally sensitive to attacks, because they are not the best choice of encoder, and hence easy to be changed when re-encoding the video. We proposed to strengthen the embedded watermark by modifying the coded blocks. After modifying the coded blocks, all the watermarked reference indexes became the best choice of encoding the coded blocks. Consequently, the watermark robustness was improved greatly.

In this paper, we try to extend the method to MPEG-2 video coding standard. MPEG-2 bit-stream does not have reference index, so it is impossible to directly use the previous method. But we know that motion vector is like reference index and also indicates the motion information of video object. So we can take motion vector as the embedding object. Considering the difference between H.264 and MPEG-2, many modifications to the embedding algorithm are needed. For instance, the method of modifying the coded blocks should be changed due to the different criterion of motion estimation.

3   The Proposed Video Watermarking for MPEG-2

3.1 Motion Vector in MPEG-2 Video

Motion vector reflects the moving displacement of the coded block in current frame, and the best prediction block in reference frame [8]. MPEG-2 encoder will record the

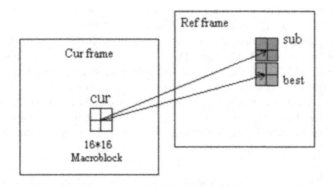

Fig. 1. Process of searching matching macroblock

distances between current block and every searching block. Then it will pick up the block of minimal distance within searching scope and regard this block as the predicted block of current block. Schematic diagram for the searching process is shown in Fig.1.

In Fig.1, *best* block represents the best prediction block chosen by encoder and *sec* block is the suboptimal prediction block.

In MPEG-2, the algorithm to measure the distance between two blocks is SAD (Sum of Absolute Difference), which is given by

$$d = \text{distance}(D, C) = \sum_{i=0}^{255} abs(D_i - C_i), \qquad (1)$$

where D_i and C_i represent a pixel of block D and current block C respectively.

Referring to Fig.1, the best prediction block is nearer to the current block than any other prediction block, which can be represented by

$$\text{distance}(D_{best}, C) < \text{distance}(D_{any}, C) \qquad (2)$$

Motion vector is calculated as follows.

$$\overrightarrow{MV} = (H, V) = (ibest - icur, \ jbest - jcur), \qquad (3)$$

where H, V are horizontal and vertical component of motion vector respectively, *ibest* and *jbest* denote the coordinate of *best* block ,while *icur* and *jcur* denote coordinate of *cur* block.

3.2 Watermark Embedding

From section 3.1, we can see that MPEG-2 encoder will choose the block with minimal distance as the prediction block and then calculate the motion vector. In literature [11], most motion vector based watermarking algorithms embedded watermark bit by slightly modifying the motion vector. The modified motion vector is not the best choice of the encoder. Could the modified motion vector which carries the watermark bit be kept when the watermark video is recompressed? We observed that if only altering the motion vectors to embed watermark, the motion vector will be changed, and consequently the watermark bit will not be extracted correctly. Table 1 demonstrates the experimental results tested on various video sequences. In Table 1, all the sequences are coded and watermarked at 8Mbps. The watermark embedding algorithm is similar to the method in [11]. Then the watermarked video is recompressed with different bit rate. From Table 1, we can see that with the recompression bit rate decrease, very small proportion of watermarked motion vectors can be correctly extracted. We think it is because the altered motion vectors are not the best choice of encoding the current coded blocks. In order to improve the robustness, the coded block will be modified. So the altered motion vectors become the best choice of encoder.

Table 1. Proportion of watermarked MVs that not be changed during recompression

Recompression bit rate	Average Proportion (%)
8M	37
6.8M	31
5.6M	25
4.4M	23
3.2M	19
2M	14

The framework of the robust watermarking scheme is shown in Fig.2,

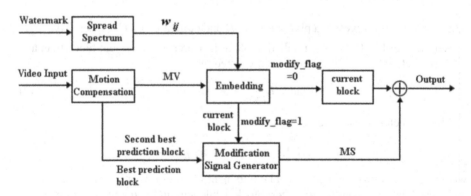

Fig. 2. Watermarking Framework

where w_{ij} is the spread spectrum watermark signal, and modify_flag represents if the current coded block, *cur* block, needs to be modified.

During encoding the video, we embed the watermark information into motion vectors. Some motion vectors may not fit the watermark bit w_{ij}. In this case, we generate modification signal to modify the current coded block in order that encoder will select a new motion vector, which can fit the w_{ij}. The modification signal is generated by

Modification Signal Generator, which needs 3 inputs, best prediction block, second best prediction block, and current block. Best prediction block has been mentioned in Fig.1. Second best prediction block is a prediction block which is pointed to the new motion vector. The detailed description is given as follows.

Firstly, the watermark is preprocessed by spread spectrum method [9], which could help to improve the watermark robustness effectively. The method of spread spectrum is given by

$$w_{ij} = w_i \oplus p_{ij} \qquad (i=1,2...L_1, j=1,2...L_2), \qquad (4)$$

where L_1 is the length of original watermark w and L_2 is the length of spread spectrum. w_{ij} is generated by XOR operation between original watermark bit w_i and random sequence p_{ij}.

Before embedding, we will decide whether to modify the current block or not according to w_{ij} and motion vector as Eq.5.

$$Modify\_flag = \begin{cases} 0, & \text{for} \quad ((|H|+|V|)\text{mod }2) = w_{ij} \\ 1, & \text{for} \quad ((|H|+|V|)\text{mod }2) \neq w_{ij} \end{cases} \qquad (5)$$

where $|H|$ and $|V|$ are absolute value of H and V respectively. If $modify\_flag$=1, w_{ij} is regarded as embedded into motion vector directly. If not, we will change MV to fit the condition by modifying current block.

Here, we define a substitute block sec_block, shown as second best prediction block in Fig.2.

$$sec\_block= \text{address\_dmin } (E) \qquad (6)$$

where

$$E = \{Block_i \mid (| H_i |+| V_i |) \text{ mod } 2 \neq (| H_{best} |+| V_{best} |) \text{ mod } 2\} \qquad (7)$$

Aggregation E stands for blocks whose absolute sum of motion vector mod 2 is not equal to that of the best prediction block. address_dmin( ) denotes the address of the block with minimal distance. From Eq.7, we know that the value of absolute sum of sec_block' motion vector mod 2 is different from that of $best\_block$.

The system will generate MS according to the relationship between the cur_block, $best\_block$ and sec_block, and then add MS to cur_block. After modifying the cur block, sec_block will become the best predicted block when recompression. Now, the new MV is suitable for embedding w_{ij}.

3.3 Block Modifying Algorithm

The modification signal, MS, in Fig.2 is related to 3 parameters, cur_block, $best\_block$ and sec_block. For convenience, we use the following denotations to represent the blocks.

$$C = cur\_block \tag{8}$$

$$B = best\_block \tag{9}$$

$$S = sec\_block \tag{10}$$

MS is determined by the distances among blocks, C, B and S. The relationships between C, B and S are demonstrated in Fig.3, where $m_1 m_2$ is the perpendicular bisector of BS, and it divides the space into two parts. In Fig.3, we can see that $diatance(B,C) < diatance(S,C)$.

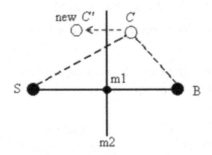

Fig. 3. Geometrical Position between C, B and S

Now, C is on the right side of $m_1 m_2$. Our goal is to drive C to cross line $m_1 m_2$, reaching the left half-plane, like the position of new C', and make distance $(S, C') <$ distance (B, C').

Pixel C_i in C should be modified according to C_i of *sec_block* and B_i of *best_block*. The relationships between them are specified in Fig.4.

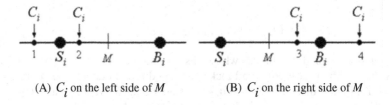

(A) C_i on the left side of M (B) C_i on the right side of M

Fig. 4. Relationship among C_i, S_i and B_i

where M is the midpoint of segment $S_i B_i$.

$$M = \frac{1}{2}(S_i + B_i) \tag{11}$$

Modification signal is generated for case A and case B in Fig.4 by the geometrical method.

a) For the case of Fig.4 (A), C_i is at the position 1 or 2, and we can get that, $|C_i - S_i|$ < $|C_i - B_i|$. In this case, the block needn't be modified in principle. But, we found that if we modify this pixel, then the modifying amplitude of other pixel can become smaller and the quality of watermarked video can be better. So we present the **Modification Algorithm 1** for case A.

$$C'_i = \begin{cases} C_i - \lambda_1 & if\,(C_i \geq S_i) \\ C_i + \lambda_1 & if\,(C_i < S_i) \end{cases} \tag{12}$$

where $\lambda_1 \in \{x \mid 0 < x < abs(S_i - C_i)\}$, and the value of λ_1 is related to the strength of modification, and it is appropriate to set λ_1 below 15. That is: max (λ_1) <15.

b) For case B, when C_i is at the position as 3 or 4 in Fig.4 (B), C_i should be modified to reach the left side of M. And **Modification Algorithm 2** for case B is as follows.

$$C'_i = M - \lambda_2 \quad (-5 < \lambda_2 < 5) \tag{13}$$

In case B, over modification may occur because the distance between C_i and C'_i is too far. So we must limit the modified range to prevent the great degradation of video quality. The experimental results demonstrate that if ($|C'_i - C_i| < 20$), the performance of our scheme works well and the degradation value of PSNR (Power Signal-to-Noise Ratio) is less than 1 db.

In the process of modifying, encoder will compare the two numbers diatance(B,C') and diatance(S,C') after every time of modification. At the beginning, the value of difference $dif(B,S)$ will be recorded.

$$dif(B, S) = \text{diatance(S,C')-diatance(B,C')} \tag{14}$$

Then, after modifying each pixel, the convergence condition is

$$dif(B, S) = dif(B, S) - d_i \tag{15}$$

In each iteration, d_i is calculated by Eq.(16)

$$d_i = \begin{cases} 2\lambda_1 & for(case\ \ A) \\ (|S_i - C_i| - |B_i - C_i|) - (|S_i - C'_i| - |B_i - C'_i|) & for(case\ \ B) \end{cases} \tag{16}$$

We define a threshold T (negative) as the finishing condition for modification. When $dif(B,S)$ meets the condition that $dif(B,S) < T$, the process is completed.

3.4 Watermark Extraction

Watermark can be extracted directly from bitstream by decoder. The extraction process is the inverse of watermark embedding process. The method for watermark extraction is simple, described as below.

$$\hat{w}_{ij} = \begin{cases} 1, & for \quad ((|H|+|V|)\mathrm{mod}\ 2) = 1) \\ 0, & for \quad ((|H|+|V|)\mathrm{mod}\ 2) = 0) \end{cases} \tag{17}$$

where $\hat{w}_{ij}$ is the retrieved watermark from the decoder.

And then random sequence P_{ij} and $\hat{w}_{ij}$ are operated by XOR before recovering the original watermark bit w_i .

4 Experimental Results

Standard MPEG-2 encoder is used in the experiments. Three groups of video are selected for tests.

First group,   resolution: 720*480, football, cheer, flower.   Bit rate:8 M/s
Second group,   resolution: 704*576, basketball, cross_street.   Bit rate:10 M/s
Third group,   resolution: 352*288, mobile , canoa , bus.   Bit rate:2 M/s

4.1 Watermark Imperceptibility Test

The length of spread spectrum in the first and second group is 170 bits, while the third group is 60 bits. The decrease of PSNR is shown in Table 2.

As shown in Table 2, the proposed algorithm has little influence on video quality. We can also see that the more blocks are modified, the more PSNR decreases. For instance, the decrease of PSNR of video cheer that has plenty of motion vectors is greater than that has less motion vectors, such as flower. Fig.5 shows the imperceptibility of watermark.

Table 2. Imperceptibility Test

Video Sequence	Spread Spectrum	Decrease of PSNR
cheer	170 bits	0.4483 db
football	170 bits	0.5041 db
flower	170 bits	0.2826 db
basketball	170 bits	0.3073 db
cross street	170 bits	0.4501 db
mobile	60 bits	0.1495 db
canoa	60 bits	0.1047 db
bus	60 bits	0.0754 db

(a) One watermarked frame of mobile

(b) The corresponding original frame

(c) One watermarked frame of canon

(d) The corresponding original frame

Fig. 5. Demonstration of invisibility

4.2 Watermark Robustness Test

Bit Error Rate (BER) can be used for illustrating robustness of watermarking when it encounters attacks. In order to test the robustness of our watermarking scheme, we carry out attacks testing as follows [9]. The parameters in each attack is expressed as starting value:step:end value. For example, in rotation attack, the rotation degree if changed from 0.5 to 3 by step 0.5.

The attacks are as follows:

1) Recompression: Bit rate decrease percent: τ = 0:10:70
2) Rotation: Degree: D=0.5:0.5: 3
3) Luminance Increase: Increasing the video with L_d = 0:10:60

4) Luminance Decrease: Decreasing the video with L_i = 0:-10:-60

5) AWGN (additive white gaussian noise): σ_a =1: 3: 16

6) Gaussian Blurring: σ_g =0.4:0.2:1.6

The robustness to these attacks is shown in Figure 6-11. The following conclusions can be drawn from the above tests:

1) The scheme we propose has good robustness, especially for recompression and luminance change (Fig.6, Fig.8 and Fig.9). In general, the watermark can still survive after some common attacks mentioned above.
2) The watermark embedded in the video with rich motion vectors can be robust to strong attacks. Because there are more motion vectors for embedding watermark bits in, such as the video cheer, basketball and so on. On the contrary, the watermark in the video with less motion vectors will be sensitive to the attacks.

3) The length of spread spectrum plays an important role in the robustness of watermarking. From the results of the first and third groups of videos, we can see the increase of spread spectrum length has remarkably improved watermarking resistance. In Fig.5, when recompression bit rate drops to half of the embedding compression bit rate, the watermark in the first and second groups of videos almost survives. However, the BER of the third group increases to more or less 10%. Hence, the robustness of the video with less motion vectors can be improved by increasing the length of spread spectrum.

4) In Fig.10 and Fig.11, when *Standard Deviation* of AWGN *is* 14 and σ_g of Gaussian Blurring is 1.0, the watermark can still be extracted with low BER.

5) In order to test the performance of block-modifying scheme, we compare it with the scheme that embeds the watermark directly without modifying current block. The results are shown in Fig.12 We can see that the robustness to recompression is improved efficiently by the method of modifying blocks.

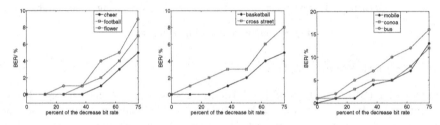

Fig. 6. Robustness against Recompression Attack

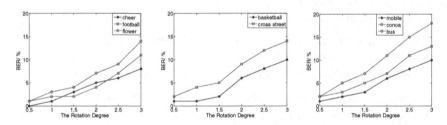

Fig. 7. Robustness against Rotation

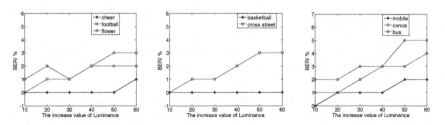

Fig. 8. Robustness against Luminance Increase

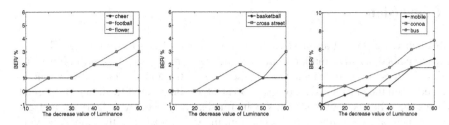

Fig. 9. Robustness against Luminance Decrease

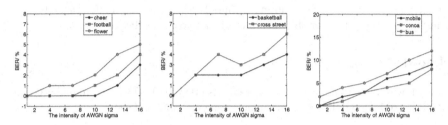

Fig. 10. Robustness against AWGN Attack

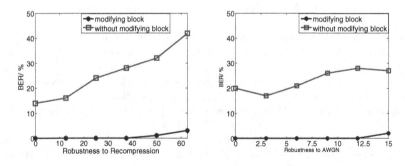

Fig. 11. Robustness against Gaussian Blurring

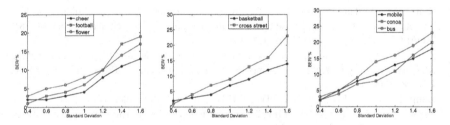

Fig. 12. Compare our scheme with the scheme without modifying block

5 Conclusion

In this paper, we present a robust video watermarking scheme based on MPEG-2. The idea is to embed the watermark into motion vectors by modifying the current block. The motion vectors used to embed watermark by slightly altering the value would be changed when the video is recompressed. So an algorithm of modification is proposed to improve the robustness of watermark, which is based on the SAD algorithm and geometrical method. According to this algorithm, the visual quality of the embedded video is well maintained. The performance of the proposed scheme is evaluated through experiments which clearly show a good robustness against a variety of attacks. Our future work includes embedding the watermark into B-frame to exploit the capacity and solving the non-embedding problem in intra-block to enhance the robustness.

Acknowledgements

This work was supported by NSFC under Grants 60633030, 973 Program under Grant 2006CB303104 and GDIID Program under Grant GDIID2008IS046.

References

1. Kutter, M., Jordan, F., Ebrahimi, T.: Proposal of a watermarking technique for hiding/retrieving data in compressed and decompressed video. Technical report M2281, ISO/IEC document, JTC1/SC29/WG11 (1997)
2. Zhang, J., Li, J.G., Zhang, L.: Video Watermark Technique in Motion Vector. In: Proc of the XIV Brazilian Symposium on Computer Graphics and Image Processing, 2001, pp. 179–182 (2001)
3. Kung, C.H., Jeng, J.H., Lee, Y.C., Hsiao, H.H., Cheng, W.S.: Video Watermarking Using Motion Vector. In: Proc. of 16th IPPR Conference on computer vision, graphics and image processing, 2003, pp. 547–551 (2003)
4. Liu, Z.N., Liang, H.Q., Niu, X.X., Yang, Y.X.: A Robust Video Watermarking in Motion Vectors. In: Proc. of ICSP 2004, vol. 3, pp. 2358–2361 (2004)
5. Hartung, F., Girod, B.: Watermarking of uncompressed and compressed video. Signal Processing 66(3) (May 1998)
6. Antonio, C.H., Mariko, N.M., Luis, R.C.: Robust Video Watermarking Using Perceptual Information and Motion Vector. In: Proc. of IEEE Northeast Workshop 2007, pp. 811–814 (2007)
7. Ling, H.F., Lu, Z., Zou, F.: New real-time watermarking algorithm for compressed video in VLC domain. In: Proceedings of ICIP 2004, pp. 2171–2174 (2004)
8. Zhang, J., Li, J., Zhang, L.: Video Watermark Technique in Motion Vector. In: Computer Graphics and Image Processing 2001, pp. 179–182 (2004)
9. Li, J., Liu, H.M., Huang, J.W., Zhang, Y.P.: A Robust Watermarking Scheme for H.264. In: Proc. of the7th International Workshop on Digital Watermarking 2008, pp. 9–23 (2008)
10. George, M., Chouinard, J., Georganas, N.: Digital watermarking of images and video using direct sequence spread spectrum techniques. In: Proc. of 1999 IEEE Canadian Conf. Electrical and Computer Engineering, May 1999, vol. 1, pp. 116–121 (1999)
11. Qiu, G., Marziliano, P., Ho, A.T.S., He, D., Sun, Q.B.: A Hybrid Watermarking Scheme for H.264/AVC Video. In: Proc. of Pattern Recognition, ICPR 2004, vol. 4, pp. 865–869 (2004)

Temporal Statistic Based Video Watermarking Scheme Robust against Geometric Attacks and Frame Dropping

Chong Chen, Jiangqun Ni[*], and Jiwu Huang

School of Information Science and Technology, Sun Yat-Sen University
Guangzhou 510275, P.R. China
Tel.: 86-20-84036167
issjqni@mail.sysu.edu.cn

Abstract. Robustness against geometric attacks is still considered to be one of the major challenging issues in the development of watermarking algorithm, especially for video watermarking. This paper presents a multi-bit video watermarking scheme resilient to geometric attacks and frame dropping by utilizing the geometric invariant sequence generated from the average dc energy of the input video and the temporal statistic described by its histogram. Firstly, the average dc energy of frame is introduced and three of its geometric invariance natures, i.e. rotation, scaling and translation, are proved. Then the watermarks are embedded into the histogram of average dc energy sequence of video frame. The embedding strategy is implemented by reassigning the populations in groups of two consecutive bins in the histogram. The simulation results demonstrate that the proposed watermarking scheme achieves satisfactory performances against geometric and common signal processing attacks, and intense frame dropping and averaging.

1 Introduction

In the design of robust image watermarking algorithm, one of the major challenges is to increase its performance against geometric attacks such as rotation, scaling, translation, cropping, etc. The geometric attacks are effective in that they can destroy synchronization in a watermarked image, which is necessary in watermark detection and decoding [1]. Several major approaches to resisting geometric attacks are reported in the literatures [2-15]. The first approach hides the watermark signal in the invariant domain of the host signal. In [3], Ruanaidh *et al.* proposed a watermarking scheme based on transform invariants via applying Fourier-Mellin transform to the magnitude spectrum of the original image. However, the resulting stego-image quality is poor due to interpolation errors. The second approach exploits the self-reference principle based on an auto-correlation function (ACF) or the Fourier magnitude spectrum of a periodical watermark [6]. The third approach incorporates the template for watermark synchronization. In [8], Kang and Huang proposed a DWT-DFT composite watermarking scheme, where the messages and templates are embedded into DWT

---

[*] Corresponding author.

A.T.S. Ho et al. (Eds.): IWDW 2009, LNCS 5703, pp. 81–95, 2009.

and DFT domain, respectively. Relatively high robustness is observed against both affine transformation and JPEG compression.

For video watermarking, new challenges show up and have to be addressed. The additional temporal dimension of video poses extra robustness requirements for watermarking algorithm. The attackers may use temporal attacks such as inter-frame filtering, frame dropping, frame interpolation/averaging and frame swapping to destroy watermark. Therefore, robustness against temporal attacks is also required for video watermarking. Real-time implementation is another important issue for video watermarking. To obtain a smooth video stream, frames are generally sent at a relatively high rate, say 25 fps. Therefore, the computational complexity of video watermarking algorithms should be extremely low to meet the requirement of real-time implementation.

Aiming at solving the robustness issue under both intra-frame geometric and temporal attacks, a multi-bit video watermarking scheme with low complexity is proposed, which is based on the average dc energy sequence of video frame and embeds the watermarks into the temporal statistical features described by the histogram specification of the dc energy sequence.

The average dc energy of frame is designed to tackle the issue of de-synchronization introduced by intra-frame geometric attacks such as rotation, scaling and translation (RST). It is well known that, when a video frame undergoes geometric attacks, there exist three kinds of effects. Firstly, some or all of the pixel positions may be modified (*e.g.*, RST). Secondly, some or all of the pixel values may be altered slightly by interpolation. Finally, the pixel number of the frame may be increased or decreased linearly (*e.g.*, scaling the size of frame) or nonlinearly (*e.g.*, cropping or filling with black pixels, *etc*). However, all geometric operations follow a rule that the frame after geometric attacks must preserve the content to keep visual coherence. Therefore, the average dc energy of video frame is introduced as a geometric invariant. The histogram generated from the average dc energy sequence of video frame can effectively resist against temporal attacks, such as frame dropping, frame averaging and frame swapping. In [17], the authors proved that the audio mean and histogram shape (interpreted as the ratios in the number of samples between groups of three consecutive bins) are invariant to time scaling modifications (TSM) and cropping operations. The principle is then used to design robust audio watermarking scheme by embedding watermark in the histogram of audio samples. Inspired by the works in [17], we propose to design geometrically and temporally resilient video watermarking algorithm by taking advantage of histogram of average dc energy sequence. To implement the scheme, the average dc energy of each video frame is calculated to generate the histogram, then the watermarks are embedded by modifying the ratios of the number of average dc energy between groups of neighboring two bins, rather than three bins in [17]. As the complexity of the proposed scheme is extremely low and works in spatial domain, the requirement for real-time implementation can be met.

Extensive simulation results demonstrate that the proposed video watermarking scheme is robust against intra-frame attacks, such as RST and common signal processing operations, and temporal attacks, such as random frame dropping, frame averaging and frame swapping. We also test the performance against jointly geometric attacks, the result is also satisfactory.

The reminder of this paper is organized as follows. In Section 2, the geometric invariant – average dc energy is introduced and its RST invariance is justified. The proposed video watermarking scheme is given in Section 3. The simulation results and analysis are presented in Section 4. Finally, we draw the conclusion in Section 5.

2 The Average DC Energy and Its Geometric Invariance

Besides the geometric invariance nature, the average dc energy of image is insensitive to many content-preserving image processing operations such as low-pass filtering, JPEG compression and noise addition. Therefore the average dc energy of frame is employed to resist against intra-frame attacks in the proposed video watermarking scheme.

2.1 Average DC Energy

Let $I(x,y,t)$ to be the gray-level luminance value of the pixel in position (x,y) of the tth frame. The video signal can be expressed as a set

$$Video = \left\{ I(x,y,t) \mid x = 1,\cdots,R;\, y = 1,\cdots,C;\, t = 1,\cdots,F \right\} \tag{1}$$

where R and C are the number of rows and columns of the tth frame, respectively. And F denotes the frame number of the video. The mean of the luminance value in the tth frame is computed as

$$m(t) = \frac{1}{R \cdot C} \sum_{x=1}^{R} \sum_{y=1}^{C} I(x,y,t) \tag{2}$$

With $m(t)$, the dc energy of the tth frame can be calculated with (3)

$$e_{dc}(t) = \sum_{x,y} (m(t))^2 = \sum_{x,y} \left(\frac{1}{R \cdot C} \sum_{x=1}^{R} \sum_{y=1}^{C} I(x,y,t) \right)^2 = \frac{1}{R \cdot C} \left(\sum_{x=1}^{R} \sum_{y=1}^{C} I(x,y,t) \right)^2 \tag{3}$$

The average dc energy $\overline{e}_{dc}(t)$ can then be defined as:

$$\overline{e}_{dc}(t) = \frac{1}{R \cdot C} e_{dc}(t) = \left(\frac{1}{R \cdot C} \sum_{x=1}^{R} \sum_{y=1}^{C} I(x,y,t) \right)^2 \tag{4-1}$$

It is easy to show that the average dc energy $\overline{e}_{dc}(t)$ is the square of $m(t)$, i.e.,

$$\overline{e}_{dc}(t) = m^2(t) \tag{4-2}$$

The definition in (4-1) also shows the average dc energy is irrelevant to the pixel position of the frame, which leads to the fact that average dc energy is rotation and translation invariant. In the next section we will prove mathematically that the average dc energy is not only invariant to rotation and translation, but also resistant to scaling operation.

2.2 Geometric Invariance of Average DC Energy

In this section, the geometric invariance nature of average dc energy is justified. For geometric operations, we mainly focus on rotation, scaling and translation.

1) Rotation and Translation Invariance

For rotation and translation operation, the pixel value remains unchanged although the pixel location changes completely. If the effect of interpolation is ignored and the frame size kept unchanged after rotation and translation, the average dc energy is exactly invariant due to its irrelevance to the pixel position.

For pixel $I(x, y, t)$ of tth frame, assume the coordinates (x, y) change to (x', y') due to rotation or translation. If the interpolation error during geometric operation is not considered, the pixel value keeps unchanged, $i.e.$,

$$I(x, y, t) = I(x', y', t) \tag{5}$$

Let $\bar{e}'_{dc}(t)$ denote the average dc energy after rotation or translation, by making use of (5), we have

$$\bar{e}'_{dc}(t) = \left(\frac{1}{R \cdot C} \sum_{x'=1}^{R} \sum_{y'=1}^{C} I(x', y', t) \right)^2 = \left(\frac{1}{R \cdot C} \sum_{x=1}^{R} \sum_{y=1}^{C} I(x, y, t) \right)^2 = \bar{e}_{dc}(t) \tag{6}$$

For practical implementation of rotation and translation, black pixels (zero-value pixels) are usually padded in surrounding area in order to keep the frame shape/size. In this case the average dc energy is different from the original one. Suppose $\bar{e}'_{dc}(t)$ is the average dc energy of the tth frame after geometric operation, R' and C' are its rows and columns, respectively, we have

$$\bar{e}'_{dc}(t) = \left(\frac{1}{R' \cdot C'} \sum_{x'=1}^{R} \sum_{y'=1}^{C} I(x', y', t) \right)^2 = \left(\frac{1}{R' \cdot C'} \sum_{\substack{x', y' \\ 1 \le x' \le C' \\ 1 \le y' \le R'}} I(x', y', t) \right)^2$$

$$= \left(\frac{1}{R' \cdot C'} \right)^2 \left(\sum_{content} I(x', y', t) + \sum_{padding} I(x', y', t) \right)^2$$

$$= \left(\frac{1}{R' \cdot C'} \right)^2 \left(\sum_{content} I(x', y', t) + 0 \right)^2$$

$$= \left(\frac{1}{R' \cdot C'} \right)^2 \left(\sum_{x=1}^{R} \sum_{y=1}^{C} I(x, y, t) \right)^2$$

$$= \left(\frac{R \cdot C}{R' \cdot C'} \right)^2 \cdot \left(\frac{1}{R \cdot C} \sum_{x=1}^{R} \sum_{y=1}^{C} I(x, y, t) \right)^2 = K \cdot \bar{e}_{dc}(t) \tag{7}$$

where $K = \left((R \cdot C) / (R' \cdot C') \right)^2$. The result in (7) implies that $\bar{e}'_{dc}(t)$ is linear to $\bar{e}_{dc}(t)$.

2) Scaling Invariance

For scaling operation, the general case of non-proportional scaling over the tth frame is considered. Without loss of generality, we investigate the scaling operation in continuous domain. Assume $\{I_t(i, j)\}$ is the tth frame, $\{I_t'(i', j')\}$ is the scaled frame with vertical and horizontal scaling factor α and β. If the effects introduced by interpolation are also ignored, we have $I_t'(i', j') = I_t(i/\alpha, j/\beta)$. The height and width of the scaled frame are $R' = \alpha R$ and $C' = \beta C$. Let $\bar{e}_{dc}'(t)$ be the average dc energy of the tth frame after scaling, we have

$$
\begin{aligned}
\bar{e}_{dc}'(t) &= \left(\frac{1}{R' \cdot C'} \int_{j=0}^{C'} \int_{i=0}^{R'} I_t'(i', j') \, di \, dj \right)^2 \\
&= \left(\frac{1}{\alpha R \cdot \beta C} \int_{j=0}^{\beta C} \int_{i=0}^{\alpha R} I_t(i/\alpha, j/\beta) \, di \, dj \right)^2 \\
&= \left(\frac{1}{R \cdot C} \int_{j=0}^{\beta C} \int_{i=0}^{\alpha R} I_t(i/\alpha, j/\beta) \, d\left(\frac{i}{\alpha}\right) d\left(\frac{j}{\beta}\right) \right)^2 \\
&= \left(\frac{1}{R \cdot C} \int_{j_1=0}^{C} \int_{i_1=0}^{R} I_t(i_1, j_1) \, di_1 \, dj_1 \right)^2 \\
&= \bar{e}_{dc}(t)
\end{aligned}
\tag{8}
$$

Equation (8) reveals the fact that the average dc energy is mathematically invariant to scaling operation.

In general, the average dc energy of a frame is RST-invariant. Recall that it is also resilient to common signal processing attack, it would be very robust against both geometric and signal processing when embedding watermark signal into the average dc energy sequence.

3   The Proposed Video Watermarking Scheme

In this section, we develop a multi-bit video watermarking scheme by using average dc energy sequence of video frame and its histogram. The scheme aims at obtaining robustness against both intra-frame geometric and signal processing attacks as well as temporal attacks, such as frame dropping/averaging/swapping. Xiang et al. in [17] proposed an audio watermarking algorithm based on audio histogram. The authors take advantage of the audio mean and histogram shape, which are invariant to time scaling modifications (TSM) and cropping operations, and then embed the watermark by modifying the histogram shape. Following the spirit of Xiang's work, the algorithm in [17] is extended for robust multi-bit video watermarking. Different from [17], which embed watermark by reassigning populations in groups of three consecutive bins, the proposed scheme do it by modifying the ratios in groups of two neighboring bins. The experiment results show that both approaches have similar performance, but our implementation helps to improve the watermark capacity.

3.1 Watermark embedding Strategy

As illustrated in Fig.1, the proposed watermark embedding strategy consists of three steps, *i.e.*, average dc energy extracting, histogram generating and histogram-based embedding.

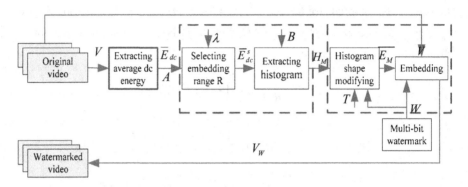

Fig. 1. Watermark embedding framework

1) Average DC Energy Extracting

Suppose the input video signal is in the format of YUV. We only consider the luminance component Y, which is denoted by $V = \{I(x, y, t) \mid t = 1, \cdots, F\}$, where F is the frame number in V. From Equation (4-1), we extract the average dc energy of each frame in V to form a sequence $\bar{E}_{dc}$, where

$$\bar{E}_{dc} = \left\{ \bar{e}_{dc}(t) \mid t = 1, \cdots, F \right\} \tag{9}$$

2) Histogram Generating

The histogram H is generated from $\bar{E}_{dc}$ by referring to its mean value $A = mean(\bar{E}_{dc}) = \dfrac{1}{F}\sum_{t=1}^{F} \bar{e}_{dc}(t)$. By selecting the elements within the range of $R = \left[(1-\lambda)A,\ (1+\lambda)A\right]$ from $\bar{E}_{dc}$, another sequence $\bar{E}_{dc}^{s}$ is generated. Here, $\bar{E}_{dc}^{s}$ is described by $\bar{E}_{dc}^{s} = \left\{ \bar{e}_{dc}(t) \mid \bar{e}_{dc}(t) \in R; t = 1, \cdots, F_{s} \right\}$, where F_{s} is the length of sequence $\bar{E}_{dc}^{s}$ and $1 \le F_{s} \le F$. λ is a positive real number used to control the number of samples in each bin.

   The histogram H is obtained by splitting the range of $\bar{E}_{dc}^{s}$ into equal-sized bins and counting the number of samples falling in each bin. The histogram can be described by $H = \left\{ h_{M}(i) \mid i = 1, \cdots, B \right\}$, where $h_{M}(i)$ denotes the number of samples in the ith bin and satisfying both $h_M(i) \geq 0$ and $\sum_{i=1}^{B} h_M(i) = F_s$, M and B are the bin width and bin number in histogram H, respectively. In the proposed watermarking scheme, we embed one bit in every two consecutive bins of H. Therefore, if B_w bits messages are to be embedded, the bin number B is no less than $2B_w$. And λ is determined so as to ensure that the sample number in each bin is much greater than bin number B, i.e., $h_M(i) \gg B$.

3) Histogram-Based Embedding
This step can be divided into two sub-steps, including histogram shape modifying and watermark embedding.

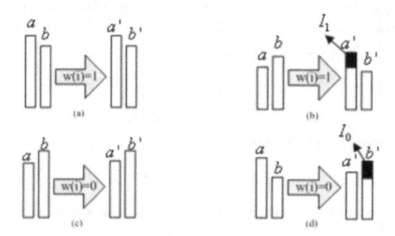

Fig. 2. Illustration of reassigning samples in four cases. I_1 and I_0 are the number of modified samples. (a) To embed bit "1" and $a/b \geq T$; $a'/b' = a/b \geq T$.(b) To embed bit "1" and $a/b < T$; then $a'/b' = (a+I_1)/(b-I_1) \geq T$. (c) To embed bit "0" and $b/a \geq T$; then $b'/a' = b/a \geq T$. (d) To embed bit "0" and $b/a < T$; then $b'/a' = (b+I_0)/(a-I_0) \geq T$.

① *Histogram shape modifying.*
The binary watermark sequence $W = \{w(i) \mid i = 1, \cdots, B_w\}$ is embedded by reassigning the number of samples between groups of consecutive two bins.

Let Bin_p and Bin_n denote two neighboring bins in the histogram H, the number of samples in Bin_p and Bin_n is a and b, respectively. One bit of message is embedded into the two consecutive bins Bin_p and Bin_n by (10), i.e.,

$$\begin{cases} \dfrac{a}{b} \geq T, & if \ w(i) = 1 \\[2mm] \dfrac{b}{a} \geq T, & if \ w(i) = 0 \end{cases} \qquad (10)$$

where T is a threshold controlling the number of modified samples and $T \geq 1$. It is obviously to show that, the larger T is, the more robust the watermarking would be and more frames would be modified. According to (10), to embed 1 bit message the shape of histogram H for average dc energy sequence should be modified in four scenarios as illustrated in Fig.2.

If $w(i)$ is bit "1" and $a/b \geq T$ (Fig.2 (a)), then the population relationship between Bin_p and Bin_n matches up with Equation (10), and no modification is needed. Similarly, if $w(i)$ is bit "0" and $b/a \geq T$ (Fig.2 (c)), no modification is required as well.

If $w(i)$ is bit "1" and $a/b < T$ (Fig.2 (b)), then the number of samples in Bin_p and Bin_n will be reassigned to meet the condition $a'/b' \geq T$, where a' and b' is the number of samples in Bin_p and Bin_n after sample reassigning, respectively. By randomly selecting I_1 samples from Bin_n and modifying their values to fall into Bin_p, we have $a' = a + I_1$ and $b' = b - I_1$. To embed bit "1", the relation $\dfrac{a'}{b'} \geq T$ should be hold, i.e.,

$$\frac{a'}{b'} = \frac{a+I_1}{b-I_1} \geq T \ \Rightarrow \ I_1 \geq \frac{T \cdot b - a}{1+T}.$$

In this way, I_1 can be determined as:

$$I_1 = \frac{T \cdot b - a}{1+T} \tag{11}$$

Similarly, if $w(i)$ is "0" and $b/a < T$ (Fig.2 (d)), I_0 samples are randomly selected from Bin_p and modified to fall into Bin_n. To meet the condition $\dfrac{b'}{a'} \geq T$, I_0 is determined as:

$$I_0 = \frac{T \cdot a - b}{1+T} \tag{12}$$

Recall M is the bin width of histogram, samples in Bin_p plus M go to Bin_n, while samples in Bin_n minus M go to Bin_p. Therefore the selected samples are modified according to (13), i.e.,

$$\begin{cases} \overline{e}_{dc}^{pw}(i) = \overline{e}_{dc}^{p}(i) + M, & 1 \leq i \leq I_0 \\ \overline{e}_{dc}^{nw}(j) = \overline{e}_{dc}^{n}(j) - M, & 1 \leq j \leq I_1 \end{cases} \tag{13}$$

where $\overline{e}_{dc}^{p}(i)$ and $\overline{e}_{dc}^{n}(j)$ are the ith selected sample in Bin_p and j^{th} selected sample in Bin_n, respectively. While $\overline{e}_{dc}^{pw}(i)$ and $\overline{e}_{dc}^{nw}(j)$ denote the modified samples and belongs to Bin_n and Bin_p, respectively. I_0 and I_1 can be determined through (12) and (11).

② *Watermark embedding.*
To describe the watermark embedding process, let $\overline{e}_{dc}(k)$ be an average dc energy selected to modify in the process of histogram shape modifying and $\overline{E}_M = \left\{ \overline{e}_{dc}(k) \mid k \in [1,I] \right\}$. For each $\overline{e}_{dc}(k)$ in $\overline{E}_M$, we re-write Equation (13) in a more general form as (14):

$$\overline{e}_{dc}^{w}(k) = \overline{e}_{dc}(k) + delta, \quad k \in [1,I] \tag{14}$$

where $\overline{e}_{dc}(k)$ lies in Bin_p or Bin_n, and $\overline{e}_{dc}^{w}(k)$ is the modified average dc energy fallen into Bin_n or Bin_p, $I = I_0$ or I_1. Depending on whether $w(i)$ is "0" or "1", $delta$ is $+M$ or $-M$.

Assume $\overline{e}_{dc}(k)$ is the tth element in $\overline{E}_{dc}^{s}$, which represents the average dc energy of tth frame, i.e.,

$$\overline{e}_{dc}(k) = \left(\frac{1}{R \cdot C} \sum_{x=1}^{R} \sum_{y=1}^{C} I_k(x,y,t) \right)^2 \tag{15}$$

By multiplying each pixel value in t^{th} frame with a scaling factor α_k^t, $\overline{e}_{dc}(k)$ is modified into $\overline{e}_{dc}^{w}(k)$, i.e.,

$$\left\{ I_k^w(x,y,t) \right\} = \left\{ \alpha_k^t \cdot I_k(x,y,t) \right\}. \tag{16}$$

We then proceed to find the scaling factor α_k^t as follows:

$$\overline{e}_{dc}^{w}(k) = \overline{e}_{dc}(k) + delta$$

$$\Rightarrow \left(\frac{1}{R \cdot C} \sum_{x=1}^{R} \sum_{y=1}^{C} I_k^w(x,y,t) \right)^2 = \left(\frac{1}{R \cdot C} \sum_{x=1}^{R} \sum_{y=1}^{C} I_k(x,y,t) \right)^2 + delta$$

$$\Rightarrow \left(\frac{1}{R \cdot C} \sum_{x=1}^{R} \sum_{y=1}^{C} \alpha_k^t \cdot I_k(x,y,t) \right)^2 = \left(\frac{1}{R \cdot C} \sum_{x=1}^{R} \sum_{y=1}^{C} I_k(x,y,t) \right)^2 + delta$$

$$\Rightarrow \alpha_k^t = \sqrt{\frac{\overline{e}_{dc}(k) + delta}{\overline{e}_{dc}(k)}} = \sqrt{\frac{\overline{e}_{dc}(k) \pm M}{\overline{e}_{dc}(k)}} \tag{17}$$

When the set of scaling factors $\left\{ \alpha_k^t \right\}$ is determined with (17), each element in $\overline{E}_M = \left\{ \overline{e}_{dc}(k) \mid k \in [1,I] \right\}$ is modified according to (16), and one bit message is embedded into the video signal $V = \left\{ I(x,y,t) \mid t = 1, \cdots, F \right\}$.

The aforementioned histogram shape modifying and watermark embedding processes are repeated until all B_w message bits are embedded to generate the watermarked video $V_w = \{I'(x, y, t) \mid t = 1, \cdots, F\}$.

3.2 Watermark Detection

The temporal attacks such as frame dropping/averaging usually affect the mean of the average dc energy sequence. Therefore a synchronization mechanism is required for the watermark detection [16]. In the proposed watermarking scheme, a synchronization code (key-based PN sequence) is used in front of the watermark sequence, as illustrated in Fig.3.

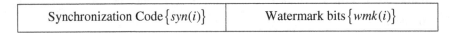

Fig. 3. The structure of embedding message

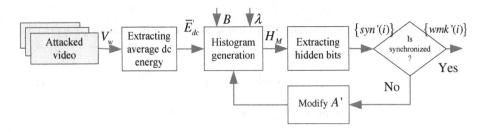

Fig. 4. Blind watermark detection framework

Fig.4 shows the proposed watermark detection framework, which is described as follows:

1) Let V_w' denote the luminance sequence of the received watermarked video, we extract the average dc energy of each frame in V_w' to generate the sequence $\overline{E}_{dc}'$.

2) Compute the mean value A' of sequence $\overline{E}_{dc}'$, which helps to avoid exhaustive search in synchronization process.

3) Let A_s' be a value in the searching space $S = \left[((1 - \Phi_1)A', (1 + \Phi_2)A'\right]$, a histogram H_M' with bin number $B = 2B_w$ in the range $R' = \left[(1 - \lambda)A_s', (1 + \lambda)A_s'\right]$ is generated, which is similar to the embedding process. The parameters Φ_1 and Φ_2 are the down and up searching factors related to the mean variation after temporal attacks, which are no less than 5%.

4) For the histogram H_M', take every two consecutive bins as groups. Hidden bits are extracted by comparing the number of samples in groups of two neighboring bins.

Let the population in two consecutive bins be a' and b', one bit message is detected according to (18), *i.e.*,

$$w_i' = \begin{cases} 1, & if \quad a'/b' \ge 1 \\ 0, & otherwise \end{cases} \tag{18}$$

5) After all hidden bits are extracted, compare the extracted synchronization code $\{syn'(i)\}$ with $\{syn(i)\}$. If they don't match with each other, A_s' is slightly modify, *e.g.* $A_s' = A_s' \pm \Delta$, where Δ is the searching step size. Then repeat 2) to 5) until the extracted $\{syn'(i)\}$ matches up with $\{syn(i)\}$ or the whole space S is completely searched.

The extracted sequence $\{wmk'(i)\}$, with whose synchronization code is best matched, is recognized as the watermark signal. As no original video is referred to, blind watermark detection is achieved. Besides, considering that both the embedding and detection of the proposed video watermarking scheme have extremely low computation complexity, the requirement for real-time implementation can also be met.

4 Simulation Results and Analysis

Two test videos "*highway*" and "*combine_video*" are utilized in our simulation. "*Combine_video*" is a composite video consisting of several video fragments with different scenes, while "*highway*" has far less varied scenes. Both videos are QCIF (176×144) and in YUV format with length of 8000 frames. 20 bits messages (including 5 bits key-based PN sequence for synchronization) are embedded into the Y component of both test videos by using the threshold $T = 5$. Fig.5 gives the typical snapshots of the original and watermarked video frames for the two test videos, which are visually indistinguishable. The average PSNRs of the modified frames are 56.52dB and 49.52dB for "*highway*" and "*combine_video*", respectively. Note that, with the proposed watermarking scheme, many video frames remain un-modified. Therefore, only the modified frames are used to calculate the PSNR.

      (a)   (b)   (c)   (d)

Fig. 5. Snapshots from *Highway* and *Combine_video*. (a) and (b) are original and watermarked frames from *Highway,* respectively. (c) and (d) are original and watermarked frames from *Combine_video*, respectively.

During our simulations, we evaluate the robustness performance of the proposed video watermarking scheme in terms of BER (bit error rate), which is defined as the ratio between the number of error bits and the number of watermark bits. The following sections show the performances against common signal processing operations, geometric attacks, and temporal attack such as frame dropping/averaging/swapping.

4.1 Performance against Common Signal Processing Operations

In this section we test robustness performance against intra-frame signal processing operations, including additive Gaussian white noise (AGWN), Gaussian lowpass filtering and median filtering. For the tested signal processing attacks, all frames of the watermarked video undergo the same attack in our simulation. The AWGN attack uses an additive Gaussian noise of zero mean and variance ranging from 0.1 to 10.0. While 3×3 templates are employed for Gaussian lowpass filtering and median filtering. The performances are summarized in Table 1.

Table 1. Performance against common signal processing attacks

Attack Type	Description	Video	
		Highway (BER)	*combine_video* (BER)
AGWN	Variance = 0.1~10.0	0	0
Gaussian lowpass filtering	3×3 template	0	0
Median filtering	3×3 template	0	0

Notice the proposed scheme has excellent performance against AGWN attack, the BER is zero even when the AWGN has a variance of 10. The reason is that the average dc energy of frame is the square of its mean and the mean is invariant to any mean zero additive noise. This can also explain the robustness of the proposed scheme against lowpass and median filtering attacks.

4.2 Robustness against Geometric Attacks

Robustness against geometric attacks is the major concern of the proposed video watermarking scheme. In our simulation, the performance against geometric attacks such as rotation, scaling, translation, and their joint attacks are tested. As implemented in Section 4.1, all frames of the watermarked video undergo the same geometric attack. Table 2 gives the performances against geometric attacks.

The excellent performance against geometric attacks can be explained by the fact that the watermark messages are embedded into the average dc energy sequence of the video. And the geometric invariance of the dc energy is mathematically proved in Section 2.

Table 2. Performance against geometric attacks (rotation, scaling and translation)

Attack Type	Description	Video	
		Highway (BER)	*combine_video* (BER)
Rotation	Rotation of 45^0	0	0
Translation	Shifting of 20 rows + 20 columns	0	0
Scaling	Scaling of 20%~180%	0	0
Rotation and scaling	Rotation of 20^0 and scaling back to the same size	0	0
Scaling and translation	scaling of 80% and shifting of 20 rows and 20 columns	0	0

4.3 Robustness against Temporal Attacks

The temporal operations, such as temporal cropping, frame swapping, frame dropping, frame averaging/interpolation and inter-frame filtering, can efficiently undermine the watermarked video by destroying its synchronization. An attacker can destroy the watermark while maintain the visual quality of the watermarked video by swapping, dropping and filtering some frames of the video or by replacing them through frame interpolation.

For frame dropping attack, two tests are designed: (1) one of each consecutive two frames is dropped. For the watermarked video of 8000 frames, totally 4000 frames are dropped. (2) randomly drop n frames from the watermarked video.

For frame averaging/interpolation attack, one of each consecutive two frames is dropped. The missing frames are replaced by the average of two neighboring frames. Specifically, we drop the odd indexed frames and replacing the missing frames with the average of the two neighboring frames, i.e., $F_{2n+1} = (F_{2n} + F_{2n+2})/2$.

For frame swapping, we randomly change the position of each frame in the video and test its performance.

For inter-frame filtering attack, a low pass filter with the transfer function of $H(z) = (1 + z^{-2})/2z^{-1}$ is used, which means each frame in the video is replaced by the mean of its neighboring two frames.

The performance against temporal attacks is summarized in Table 3.

Table 3. shows that the proposed video watermarking scheme is robust against frame dropping, frame averaging and swapping. The good performance against swapping is due to the fact that the histogram is independent of frame position. For frame averaging and dropping attacks, the reason for its good performance is that the average dc energy sequence after frame dropping/averaging has similar distribution as that of the original one. Notice that the performance "*combine_video*" under frame dropping is not so good as that of "*highway*", the reason is that the varied scenes in "*combine_video*" increase the range of average dc energy, and therefore decrease the sample number in each bin, which makes the histogram more vulnerable under frame dropping attack. As the histogram shape is modified during inter-frame filtering, the proposed scheme is not very robust against inter-frame filtering, which coincides with the results in Table 3.

Table 3. Performance against to temporal attacks

Attack Type	Description	Video	
		Highway (BER)	combine_video (BER)
Dropping	One of each consecutive two frames	0	13.33
Dropping	Randomly selected n frames	0 ($n = 1 \sim 712$)	0 ($n = 1 \sim 638$)
Averaging	The odd indexed frames are replaced by the average of two neighboring frames	0	0
Swapping	Randomly change frame position	0	0
Inter-frame filtering	Lowpass filter with $H(z) = \left(1 + z^{-2}\right)/2z^{-1}$	40	13.33

5 Conclusions

In this paper we present a robust multi-bit video watermarking scheme against general content-preserving signal processing operations, geometric and temporal attacks. The average dc energy of video frame is proven to be a geometric invariant and resilient to common signal processing operation. The watermark is embedded by modifying the histogram shape of average dc energy sequence in the video such that it is also robust against temporal attacks such as frame dropping, frame averaging and frame swapping. The visual quality of the watermarked video is quite satisfactory due to the facts that (1) many frames of the video remain unchanged; (2) the selected frames are modified to its neighboring bin so that the modification is negligible. In addition, the extremely low computation complexity of the proposed scheme makes it possible to implement in real-time. Extensive simulations are carried out to demonstrate the feasibility and effectiveness of the proposed video watermarking scheme.

Acknowledgment

The authors appreciate the supports received from NSFC (60773200, 60633030), 973 Program (2006CB303104) and NSF of Guangdong (7003722).

References

1. Dong, P., Brankov, J.G., Galatsanos, N.P., Yang, Y.Y., Davoine, F.: Affine transformation resistant watermarking based on image normalizaton. IEEE Trans. Image Process 14(12), 2140–2150 (2005)
2. Lin, C.Y., Wu, M., Bloom, J.A., Cox, J., Miller, M.L., Lui, Y.M.: Rotation, Scale and Translation Resilient Watermarking for Images. IEEE Trans. on Image Processing 10, 767–782 (2001)

3. Ruanaidh, J., Pun, T.: Rotation, Scale and Translation Invariant Spread Spectrum Digital Image Watermarking. Signal Processing 6(3), 303–317 (1998)
4. Ruanaidh, J.J.K.Ó., Pun, T.: Rotation, scale and translation invariant digital image watermarking. In: Proc. ICIP 1997, IEEE Int. Conf. Image Processing, Santa Barbara, CA, October 1997, pp. 536–539 (1997)
5. ISetyawan, G.K., Lagendijk, R.L.: Synchronization-insensitive video watermarking using structured noise pattern. In: Proc. SPIE, Security and Watermarking of Multimedia Contents IV, San Jose, CA, pp. 520–530 (2002)
6. Kutter, M.: Watermarking Resistance to Translation, Rotation and Scaling. In: Proc. of SPIE: Media Systems Applications, vol. 3528, pp. 423–431 (1998)
7. ISetyawan, et al.: Perceptual quality evaluation of geometrically distorted images using relevant geometric transformation modeling. In: Proc SPIE, Security and Watermarking of Multimedia Contents V, vol. 5020 (2003)
8. Kang, X., Huang, J., Shi, Y., Lin, Y.: A DWT-DFT composite watermarking scheme robust to both affine transform and JPEG compression. IEEE Trans. Circuits Syst. Video Technol. 13(8), 776–786 (2003)
9. Pereira, S., Pun, T.: Robust template matching for affine resistant image watermarks. IEEE Trans. Image Process. 9(6), 1123–1129 (2000)
10. Pereira, S., Pun, T.: An iterative template matching algorithm using the Chirp-Z transform for digital image watermarking. Pattern Recognit. 33, 173–175 (2000)
11. Kutter, M., Bhattacharjee, S.K., Ebrahimi, T.: Towards second generation watermarking schemes. In: Proc. IEEE Int. Conf. Image Process., pp. 320–323 (1999)
12. Alghoniemy, M., Tewfik, A.: Geometric distortion correction through image normalization. In: Proc. IEEE Int. Conf. Multimedia Expo, vol. 3, pp. 1291–1294 (2000)
13. Kim, H.S., Lee, H.K.: Invariant image watermark using Zernike moments. IEEE Trans.Circuits Syst. Video Technol. 13(8), 766–775 (2003)
14. Loo, P., Kingsbury, N.: Motion-estimation-based registration of geometrically distorted image for watermark recovery. In: Proc. SPIE, Security and Watermarking of Multimedia Contents III, San Jose, CA, pp. 606–617 (2001)
15. Delannay, D., Delaigle, J.-F., Macq, B., Barlaud, M.: Compensation of geometrical deformations for watermark extraction in the digital cinema application. In: Proc. SPIE, Security and Watermarking of Multimedia Contents III, San Jose, CA, pp. 149–157 (2001)
16. Xiang, S., Huang, J., Yang, R.: Time-scale invariant audio watermarking based on the statistical features in time domain. In: Camenisch, J.L., Collberg, C.S., Johnson, N.F., Sallee, P. (eds.) IH 2006. LNCS, vol. 4437, pp. 93–108. Springer, Heidelberg (2007)
17. Xiang, S., Huang, J.: Histogram-based audio watermarking against time-scale modification and cropping attacks. IEEE Trans. Multimedia 9(7), 1357–11372 (2007)
18. Liu, H., Chen, N., Huang, J., Huang, X., Shi, Y.Q.: A robust DWT based video watermarking algorithm. In: Proc. IEEE Int. Symp. Circuits Systems, May 26-29, 2002, vol. 3, pp. 631–634 (2002)
19. Su, K., Kundur, D., Hatzinakos, D.: A content dependent spatially localized video watermark for resistance to collusion and interpolation attacks. In: Proc. Int. Conf. Image Processing, October 7-10, 2000, vol. 1, pp. 818–821 (2000)
20. Zhao, Y., Lagendijk, R.L.: Video watermarking scheme resistant to geometric attacks. In: Proc. Int. Conf. Image Processing, September 22–25, 2002, vol. 2, pp. 145–148 (2002)

Blind Digital Watermarking of Low Bit-Rate Advanced H.264/AVC Compressed Video

Dawen Xu[1,3], Rangding Wang[2], and Jicheng Wang[1]

[1] Department of Computer Science and Technology, Tongji University,
Shanghai, 201804, China
[2] CKC software lab, Ningbo University, Ningbo, 315211, China
[3] School of Electronics and Information Engineering,
Ningbo University of Technology, Ningbo, 315016, China
dawenxu@126.com

Abstract. H.264/AVC is becoming a popular video codec for its better compression ratio, lower distortion and applicability to portable electronic devices. Thus, issues of copyright protection and authentication that are appropriate for this standard become very important. In this paper, a blind video watermarking algorithm for H.264/AVC is proposed. The watermark information is embedded directly into H.264/AVC video at the encoder by modifying the quantized DC coefficients in luminance residual blocks slightly. The watermark embedded in the residuals can avoid decompressing the video and to decrease the complexity of the watermarking algorithm. To reduce visual quality degradation caused by DC coefficients modifying, block selection mechanism is introduced to control the modification strength. Experimental results reveal that the proposed scheme can achieve enough robustness while preserving the perceptual quality.

Keywords: video watermarking, H.264/AVC, intra prediction, copyright protection, compressed domain.

1 Introduction

Nowadays, with the thriving internet technology, how to protect the copyright of the digitalized information is becoming more and more attractive. Digital watermarking technology [1, 2] has been proposed as an effective method to protect the authenticity of the intellectual property. The principle of watermarking is to embed a digital code (watermark) within the host multimedia, and to use such a code to prove ownership, to prevent illegal copying. The watermark code is embedded by making imperceptible modification to the digital data.

Video watermarking techniques can be classified as spatial-domain, transform-domain or compressed-domain. In spatial domain watermarking systems, the watermark is embedded directly in the spatial domain (pixel domain) [3]. In transform domain watermarking systems, watermark insertion is done by transforming the video signal into the frequency domain using DFT [4], DCT [5] or DWT [6]. Since most digital video products are distributed and stored in compressed format, compressed-domain video watermarking

A.T.S. Ho et al. (Eds.): IWDW 2009, LNCS 5703, pp. 96–109, 2009.

is especially attractive. In [7, 8], the spatial spread-spectrum watermark is embedded directly to compressed MPEG-4 and MPEG-2 bitstreams by modifying DCT coefficients. In [9], the robust watermark is embedded in motion vectors of the bitstream based on the relationships between one-pixel accuracy and half-pixel accuracy motion vectors at the encoder. In [10], watermark embedding is performed in the variable length codeword (VLC) domain. In [11], the fragile watermark is embedded in a VLC by changing that VLC to an unused code word. Above typical compressed-domain video watermarking methods were focusing on MPEG standards. Unfortunately, these video watermarking algorithms cannot be applied directly to H.264/AVC because of differences in the standards. For a more detailed description of H.264, please refer to [12] and [13].

Recently, a few watermarking algorithms on H.264/AVC have appeared in the open literature. Qiu [14] proposed a hybrid watermarking scheme for H.264/AVC by embedding the robust watermark into DCT domain and the fragile watermark into motion vectors respectively. The algorithm is not robust against common watermarking attack. A blind watermarking algorithm by embedding the watermark in the H.264 I frames is presented in [15]. The scheme can survive H.264 compression attacks with more than a 40:1 compression ratio, but requires decompressing the video to embed the watermark. In order to enhance the robustness, the authors in [16] employ a human visual model adapted for a 4×4 DCT block to increase the payload and robustness. The algorithm can achieve high robustness, but its computational complexity is high. The authors in [17] proposed a robust video watermarking scheme of H.264/AVC using a grayscale watermark pattern. In this scheme, a grayscale watermark pre-processing technique is performed. Thus for these techniques it is extremely difficult to perform watermark embedding/detection in real-time.

In general, H.264/AVC coding standard adopts many new features such as intra-prediction, integer 4×4 DCT transform, variable block size motion estimation, and new entropy coding methods of context-adaptive binary arithmetic coding (CABAC) and context-adaptive variable length coding (CAVLC) [12]. These can be exploited for watermarking purpose. Kapotas [18] exploited the IPCM encoded macroblocks during the intra prediction stage to hide the desired data. This method is suited to content-based authentication and covert communication applications. Hu [19] exploited the intra 4×4 prediction modes to hide information. Information hiding is implemented by modifying the intra prediction modes of qualified intra 4×4 luma blocks. Future work will focus on the watermarking scheme using new features of H.264/AVC. In this paper, a blind watermarking algorithm exploited intra prediction of H.264/AVC is proposed. The watermark is embedded in the DC coefficients of intra-coded macroblocks. Because our scheme performed directly in quantized residual coefficients, only inverse entropy coding is needed before watermark detection. So watermark detection can be achieved in real-time. Since human eyes are highly sensitive to the modification of DC values, a block selection mechanism is introduced to prevent from obvious degradation of visual quality.

The rest of the paper is organized as follows. In Section 2, the watermark embedding and detection algorithms are described. In Section 3, experimental results and performance analysis are presented aiming at demonstrating the validity of the proposed scheme. Finally, the conclusions are drawn in Section 4.

2 The Proposed Scheme

2.1 Embedding Position Selection

Similar to I-, P-, and B-pictures defined for MPEG-2, H.263, and MPEG-4, the H.264/AVC syntax supports I-, P- and B-slices. In an I-slice, all macroblocks are encoded in Intra mode. Intra prediction means that the samples of a macroblock (MB) are predicted by using only information of already transmitted macroblocks of the same image. In H.264/AVC, two different types of intra prediction are possible for the prediction of the luminance component Y. The first type is called Intra_4×4 and the second one Intra_16×16. The Intra_4×4 type is based on predicting each 4×4 luminance block separately and is well suited for coding of parts of a picture with significant detail. The Intra_16×16 type, on the other hand, performs prediction of the whole 16×16 luminance block and is more suited for coding very smooth areas of a picture [12, 20]. Based on the foundation of human visual system (HVS), human eye is less sensitive to noise in edge and detail regions rather than in smooth areas. Therefore macroblocks using Intra_4×4 mode are used for embedding watermark.

Similar to previous video coding standards, H.264/AVC utilizes transform coding of the prediction residual. However, in H.264/AVC, the transformation is applied to 4×4 blocks (instead of 8×8 blocks used in previous standards), and a separable integer transform with similar properties as a 4×4 DCT is used. Where should watermark be embedded in the DCT domain? In [21], Huang proposed that DC components are more suitable for watermarking than any AC components. In [22], Liu choose the DC coefficients of DCT blocks in each intra frame to embed watermark. This scheme in MPEG-2 compressed domain has some advantages (please refer to [22]). In this paper, we also apply DC-based embedding strategy for H.264/AVC standard. Because the watermark embedded in DC components is more robust than that in AC components.

2.2 Watermark Embedding

In this study, watermark information is the extended m-sequence denoted by $W = \{w(l) \mid w(l) \in \{+1, -1\}, l = 1, 2, ..., M\}$. Extended m-sequences have good balance (zero mean), random appearance, resilience to filtering, cropping and individual bit errors, optimal autocorrelation properties and constrained cross-correlation [23].

Watermark embedding procedure is described as follows:

(1) Calculate the mean of the non-zero quantized DC coefficients in the $i \cdot th$ MB.

$$D(i) = \frac{1}{k_i} \sum_{j=1}^{k_i} |dc_{i,j}| \qquad (1)$$

where, k_i is the number of the non-zero DC coefficients in the $i \cdot th$ MB, $dc_{i,j}$ is the $j \cdot th$ non-zero DC coefficient in the $i \cdot th$ MB.

(2) Calculate the mean value of the sequence $D = \{D(i), i = 1, 2, ..., N\}$.

$$\overline{D} = \frac{1}{N} \sum_{i=1}^{N} D(i) \qquad (2)$$

(3) The magnitude relationships between $D(i)$ and $\overline{D}$ can be determined as follows:

$$diff_m(i) = sign\left(D(i) - \overline{D}\right) \tag{3}$$

where $sign(x)$ is defined as

$$sign(x) = \begin{cases} +1 & if \cdot x \geq 0 \\ -1 & if \cdot x < 0 \end{cases} \tag{4}$$

(4) Watermark embedding is performed accord to the relationship between $diff_m(i)$ and watermark sequence $w(i)$. The detailed embedding scheme is as follows:

Case 1: When $diff_m(i) = w(i)$, DC coefficients in the $i \cdot th$ MB keep unchanged.

Case 2: Otherwise, $D(i)$ is modulated by $Q(i)$ as

$$D^w(i) = D(i) + w(i) \cdot Q(i) \tag{5}$$

where $Q(i)$ is modification quantity should be determined, $D^w(i)$ is the modulated result of $D(i)$. Then the mean value of the sequence $D^w(i)$ can be derived as

$$\overline{D}^w = \frac{1}{N}\sum_{i=1}^{N} D^w(i) = \frac{1}{N}\sum_{i=1}^{N} D(i) + \frac{1}{N}\sum_{i=1}^{N} w(i) \cdot Q(i) \approx \overline{D} \tag{6}$$

The new relationship between $D^w(i)$ and $\overline{D}^w$ is

$$\begin{aligned} diff_m^w(i) &= sign\left(D^w(i) - \overline{D}^w\right) \\ &= sign\left((D(i) + w(i) \cdot Q(i)) - \overline{D}\right) \\ &= sign\left((D(i) - \overline{D}) + w(i) \cdot Q(i)\right) \end{aligned} \tag{7}$$

After modulating by Eq. (5), it should be insure that the sign of $diff_m^w(i)$ is the same as corresponding watermark bit $w(i)$ [10]. Based on this purpose, Eq. (7) can be rewritten as

$$\left(D(i) - \overline{D}\right) + w(i) \cdot Q(i) = sign(w(i)) \cdot T \tag{8}$$

where T can be determined as follows:

$$T_{\min} = \min\left\{\left|D(1) - \overline{D}\right|, \cdots, \left|D(N) - \overline{D}\right|\right\}$$

$$T_{\max} = \max\left\{\left|D(1) - \overline{D}\right|, \cdots, \left|D(N) - \overline{D}\right|\right\}$$

$$T = \lambda \cdot T_{\min} + (1 - \lambda) \cdot T_{\max} \quad 0 \leq \lambda \leq 1 \tag{9}$$

where λ is a factor used to control the image quality and robustness. For avoiding the distortion of the embedded video, we set $T = 1$ directly.

According to Eq. (8), $Q(i)$ can be determined as

$$Q(i) = \begin{cases} T - (D(i) - \overline{D}) & \text{if } w(i) = +1 \\ T + (D(i) - \overline{D}) & \text{if } w(i) = -1 \end{cases} \qquad (10)$$

Therefore, Eq. (10) can be substituted into Eq. (5) to perform watermark embedding. From the above description, the mean of the non-zero DC coefficients in the $i \cdot th$ MB has been modulated by $w(i) \cdot Q(i)$. The modification of the mean $D(i)$ should be carried out by modifying all the constituent DC coefficients in the $i \cdot th$ MB. That is to say, in order to finish watermark embedding, $dc_{i,j}$ should be modulated as follows:

$$dc_{i,j}^w = \begin{cases} dc_{i,j} + (T - (D(i) - \overline{D})) & \text{if } w(i) = +1 \text{ and } dc_{i,j} > 0 \\ dc_{i,j} - (T - (D(i) - \overline{D})) & \text{if } w(i) = +1 \text{ and } dc_{i,j} < 0 \\ dc_{i,j} - (T + (D(i) - \overline{D})) & \text{if } w(i) = -1 \text{ and } dc_{i,j} > 0 \\ dc_{i,j} + (T + (D(i) - \overline{D})) & \text{if } w(i) = -1 \text{ and } dc_{i,j} < 0 \end{cases} \qquad (11)$$

where $dc_{i,j}^w$ are modulated DC coefficients. Here, $dc_{i,j}$ may be modified to 0, which will result different mean value in Eq. (1). In this case, the decoder will be not able to recover the watermark exactly. So if modulated DC coefficient equals to 0 (i.e, $dc_{i,j}^w = 0$), we reset $dc_{i,j}^w$ to $sign(dc_{i,j})$.

Until now, the watermark embedding in $i \cdot th$ MB is finished. The above process is repeated until the whole watermark sequence is embedded.

2.3 Performance Improvement

According to Eq. (5) and Eq. (8), $D^w(i)$ can be rewritten as

$$D^w(i) = D(i) + w(i) \cdot Q(i) = \overline{D} + sign(w(i)) \cdot T \qquad (12)$$

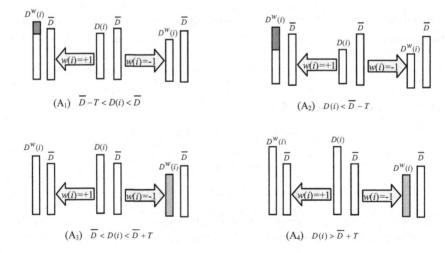

(A_1) $\overline{D} - T < D(i) < \overline{D}$

(A_2) $D(i) < \overline{D} - T$

(A_3) $\overline{D} < D(i) < \overline{D} + T$

(A_4) $D(i) > \overline{D} + T$

Fig. 1. Watermarking modulation at different regions

When $diff_m(i)$ is not identical to $w(i)$ and $|D(i)-\overline{D}|$ is very large (For example, A_2 and A_4 in Fig. 1), watermark embedding will cause degradation of visual quality. Das [24] reorganize the blocks such that energy of each subregion is close. But its computational complexity is comparatively high. Here, block selection mechanism is performed directly. We set threshold $T_\psi = 2$. If $diff_m(i)$ is not identical to $w(i)$ and $|D(i)-\overline{D}| > T_\psi$, then this MB will not be used to embed watermark. According to experimental results, we can find that the mean of the non-zero quantized DC coefficients in each MB is close. The process may discard few MBs which not suitable for watermark embedding. So watermarking capacity will not be reduced apparently.

2.4 Watermark Detection

The watermark signal detection process is fast and simple. Because watermark signal is embedded in quantized residual coefficients, inverse quantization, inverse DCT, and full decoding are not performed on the watermarked bitstreams. On the contrary, only inverse entropy coding is required to obtain quantized residual coefficients. Thus, real-time detection can be achieved.

The watermark is detected from the H.264/AVC compressed video stream by going through following steps:

(1) The bitstream is partially decoded to obtain the quantized DCT coefficients.
(2) Calculate the mean value $D_a^w(i)$ of the non-zero DC coefficients in the $i \cdot th$ MB and the mean value $\overline{D}_a^w$ of the sequence $D_a^w = \{D_a^w(i), i=1,2,...,N\}$. Watermark can be determined as follows:

$$w_s(l) = sign\left(D_a^w(l) - \overline{D}_a^w\right)$$
$$= \begin{cases} +1 & if \cdot D_a^w(l) - \overline{D}_a^w \geq 0 \\ -1 & if \cdot D_a^w(l) - \overline{D}_a^w < 0 \end{cases} \quad l = 1,2,...,M \qquad (13)$$

(3) For comparing the similarities between the original and extracted watermark signals, the normalized cross-correlation function is computed as

$$Sim(w, w_s) = \frac{\sum_{i=1}^{M} w(l) \cdot w_s(l)}{\sqrt{\sum_{l=1}^{M} w^2(l)} \sqrt{\sum_{l=1}^{M} w_s^2(l)}} \qquad (14)$$

To decide whether watermark is present or not, we need to compare the similarity with a threshold. Similarity is greater than a minimum threshold indicates the presence of the watermark.

2.5 False Positive Analysis

The probability of false positive is defined as [25]

$$P_{fp} = P\{Sim(w, w_s) \geq T_\rho \mid no\ watermark\} \qquad (15)$$

where $P\{A \mid B\}$ is the conditional probability that event A occurs given that event B has occurred already.

Since $w(l)$ and $w_s(l)$ are either 1 or -1, accordingly, $w^2(l) = w_s^2(l) = 1$. So Eq. (14) can be re-written as

$$Sim(w, w_s) = \frac{\sum_l w(l)w_s(l)}{\sqrt{\sum_l w^2(l)}\sqrt{\sum_l w_s^2(l)}} = \frac{\sum_l w(l)w_s(l)}{M} \tag{16}$$

Suppose n bits error occurs when extracting watermark data. Then, $m = M - n$ bits are identical to the original watermark data. The equation is easily derived as

$$\sum_i w(l)w_s(l) = m - n = M - 2n \tag{17}$$

If Eq. (16) and Eq. (17) are substituted into Eq. (15), the probability of false positive can be further derived as

$$P_{fp} = P\{Sim(w, w_s) \geq T_\rho \mid no\ watermark\}$$

$$= \left\{ \frac{\sum_l w(l)w_s(l)}{M} \geq T_\rho \middle| no\ watermark \right\} \tag{18}$$

$$= \left\{ \frac{M - 2n}{M} \geq T_\rho \middle| no\ watermark \right\}$$

When $n \leq M(1 - T_\rho)/2$, the false positive error will occur. Thus, we have

$$P_{fp} = \sum_{n=0}^{\lceil M(1-T_\rho)/2 \rceil} P\left\{ \sum_l w(l)w_s(l) = M - 2n \middle| no\ watermark \right\}$$

$$= \sum_{n=0}^{\lceil M(1-T_\rho)/2 \rceil} \binom{M}{n} \cdot p^n(1-p)^{M-n} \tag{19}$$

where $\binom{M}{n} = \frac{M!}{n!(M-n)!}$, p is the probability of error occur when some watermark extraction is performed. Since watermark values are either 1 or -1, so $p = 0.5$. Therefore,

$$P_{fp} = \sum_{n=0}^{\lvert M(1-T_\rho)/2 \rvert} \binom{M}{n} \cdot 0.5^M \tag{20}$$

Similarly, the probability of false negative can be determined as

$$P_{fn} = P\{Sim(w, w_s) < T_\rho \mid watermark\}$$

$$= \sum_{n=\lceil M(1-T_\rho)/2 \rceil+1}^{M} \binom{M}{n} \cdot 0.5^M \tag{21}$$

Generally, a desired probability of false positive is given, the detection threshold T_ρ can be determined according to Eq.(20). The determination of threshold should consider the trade-off between false positive and false negative. An increase in T_ρ will reduce P_{fp}, but will increase P_{fn}. For our simulation results T_ρ is set to 0.15.

3   Experimental Results and Analysis

The proposed watermarking scheme has been integrated into the H.264/AVC JM-12.2 reference software [26]. We used three standard video sequences (Foreman, Carphone and Container) in QCIF format (176×144) at a rate 30 frames/s for our simulation. The first 30 frames of the video sequences are used in the experiments. The GOP (Group of Pictures) structure consisted of an Intra (I-) frame followed by 4 Inter (P-) frames.

3.1   Visibility Experiments

An original frame from each video is shown in Fig.2. The corresponding watermarked frames are shown in Fig.3. In the experiments, no visible artifacts can be observed in all of the test video sequences. Fig.4 illustrates the Y-PSNR (peak signal-to-noise ratio) variation of 30 frames induced by the watermark embedding. The simulation results show that the PSNR of each watermarked frame is greater than 36dB. The PSNR curves for the two sequences (with and without the watermark) are very close and the PSNR variations are smoother, indicating little influence on the video quality. Fig.6 displays the average PSNR and bit rate comparison results. The test sequences are encoded with fixed quantization parameters QP= [24, 28, 32, 36, 40], corresponding to typical QPs for low bit-rate applications [14]. Simulation results show that watermark embedding increases the bit rate of the video about 0.51%, 3.73%, 3.78% for the sequence Foreman, Carphone and Container encoded with QP=28.

Comparing with the existing schemes, the number of watermark bits embedded in an I-frame and the robustness of our scheme are higher than that in [27], but the increase of bit rate is also higher (shown in Table.1). More experimental results against attacks are shown in Section 3.2.

(a) "Foreman"   (b) "Carphone"   (c) "Container"

Fig. 2. Original frames

(a) "Foreman" (36.97dB)   (b) "Carphone" (37.75dB)   (c) "Container" (37.32dB)

Fig. 3. Watermarked frames

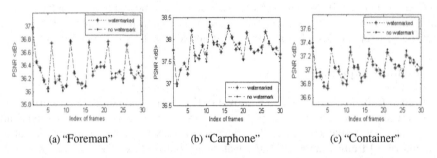

(a) "Foreman"   (b) "Carphone"   (c) "Container"

Fig. 4. The variation of Y-PSNR induced by the watermark embedding

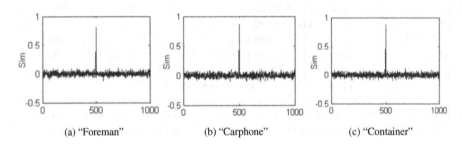

(a) "Foreman"   (b) "Carphone"   (c) "Container"

Fig. 5. Detector response

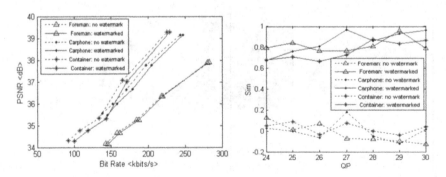

Fig. 6. PSNR and bit rate comparison results   **Fig. 7.** *Sim* curves

Table 1. Performance comparison between our scheme and [27]

Video	Watermark Bits		Re-encoding Recovery Rate		Bit Rate Increase	
Sequence	Method in [27]	Our scheme	Method in [27]	Our scheme	Method in [27]	Our scheme
Carphone	44	59	58%	78.16%	0.80%	3.73%
Claire	22	35	83%	77.46%	0.44%	3.57%
Mobile	85	118	85%	77.87%	0.23%	0.51%
Mother	42	44	68%	82.73%	0.69%	4.37%
Table	38	77	62%	85.94%	0.31%	2.28%
tempete	81	113	83%	84.83%	0.44%	0.79%

3.2 Robustness Experiments

This study generated 1000 different sets of watermark sequences using random seed, and calculated the correlation between these sequences and the watermark extracted from the watermarked images. Without any attack, the detection responses are shown in Fig.5, and the 500th is the original watermark sequence. From the figures, only one peak exists, and the peak is greater than the threshold T_ρ. It is observed that the original watermarks can be correctly detected.

We compared *Sim* curves that were generated from watermarked and un-watermarked video sequences (shown in Fig.7). In this figure, the horizontal axis indicates the quantization parameter QP, and the vertical axis indicates the correlation value. It is easy to distinguish the watermarked video sequences from the un-watermarked video sequences according to T_ρ.

To test robustness against different attacks, several attacks, including re-encoding with different QP, frame rate changing, frame swapping, and additive noise attack are performed to verify the performance of our video watermarking algorithm.

1) *Recompression.* Watermarked video streams are decoded and re-encoded with different *QP*. The original sequences are coded with *QP*=28. The test results are shown in Fig. 8. It is observed that *Sim* is high enough for correct detection.

2) *Adding Gaussian noise.* Gaussian noise with different strength is added to the watermarked video. Fig. 9 shows the *Sim* values between the original and the extracted sequence. It is found that the video frames have visible distortion when the PSNR decreases down to 30dB, but the detection response is higher than threshold T_ρ (see Fig. 9). The results show that the proposed algorithm is robust to additive Gaussian noise attack.

3) *Frame rate changing.* We also performed frame rate changing attacks on the watermarked videos. When frame rate changes from 30 to 15 frames/s, the watermark detection results are shown in Fig.10. The algorithm is robust against frame rate changing.

4) *Frame swapping.* Frame swapping is performed by taking two random frames from the sequence and swapping them. The *Sim* values after frame swapping are shown in Fig.11. The x-coordinate denotes the number of frames swapped. The proposed method achieves high robustness against frame swapping attack.

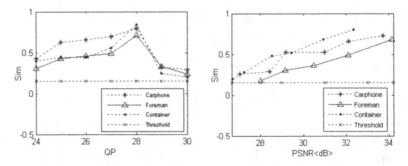

Fig. 8. *Sim* values after recompression   **Fig. 9.** *Sim* values after noise attack

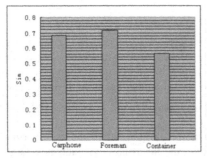
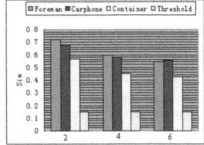

Fig. 10. *Sim* after Frame rate changing attacks   **Fig. 11.** *Sim* after Frame swapping attacks

3.3 Real-Time Performance Evaluation

The proposed watermarking scheme is performed without high computational complexity and difficulty in detecting watermark information. The time cost is calculated and shown in Fig.12. The watermarking algorithm is run on a PC with a Pentium

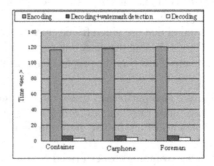

Fig. 12. Comparison of the time cost

2.8GHz CPU under Windows XP. Our experiments show that the proposed scheme does not introduce serious delays in the encoding process. Since entropy decoding does not incorporate the inverse transform, it is performed very fast. From the results, we can find that our watermark detection can almost be performed in real-time.

4 Conclusions

In this paper, a blind video watermarking algorithm based on H.264/AVC codec is presented. The video is watermarked during H.264/AVC compression process. In the embedding procedure, watermark signals are embedded directly in quantized residual coefficients to satisfy the requirement of real-time detection. The watermarked H.264/AVC video streams maintain the good visual quality and almost the same bit rate. We also test the robustness of our proposed algorithm to several common signal processing attacks such as requantization, frame rate changing, frame swapping, and additive noise attacks. Simulation results show that the proposed algorithm is robust against these attacks.

Currently, the proposed scheme is implemented only in H.264/AVC baseline profile. In future work, we will extend watermarking scheme into all profiles. Also the scheme to resist video transcoding [28] and collusion attacks is under investigation.

Acknowledgements

We want to thank three anonymous reviewers for their helpful comments and suggestions. This work is supported by the National Natural Science Foundation of China (60672070, 60873220), Zhejiang Provincial Natural Science Foundation of China (Y1080221), Ningbo Science &Technology Project of China (2006B100067) and Scientific Research Fund of Zhejiang Provincial Education Department (Y200803979).

References

1. Cox, I.J., Kilian, J., Leighton, T., Shamoon, T.: Secure spread spectrum watermarking for multimedia. IEEE Transactions on Image Processing 6(12), 1673–1687 (1997)
2. Langelaar, G.C., Setyawan, I., Lagendijk, R.L.: Watermarking digital image and video data: A satate-of-the-art overview. IEEE Signal Processing Magazine 17(5), 20–46 (2000)
3. Xu, D.W., Wang, R.D., Wang, J.C.: Video watermarking based on spatio-temporal JND profile. In: 7th International Workshop on Digital Watermarking (IWDW 2008), Busan, Korea, pp. 338–351 (2008)
4. Lee, Y.Y., Jung, H.S., Lee, S.U.: Multi-bit video watermarking based on 3D DFT using perceptual models. In: Kalker, T., Cox, I., Ro, Y.M. (eds.) IWDW 2003. LNCS, vol. 2939, pp. 301–315. Springer, Heidelberg (2004)

5. Wang, Y.L., Pearmain, A.: Blind MPEG-2 video watermarking robust against geometric attacks: a set of approaches in DCT domain. IEEE Transactions on Image Processing 15(6), 1536–1543 (2006)

6. Coria, L.E., Pickering, M.R., Nasiopoulos, P., Ward, R.K.: A video watermarking scheme based on the dual-tree complex wavelet transform. IEEE Transactions on Information Forensics and Security 3(3), 466–474 (2008)

7. Alattar, A.M., Lin, E.T., Celik, M.U.: Digital watermarking of low bit-rate advanced simple profile MPEG-4 compressed video. IEEE Transactions on Circuits and Systems for Video Technology 13(8), 787–800 (2003)

8. Biswas, S., Das, S.R., Petriu, E.M.: An adaptive compressed MPEG-2 video watermarking scheme. IEEE Transactions on Instrumentation and Measurement 54(5), 1853–1861 (2005)

9. Wang, H.X., Li, Y.N., Lu, Z.M., Sun, S.H.: Compressed domain video watermarking in motion vector. In: Khosla, R., Howlett, R.J., Jain, L.C. (eds.) KES 2005. LNCS (LNAI), vol. 3682, pp. 580–586. Springer, Heidelberg (2005)

10. Lu, C.S., Chen, J.R., Fan, K.C.: Real-time frame-dependent video watermarking in VLC domain. Signal Processing: Image Communication 20(7), 624–642 (2005)

11. Mobasseri, B.G., Berger, R.J.: A foundation for watermarking in compressed domain. IEEE Signal Processing Letters 12(5), 399–402 (2005)

12. Wiegand, T., Sullivan, G.J., Bjntegaard, G., Luthra, A.: Overview of the H.264/AVC video coding standard. IEEE Transactions on Circuits and Systems for Video Technology 13(7), 560–576 (2003)

13. Schwarz, H., Marpe, D., Wiegand, T.: Overview of the scalable video coding extension of the H. 264/AVC standard. IEEE Transactions on Circuits and Systems for Video Technology 17(9), 1103–1120 (2007)

14. Qiu, G., Marziliano, P., Ho, A.T.S., He, D.J., Sun, Q.B.: A hybrid watermarking scheme for H.264/AVC video. In: Proceedings of the 17th International Conference on Pattern Recognition, Cambridge, UK, vol. 4, pp. 865–868 (2004)

15. Wu, G.Z., Wang, Y.J., Hsu, W.H.: Robust watermark embedding detection algorithm for H.264 video. Journal of Electronic Imaging 14(1), 1–9 (2005)

16. Noorkami, M., Mersereau, R.M.: A framework for robust watermarking of H.264-encoded video with controllable detection performance. IEEE Transactions on Information Forensics and Security 2(1), 14–23 (2007)

17. Zhang, J., Ho, A.T.S., Qiu, G., Marziliano, P.: Robust video watermarking of H. 264/AVC. IEEE Transactions on Circuits and Systems 54(2), 205–209 (2007)

18. Kapotas, S.K., Skodras, A.N.: Real time data hiding by exploiting the IPCM macroblocks in H.264/AVC streams. Journal of Real-Time Image Processing 4(1), 33–41 (2009)

19. Hu, Y., Zhang, C.T., Su, Y.T.: Information hiding based on intra prediction modes for H.264/AVC. In: IEEE International Conference on Multimedia and Expo, Beijing, China, pp. 1231–1234 (2007)

20. Ostermann, J., Bormans, J., List, P., Marpe, D., Narroschke, M., Pereira, F., Stockhammer, T., Wedi, T.: Video coding with H.264/AVC: tools, performance, and complexity. IEEE Circuits and Systems Magazine 4(1), 7–28 (2004)

21. Huang, J.W., Shi, Y.Q., Shi, Y.: Embedding image watermarks in DC components. IEEE Transactions on Circuits and Systems for Video Technology 10(6), 974–979 (2000)

22. Liu, H.M., Shao, F.L., Huang, J.W.: A MPEG-2 video watermarking algorithm with compensation in bit stream. In: Safavi-Naini, R., Yung, M. (eds.) DRMTICS 2005. LNCS, vol. 3919, pp. 123–134. Springer, Heidelberg (2006)

23. Van Schyndel, R.G., Tirkel, A.Z., Osborne, C.F.: Towards a robust digital watermark. In: Second Asian Conference on Computer Vision, Singapore, vol. 2, pp. 504–508 (1995)
24. Das, T.K., Maitra, S., Mitra, J.: Cryptanalysis of optimal differential energy watermarking (DEW) and a modified robust scheme. IEEE Transactions on Signal Processing 53(2) (2005)
25. Kundur, D., Hatzinakos, D.: Digital watermarking using multiresolution wavelet decomposition. In: IEEE International Conference on Acoustics, Speech and Signal Processing, Seattle, Washington, vol. 5, pp. 2969–2972 (1998)
26. Suhring, K.: H.264/AVC Joint Model 8.6 (JM-8.6) Reference Software, http://iphome.hhi.de/suehring/tml/
27. Noorkami, M., Mersereau, R.M.: Compressed-domain video watermarking for H.264. In: IEEE International Conference on Image Processing, Genoa, Italy, vol. 2, pp. 11–14 (2005)
28. Shen, H.F., Sun, X.Y., Wu, F.: Fast H.264/MEPG-4 AVC transcoding using power-spectrum based rate-distortion optimization. IEEE Transactions on Circuits and Systems for Video Technology 18(6), 746–755 (2008)

Fast Embedding Technique for Dirty Paper Trellis Watermarking

Marc Chaumont

University of Nîmes, Place Gabriel Péri, 30000 Nîmes, France
University of Montpellier II, Laboratory LIRMM, UMR CNRS 5506,
161, rue Ada, 34392 Montpellier cedex 05, France
marc.chaumont@lirmm.fr
http://www.lirmm.fr/~chaumont

Abstract. This paper deals with the improvement of the Dirty Paper Trellis Code (DPTC) watermarking algorithm. This watermarking algorithm is known to be one of the best among the high rate watermarking schemes. Nevertheless, recent researches reveal its security weakness. Previously, we proposed to reinforce its security by using a secret space before the embedding. This secret space requires to compute projections onto secrets carriers. When dealing with high rate watermarking, the CPU cost for those projections is dramatically high. After introducing the watermarking scheme, we then propose two Space Division Multiplexing (SDM) approaches which reduce the complexity. Evaluations are achieved with four different attacks and show that our proposal gives better robustness results with SDM approaches.

1 Introduction

Dirty Paper Trellis Codes (DPTC) [1] watermarking is one of the most efficient high rate schemes. Nevertheless, it suffers of two major drawbacks: its CPU computational complexity for the embedding part and its security weakness. In this paper we propose to carry on the work proposed in [2] which gives a nice way to improve those two drawbacks while preserving a good robustness.

The recent work of Bas and Doërr [3] about security of DPTC [1] shows that in the Kerckhoffs's framework [4], i.e. when the embedding and extracting algorithms are known by an attacker, the trellis codebook may be retrieved observing a large number of watermarked images. Those conclusions are drawn based on a simplified version of the DPTC algorithm (non random-ordering of DCT coefficients) but show a certain security weakness of DPTC [1]. In [2], we proposed to use a *private embedding space* in order to better hide the structure of the trellis. Moreover, we provided a fast embedding strategy.

The *private space* is obtained by vector projections. If achived directly, the vector projections give a quadratic CPU complexity. In that paper, we propose two different Space Division Multiplexing (SDM) approaches in order to reduce the quadratic complexity to a linear one.

A.T.S. Ho et al. (Eds.): IWDW 2009, LNCS 5703, pp. 110–120, 2009.
© Springer-Verlag Berlin Heidelberg 2009

In section 2, we briefly present the embedding space and the embedding approach already presented in [2]. In section 3, we present two SDM approaches in order to reduce the projections complexity. Finally, in section 4 we evaluate the schemes and conclude to the good behavior of the SDM approaches.

2 New Embedding Approach

In this section, we remind the embedding space and the embedding approach proposed in [2].

2.1 Embedding Space

The embedding space is obtained by first, a wavelet transform of the image, and second, a projection of the host signal $\mathbf{x}$ of dimension N_{wlt} ($\mathbf{x}$ is the concatenation of sub-bands coefficients except LL sub-band's coefficients) onto N_{sec} carriers of same dimension. Carriers are denoted $\mathbf{u}_i$ with $i \in [0, N_{sec} - 1]$. Note that a projection is just a scalar product. Figure 1 illustrates the construction of the host signal $\mathbf{x}$ and the host vector (secret space) $\mathbf{v_x}$. The obtained vector $\mathbf{v_x}$ may then be used for the *informed-coding* and *informed-embedding* (see Section 2.2).

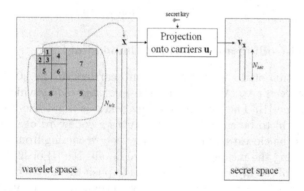

Fig. 1. Construction scheme of the secret embedding space

The carriers $\mathbf{u}_i$ are built from normalized bipolar pseudo-random sequences. For computational complexity reasons, carriers are neither orthonormalized nor drawn from a Gaussian distribution. This is not a weakness since in high dimension, carriers are orthogonal and Gaussian property is not essential. Nevertheless, computational complexity is still high since computing the N_{sec} coefficients of the secure space requires to compute $N_{wlt} \times N_{sec}$ multiplications (resp. sums).

Knowing that $N_{wlt} = N \times (1 - 1/2^{2l})$ and $N_{sec} = N \times payload \times N_{arc}$, it gives[1] $N^2 \times payload \times N_{arc} \times (1 - 1/2^{2l})$ multiplications (resp. sums). The computational complexity is thus quadratic in function of the image size N.

---

[1] l is the number of wavelet decompositions, *payload* is the number of embedded bits by pixel, and N_{arc} is the number of output coefficients labeling an arc of the trellis.

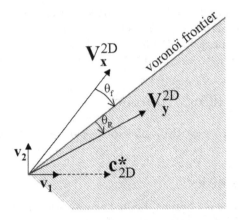

Fig. 2. Rotation-based embedding in the Miller, Cox and Bloom plane

As an illustration, with a 256×256 image, $l = 3$ levels, *payload* $= 1/64$ bbp, and $N_{arc} = 12$ coefficients, there are 792 723 456 multiplications (resp. sums). Let us remark that it is impossible to reduce the number of multiplications and additions (thus it is impossible to reduce the complexity), and thus it is not useful to use a particular matrix multiplication routine.

2.2 Informed-Coding and Informed-Embedding

After the projection of the host vector $\mathbf{x}$ onto carriers' $\mathbf{u}_i, i \in [0, N_{sec} - 1]$, we obtain the host vector $\mathbf{v_x}$. We then run the *informed-coding* which is the same as the original one [1]. The informed-coding takes as input the host vector $\mathbf{v_x}$ and the message m to be embedded and returns a codeword $\mathbf{c}^*$. This vector $\mathbf{c}^*$ (of size N_{sec}) is the closest one to $\mathbf{v_x}$ among vectors coming from the codebook $\mathcal{C}$, and representing the message m. For more details see [1] or [2].

The objective of the *informed-embedding* is to push the host vector $\mathbf{v_x}$ into the Voronoï region of $\mathbf{c}^*$ in order to obtain the watermarked vector $\mathbf{v_y}$. Many solutions exist which are either too CPU consuming [1], either too sub-optimal considering robustness-distortion tradeoff [5][2], [6]. In [1], a Monte-Carlo approach is used which requires many iterations of Viterbi decoder. On a Pentium 3 GHz, for a 256×256 image and a message size of 1024 bits, watermarking takes from half an hour to two hours depending on the robustness threshold. In [5] and [6], the Viterbi decoder is only used once or twice. On a Pentium 3 GHz, for a 256×256 image and a message size of 1024 bits, watermarking takes less than one minute. Nevertheless, those two last approaches degrade the image quality and are thus not fully satisfying.

Our previous approach [2] is a good compromise between complexity and robustness. It is illustrated in Figure 2 in the plane defined by $\mathbf{v_x}$ and $\mathbf{c}^*$ (those

---

[2] Paper [5] purpose is not informed-embedding but it uses a simple embedding solution.

two vectors are noted $\mathbf{v_x^{2D}}$ and $\mathbf{c_{2D}^*}$). This plane is usually named the Miller, Cox and Bloom plane (*abbr.* MCB plane).

Our approach consists in dichotomously reducing the angle between the host vector $\mathbf{v_x}$ and the codeword $\mathbf{c^*}$ until obtaining the smallest angle (noted θ_f) regarding all the other angles. Then, one penetrates inside the Voronoï region with a given angle θ_R. Our informed embedding is thus a rotation of $\mathbf{v_x}$ with an oriented angle equals to $\max(\theta_f + \theta_R, (\widehat{\mathbf{v_x}, \mathbf{c^*}}))$. This rotation gives the marked vector $\mathbf{v_y}$.

We then compute the watermark vector $\mathbf{v_w} = \mathbf{v_y} - \mathbf{v_x}$, retro-project it onto carriers in order to obtain the watermark signal $\mathbf{w}$ and then compute the watermarked signal $\mathbf{y} = \mathbf{x} + \mathbf{w}$. The inverse wavelet transform of $\mathbf{y}$ gives the watermarked image. At the extraction we project wavelet coefficients onto secret carriers and then retrieve the closest codeword (and thus the message) from the codebook $\mathcal{C}$.

3   Space Division Multiplexing (SDM) Approaches

As explained in Section 2, the projections of the host signal $\mathbf{x}$ onto secret carriers are quadratic in (computational) complexity. In order to reduce this complexity to a more reasonable linear function, we decide to divide the wavelet space into disjoint *regions* and to use a carrier for each *region*. Figure 3 illustrates this concept. There is still N_{sec} carriers but their non-zero values are limited to a small *region*. Let $\bar{s} = N_{wlt}/N_{sec}$ be the mean *region* size. The number of multiplications (resp. sums) in order to compute the secret space is now approximately $N_{sec} \times \bar{s} = N_{wlt} = N \times (1 - 1/2^{2l})$. The computational complexity is thus linear in function of the image size N. This division approach is called Space Division Multiplexing (SDM) [7].

We thus propose two approaches for SDM. In the first one, we build regions of equal size for each wavelet level (but not necessarily of equal size between the

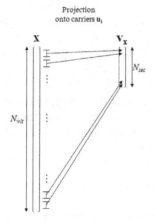

Fig. 3. General Space Division Multiplexing principle

levels) and then re-arrange $\mathbf{v_x}$ coefficients in order to obtain a fair distribution. We call this approach the **structured SDM** (see Section 3.1). In the second approach, we build regions of quasi-equal sizes. We name this approach the **random SDM** (see Section 3.2).

3.1   Structured SDM

In order to obtain region sizes belonging to $\mathbb{N}^*$, we solve the equation below (in the case of a 3-level wavelet decomposition):

$$\left(3.\frac{N}{4}\right)\frac{1}{s_{789}} + \left(3.\frac{N}{16}\right)\frac{1}{s_{456}} + \left(3.\frac{N}{64}\right)\frac{1}{s_{123}} = N_{sec} \quad (1)$$

where $s_{789} \in \mathbb{N}^*$ is the size of regions in the wavelet sub-bands 7, 8 or 9 and so on (see Figure 1 for sub-bands numbering). Note that the regions sizes depend on the wavelet level.

Knowing that $N_{sec} = N \times payload \times N_{arc}$, Equation 1 is independent from the image size (3-level wavelet decomposition):

$$16 \times s_{123} \times s_{456} + 4 \times s_{789} \times s_{123} + s_{789} \times s_{456}$$
$$-\frac{64}{3} \times payload \times N_{arc} \times s_{123} \times s_{456} \times s_{789} = 0.$$

The retained solution among all the possible solutions is the one for which regions sizes are closest to[3] $\overline{s} = N_{wlt}/N_{sec}$. If no integer solution is found, we use overlapping on regions borders.

Before projecting the host signal $\mathbf{x}$ onto carriers, we pseudo-randomly shuffle its coefficients by group of wavelet level (see Figure 4). This ensures a good spreading of the influences coming from coefficients of the secret space. Moreover, it improves the security, the robustness (since it breaks spatial dependencies) and the psycho-visual impact.

After the projection of the host signal $\mathbf{x}$ onto carriers $\mathbf{u}_i$ (carriers are built with this Space Division Multiplexing approach), we obtain the host vector $\mathbf{v_x}$. In order to better balance the influence distribution of the $\mathbf{v_x}$ vector coefficients, we re-arrange it. Indeed, the first coefficients of $\mathbf{v_x}$ are related to the low frequency wavelet sub-bands 1, 2 and 3, the next coefficients are related to higher frequency sub-bands 4, 5, and 6 etc. Thus the vector $\mathbf{v_x}$ is re-arranged such that in each consecutive group of N_{arc} coefficients, the probability distribution of influence is the same (see in Figure 4, the distribution influence re-arrangement).

For example, with 3-level wavelet decomposition, in a block of N_{arc} coefficients of $\mathbf{v_x}$, the probability of coefficients coming from the different sub-bands are:

$$p_{1,2,3} = \frac{\frac{3N}{64s_{1,2,3}}}{N_{sec}}, \quad p_{4,5,6} = \frac{\frac{3N}{16s_{4,5,6}}}{N_{sec}}, \quad p_{7,8,9} = \frac{\frac{3N}{4s_{7,8,9}}}{N_{sec}} \quad (2)$$

---

[3] With 3 level wavelet decomposition, $payload = 1/64$ and $N_{arc} = 12$, the retained solution is $s_{7,8,9} = 6$, $s_{4,5,6} = 4$, $s_{1,2,3} = 3$.

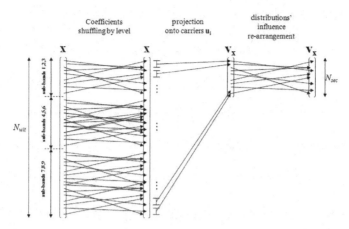

Fig. 4. Structured SDM: Space Division Multiplexing and re-arrangements for the projection onto carriers

In a block of N_{arc} coefficients of $\mathbf{v_x}$, the number of coefficients influencing the wavelet coefficients from sub-bands 1, 2, 3 (resp. 4, 5, 6 and 7, 8, 9), are thus respectively[4]:

$$
\begin{aligned}
n_{1,2,3} &= p_{1,2,3} \times N_{arc} = \frac{3}{64 s_{1,2,3} \times payload}, \\
n_{4,5,6} &= p_{4,5,6} \times N_{arc} = \frac{3}{16 s_{4,5,6} \times payload}, \\
n_{7,8,9} &= p_{4,8,9} \times N_{arc} = \frac{3}{4 s_{7,8,9} \times payload}
\end{aligned}
\tag{3}
$$

Note that each block of N_{arc} should respect this distribution but coefficients are again pseudo-randomly arranged in order to keep a good security level.

3.2 Random SDM

With the random SDM approach, we compute regions with no overlap, that fully cover the host vector $\mathbf{x}$ and whose sizes are integer and close to $\bar{s} = N_{wlt}/N_{sec}$. We talk of quasi-equal regions sizes (see Figure 5).

There are N_{sec} regions. A region r_i, with $i \in [0, N_{sec} - 1]$, is thus a set of contiguous wavelet coefficients, such that:

$$
r_i = \{\mathbf{x}[i] | i \in [\lfloor i.\bar{s} \rfloor, \lfloor (i+1).\bar{s} \rfloor - 1]\},
\tag{4}
$$

where $\mathbf{x}[i]$, with $i \in [0, N_{wlt} - 1]$, is a wavelet coefficient of the host vector $\mathbf{x}$.

Note that before proceeding to the projection, the host signal $\mathbf{x}$ is pseudo-randomly shuffled in order to: break spatial dependencies, keep a good security level, and improve the robustness and the psycho-visual impact. The shuffled host signal $\mathbf{x}$ is then projected onto N_{sec} carriers using SDM with quasi-equal regions' sizes (see Equation 4 for regions definition). The host vector $\mathbf{v_x}$ is the result of this projection.

---

[4] With 3 level wavelet decomposition, $payload = 1/64$ and $N_{arc} = 12$, the retained solution is $n_{7,8,9} = 8$, $n_{4,5,6} = 3$, $n_{1,2,3} = 1$.

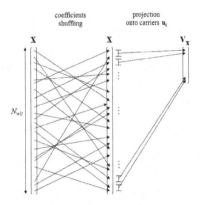

Fig. 5. Random SDM

4   Results

Tests were carried on the first 100 images of the BOWS2 data-base[5] with images resized to 256×256[6]. Those images are 8-bits grey-level images and are personal photos.

The trellis structure has 128 states with 128 arcs per states. Outputs arcs labels are drawn from a Gaussian distribution and there are $N_{arc} = 12$ coefficients by output arc. The used payload is $payload = 1$ bit for 64 coefficients which is the same as the original DPTC algorithm [1]. The number of embedded bits is thus 1024 bits. Wavelet transform is a 9/7 Daubechies with $l = 3$ decompositions levels. Except the LL sub-band, all the other sub-bands are used to form the host signal $\mathbf{x}$. With 256×256 images, the wavelet space size is thus $N_{wlt} = 64\,512$ coefficients. Knowing that the payload is $payload = 1/64$ $bits\ per\ pixel$ and that the number of outputs coefficients for an arc is $N_{arc} = 12$ coefficients, private space size is thus $N_{sec} = 1024 \times 12 = 12\,288$ coefficients.

Four kinds of robustness attacks have been applied: Gaussian noise attack, filtering attack, valumetric attack and jpeg attack. The Bit Error Rate (BER) is the number of erroneous extracted bits divided by the total number of embedded bits. The BER is computed for each attack. Three algorithms compete with a mean distortion close to 42.4 dB:

- the algorithm detailed in [2], having **carriers of high dimension** and whose projection complexity is quadratic. For this method the mean embedding PSNR is 42.42 dB and the inside angle penetration is $\theta_R = 0.1$ radian;
- the **structured SDM** algorithm (see Section 3.1). For this method the mean embedding PSNR is 42.23 dB and the inside angle penetration is $\theta_R = 0.05$ radian.

---

[5] BOWS2 data-base is located at http://bows2.gipsa-lab.inpg.fr/.

[6] The images sub-sampling has been achieved with xnview program and using Lanczos interpolation.

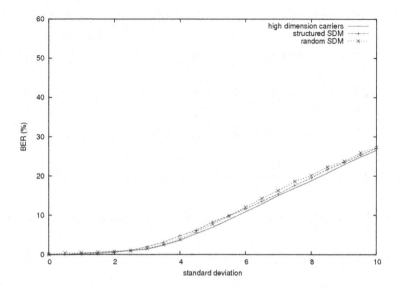

Fig. 6. Gaussian attack : BER for attack on the **high dimension carriers** algorithm
[2], on the **structured SDM** algorithm and on the **random SDM** algorithm

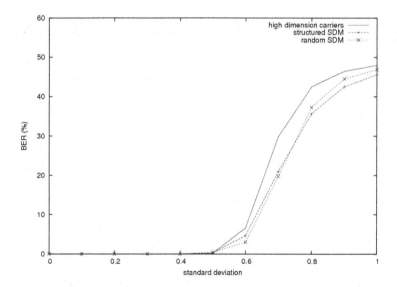

Fig. 7. Filtering attack : BER for attack on the **high dimension carriers** algorithm
[2], on the **structured SDM** algorithm and on the **random SDM** algorithm

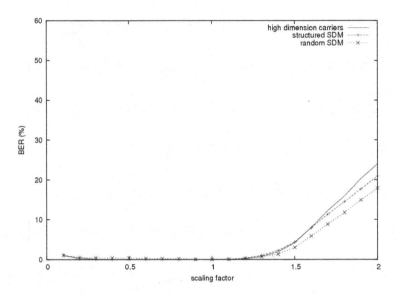

Fig. 8. Valumetric attack : BER for attack on the **high dimension carriers** algorithm [2], on the **structured SDM** algorithm and on the **random SDM** algorithm

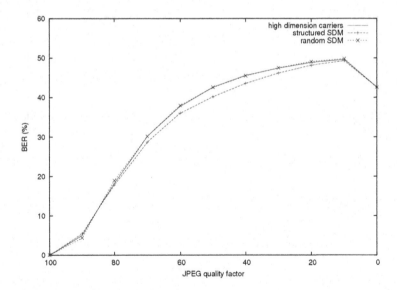

Fig. 9. Jpeg attack : BER for attack on the **high dimension carriers** algorithm [2], on the **structured SDM** algorithm and on the **random SDM** algorithm

– and the **random SDM** algorithm (see Section 3.2). For this method, the mean embedding PSNR is 42.15 dB and the inside angle penetration is $\theta_R = 0.11$ radian.

In Figures 6, 7, 8, 9, we observe that the two SDM approaches perform equal or even better results than the high dimension carriers algorithm [2]. Results are similar for the Gaussian and the jpeg attacks, but for the filtering and the scaling attacks, the SDM approaches are better. This is a very interesting result since the high dimension carriers approach [2] is more complex (quadratic complexity) than the two SDM approaches. The high dimension carriers approach [2] may then be replaced with a faster (linear complexity) SDM approach.

If we compare the *structured SDM* approach with the *random SDM* approach, for the filtering and the scaling attacks, we observe that under 10% BER, the *random SDM* (i.e. the less complex approach) performs the best results. We conclude that in order to achieve the projection onto carriers, one should use *random SDM* since it is linear in complexity and it gives better robustness results than the *structured SDM* approach and the high dimension carriers' approach [2].

On a Pentium 3 GHz, for a 256×256 image and a message size of 1024 bits, watermarking takes less than one minute for the two SDM approaches and from half an hour to two hours for the original Miller *et al.* algorithm [1]. In [2], we show that our general scheme (using a secret space and a rotation-based embedding) has good robustness performances (except facing jpeg attack) compared to the original algorithm [1] or the Lin *et al.* approach [6]. We conclude that our scheme [2], enriched with the SDM technique, provides a good distortion - payload - robustness and complexity compromise.

Moreover, we believe that it is as least as difficult for an attacker to retrieve the codebook for our *random SDM* approach as for the Miller *et al.* one [1]. Indeed, the original approach only shuffles a subset of the DCT host coefficients whereas our approach shuffles and projects onto random carriers almost all the wavelet host coefficients.

5   Conclusion

In this paper, we introduce a new Dirty Paper Trellis Code (DPTC) algorithm having a security space built by projecting the wavelet coefficients onto secret carriers. In comparison to the original DPTC algorithm [1], our scheme is as least as secure and the visual degradation is better adapted to the human psycho-visual system. After introducing the general problem of projections, we have proposed two Space Division Multiplexing (SDM) algorithms in order to decrease the projections complexity to a more reasonable linear computational complexity. We evaluated robustness with and without SDM approaches and observed that projection with SDM approaches give more robust results than projecting with high dimension carriers. We finally observe that the *random SDM* approach, which is the less complex approach, is the more robust.

Acknowledgements

This investigation was supported by the VOODDO project which is a French national project of the ANR (*Agence Nationale de la Recherche*) "Contenu et Interaction". We would also like to thank the Languedoc-Roussillon Region.

References

1. Miller, M.L., Doërr, G.J., Cox, I.J.: Applying Informed Coding and Informed Embedding to Design a Robust, High Capacity Watermark. IEEE Transactions on Image Processing 13(6), 792–807 (2004)
2. Chaumont, M.: A Novel Embedding Technic for Dirty Paper Trellis Watermarking. In: IEEE International Conference On Image Processing, ICIP 2009, Cairo, Egypt (submitted)(November 2009)
3. Bas, P., Doërr, G.: Evaluation of an Optimal Watermark Tampering Attack Against Dirty Paper Trellis Schemes. In: 10th ACM workshop on Multimedia and Security, MM&Sec 2008, Oxford, United Kingdom, September 2008, pp. 227–232 (2008)
4. Kerckhoffs, A.: La Cryptographie Militaire. Journal des Sciences Militaires IX, 5–38 (January 1883); pp. 161–191 (February 1883)
5. Wang, C., Doërr, G., Cox, I.J.: Toward a Better Understanding of Dirty Paper Trellis Codes. In: IEEE International Conference on Acoustics, Speech and Signal Processing, ICASSP 2006, Toulouse, France, May 2006, vol. 2, pp. 233–236 (2006)
6. Lin, L., Cox, I.J., Doërr, G., Miller, M.L.: An Efficient Algorithm for Informed Embedding of Dirty Paper Trellis Codes for Watermarking. In: IEEE International Conference on Image Processing, ICIP 2005, Genova, Italy, September 2005, vol. 1, pp. 697–700 (2005)
7. Cox, I., Miller, M., Bloom, J., Fridrich, J., Kalker, T.: 5. in Multimedia Information and Systems. In: Digital Watermarking and Steganography, 2nd edn., pp. 110–117. Morgan Kaufmann, San Francisco (2007)

A Homomorphic Method for Sharing Secret Images

Naveed Islam[1], William Puech[1], and Robert Brouzet[2]

[1] LIRMM Laboratory, UMR 5506 CNRS, University of Montpellier II
34392 Montpellier France
[2] I3M Laboratory, UMR 5149 CNRS, University of Montpellier II
34392 Montpellier France

Abstract. In this paper, we present a new method for sharing images between two parties exploiting homomorphic property of public key cryptosystem. With our method, we show that it is possible to multiply two encrypted images, to decrypt the resulted image and after to extract and reconstruct one of the two original images if the second original image is available. Indeed, extraction and reconstruction of original image at the receiving end is done with the help of carrier image. Experimental results and security analysis show the effectiveness of the proposed scheme.

Keywords: Cryptosystem, Homomorphism, Image encryption.

1 Introduction

With the development of new communication technologies, Internet transfer of visual data (images, videos or 3D objects) for different types of multimedia applications has grown exponentially. However, digital communication is increasingly vulnerable to malicious interventions or monitoring like hacking or eavesdropping. The security of these sensitive visual data in applications like safe storage, authentication, copyright protection, remote military image communication or confidential video conferencing require new strategies for secure transmission over insecure channel. There are two common techniques used for secure transmission of data namely cryptography and watermarking. Cryptography ensures the security by scrambling the message using some secret keys [9]. Homomorphic cryptosystems are special type of cryptosystems which preserve group operations performed on ciphertexts. A homomorphic cryptosystem has the property that when any specific algebraic operation is performed on the data input before encryption, the resulting encryption is same as if an algebraic operation is performed on the data input after encryption [8]. Homomorphic property of public key cryptosystems has been employed in various data security protocols like electronic voting system, bidding protocols, cashing systems and asymmetric finger printing of images [4]. The use of carrier image for the encryption of image has been presented in [6] using private key cryptosystem in frequency domain. For the authentication of images, copyright protection, watermarking techniques are used, these watermarking techniques along with cryptographic technique gives

A.T.S. Ho et al. (Eds.): IWDW 2009, LNCS 5703, pp. 121–135, 2009.
© Springer-Verlag Berlin Heidelberg 2009

enough level of security [7]. In this paper, we exploit the multiplicative homomorphic property of RSA cryptosystem for sharing secret images using carrier image for both transfer and extraction of original image.

This paper is organized as follows. In Section 2, we first give a brief introduction of cryptographic techniques focusing on asymmetric encryption of RSA with special reference to its homomorphic property and then we explain how to apply it to an image. The proposed algorithm is detailed in Section 3 and experimental results along with security analysis of the proposed scheme are studied in Section 4. Finally, Section 5 gives summary and concluding remarks.

2   Previous Works

Extra storage capacities and special computation is required for visual data types such as images, videos or 3D objects, due to the large amount of data. Nowadays cryptographic techniques for image security are widely used for secure transfer. In image domain, there may be full encryption or selective encryption of the image depending on the application. Since many applications require real time performances, partial encryption is mostly used [10]. Cryptographic techniques can be divided into symmetric encryption (with secret keys) and asymmetric encryption (with private and public keys).

In symmetric cryptosystems, the same key is used for encryption and decryption. Symmetric key cryptosystems are usually very fast and easy to use. Since same key is used for encryption and decryption, the key needs to be secure and must be shared between emitter and receiver.

2.1   Asymmetric Encryption

In asymmetric cryptosystem, two different keys are necessary: the public and the private keys. With the receiver public key, the sender encrypt the message and send it to the receiver who decrypt the message with his private key. Some known algorithms are RSA, El Gamal and Paillier cryptosystems [9,3,5]. RSA and El Gamal are public-key cryptosystems that support the homomorphic operation of multiplication modulo n and Paillier cryptosystem support homomorphic addition and subtraction of encrypted messages.

RSA is a well known asymmetric cryptosystem, developed in 1978. The general procedure consists of selecting two large prime numbers p and q, calculating their product $n = p \times q$ and selecting an integer e, which is relative prime to $\Phi(n)$ and with $1 < e < \Phi(n)$, where $\Phi(n)$ is the Euler's function. We need to calculate d, the inverse of e with $d \equiv e^{-1} mod \ \Phi(n)$. The public key is composed of the couple (e, n) and the private key of the couple (d, n). For the encryption, the plaintext M is partitioned into blocks m_i such that $m_i < n$ and for each plaintext m_i we get a ciphertext c_i:

$$c_i = m_i^e \ mod \ n. \tag{1}$$

For the decryption, with the ciphertext c_i we can obtain the original plaintext m_i by the equation:

$$m_i = c_i^d \bmod n. \tag{2}$$

Example: assume primes p and q are given as $p = 7, q = 17$ therefore $n = p \times q = 7 \times 17 = 119$, let $e = 5$, which follows that $gcd(\Phi(p * q), 5) = 1$ and for $e = 5$, we found $d \equiv e^{-1} \bmod \Phi(n) = 77$. Let the input plain texts be $m_1 = 22$ and $m_2 = 19$. Therefore the encryption of m_1 is given as: $c_1 = 22^5 \bmod 119 = 99$ and the encryption of m_2 is given as: $c_2 = 19^5 \bmod 119 = 66$.

2.2 Multiplicative Homomorphism

Most of the asymmetric cryptosystems follow either additive homomorphism or multiplicative homomorphism. An encryption algorithm $E()$ is said to be homomorphic if it obeys the following condition [2]:

$$E(x \oplus y) = E(x) \otimes E(y), \tag{3}$$

where $\oplus$ and $\otimes$ can be addition, subtraction or multiplication and not necessary the same between the plaintexts and the ciphertexts. But usually the former operation is either addition or multiplication or exclusive or while the latter is multiplication.

The encryption algorithm RSA follows multiplicative homomorphism:

$$E(m_1) \times E(m_2) = E(m_1 \times m_2). \tag{4}$$

Example: with the values of the example presented in Section (2.1) we have $c_1 \times c_2 = 99 \times 66 \bmod 119 = 108$. Multiplying the two plaintexts will give a third text m_3 given as: $m_3 = m_1 \times m_2 = 22 \times 19 \bmod 119 = 61$. The encryption of m_3 is given by: $c_3 = 61^5 \bmod 119 = 108$ which equals to the multiplication of two ciphertexts. Hence RSA support homomorphic operation of multiplication modulo n, presented in equation (4).

2.3 Image Encryption

Extreme care must be taken while calculating the values of the keys because the security of encrypted image depends on the size and the value of the public key and small or bad keys can produce encrypted images which contain information of the original images [1]. An effective way for image security using asymmetric cryptographic techniques is block-based image encryption. In block-based image encryption schemes the block size is selected according to the size of the key, so that encrypted data provide sufficient level of security in shape of key size and no extra payload in shape of increase in image size appears. Also the creation of block and then encryption should be made in such away that the ciphered image does not reveals any structural information about the data in the image. For the proposed method, the image is transformed into a coefficient image, where each coefficient has size equal to the size of the block in the original image and the block size depends on the key size being selected for encryption and decryption. If length of the encryption key is γ bits then the number of pixels in the block is given by:

$$b = \lceil \gamma/k \rceil, \tag{5}$$

where k is the number of bits of a single pixel. Let an image of size $M \times N$ pixels $p(i)$, where $0 \leq i < M \times N$, the construction of the coefficient values from the original image pixels $p(i)$ is given as:

$$B(i) = \sum_{j=0}^{b-1} p(i * b + j) \times 2^{kj}, \tag{6}$$

where $0 \leq i < \lceil M \times N/n \rceil$ for the coefficient image.

For RSA cryptosystem, to be applied on each coefficient, let $B(i)$ be the ith constructed coefficient of an image, then the encryption of $B(i)$ is given by:

$$B'(i) = E_k(B(i)) = B(i)^e \bmod n, \tag{7}$$

where $B(i)$ and $B'(i)$ are coded on γ bits of each coefficient. After decryption of $B(i)$, the decomposition of the transformed coefficients to get the original pixels is given by:

$$\begin{cases} \text{if } j = 0 \\ p(i \times b + j) = B(i) \bmod 2^k \\ \text{else} \\ p(i \times b + j) = \left(B(i) \bmod 2^{k(j+1)} - \sum_{l=0}^{j-1} p(l) \right) / 2^{kj} \end{cases}$$

3   Proposed Homomorphic Based Method

3.1   Standard Protocol for Image Transmission

The standard protocol for secure image or message transfer is based on the security of the keys. In standard procedure, if a user P1 wants to send image M1 to user P2, he will first encrypt the image with the public key of the receiver i.e. P2. This encrypted image will be then transmitted to the user P2 over unsecured transmission channel. At the receiving end, in order to read the image, the user P2 will decrypt the image with his private key, as shown in Fig. 1.

For authentication, the protocol is a little bit changed, the sender must first encrypt the sending image with his private key and then again encrypt with the receiver public key, the first encryption allow him to sign the sending message. Similarly the receiver first decrypt the message with his private key and then for authentication he will use the public key of the sender for decryption, as illustrated in the Fig. 2. But here two keys are required by each user and also the processing time for encrypting and decrypting increases.

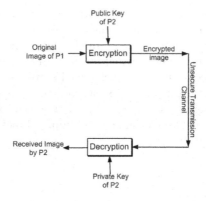

Fig. 1. Standard way for image transmission

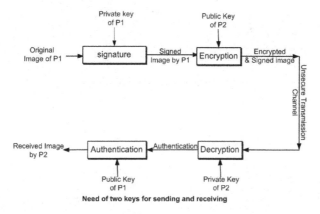

Fig. 2. Standard way for image transmission along with authentication

3.2   Overview of Proposed Method

The purpose of our scheme is to securely transfer and to share a secret image between two persons. Even if an intruder gets a copy of the protected transmitted image he can not be able to extract the original image. A block diagram of encryption step of proposed technique is given in Fig. 3.

Each user takes an image of same size and transform it into a coefficient image using equation (6), where each coefficient represents the total number of pixels in a single block, we then apply asymmetric algorithm of RSA on each coefficient of the transformed image. Note that the same key is used for encryption process separately for both images. After the two images have been encrypted, we take modulo multiplication of the two encrypted images to get a third encrypted image. Because of the homomorphic property of RSA, this third encrypted image must be the same if we had first multiplied the two original images to get a third image and then applying RSA algorithm. The third encrypted image or its decrypted version can be transferred over any insecure channel. Since the third image contains components of both first and second original images, one can extract any one of the two original images if other image is available. At the receiving end, as a user has one of the original images and he received the third image, he can extract the second original image with the help of his own image. This extracted image contains noise elements because some encrypted pixels can give multiple solutions during the extraction. So, we apply a reconstruction algorithm in order to remove the maximum of the noise pixels and get better pixels. Fig. 4 shows the block diagram of the proposed method for decryption.

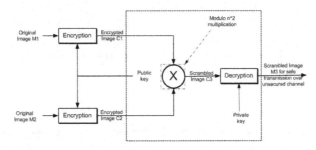

Fig. 3. Overview of encryption step

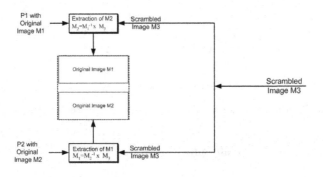

Decryption without Key

Fig. 4. Decryption of scrambled image without use of public or private keys

3.3 Encryption Step

For each block of the two original images M_1 and M_2 we apply the RSA encryption as described in equation (7). The image M_1 is considered to be available at both ends. But before encryption, some preprocessing must be done due to limitation on encryption algorithm and image data size.

After the encryption of the two original images M_1 and M_2 we get the two encrypted images C_1 and C_2 as illustrated in Fig. 3. We can then scramble these two encrypted images by applying a modulo multiplication between them. Since each block of the two encrypted images C_1 and C_2 has value between 0 and

$2^\gamma - 1$, after the multiplication of the two encrypted images we must apply the modulo operation to get scrambled pixels of C_3 encodable on γ bits:

$$B'_3(i) = B'_1(i) \times B'_2(i) \bmod n. \tag{8}$$

This encrypted image C_3 can be decrypted with the private key to produce M_3. This M_3 is our intended image to be transferred by the sender to the receiver through insecure channel.

3.4 Extraction and Reconstruction

The block diagram of the proposed method for extraction and reconstruction is shown in Fig. 5. At the receiving end, for example user P_1 has M_1 and receives M_3 and then wants to extract M_2. Due to the multiplicative homomorphic property of RSA, from the equation (8), we have also:

$$B_3(i) = B_1(i) \times B_2(i) \bmod n. \tag{9}$$

We can do inverse modulo operation of equation (9), which gives single values for the coefficients $B_1(i)$ of M_1 which are relative prime to n and multiple solutions for the coefficients $B_1(i)$ which are non relative primes to n. For these particular cases the reconstruction step consists in choosing the best value among the multiple solutions for particular blocks in order to try to reconstruct an image the nearest to the original image M_2.

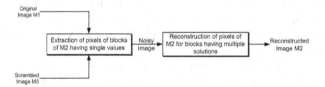

Fig. 5. Extraction and reconstruction of image M2 having pixels of image M1

In order to explain the principles that make the extraction of the second image M_2 possible, let us consider that p and q are primes such that $p < q$, and $n = p \times q$. Let $B_1(i)$, $B_2(i)$ and $B_3(i)$ three integers between 0 and $n - 1$, satisfying equation (9) or the three respective encrypted values $B'_1(i)$, $B'_2(i)$ and $B'_3(i)$ satisfying equation (8).

Then, if M_1 and M_3 are given and we want to extract M_2, it is similar to say that $B_1(i)$ and $B_3(i)$ are given and we want to extract $B_2(i)$, we are interesting in solution of the above modular equation if $B_2(i)$ is not known. To extract $B_2(i)$, we have two cases:

First case: $B_1(i)$ and n are relatively primes. In this case, $B_1(i)$ has inverse modulo n and therefore the above equation possesses a single solution modulo n. Thus, there is a single integer solution since $B_2(i)$ is supposed to be less than n, therefore:

$$B_2(i) \equiv B_1(i)^{-1} \times B_3(i) \bmod n. \tag{10}$$

Second case: $B_1(i)$ **and** n **are not relatively primes.** In this case, the only common divisors possible to $B_1(i)$ and n, are p and q. That is, $B_1(i)$ is multiple of p or q. Suppose that $B_1(i)$ is multiple of p, then $B_1(i) = k \times p$, for $k \in \{1, \ldots, q-1\}$. Thus, p divides $B_1(i)$ and n, and from the equation (9) necessarily p also divides $B_3(i)$. We can then write $B_3(i) = p \times \tilde{B}_3(i)$. The equation (9) signifies that there exist an integer l such:

$$k \times p \times B_2(i) = p \times \tilde{B}_3(i) + l \times p \times q, \tag{11}$$

and thus dividing by p gives:

$$k \times B_2(i) = \tilde{B}_3(i) + l \times q. \tag{12}$$

Thus, we have:
$$k \times B_2(i) \equiv \tilde{B}_3(i) \bmod q. \tag{13}$$

Since k is strictly less then q, it is relatively prime to q and thus invertible modulo q, therefore:

$$B_2(i) = k^{-1} \times \tilde{B}_3(i) \bmod q. \tag{14}$$

This single solution modulo q leads to p solutions for the block $B_2(i)$: one before q, one between q and $2q$ and so on; in the case of $B_1(i)$ is multiple of q, we have in the same way q solutions.

Since we would not have all single solutions for these noisy pixels of M_2, indeed a lot of blocks would be factor of the initial primes p and q, so they would give multiple solutions for each noisy block of M_2, and these solutions must be less than or equal to $\{1, \ldots, q\}$ and the original value of the noisy pixel of M_2 belongs to this solution set.

In order to select the best value from the solution set for the noisy pixel and to remove the noisy pixels from the extracted M_2, we take advantage of the homogeneity of the visual data, as usually there is high degree of coherence between the neighbors of image data. So we take mean of the non-noisy neighbors of noisy pixels of M_2 and this mean value is compared with each value of the solution set for the corresponding pixel, and then select the value from the solution set which is giving us the least distance from mean value.

4   Experimental Results and Discussions

We have tested the proposed algorithm on 200 gray level images (8 bits/pixel) of size 512×512 pixel. We have randomly partitioned the 200 gray level images into two groups (100 each), transferring image group and reconstruction image group, then we randomly selected two images M_1 and M_2, one for the transfer purpose and second for reconstructed purpose. For our experimentation we have chosen the keys which follows the basic properties of RSA cryptosystem. We transformed each image into coefficient image where each coefficient is representing block of pixels using equation (6) and then encrypt each coefficient of the two images M_1 and M_2 with RSA by using equation (7).

After encryption of M_1 and M_2 we have scrambled the two corresponding encrypted images C_1 and C_2 by applying a multiplication modulo n to get a new scrambled image C_3. This scrambled image C_3 can be decrypted to produce M_3. These two images C_3 and M_3 are our intended images to be safe transferred by the sender to the receiver through insecure channel.

4.1   A Full Example

In Fig. 6 we visually present an example of the proposed method. Fig. 6.a and 6.b present two standard gray level original images of Lena and Barbara, each of

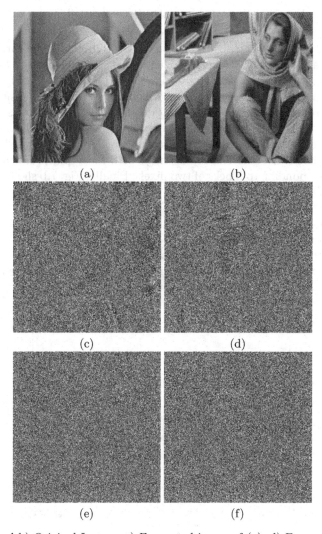

Fig. 6. a) and b) Original Images, c) Encrypted image of (a), d) Encrypted image of (b), e) Image obtained from multiplication of (c) and (d), f) Decrypted image of (e)

(a)   (b)

Fig. 7. a) Extracted image, b) Reconstructed image

size 512×512 pixels (8 bits/pixel), Fig. 6.c and 6.d illustrate the corresponding encrypted images and Fig. 6.e corresponds to the scrambled image from multiplication of the two encrypted images Fig. 6.c and 6.d. Finally, Fig. 6.f shows the resultant decrypted image of Fig. 6.e, which can be used for transfer purpose. Fig. 6.c-f are represented after decomposition of blocks in order to visualize pixel values.

In Fig.7, we show the extraction and reconstruction of the shared secret image. Fig. 7.a illustrates the extracted image with noisy pixels having multiple solutions corresponding to blocks of two pixels. Finally, Fig. 7.b shows the reconstructed image which is very near of the original image M_2. The peak signal to noise ratio (PSNR) between the original image, Fig. 6.a, and the reconstructed one, Fig. 7.b equals to 47.8 dB. This value shows high degree of resemblance between the original and the reconstructed image.

The strength and effectiveness of the proposed method applied to 100 images in terms of PSNR value between the original and the reconstructed images is shown in Fig. 8. and the mean value for the PSNR is 45.8 dB.

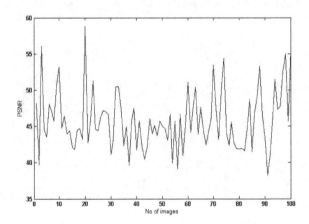

Fig. 8. Graphical display of PSNR values of 100 images

4.2   Comparison with XOR-Based Method

Exclusive-OR (XOR) is a binary operator which has the property that if it is applied between two numbers, and if one of the number is available after performing this operation on then we can get the second number by using resultant number and one of the two numbers. If we apply the XOR operation between two images M_1 and M_2 and transfer the resultant image through insecure channel, we can get any one of the image, if we have the second image: $M_{XOR} = M_1 \otimes M_2$ thus $M_1 = M_{XOR} \otimes M_2$ or $M_2 = M_{XOR} \otimes M_1$.

We can encounter two problems with this approach. First the resultant image M_{XOR} contains a lot of information about the two original images, for example if we applied the XOR operation between M_{XOR} and a homogeneous image (for example with all pixels equal to 128) then the resulted image can give a lot information about the two original intended images, as shown in Fig. 9.a while if the same homogeneous image is used as an attack on the proposed method we would have a resultant scrambled image with no worth-full information contents, as shown in Fig. 9.b.

(a)   (b)

Fig. 9. a) Resultant image after attack by using a homogeneous image (grey level = 128) on XOR image M_{XOR}, b) Resultant image after attack by using a homogeneous image (grey level = 128) on the transferred image

The second problem is that XOR is not a homomorphic operator. Suppose we have encrypted images M_1 and M_2 and we apply XOR operation between C_1 and C_2 to produce C_{XOR}, now decrypting C_{XOR} gives M'_{XOR}, but when we apply XOR operation between M_{XOR} and M_1 the result does not produce the original image M_2.

4.3   Security Analysis

Analysis of Entropy and Local Standard Deviation: The security of the encrypted images can be measured by considering the variations (local or global) in the protected images. Considering this, the information content of image can be measured with the entropy $H(X)$, where entropy is a statistical measure of randomness or disorder of a system which is mostly used to characterize the

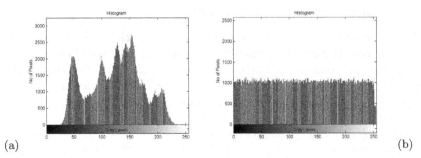

Fig. 10. a) Histogram of original image of Lena, b) Histogram of scrambled image Fig. 6.e

texture in the input images. If an image has 2^k gray levels α_i with $0 \leq i \leq 2^k$ and the probability of gray level α_i is $P(\alpha_i)$, and without considering the correlation of gray levels, the entropy $H(X)$ is defined as:

$$H(X) = -\sum_{i=0}^{2^k} P(\alpha_i)log_2(P(\alpha_i)). \tag{15}$$

If the probability of each gray level in the image is $P(\alpha_i) = \frac{1}{2^k}$, then the encryption of such image is robust against statistical attacks, and thus $H(X) = log_2(2^k) = k$ bits/pixel. In the image the information redundancy r is defined as:

$$r = k - H(X). \tag{16}$$

When $r \approx 0$, the security level is acceptable. Theoretically an image is an order-M Markov source, with M the image size. In order to reduce the complexity, the image is cut in small block of size n and considered as an order-n Markov source. The alphabet of the order-n Markov source, called X' is β_i with $0 \leq i < 2^{k^n}$ and the order-n entropy $H(X')$ is defined as:

$$H(X') = H(X^n) = -\sum_{i=0}^{2^{k^n}} P(\beta_i)log_2(P(\beta_i)). \tag{17}$$

We used $2^k = 256$ gray levels and blocks of n=2 or 3 pixels corresponding to a pixel and its preceding neighbors. In order to have minimum redundancy i.e. $r \approx 0$, in equation (16), we should have k=8 bits/pixel for equation (15) and k=16 or 24 bits/block for equation (17).

Similarly we also analyzed the variation of the local standard deviation $\sigma(j)$ for each pixel $p(j)$ taking account of its neighbors to calculate the local mean $\overline{p(j)}$, the formula for local standard deviation is given as:

$$\sigma(j) = \sqrt{\frac{1}{m}\sum_{i=1}^{m}(p(i) - \overline{p(j)})}, \tag{18}$$

where m is the size of the pixel block to calculate the local mean and standard deviation, and $0 \leq j < M$, if M is the image size.

In Fig. 10, we show the histogram of the original image of Lena and the histogram of the scrambled transmitted image, where the histogram of the transmitted safe image is different to the histogram of the original image. In Fig. 10.b, we can see a uniform distribution of the gray level values among the pixel coordinates of the transmitted image while in the histogram of original image Fig. 10.a, there is single blob of gray level values which signifies some shape or object. Similarly from equation (15) we get high entropy H(X) of 7.994 bits/pixel (H(X)= 7.45 bits/pixel for the original image of Lena). The information redundancy r, in equation (16) then equals to 0.006 bit/pixel. The order-2 entropy, $H(X^2)$ of equation (17) equals to 15.81 bits/block for Fig. 10.d (12.33 bits/block for the original image). The information redundancy r, is then less than 0.19 bit/block.

From equation (18) we also analyzed the variation of the local standard deviation σ for each pixel while taking its neighbors into account. The mean local standard deviation equals to 67.35 gray levels for the final scrambled image of Fig. 10.d, where as the mean local standard deviation equals to 6.21 gray levels for the original Lena image. These analysis show that the final scrambled image is protected against statistical attacks.

Correlation of Adjacent Pixels: Visual data is highly correlated i.e. pixels values are highly probable to repeat in horizontal, vertical and diagonal directions. Since RSA public-key cryptosystem is not random in nature, so it give same results for the same values of the inputs. It means that if an image region is highly correlated or having same values, then the public-key encryption will produce the same results, and a cryptanalyst can easily understand the information content related to the original image. A cryptosystem is considered robust against statistical attacks if it succeeds in providing low correlation between the neighboring pixels or adjacent pixels. The proposed encryption scheme generates a ciphered image with low correlation among the adjacent pixels. A horizontal correlation of a pixel with its neighboring pixel is given by a tuple (x_i, y_i) where y_i is the horizontal adjacent pixel of x_i. Since there is always three directions in images i.e. horizontal, vertical and diagonal, so we can define correlation in horizontal direction between any two adjacent pixels as:

$$corr_{(x,y)} = \frac{1}{n-1} \sum_0^n (\frac{x_i - \overline{x_i}}{\sigma_x})(\frac{y_i - \overline{y_i}}{\sigma_y}), \qquad (19)$$

Table 1. Correlation of horizontal and vertical adjacent pixels in two images

	Plain image	Encrypted image
Horizontal	0.9936	0.1693
Vertical	0.9731	-0.0010

where n represents the total number of tuples (x_i, y_i), $\overline{x_i}$ and $\overline{y_i}$ represent the mean and σ_x and σ_y represent standard deviation respectively. In Table (1), we can see correlation values of Lena image and the transmitted scrambled image. It can be noticed from the table that the proposed scheme retains small correlation coefficients in horizontal and vertical directions.

Key Sensitivity Test: Robustness against cryptanalyst can be improved if the cryptosystem is highly sensitive towards the key. The more the visual data is sensitive towards the key, the more we would have data randomness i.e. high value for the entropy and thus the lower we would have visual correlation among the pixels of the image. For this purpose, a key sensitivity test is assumed where we pick one key and then applied the proposed technique for encryption and then make a one bit change in the key and again applied the proposed encryption technique. Numerical results show that the proposed technique is highly sensitive towards the key change, that is, a totally different version of scrambled image is produced when the keys are changed, as shown in Fig. 11. Also from equation (19), we get a correlation value of 0.1670, which means there is negligible amount of correlation among the pixels of the ciphered image with different keys.

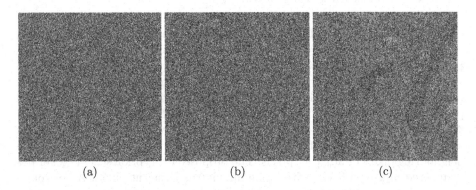

(a)   (b)   (c)

Fig. 11. Key sensitivity test: a) Encrypted image with key, K2, b) Image encrypted with K1 and decrypted with K2, c) Reconstructed image with key K2

Also, if we encrypt an image with one key $K1$ and decrypt with a another key $K2$ and then apply the proposed scheme for the reconstruction of the original image, we can not get the original image, this observation can be seen in Fig. 11.b and 11.c.

5   Conclusions

In this paper, we proposed a method for sharing secret images during a transfer using carrier exploiting multiplicative homomorphic property of RSA algorithm. It has been observed that extraction of the original image from the transferred image is possible with the help of carrier image. For the reconstruction of the shared image, we have demonstrated that we have two particular cases. In the first case, we have a single solution and in the second case we have multiple solutions but only one corresponds to the original value. Experimental results showed that the reconstructed image after the extraction is visually indistinguishable of the original image. We can use this method on any public key cryptosystem satisfying multiplicative or additive homomorphic property.

References

1. Borie, J.C., Puech, W., Dumas, M.: Encrypted Medical Images for Secure Transfer. In: ICDIA 2002, Diagnostic Imaging and Analysis, Shanghai, R.P. China, August 2002, pp. 250–255 (2002)
2. Fontaine, C., Galand, F.: A Survey of Homomorphic Encryption for Nonspecialists. EURASIP Journal Information Security 2007(1), 1–15 (2007)
3. Gamal, E.: A Public-Key Cryptosystem and a Signature Scheme Based on Discrete logarithms. IEEE Transactions on Information Theory, 469–472 (1985)
4. Kuribayashi, M., Tanaka, H.: Fingerprinting Protocol for Images Based on Additive Homomorphic Property. IEEE Transactions on Image Processing 14(12), 2129–2139 (2005)
5. Paillier, P.: Public-Key Cryptosystems Based on Composite Degree Residuosity Classes. In: Stern, J. (ed.) EUROCRYPT 1999. LNCS, vol. 1592, pp. 223–238. Springer, Heidelberg (1999)
6. Prasanna, S.R.M., Rao, Y.V.S., Mitra, A.: An Image Encryption Method with Magnitude and Phase Manipulation using Carrier Images. International Journal of Computer Vision 1(2), 132–137 (2006)
7. Puech, W., Rodrigues, J.M.: A New Crypto-Watermarking Method for Medical Images Safe Transfer. In: Proc. 12th European Signal Processing Conference (EU-SIPCO 2004), Vienna, Austria, pp. 1481–1484 (2004)
8. Rappe, D.K.: Homomorphic Cryptosystems and their Applications. Cryptology ePrint Archive, Report 2006/001 (2006)
9. Schneier, B.: Applied cryptography. Wiley, New-York (1995)
10. Uhl, A., Pommer, A.: Image and Video Encryption: From Digital Rights Management to Secured Personal Communication. Springer, Heidelberg (2005)

Dot-Size Variant Visual Cryptography

Jonathan Weir and Wei-Qi Yan

Queen's University Belfast, Belfast, BT7 1NN, UK

Abstract. In this paper, we propose a scheme by which a secure random share can be generated using a dot-size variant form of visual cryptography (VC). We generate two extended style VC shares, when the share is viewed, it appears as a normal random visual cryptography share. However, this scheme is designed with spatial filtering in mind, this is the dot-size variant part of the scheme. Dot-size variant means that instead of having single black and white dots which make up a VC share, we use a cluster of smaller dots to represent these black and white pixels. This means that after printing, if the share is scanned or photocopied or even viewed with a mobile phone or digital camera, the smallest dots in the scheme are filtered. This loss of information during the copying process allows the original share to have additional security in that accurate copies cannot be created, as well as the fact that due to this loss, the copied share looks totally different from the original. This technique can be used to detect possible counterfeit shares and copies as they will be noticeably different from the original. One major advantage of our scheme is that it works with traditional print techniques and required no special materials. We present our results within this paper.

1 Introduction

Many printed images which are used for a particular type of product verification or identification do not contain overly robust methods of copy protection, particularly from scanning and photocopying and more recently, attacks from high quality digital cameras and even mobile phone cameras. Assailants could easily make a very fast copy of potentially sensitive information and make many apparently legitimate replicas and the original would practically be impossible to tell from the copies.

There are a number of different methods available to content providers which could be employed to prevent this type of fast digital copying misuse [1], namely steganography [2,3] and watermarking combined with visual cryptography [4,5,6]. This paper deals primarily from a pure visual cryptography point of view for data protection.

Within typical secret sharing using traditional visual cryptography (VC) methods [7], a single secret s is encoded into n shares, if any k of these shares are superimposed, the secret can be recovered. This is known as k-out-of-n secret sharing. Superimposing any $k - 1$ of the these shares keeps the secret completely hidden.

A.T.S. Ho et al. (Eds.): IWDW 2009, LNCS 5703, pp. 136–148, 2009.
© Springer-Verlag Berlin Heidelberg 2009

Within this paper, we present a scheme which uses an extended form of visual cryptography [8] which has been adapted to incorporate our dot-size variant VC scheme which attempts to reduce the risk of security problems that can arise from assailants who try to capture specific types of data, whether it is from document copying using scanning and photocopying techniques, or whether it comes in the form of digital photographs of documents using a digital camera.

The key point that we will highlight in this paper deals with the variant dot sizes. The difference in dot sizes will help to cause inaccuracies when copies of documents which contain these dot-size variant VC shares are scanned or photocopied. The scanner or photocopier will filter the smaller dots completely, which removes a critical part of the image. After having removed these smaller dots, the inaccurate copy looks extremely different when compared to the original.

Spatial filtering is the principle concept behind our proposed scheme. The idea being that a correctly designed share, when copied with a certain device, will filter smaller insignificant parts of the image, which are actually very important to the overall shares appearance. This would be akin to a lowpass filter which has the overall effect of smoothing or blurring an image. Further discussion on spatial filtering is detailed in Section 2.

This type of spatial filtering, as far as we are aware, has never been actively researched within the visual cryptography domain. We believe the techniques developed within this paper provide a novel contribution to the current VC techniques that are in use and essentially improve upon previous work.

A flowchart outlining our proposed technique can be viewed in Figure 1. It is fully explained within Section 3.

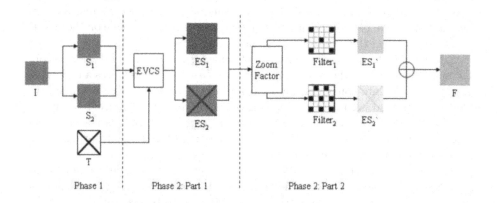

Fig. 1. Flowchart of our proposed scheme

The remainder of this paper is set out as follows; Section 2 outlines the related work pertaining to our work. Section 3 details our contribution, explaining how the new schemes work. The results are presented within Section 4 and the conclusions are drawn in Section 5.

2 Related Work

Visual cryptography is a cryptographic scheme, which can decode concealed images without any cryptographic computation and was originally created by Naor and Shamir [7]. The encryption technique is expressed as a *k-out-of-n* secret sharing problem. Given the secret, n transparencies are generated so that the original secret is visible if any k of them are stacked together. The image remains hidden if fewer than k transparencies are superimposed. As the name, visual cryptography suggests, it is related to the human visual system. When the k shares are stacked together, the human eyes do the decryption. This allows anyone to use the system without any knowledge of cryptography and without performing any computations whatsoever.

Extended visual cryptography schemes allow the construction of visual secret sharing schemes within which the shares are meaningful as apposed to the shares consisting of random noise. After the set of shares are superimposed, this meaningful information disappears and the secret is recovered. This is the basic premise for the extended form of visual cryptography.

An extended visual cryptography scheme (EVCS) proposed by Ateniese et al. [8] is based on two types of access structure. A qualified access structure Γ_{Qual} and a forbidden access structure Γ_{Forb} in a set of n participants. The technique encodes the participants in that if any set, which is a member of the qualified access structure and those sets are superimposed, the secret is revealed. However, for any set which is a member of the forbidden access structure and has no information on the shared secret, meaning that no useful information can be gleaned from stacking the participants. The main difference between basic visual cryptography and extended visual cryptography is that a recognizable image can be viewed on each of the shares; once the shares have been superimposed (provided they are part of the qualified access structure), the image on the shares will disappear and the secret will become visible.

With EVCS, the first n shares represent some form of meaningful information. The secret is normally the last to be dealt with $(n+1)$. This requires a technique that has to take into consideration the colour of the pixel in the secret image we want to obtain, so when the n shares are superimposed, their individual images disappear and the secret image can be seen. In general, this can be denoted by $C_c^{c_1 \cdots c_n}$ with $c, c_1, \cdots, c_n \in \{b, w\}$, the collection of matrices from which we can choose a matrix to determine the shares, given c_i being the colour of the ith innocent image and c being the colour of the secret image. In order to implement this scheme, 2^n pairs of such collections, one for each possible combination of white and black pixels in the n original images need to be generated.

It is assumed that no information is known on the pixel values of the original image that is being hidden. The only thing that is known is that the pixels can be black or white. No probability distribution is known about the pixels. There is no way to tell if a black pixel is more likely to occur than a white pixel. Three conditions must be met when it comes to encrypting the images. Firstly, images that belong to the qualified set access structure, should, when superimposed, reveal the secret image. Secondly, by inspecting the shares, no hint should be available about what secret is hidden within the shares. Finally, the image within the shares should not be altered in anyway, that is, after the n original images have been encoded, they should still be recognizable by the user.

A stronger security model for EVCS is one in which the shares associated to a forbidden subset can be inspected by the user, meaning that the secret image will still remain totally hidden even if all n shares are previously known by the user. A systematic approach to fully address a general (k, n) problem was proposed in [9].

Improving the shares quality [10] to that of a photo realistic picture has been examined within extended visual cryptography. This is achieved using gray subpixels rather than black and white pixels in the form of halftoning. Removing the need for pixel expansion within VC has also been examined. Ito et al. [11] remove the need for this pixel expansion by defining a scheme which uses the traditional (k, n) sharing where m (the number of subpixels in a shared pixel) is equal to one.

A probabilistic method to deal with size invariant shares is proposed in [12] in which the frequency of white pixels is used to show the contrast of the recovered image. The scheme is non-expansible and can be easily implemented on a basis of conventional visual secret sharing (VSS) scheme. The term non-expansible means that the sizes of the original image and shadows are the same. Many others have also researched this area of invariant share sizes and invariant aspect ratios [13,14,15].

In terms of EVCS, our scheme uses the final result of an extended scheme as the image that should be resilient to copying. The original secret is recovered and used. However, each of the layers used to make up the final secret (the qualified subsets) has the dot-size variant patterns applied to each. That way the recovered share looks like the original secret, until it is copied, which changes the overall appearance, ie, filtering the specifically smaller dots on the layers. Many previously discussed schemes work towards invariant size and reduced share sizes, our scheme approaches this VC problem from the opposite end, by enlarging the shares and employing different pixel patterns for each share. Its primary use is within the printing industry. By printing these shares in very high quality (high dots per inch), they possess the anti-copy properties described within this paper. Our schemes primary application deals purely with anti-copying methods. If a phone or digital camera takes a picture of the share, it should render it useless if the user wishes to make copies of it. The same should be true for photocopying and scanning techniques. We attempt to use the principles of spatial filtering in the design of our shares.

A typical spatial filter consist of two things, a neighbourhood and a predefined operation that is performed on the neighbourhood pixels. Filtering creates a new area within the neighbourhoods coordinates with the results of applying the predefined operation. We focus on the mechanics of linear spatial filtering using various $n \times m$ neighbourhood masks. The filter we look at in this paper involves a 5×5 filter, the reason being that it is more intuitive and easier to work with due to its center falling on integer values. We attempt to use this principle of spatial filtering combined with visual cryptography to construct sufficiently secure dot-size variant shares which become filtered when some forms of copying are attempted.

3 Our Contributions

Based on the extended form of visual cryptography, our proposed scheme works as detailed in Figure 1. Firstly, there are two phases to this scheme. The first phase involves creating two random shares with basic traditional VC techniques. The hidden text or message you wish to appear in the copied shares should also be selected at this stage. The second phase involves two parts, firstly an extended form of VC is applied to both shares created from phase one along with the text and then secondly the resultant extended VC shares are combined with our variant dot-size system.

Two schemes are presented and detailed below based on our dot-size variant scheme. The first scheme is a densely populated pixel scheme, the other is a sparsely populated scheme. Essentially, both schemes work in exactly the same way, they are detailed here to show that the scheme works with both types of pixels depending on the distance between the pixels. The densely populated pixel scheme uses, a dense set of pixel patterns and the sparsely populated pixel scheme uses a sparse set of pixel patterns.

Initially the scheme generates two random shares S_1 and S_2. They are obtained from a simple random binary image I with no visual meaning. In order to create each share, a traditional *2-out-of-2* VC method is employed. The input image required to generate these shares does not matter. It can be anything, typically we just use an automatically generated random image which allows the shares to be generated.

S_1 is used as the main secret in the extended part of the scheme. S_2 is also used in the second phase. It is combined with the text T you wish to appear when the final printed image is copied or viewed with a number of devices, such as a photocopier or digital camera. Figure 2 shows each of these generated shares along with the secret text image used in the extended phase of our scheme.

In phase two, we use a $(2, 2)$-EVCS scheme to conceal S_1 within the two other images S_2 and T. Share one is passed to the extended scheme as the secret, S_2 and T act as the corresponding halftone cover images. After the EVCS scheme

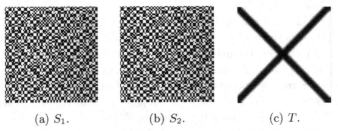

(a) S_1.   (b) S_2.   (c) T.

Fig. 2. Shares generated after phase one along with the text image

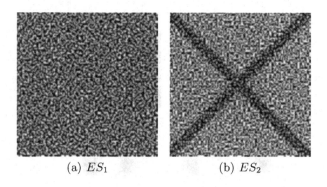

(a) ES_1 (b) ES_2

Fig. 3. Extended VC phase of the proposed scheme

has been performed on each of the two cover images we obtain the new extended shares ES_1 and ES_2 which are visible in Figure 3.

The next part of phase two involves our new dot-size variant scheme. Both ES_1 and ES_2 need to be modified with the properties of this new scheme. This is the phase which generates the new dot-size variant shares which allow the superimposed shares to appear as normal under general viewing conditions and when copied, allow the hidden text to appear.

The idea behind the dot-size variant scheme is that each pixel within the original extended shares is expanded into a 5×5 block. This is the Zoom Factor stage at the start of Phase 2: Part 2. Within this zooming stage different block styles are chosen which contain specific patterns which are used to represent a black or white pixel, these patterns are known as $Filter_1$ and $Filter_2$. The reason these size of blocks were chosen, is that they contain the minimum amount of information to make this scheme effective. With a 3×3 block, the patterns generated cannot contain enough information in order to successfully invalidate the share after copying has been performed. Anything larger than 5×5 works but results in even larger shares, so there is no need to include them here.

The aforementioned filter patterns used to construct the new shares are discussed below. Only the black pixels are replaced in the larger shares, the white pixels are scaled to their new size and are made up from only white pixels. A range of different pixel patterns can be used within this zoom stage. The key thing to remember when choosing a pixel pattern is that there cannot be too much difference between each set of patterns. This comes down to the difference in contrast, a highly important part of any VC scheme [16,17,18].

For example, if solid black pixels are used for share one (this would imply densely populated pixels) in a 5×5 grid, there can only be a difference of three pixels when designing the pattern for share two. The same is true for the sparse pixel set. Potential pattern sets are displayed in Figure 4. Figure 4(a) shows the black solid 5×5 pixel pattern and Figure 4(b) shows the slightly less dense version from the same dense pixel set. Figure 4(c) and Figure 4(d) illustrate an example of a sparse pixel set. All figures have been zoomed by a factor of eight from their original size for clarity.

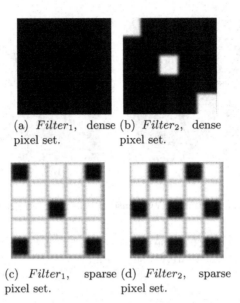

(a) *Filter₁*, dense pixel set. (b) *Filter₂*, dense pixel set.

(c) *Filter₁*, sparse pixel set. (d) *Filter₂*, sparse pixel set.

Fig. 4. Corresponding pattern sets for a densely populated pixel pattern

After the pixel patterns $Filter_1$ and $Filter_2$ have been chosen based on the type of sets used (dense or sparse) each extended share is required to be modified with the corresponding filter set. Each zoomed share is read in and has the corresponding pixel sets applied. Figure 5 shows the resultant shares after a 5 × 5 sparse pixel set has been applied to it. The pattern from Figure 4(c) has been applied to ES_1 from Figure 3(a), while Figure 4(d) has been applied to ES_2 from Figure 3(b). The final modified extended shares ES_1' and ES_2' can be viewed in Figure 5(a) and 5(b) respectively. The final share F can be viewed in the next section in Figure 6, which shows the result from superimposing ES_1' and ES_2'.

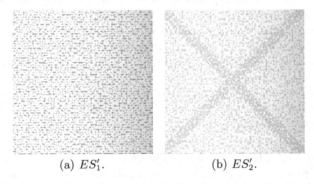

(a) ES_1'.   (b) ES_2'.

Fig. 5. Results from applying the sparse pixel patterns to each extended share after zooming

The final share F could be used as an identification mark on a document, which would highlights whether or not copies have been made of the document.

It is this slight difference in density and ultimately the contrast that allows the message to remain hidden from human sight, but allows it to become visible when attempts are made to copy the shares. The difference in pixel locations become filtered, therefore leaving a lighter background which allows the denser sections of the image to become visible.

4   Experimental Results

Due to the nature of this scheme, it is primarily designed for printed images and would be best used within a printing application. To achieve the best results, a high quality printer should be used which should be capable of printing at a high resolution. All of the printed examples in the results section where all printed at 1200 DPI (dots-per-inch). This produces suitably sized, printed images which are clear and are not too large after printing. This high resolution printing prevents accurate copies being made using a mobile phone camera, which, when used on these printed images, tend to blend and filter the smaller dots which results in the resultant marks on the photo. This is why some of the text may be visible within some of the created shares from our results, becuase we cannot display the images at 1200 DPI or greater without printing them first.

Within this section, we present our experimental results. The results are presented which highlight the spurious nature of the copies obtained with a variety of devices previously mentioned. The dense and sparse set schemes are both presented and the corresponding results are published.

Figure 6 provides the results of a 5×5 sparse set of shares with an "X" running through the center of the image. When the original share in Figure 6 is printed at 1200 DPI and a copy of it is made on a digital camera, the difference is clear. Figure 7 shows the resultant image from the digital camera, which was taken using the cameras 7 megapixel setting. A darker "X" shape is clearly visible which stands out quite substantially when compared to the original.

Figure 8 was generated from the 5×5 dense pixel set. To illustrate the anti-copying techniques based on photocopy, we employ an artistic filter from the GNU Image Manipulation Program which makes use of a photocopy filter for any given image. The filters settings where kept at their defaults. The results from applying this filter to the image in Figure 8 can be viewed in Figure 9. The difference from the original is clear and obvious. The text in the original is almost impossible to detect, whereas the copy has a very visible text running through it. This is entirely down to the difference in contrast between the original share and the copy due to the filtering of the small dots.

In order to measure the contrast, we use luminance of the image. The luminance of an image describes the amount of light that passes through or is emitted from a particular area of an image. That is, the measure of energy an observer perceives from a light source. The general equation for luminance is defined as (1):

$$L_v = \frac{d^2 F}{dAd\Omega cos\theta} \tag{1}$$

where L_v is the luminance, F is luminous flux, θ is the angle between the surface normal and the specified direction, A is the surface area of the image and Ω is the solid angle.

We use this luminance value to help determine the images contrast C and to show that the difference is sufficient in the copied image when compared to the original to warrant a practical use for this type of technique. Typically, we use the standard contrast equation (2) to help determine this metric along with applying a specific variation of it, the Weber contrast (3):

$$C = \frac{\text{Luminance Difference}}{\text{Average Luminance}} \tag{2}$$

$$C = \frac{I - I_b}{I_b} \tag{3}$$

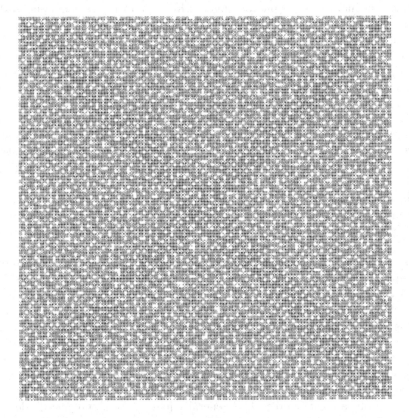

Fig. 6. The resultant share generated by the process using a sparse share

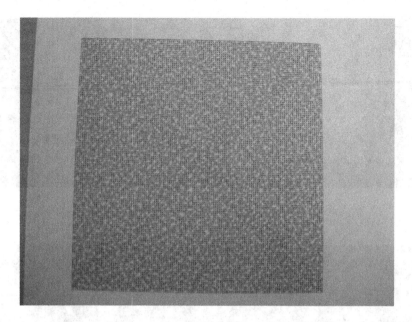

Fig. 7. Photographic copy of the share with "X" running through the center of it

where I and I_b represent the luminance of the features (the hidden text in this case) and the background luminance (the random noise), respectively. The Weber function was chosen because the background in most cases remains largely uniform, meaning its value can be used as the average luminance.

A comparison was done between the contrast in the original share and the photocopy, a number of areas were selected. Each of the areas are paired, so a comparison could be done between the area that contains nothing meaningful and an area which contains the hidden text. The comparison measures the amount of black pixels in each area, as a percentage, and measures the difference. It is this difference which gives rise to the visible results after copying has occurred.

The four areas of interest are of size 128×128 and where taken at the following coordinates $(0, 0)$, $(148, 1372)$, $(3890, 1374)$, and $(3736, 1374)$ on Figure 8. The shares overall size is 4520×1660. The four original share areas are represented by $O_i = O_1, \ldots, O_4$ while the corresponding four photocopied share areas are represented by $P_i = P_1, \ldots, P_4$. The contrast as a percentage, for an area, O_1 for the binary shares is calculated using (4).

$$O_1 = 100 \cdot \sum_{x=1}^{W} \sum_{y=1}^{H} \frac{b_{xy}}{W \times H} \qquad (4)$$

where x and y are the pixel coordinates, b represents a black pixel and W and H are the width and height of the area being computed. The same equation is

Fig. 8. The resultant share using densely positioned pixels

Fig. 9. A photocopy filter applied to a dense share

used for all the areas, these percentages are subtracted, giving the final contrast percentage difference.

The contrast is obtained in each area of each share, in both the original and the photocopy and then the difference is computed between these areas. O_1 and O_2 are similar regions within the original, one area from the background and one area from the foreground, the same is true for O_3 and O_4 as well as the corresponding photocopied shares notation. Table 1 presents the contrast analysis results. Each of the corresponding areas are grouped accordingly in the table.

From these results, it is possible to see that when the printed images are viewed with a mobile phone camera or digital camera, the hidden text becomes available. It becomes darker and easier to see, making it very difficult to obtain an accurate copy. The same principle is true for the photocopied images. This is due to the difference in contrast. Each of the devices used filtered the small dots which increases the contrast difference in particular areas of the image. It is this increase in contrast difference which allows this scheme to work successfully, which is confirmed by the results obtained in Table 1. Take for example the

Table 1. Contrast analysis between the original share and the photocopy

area	black (%)	difference (%)
O_1	83.1%	2.7%
O_2	85.8%	
P_1	70.2%	6.1%
P_2	76.3%	
O_3	83.0%	2.9%
O_4	85.9%	
P_3	70.4%	6.5%
P_4	76.9%	

P_1 and P_2 results, the difference between the background noise and the hidden text is 6.1%, which is extremely large compared to the original having just a difference of 2.7% within the same area. There is over twice the difference in contrast, this greater difference confirms the visible changes of appearance in the copied shares.

5   Conclusion

In this paper we propose a novel dot-size variant visual cryptography scheme which attempts to reduce the likelihood of successful image or document copying using a number of devices. Our technique provides a practical application of VC in the area of anti-copying. Visually, the share itself looks normal, however after a copy of the share is taken, the small dots are filtered, revealing the hidden message. This potentially allows for improved security when it comes to the area of document authentication and identification. This can clearly be observed from the results, making it quite difficult to copy these types of shares using readily available copying devices. Further development of these schemes would potentially improve these techniques, especially in the area of reducing the overall size of the shares which could grow quite large depending on the type of data that is required to be concealed during the embedding process.

References

1. Memon, N., Wong, P.W.: Protecting digital media content. Communications of the ACM 41(7), 35–43 (1998)
2. Chang, C.C., Tseng, H.W.: A steganographic method for digital images using side match. Pattern Recognition Letters 25(12), 1431–1437 (2004)
3. Liu, C.L., Liao, S.R.: High-performance jpeg steganography using complementary embedding strategy. Pattern Recognition 41(9), 2945–2955 (2008)
4. Fu, M.S., Au, O.: Joint visual cryptography and watermarking. In: ICME 2004, vol. 2, pp. 975–978 (2004)
5. Hassan, M.A., Khalili, M.A.: Self watermarking based on visual cryptography. In: Proceedings of World Academy of Science, Engineering and Technology, vol. 8, pp. 159–162 (2005)

6. Wu, C.W., Thompson, G.R., Stanich, M.J.: Digital watermarking and steganography via overlays of halftone images, vol. 5561, pp. 152–163. SPIE (2004)
7. Naor, M., Shamir, A.: Visual cryptography. In: De Santis, A. (ed.) EUROCRYPT 1994. LNCS, vol. 950, pp. 1–12. Springer, Heidelberg (1995)
8. Ateniese, G., Blundo, C., Santis, A.D., Stinson, D.R.: Extended schemes for visual cryptography. Theoretical Computer Science 250, 1–16 (1996)
9. Ateniese, G., Blundo, C., Santis, A.D., Stinson, D.R.: Visual cryptography for general access structures. Information and Computation 129(2), 86–106 (1996)
10. Yang, C.-N., Chen, T.-S.: Extended visual secret sharing schemes with high-quality shadow images using gray sub pixels. In: Kamel, M.S., Campilho, A.C. (eds.) ICIAR 2005. LNCS, vol. 3656, pp. 1184–1191. Springer, Heidelberg (2005)
11. Ito, R., Kuwakado, H., Tanaka, H.: Image size invariant visual cryptography. IEICE Transactions E82-A(10), 2172–2177 (1999)
12. Yang, C.N.: New visual secret sharing schemes using probabilistic method. Pattern Recognition Letters 25(4), 481–494 (2004)
13. Yang, C.N., Chen, T.S.: Aspect ratio invariant visual secret sharing schemes with minimum pixel expansion. Pattern Recognition Letters 26(2), 193–206 (2005)
14. Yang, C.N., Chen, T.S.: New size-reduced visual secret sharing schemes with half reduction of shadow size. IEICE Transactions 89-A(2), 620–625 (2006)
15. Yang, C.-N., Chen, T.-S.: Visual secret sharing scheme: Improving the contrast of a recovered image via different pixel expansions. In: Campilho, A., Kamel, M.S. (eds.) ICIAR 2006. LNCS, vol. 4141, pp. 468–479. Springer, Heidelberg (2006)
16. Hofmeister, T., Krause, M., Simon, H.U.: Contrast-optimal k out of n secret sharing schemes in visual cryptography. Theoretical Computer Science 240(2), 471–485 (2000)
17. Blundo, C., D'Arco, P., Santis, A.D., Stinson, D.R.: Contrast optimal threshold visual cryptography schemes. SIAM Journal on Discrete Mathematics 16(2), 224–261 (2003)
18. Yang, C.-N., Wang, C.-C., Chen, T.-S.: Real perfect contrast visual secret sharing schemes with reversing. In: Zhou, J., Yung, M., Bao, F. (eds.) ACNS 2006. LNCS, vol. 3989, pp. 433–447. Springer, Heidelberg (2006)

High Capacity Data Hiding in Binary Document Images

N.B. Puhan[1], A.T.S. Ho[2], and F. Sattar[1]

[1] School of Electrical and Electronic Engineering
Nanyang Technological University, Singapore, 639798
[2] Department of Computing
Faculty of Engineering and Physical Sciences
University of Surrey, Guildford, Surrey, UK
puhan@ntu.edu.sg, a.ho@surrey.ac.uk, efsattar@ntu.edu.sg

Abstract. In this paper, we propose a high capacity data hiding method in binary document images towards semi-fragile authentication. Achieving high capacity in binary images with strict imperceptibility criterion is found to be a difficult task. In this method, noise type pixels are selected for pixel-wise data embedding using a secret key. The data hiding process through pixel flipping introduces some background noise in watermarked images and could preserve relevant information. The reversible nature of noise pixel patterns used in flipping process enables blind detection and provides high watermark capacity illustrated in different test images. After extraction process, the background noise is removed to generate the noise-free version of the watermarked image.

1 Introduction

Data hiding could address important applications of multimedia security by embedding a proprietary mark which may be easily retrieved to verify about ownership and authenticity [1]. There has been a growing interest in the authentication of binary document images such as text, circuit diagrams, signature, financial and legal documents. For such images in which the pixels take on only a limited number of values, hiding significant amount of data for authentication purpose with strict imperceptibility criterion becomes more difficult.

Low *et al* [2, 3, 4] introduced robust watermarking methods for formatted document images based on imperceptible line and word shifting. The methods were applied to embed information in document images for bulk electronic publications. The line shifting method was found to have low capacity but the embedded data was robust to photocopying, scanning and printing process. The word shifting method could offer higher capacity than the line shifting method but the robustness was reduced to printing, photocopying and scanning. Brassil and O'Gorman proposed a method in [5], where the height of the bounding box enclosing a group of words could be used as a feature for embedding. This method has a better data hiding capacity than the line and word shifting methods. It was also robust to distortions caused by photocopying.

Wu and Liu hide authentication data in a binary image using a hierarchical model in which human perception was taken into consideration [6]. Distortion that occurred due to flipping of a pixel was measured by considering the change in smoothness and connectivity of a 3×3 window centered at the pixel. In a block, the total number of

A.T.S. Ho et al. (Eds.): IWDW 2009, LNCS 5703, pp. 149–161, 2009.

black pixels is modified to be either odd or even for embedding the data bits. Shuffling was used to equalize the uneven embedding capacity over the image. Koch and Zhao [7] proposed a data hiding algorithm in which a data bit '1' is embedded if the percentage of white pixels was greater than a given threshold, and a data bit '0' is embedded if the percentage of white pixels was less than another given threshold. This algorithm was not robust to attacks and the hiding capacity was low. Mei et al modified an eight-connected boundary of a connected component for data hiding [8]. A fixed set of pairs of five-pixel long boundary patterns have been identified for embedding data. A unique property of the method is that the two patterns in each pair are dual of each other. This property allowed for blind detection of the watermark in a document image.

Amamo and Misaki proposed a feature calibration method in which text areas in an image were identified and the geometry of the bounding box of each text line was calculated in [9]. Each bounding box was divided into four partitions and grouped into two sets. The average width of the horizontal strokes of characters was modified as a feature. In [10], a new perceptual measure based on curvature-weighted distance measure was proposed towards perceptual watermarking of binary document images. Puhan and Ho [11] proposed an exact authentication algorithm using the reversible property of the perceptual measure so that the possibility of any undetected content modification is removed. The method embeds an authentication signature computed from the original image into itself after identifying an ordered set of low-distortion pixels. The parity attack found in the block-wise data hiding methods becomes infeasible due to pixel-wise embedding of the authentication signature. Fragile authentication methods for tamper localization and restoration using imperceptible watermarks have been proposed in [12, 13, 14].

The above described methods could effectively address the issue of authentication and annotation using a fragile and imperceptible watermark. However, the hiding capacity achieved using the methods are not sufficient for semi-fragile authentication, where a certain level of robustness against non-intentional signal processing is required. Due to simple pixel statistics in binary document images, it is found to be difficult for a high capacity watermark embedded with strict imperceptibility criterion. In this paper, we describe an effective method for achieving high watermark capacity with relaxed imperceptibility criterion. The paper is organized as follows: in section 2 the proposed method is discussed. In section 3, the experimental results showing high capacity in several test binary images are presented. Finally, conclusions are drawn in section 4.

2 Proposed Data Hiding Method

In document images, we obtain relevant information by recognizing various patterns such as symbols, lines and curves etc. These patterns are represented by connected foreground (black) pixels against a white background and they are the source of perceived information. The existing embedding methods [6, 10, 13] use perceptual models to select a subset of foreground pixels along with certain white contour pixels so that the imperceptibility criterion can be maintained. If other foreground pixels are embedded to achieve higher capacity, there will be annoying distortion in the watermarked image. Along with, the user may face difficulty in correct interpretation of the document. In the proposed method, we select two types of pixel patterns shown in

Fig. 1. The center pixels can be black or white, while other eight pixels are white. The center pixels in these patterns do not convey important information for document images. If these pixels are altered, a background noise will be formed in the image which is similar to the salt-and-pepper noise found in case of natural images. It is known that human vision has remarkable ability to recognize different struc-tures/patterns in an image even in the presence of noise. So after embedding a watermark in these pixels, the user can still obtain relevant information about the document. Flipping of the center pixel in one pattern creates another and vice-versa; so blind detection of the embedded pixels is possible. We shall outline the proposed data hiding method in the following steps.

Embedding

1. The original image is divided into non-overlapping blocks of 3×3 pixels. Each such block is assigned a block index (I_b) in a sequential order starting from left to right and top to bottom of the image.

2. If a block matches with one of the noise pixel patterns in Fig. 1, it is consid-ered for embedding. The center pixel of such blocks is defined as noise pixel.

3. Let the set of block indices corresponding to the noise pixels be denoted as N. All bock indices in N are randomly permuted using the secret key K. Let the set containing such permuted block indices be denoted as N_p.

4. A binary watermark (W) of length L is used in embedding. The noise pixels corresponding to the first L block indices in N_p are embedded. A noise pixel is set to black if the watermark bit is 0; otherwise it is set to white.

Detection

5. To extract the embedded binary watermark sequence from an image, steps 1 and 2 are performed at the blind detector.

6. Similar to embedding, the set containing the permuted block indices (N_p^d) is detected using the secret key K.

7. The noise pixels corresponding to the first L block indices in N_p^d is extracted. The watermark bit is extracted as 0 if the noise pixel is black. Otherwise it is detected as 1.

8. All noise pixels are set to white for generating the noise-free version of the watermarked image for further use and analysis.

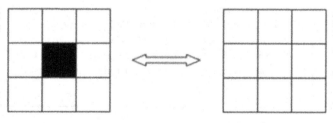

Fig. 1. Noise pixel patterns used in the proposed method; flipping of the center pixel in one pattern creates another

3   Results and Discussion

In this section, we present simulation results by embedding a binary watermark using the proposed data hiding method. The original image is shown in Fig. 2. The total number of noise pixels (i.e. the maximum capacity) in the original image is found to be 19366. The watermarked images after embedding with watermarks of different length L are shown in Fig. 3. From the figures, it is evident that a large number of watermark bits can be embedded without destroying the document information. In each case, the watermark is extracted correctly at the blind detector. The embedded data is secure and can not be extracted correctly by an adversary without using the secret key. When all noise pixels are embedded, the visual quality could get significantly affected, as shown in Fig. 3(i). Thus, a fraction of maximum capacity should be considered during embedding as a trade-off between capacity and visual quality.

To demonstrate the efficacy of the proposed method, we find data hiding capacity in several test document images (Fig. 4). The results are presented in Table 1. For each test image, it is found that a large number of bits can be embedded using the noise pixels. Both during embedding and detection, each 3×3 pixel pattern need to be matched with two noise pixel patterns. The computational complexity of the proposed method is lower than the perceptual based methods. Since simple noise patterns are employed instead of perceptual modeling, the computational complexity of the proposed method is significantly low. We have implemented the proposed method in Matlab 7.1 software and executed them on a 2.66 GHz PC running Windows XP and

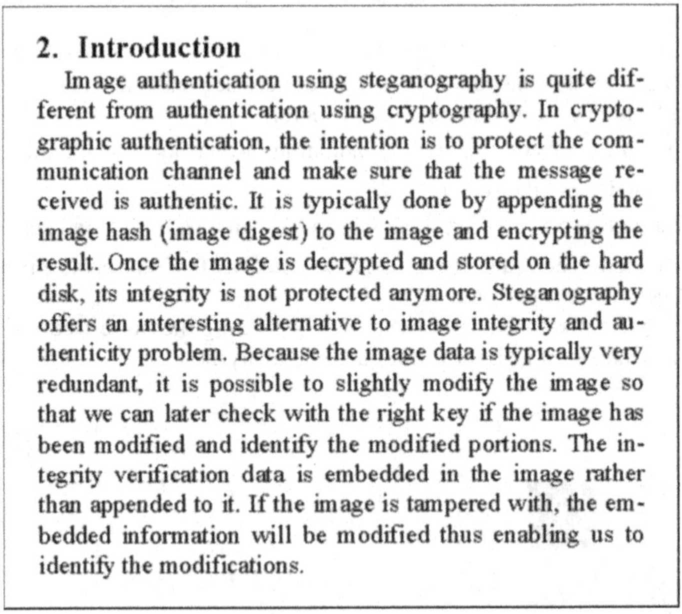

2. Introduction

Image authentication using steganography is quite different from authentication using cryptography. In cryptographic authentication, the intention is to protect the communication channel and make sure that the message received is authentic. It is typically done by appending the image hash (image digest) to the image and encrypting the result. Once the image is decrypted and stored on the hard disk, its integrity is not protected anymore. Steganography offers an interesting alternative to image integrity and authenticity problem. Because the image data is typically very redundant, it is possible to slightly modify the image so that we can later check with the right key if the image has been modified and identify the modified portions. The integrity verification data is embedded in the image rather than appended to it. If the image is tampered with, the embedded information will be modified thus enabling us to identify the modifications.

Fig. 2. Original image of 463×535 pixels

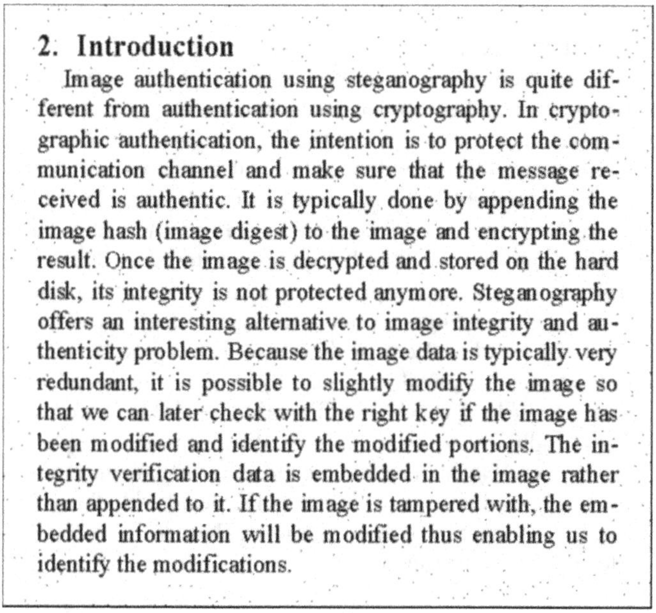

2. Introduction

Image authentication using steganography is quite different from authentication using cryptography. In cryptographic authentication, the intention is to protect the communication channel and make sure that the message received is authentic. It is typically done by appending the image hash (image digest) to the image and encrypting the result. Once the image is decrypted and stored on the hard disk, its integrity is not protected anymore. Steganography offers an interesting alternative to image integrity and authenticity problem. Because the image data is typically very redundant, it is possible to slightly modify the image so that we can later check with the right key if the image has been modified and identify the modified portions. The integrity verification data is embedded in the image rather than appended to it. If the image is tampered with, the embedded information will be modified thus enabling us to identify the modifications.

(a)

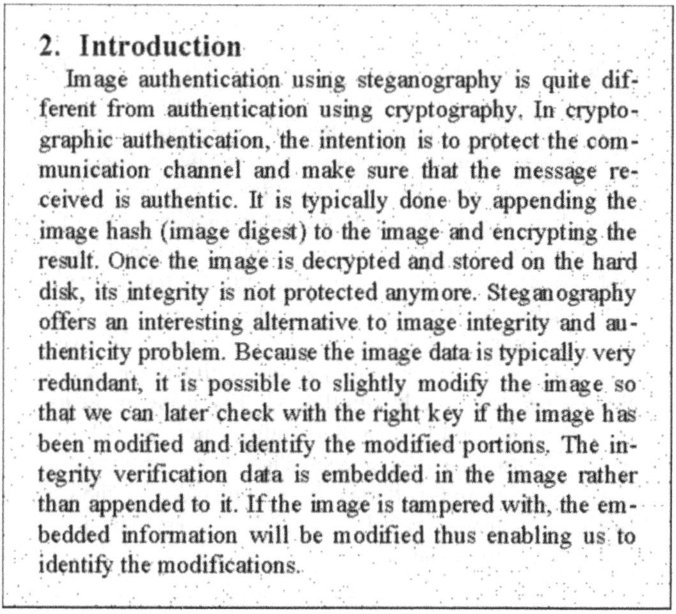

2. Introduction

Image authentication using steganography is quite different from authentication using cryptography. In cryptographic authentication, the intention is to protect the communication channel and make sure that the message received is authentic. It is typically done by appending the image hash (image digest) to the image and encrypting the result. Once the image is decrypted and stored on the hard disk, its integrity is not protected anymore. Steganography offers an interesting alternative to image integrity and authenticity problem. Because the image data is typically very redundant, it is possible to slightly modify the image so that we can later check with the right key if the image has been modified and identify the modified portions. The integrity verification data is embedded in the image rather than appended to it. If the image is tampered with, the embedded information will be modified thus enabling us to identify the modifications.

(b)

Fig. 3. The watermarked images after embedding with watermarks of different L; (a) $L=1000$, (b) $L=2000$, (c) $L=3000$, (d) $L=4000$, (e) $L=5000$, (f) $L=6000$, (g) $L=8000$, (h) $L=10000$, (i) $L=19366$

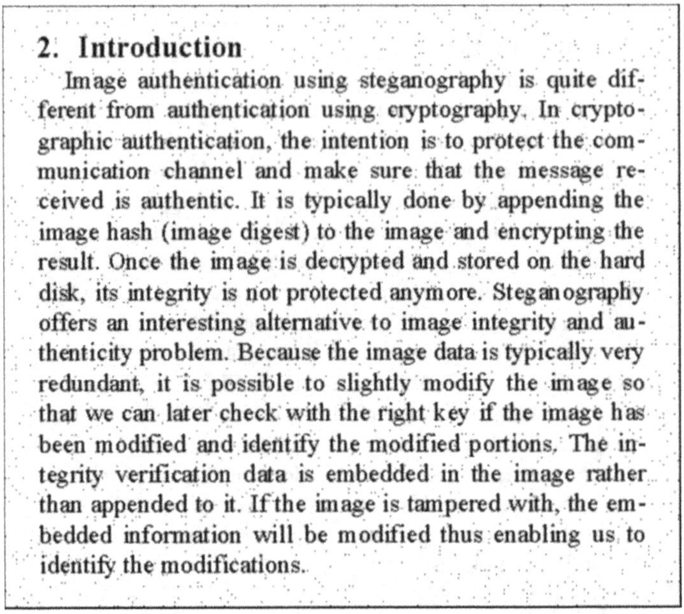

2. Introduction

Image authentication using steganography is quite different from authentication using cryptography. In cryptographic authentication, the intention is to protect the communication channel and make sure that the message received is authentic. It is typically done by appending the image hash (image digest) to the image and encrypting the result. Once the image is decrypted and stored on the hard disk, its integrity is not protected anymore. Steganography offers an interesting alternative to image integrity and authenticity problem. Because the image data is typically very redundant, it is possible to slightly modify the image so that we can later check with the right key if the image has been modified and identify the modified portions. The integrity verification data is embedded in the image rather than appended to it. If the image is tampered with, the embedded information will be modified thus enabling us to identify the modifications.

(c)

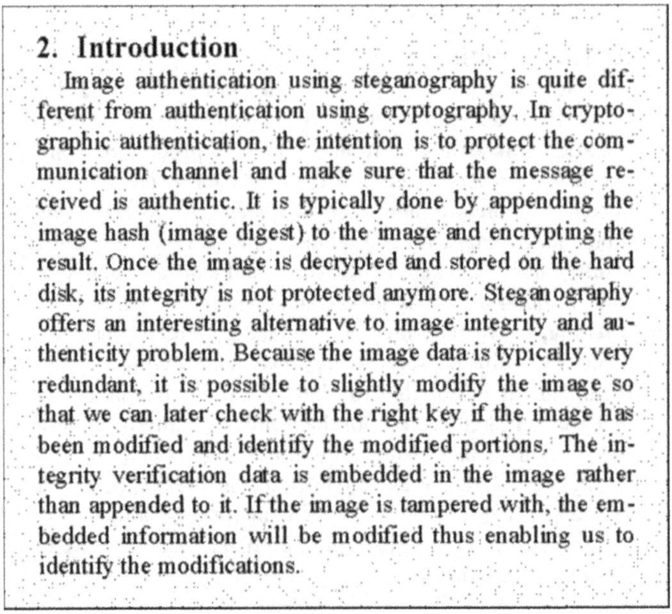

2. Introduction

Image authentication using steganography is quite different from authentication using cryptography. In cryptographic authentication, the intention is to protect the communication channel and make sure that the message received is authentic. It is typically done by appending the image hash (image digest) to the image and encrypting the result. Once the image is decrypted and stored on the hard disk, its integrity is not protected anymore. Steganography offers an interesting alternative to image integrity and authenticity problem. Because the image data is typically very redundant, it is possible to slightly modify the image so that we can later check with the right key if the image has been modified and identify the modified portions. The integrity verification data is embedded in the image rather than appended to it. If the image is tampered with, the embedded information will be modified thus enabling us to identify the modifications.

(d)

Fig. 3. (*continued*)

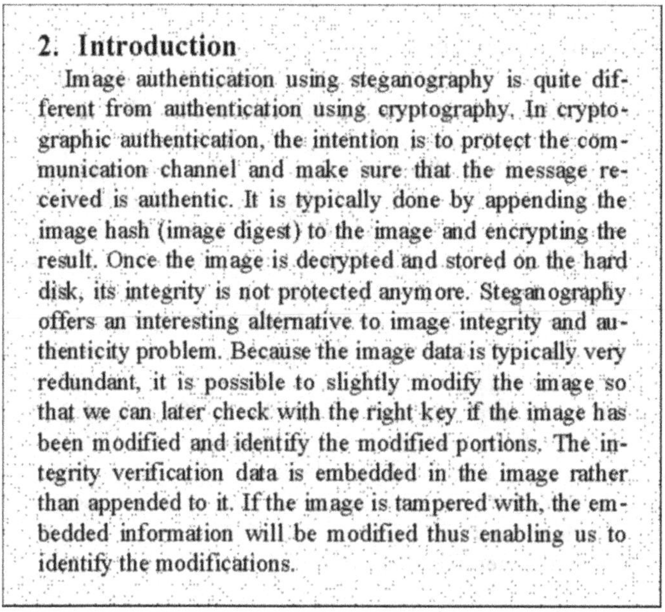

2. Introduction

Image authentication using steganography is quite different from authentication using cryptography. In cryptographic authentication, the intention is to protect the communication channel and make sure that the message received is authentic. It is typically done by appending the image hash (image digest) to the image and encrypting the result. Once the image is decrypted and stored on the hard disk, its integrity is not protected anymore. Steganography offers an interesting alternative to image integrity and authenticity problem. Because the image data is typically very redundant, it is possible to slightly modify the image so that we can later check with the right key if the image has been modified and identify the modified portions. The integrity verification data is embedded in the image rather than appended to it. If the image is tampered with, the embedded information will be modified thus enabling us to identify the modifications.

(e)

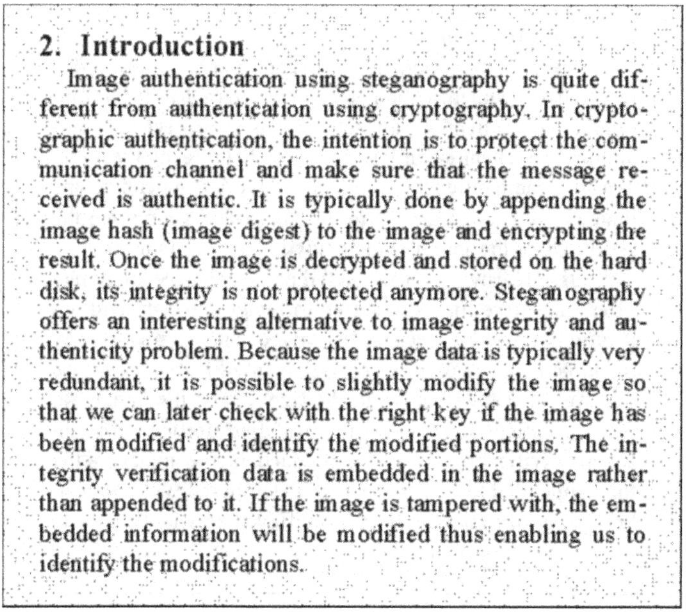

2. Introduction

Image authentication using steganography is quite different from authentication using cryptography. In cryptographic authentication, the intention is to protect the communication channel and make sure that the message received is authentic. It is typically done by appending the image hash (image digest) to the image and encrypting the result. Once the image is decrypted and stored on the hard disk, its integrity is not protected anymore. Steganography offers an interesting alternative to image integrity and authenticity problem. Because the image data is typically very redundant, it is possible to slightly modify the image so that we can later check with the right key if the image has been modified and identify the modified portions. The integrity verification data is embedded in the image rather than appended to it. If the image is tampered with, the embedded information will be modified thus enabling us to identify the modifications.

(f)

Fig. 3. (*continued*)

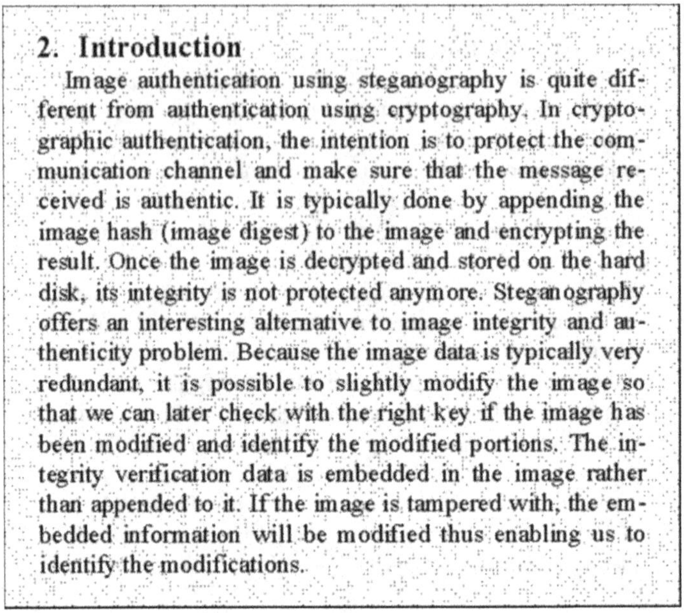

2. Introduction

Image authentication using steganography is quite different from authentication using cryptography. In cryptographic authentication, the intention is to protect the communication channel and make sure that the message received is authentic. It is typically done by appending the image hash (image digest) to the image and encrypting the result. Once the image is decrypted and stored on the hard disk, its integrity is not protected anymore. Steganography offers an interesting alternative to image integrity and authenticity problem. Because the image data is typically very redundant, it is possible to slightly modify the image so that we can later check with the right key if the image has been modified and identify the modified portions. The integrity verification data is embedded in the image rather than appended to it. If the image is tampered with, the embedded information will be modified thus enabling us to identify the modifications.

(g)

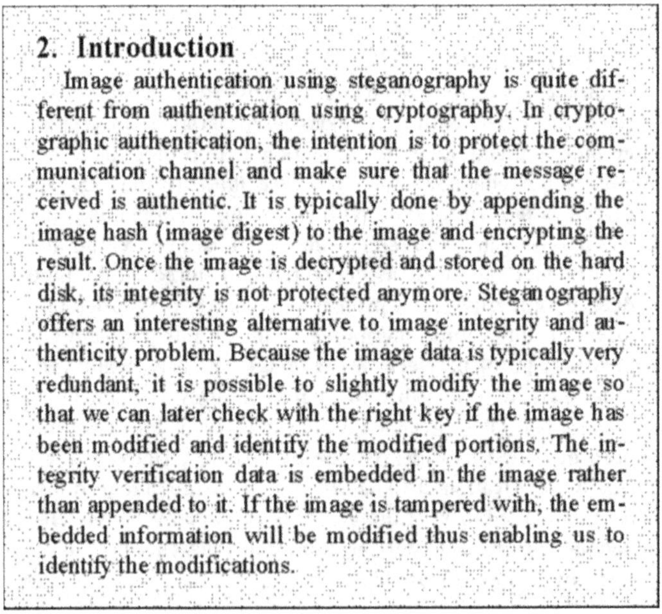

2. Introduction

Image authentication using steganography is quite different from authentication using cryptography. In cryptographic authentication, the intention is to protect the communication channel and make sure that the message received is authentic. It is typically done by appending the image hash (image digest) to the image and encrypting the result. Once the image is decrypted and stored on the hard disk, its integrity is not protected anymore. Steganography offers an interesting alternative to image integrity and authenticity problem. Because the image data is typically very redundant, it is possible to slightly modify the image so that we can later check with the right key if the image has been modified and identify the modified portions. The integrity verification data is embedded in the image rather than appended to it. If the image is tampered with, the embedded information will be modified thus enabling us to identify the modifications.

(h)

Fig. 3. (*continued*)

2. Introduction

Image authentication using steganography is quite different from authentication using cryptography. In cryptographic authentication, the intention is to protect the communication channel and make sure that the message received is authentic. It is typically done by appending the image hash (image digest) to the image and encrypting the result. Once the image is decrypted and stored on the hard disk, its integrity is not protected anymore. Steganography offers an interesting alternative to image integrity and authenticity problem. Because the image data is typically very redundant, it is possible to slightly modify the image so that we can later check with the right key if the image has been modified and identify the modified portions. The integrity verification data is embedded in the image rather than appended to it. If the image is tampered with, the embedded information will be modified thus enabling us to identify the modifications.

(i)

Fig. 3. (*continued*)

with Pentium 4 processor and 2 GB RAM. It is found that the proposed method requires 2s approximately, for both embedding and detection. The availability of a large number of noise pixels will enable to design an effective semi-fragile authentication technique. We are currently designing such a new technique exploiting the large data hiding capacity offered by the proposed method.

any change made to any bit plane will be detected. The localization properties of this simple scheme can be improved if it is applied to image blocks rather than the whole image.

One of the first fragile watermarking techniques proposed for detection of image tampering was based on inserting check-sums of gray levels determined from the seven most significant bits into the least significant bits (LSB) of pseudo-randomly selected pixels [1]. In this paper, we are going to describe one possible implementation of this idea. First, we choose a large number N that will be used for calculating the check sums. Its size directly influences the probability of making a change that might go undetected. The image is then divided into 8×8 blocks, and in each block, a different pseudo-random walk through all 64 pixels is generated. Let us denote the pixels as $p_1, p_2, ..., p_{64}$. We also generate 64 integers $a_1, a_2, ..., a_{64}$ comparable in size to N. The check sum S is calculated as

There are some obvious advantages of this approach. First, the logo itself can carry some useful visual information about the image or its creator. It can also represent a particular authentication device or software. Second, by comparing the original logo with the recovered one, one can visually inspect the integrity of the image. Third, the authentication watermark is embedded not only in the LSBs of the image but somewhat deeper (± 5 gay scales). This makes it more secure and harder to remove. Fourth, the method is fast, simple, and amenable to fast and cheap hardware implementation. This makes it very appealing for still image authentication in digital cameras.

This method, however, has a serious security gap if the same logo and key are reused for multiple images. Given two images I_1 and I_2 with gray levels $g^{(1)}$ and $g^{(2)}$ watermarked with the same key and logo L, we have

$$f_g(g^{(1)}(i,j)) = L(i,j) = f_g(g^{(2)}(i,j)) \text{ for all } (i,j).$$

Fig. 4. Test document images

The authors apply this technique to small 8×8 pixel blocks. The block is DCT transformed, and the frequency masking values $M(i,j)$ for each frequency bin $P(i,j)$ are calculated using a frequency masking model. The values $M(i,j)$ are the maximal changes that do not introduce perceptible distortions. The DCT coefficients are modified to $P_S(i,j)$ according to the following expression

$$P_S(i,j) = M(i,j) \{ \lfloor P(i,j) / M(i,j) \rfloor + r(i,j) \, \text{sign}(P(i,j)) \},$$

where $r(i,j)$ is a key-dependent noise signal in the interval $(0,1)$, and $\lfloor x \rfloor$ rounds x towards zero. Since $|P(i,j) - P_S(i,j)| \leq M(i,j)$, the modifications to DCT coefficients are imperceptible.

For a test image block with DCT coefficients $P_S'(i,j)$, the masking values $M'(i,j)$ are calculated. The error at (i,j) is estimated by the following equation

$$e' = P_S' - M' \{ r \, \text{sign}(P_S') + \lfloor P_S' / M' - (r - 1/2) \, \text{sign}(P_S') \rfloor \},$$

$$Q_{\Delta,l}(f) = 0 \text{ if } \lfloor f/(\Delta 2^l) \rfloor \text{ is even,}$$
$$Q_{\Delta,l}(f) = 1 \text{ if } \lfloor f/(\Delta 2^l) \rfloor \text{ is odd}$$

at the quantization level l. If a wavelet coefficient $f_{k,l}(m,n)$ is chosen for watermark embedding, it is modified so that

$$Q_{\Delta,l}(f_{k,l}(m,n)) = w(i) \text{ XOR } qkey(m,n),$$

where $w(i)$ is the i-th watermark bit and $qkey$ is a bit generated from the image and a secret key. The construction of the quantization function Q guarantees that one will never have to modify the coefficient at the level l by more than $\pm \Delta 2^l$. The watermark is extracted by evaluating the expression

$$w(i) = Q_{\Delta,l}(f'_{k,l}(m,n)) \text{ XOR } qkey(m,n),$$

where f' is the wavelet coefficient of the potentially tampered image. The extent of tampering is evaluated using the number of correctly recovered watermark bits $w(i)$. The

$$V\!ar\left[\frac{m_r}{N}\right] = \frac{1}{N} \cdot \frac{\binom{q}{r}\binom{S-q}{n-r}}{\binom{S}{n}} + \left(1 - \frac{1}{N}\right) \frac{\binom{q}{r}\binom{q}{r}\binom{S-2q}{n-2r}}{\binom{S}{n}} - \left[\frac{\binom{q}{r}\binom{S-q}{n-r}}{\binom{S}{n}}\right]^2. \qquad (4)$$

For the signature image of ig. 5, we have

$$\begin{cases} \text{block size} & q = 16 \times 16, \\ \text{image size} & S = 288 \times 48, \\ \text{block number} & N = \frac{S}{q} = 18 \times 3, \\ \text{flippable percentage} & p = 5.45\%. \end{cases}$$

The analytic results are shown in Fig. 8, along with the simulation results from 1000 random shuffles. The statistics of blocks with no or few flippables are also shown in Table I. The analysis and simulation are seen to agree well, and the percentage of blocks with no or few flippables is extremely low. Error correction coding can be used to handle a very small number of blocks that have no flippable pixels. As illustrated by the block

Step-2) Compute Flippability Score

The smoothness and connectivity measures are passed into a decision module to produce a flippability score. Main considerations when designing this module are 1) whether the original pattern is smooth, 2) whether flipping will increase nonsmoothness by a large amount, and 3) whether flipping will cause any change in connectivity. The changes on these patterns are generally more noticeable. Listed here are the rules used by our decision module.

1) The lowest score (i.e., not flippable) is assigned to uniformly white or black regions as well as to the isolated single white or black pixels. These trivial cases are handled first.

2) If the number of transitions along horizontal or vertical direction is zero (i.e., the pattern is smooth and regularly structured), assign zero as a final score for the current

REFERENCES

[1] M. Wu, E. Tang, and B. Liu, "Data hiding in digital binary image," in *IEEE Int. Conf. Multimedia & Expo (ICME'00)*, New York, 2000.

[2] F. A. P. Petitcolas, R. J. Anderson, and M. G. Kuhn, "Information hiding—a survey," *Proc. IEEE*, vol. 87, pp. 1062–1078, July 1999.

[3] F. Hartung and M. Kutter, "Multimedia watermarking techniques," *Proc. IEEE*, vol. 87, pp. 1079–1107, July 1999.

[4] I. J. Cox, M. L. Miller, and J. A. Bloom, *Digital Watermarking*. San Mateo, CA: Morgan Kaufmann, 2001.

[5] I. Cox, J. Kilian, T. Leighton, and T. Shamoon, "Secure spread spectrum watermarking for multimedia," *IEEE Trans. Image Processing*, vol. 6, pp. 1673–1687, Dec. 1997.

[6] C. Podilchuk and W. Zeng, "Image adaptive watermarking using visual models," *IEEE J. Select. Areas Commun.*, vol. 16, pp. 525–538, May 1998.

[7] M. Wu, H. Yu, and B. Liu, "Data hiding in images and videos: Part II—Designs and applications," *IEEE Trans. Image Processing*, vol. 12, pp. 696–705, June 2003.

The use of a suitable perceptual model is necessary to minimize the visual distortion in the marked images, because minor modification to the pixels can be perceptible since the pixels are either black or white. In this paper, a new perceptual model is proposed for binary images that is useful for data hiding applications. In our model, the distortion that occurs after flipping a pixel is estimated on the novel curvature-weighted distance difference (CWDD) measure between two contour segments. Through subjective tests the perceptual measure is validated and highly correlated with human perception.

Fig. 4. (*continued*)

proposed robust data hiding methods in formatted document images based on imperceptible line and word shifting. Their methods were applied to embed information in text images for bulk electronic publications. The line shifting method has low data hiding capacity as compared to the word shifting method but the embedded data is more robust to photocopying, scanning and printing process. Koch and Zhao [3] proposed a data hiding algorithm in which a data bit '1' is embedded if the percentage of white pixels was greater than a given threshold, and a data bit '0' is embedded if the percentage of white pixels was less than another given threshold. In [4], the proposed algorithm slightly modified interword spaces so that different lines across a text act as sampling points of a sine wave. After the modification, the

distortion measure (DRDM) for binary document images [6] that could be used for performance comparison in data hiding applications. Traditional objective distortion measures like mean square error (MSE), signal-to-noise ratio (SNR), and peak signal-to-noise ratio (PSNR) are not well correlated with human perception for binary images. All three measures only take the number of flipped pixels into account and the distortions in the binary images can be different even if the number of flipped pixels is the same.

The paper is organized as follows: Section 2 presents a contour- based metric for the proposed perceptual model. The

The purpose of the subjective test is to validate the high correlation between the model and the subjective ratings for different values of $CWDD$ measure. Using the Adobe Photoshop software, four characters 'A', 'B', 'E', 'S' are converted to binary images of size 128x128 pixels. These binary images, as shown in Fig. 1 are used as the original image set from which all test images are produced for the subjective experiments. It is difficult to produce a test image for each value of the $CWDD$ measure due to an insufficient number of flipping pixels of one particular value. To overcome this difficulty, we use the technique called *binning* to produce the test images. We divide the $CWDD$ range from [0, 8] into 9 bins. With the exception of the first one, each bin is of unity length in terms of

Here we show high correlation between the perceptual model described in Section 2 with the subjective test values obtained in Section 3. The subjective mean opinion score (MOS) was computed for each test image from the data obtained in the subjective experiments. In the plot of subjective MOS versus $CWDD_{mean}$ shown in Fig. 3, 26 points out of 34 are within the 95% confidence interval. The performance attributes Spearman rank-order correlation coefficients and correlation coefficients [8] are computed between subjective MOS and $CWDD_{mean}$ for all the test cases.

6. REFERENCES

[1] S. H. Low, N. F. Maxemchuk, and A. M. Lapone, "Document identification for copyright protection using centroid detection," *IEEE Trans. on Communication*, vol. 46, no. 3, March 1998, pp. 372-383.

[2] S. H. Low, and N. F. Maxemchuk, "Performance comparison of two text marking methods," *IEEE Journal on Selected Areas in Communications*, vol. 16, no. 4, May 1998.

[3] E. Koch, J. Zhao, "Embedding robust labels into images for copyright protection, " *Proc. International Congress on Intellectual Property Rights for Specialized Information, Knowledge &*

Digital watermarking is the art of protecting the multimedia data by inserting the proprietary mark which may be easily retrieved by the owner of the data to verify about its ownership or authenticity. A variety of digital watermarking methods have been developed for such purposes [1, 2]. For certain applications, watermarks for checking the authenticity of the multimedia data should be fragile because any corruption to watermarked data easily destroy the watermark and so the detection algorithm will be able to verify the integrity of the data being tested. Provable security of digital media can be guaranteed through the use of cryptographic signatures as the fragile watermark. Cryptographic signature has been well studied in cryptography and algorithms such as DSA, RSA and MD5 are extensively used in various authentication applications [3]. In authentication watermarking, the advantage of having the cryptographic signature hidden inside the digital data rather than appended to it is obvious. Lossless format conversion of the watermarked data does not render it inauthentic though the representation of the data is changed. Another advantage is that if the authentication information is localized, it is then possible to

Fig. 4. (*continued*)

Table 1. Data hiding capacity in test document images

Image number	Image size	Maximum capacity
1	438×519	17313
2	444×510	17289
3	462×510	19346
4	513×543	25038
5	495×549	24388
6	426×534	17852
7	549×798	37811
8	456×459	16099
9	579×474	20596
10	480×462	17001
11	561×462	19610
12	609×480	24297
13	603×495	25072
14	369×690	18720

4 Conclusion

In this paper, we proposed a data hiding method that could identify a large number of noise pixels in binary document images with blind detection. The proposed method creates watermarked images with some background noise and the noise can be erased after extraction process. The extracted image differs from the original image in positions where an original noise pixel was black. In fact, such black noise pixels occur rarely in a document image and converting them to white does not impact much on the information content. The proposed method is of low computational complexity and its large data hiding capacity will be useful for designing an effective and practical semi-fragile authentication method.

References

1. Cox, I.J., Miller, M.L., Bloom, J.A.: Digital Watermarking. Morgan Kaufmann Publishers Inc., San Francisco (2001)
2. Low, S.H., Maxemchuk, N.F., Lapone, A.M.: Document Identification for Copyright Protection Using Centroid Detection. IEEE Trans. on Communication 46(3), 372–383 (1998)
3. Low, S.H., Maxemchuk, N.F.: Performance Comparison of Two Text Marking Methods. IEEE Journal on Selected Areas in Communications 16(4), 561–572 (1998)
4. Brassil, J.T., Low, S., Maxemchuk, N.F.: Copyright Protection for the Electronic Distribution of Text Documents. Proc. of the IEEE 87(7), 1181–1196 (1999)
5. Brassil, J., O'Gorman, L.: Watermarking Document Images with Bounding Box Expansion. In: Anderson, R. (ed.) IH 1996. LNCS, vol. 1174, pp. 227–235. Springer, Heidelberg (1996)

6. Wu, M., Liu, B.: Data hiding in binary image for authentication and annotation. IEEE Transactions on Multimedia 6(4), 528–538 (2004)
7. Koch, E., Zhao, J.: Embedding Robust Labels into Images for Copyright Protection. In: Proc. International Congress on Intellectual Property Rights for Specialized Information, Knowledge & New Technologies, Vienna (1995)
8. Mei, Q., Wong, E.K., Memon, N.: Data Hiding in Binary Text Documents. In: Proc. SPIE Security and Watermarking of Multimedia Contents III, San Jose (2001)
9. Amamo, T., Misaki, D.: Feature Calibration Method for Watermarking of Document Images. In: Proc. 5th Int'l Conf on Document Analysis and Recognition, Bangalore, India, pp. 91–94 (1999)
10. Ho, A.T.S., Puhan, N.B., Marziliano, P., Makur, A., Guan, Y.L.: Perception Based Binary Image Watermarking. In: Proc. IEEE International Symposium on Circuits and Systems (ISCAS), Vancouver, Canada, May 2004, vol. 2, pp. 37–40 (2004)
11. Puhan, N.B., Ho, A.T.S.: Secure Exact Authentication in Binary Document Images. In: Proc. IET Intl. Conference on Visual Information Engineering (VIE), Bangalore, India, September 2006, pp. 29–34 (2006)
12. Kim, H.Y., de Queiroz, R.L.: Alteration-Locating Authentication Watermarking for Binary Images. In: Kalker, T., Cox, I., Ro, Y.M. (eds.) IWDW 2003. LNCS, vol. 2939. Springer, Heidelberg (2004)
13. Yang, H., Alex, C.K.: Binary Image Authentication with Tampering Localization By Embedding Cryptographic Signature and Block Identifier. IEEE Signal Processing Letters 13(12), 741–744 (2006)
14. Makur, A.: Self-embedding and Restoration Algorithms for Document Watermark. In: Proc. IEEE International Conference on Acoustics Speech and Signal Processing, vol. 2, pp. 1133–1136 (2005)

Hiding Information by Context-Based Synonym Substitution

Xueling Zheng, Liusheng Huang, Zhili Chen, Zhenshan Yu, and Wei Yang

University of Science and Technology of China, Hefei, China
zxlcc@mail.ustc.edu.cn, zlchen3@mail.ustc.edu.cn

Abstract. Many methods of linguistic steganography have been proposed by using synonym-substitution to preserve the meaning of the text. However, most of these methods replace words simply according to a static synonym set without considering the context. In this paper, we present a novel method that replaces a word by its synonym on condition that its synonym is suitable for the context. A synonym's candidates are chosen according to context, therefore, in different context the candidates can be different although the word to be replaced is the same. As a result, both of the synonym set and the encoding are dynamic. In our experiment, we use Chinese language to implement our method. The experimental results show that the method is almost twice as good as other two existing methods.

1 Introduction

It is well known that the increase of communication on the internet is unbelievable, and text, as one of most important means of communication, plays a vital role. It is natural for us to think of concealing a small amount of secrete information in the immense internet information to make sure secrete information is not so easy to find out. Therefore, many methods in linguistic steganography have been proposed. Some are based on text format [8] or text document image and the others are based on natural language processing by manipulating the lexical, semantic and/or syntactic structure of sentence [1, 10, 11].

Among all the current implementations of lexical linguistic steganography, one popular means is synonym substitution. It replaces a word by its synonym to embed secrete message and preserves the meaning of the modified sentences as much as possible. Many algorithms [2, 3, 12] are proposed and aim to make the stego-text seem innocuous to a human reader.

[4, 13] are presented to use synonym substitution for Chinese text. [4] uses Euler's Quadratic Residue Theorem to help embed watermark in the Chinese text. [4] also uses the syntactic structure of sentence to make the substitution better. [13] introduce a Chinese lexical analyzer ICTCLAS [14] to choose the substitution of replaceable words according to the context of the text. Denote $S = W_1, W_2, ..., W_n$ is a sentence and W_i is a word in S. If W_i can be replaced by W_i', it should satisfy the following qualifications. Firstly, the character string W_{i-1}, W_i', W_{i+1} should be segmented into three words W_{i-1}, W_i', W_{i+1}. At the

A.T.S. Ho et al. (Eds.): IWDW 2009, LNCS 5703, pp. 162–169, 2009.
© Springer-Verlag Berlin Heidelberg 2009

same time, the character string $S' = W_1, W_2, ..., W_i', ..., W_n$ should be segmented into n words $W_1, W_2, ..., W_i', ..., W_n$. As it is pointed out in [13], most of the previous work about synonym-substitution is designed to get correct sense by using WordNet semantic web [9]. However, WordNet is not adapted to Chinese language. Although [13] does not use WordNet, the synonym sets it used are too broad to ensure the words in the same synonym set are interchangeable. Moreover, ICTCLAS does not really consider the context of cover text. It segments the sentence according to the syntactic structure of sentence, but not the content of the sentence. Therefore, maybe a word to substitute is not suitable for the context but it is qualified under the judgment of the algorithm. From the experimental results, we know that the stego-texts do not look so natural to a human reader.

The two methods do not really consider the context during the substitution. In our algorithms, we hold the context of text as a whole. The rest of the paper is organized as follow. Section 2 provides some important notations used in our algorithms, and Section 3 depicts the design of the algorithm. The experimental results are shown in Section 4, while the conclusion and the future work are pointed out in Section 5.

2   Important Notions

2.1   Max Segmentation Length

In Chinese, words are not separated by white spaces, so we use the maximum matching algorithm to segment words from sentences. According to investigation [6] , in modern Chinese, the occurrence of two-character words is highest, reaches 0.9157, three-character words accounts for 0.051, four-character words is about 0.0275, and the words contain more than four characters is 0.0058. For this reason, we set the Max Segmentation Length in our experiment as 4 and we use MSL to present the value of Max Segmentation Length.

2.2   Context Suitability Degree (CSD)

In statistical Natural Language Processing (NLP), the co-occurrence frequency with some constraint can be used to evaluate the Collocation Degree (CD) of two words. In our algorithm, we segment the sentence of cover texts into words according to our synonym dictionary and context dictionary, and then we denote the synonym by S and n context words by $C_1, C_2, ..., C_n$ respectively. These n context words are the closest ones from S in cover text (see Fig. 1).

If we know the CD of all CS_i/S_iC, we get the sum which is S's Context Suitability Degree (CSD) of the current context. In the same way, we can calculate the CSD of S's synonyms and select S's candidates according to their CSDs. See Formula 1 to calculate a synonym's CSD. Note that CSD can be 0 if the CD of all CS_i/S_iC is 0. And the higher the CSD it is, the more suitable the word in the context.

$$CSD(S; C_1, C_2, ..., C_n) = \sum_{i=1}^{n} CD(SC_i) \tag{1}$$

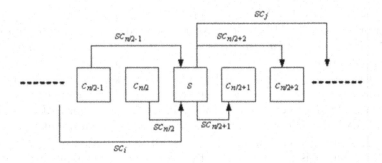

Fig. 1. The synonym and its context words in the text

In Formula 2, we set the qualifying threshold a certain value, such as 0, 5 and so on. Whether a word is a candidate of its synonym shown in context is determined by its CSD and the qualifying threshold, denote as α.

$$Candidate(word) = \begin{cases} true & \text{if } CSD(word) > \alpha \\ false & \text{if } CSD(word) \leqslant \alpha \end{cases} \tag{2}$$

2.3   Three Dictionaries

The Three Dictionaries refer to synonym dictionary, context dictionary and collocation dictionary. Every line of synonym dictionary represents an synonym set. The context dictionary is the gather of context words. And the third dictionary is collocation dictionary. Every line of collocation dictionary contains a two-word collocation phrase and a number that represents this phrase's CD.

Since choosing appropriate candidates is important for our algorithms, the three dictionaries are selected cautiously. The original synonym dictionary is a famous Chinese synonym dictionary [7], which comes from HIT IR Lab and it is free for research use. The original collocation dictionary is gotten from Sogou Labs [5], one of the famous Chinese search engine resources. The collocation dictionary is the production obtained from statistical analysis of one hundred million Chinese documents on the internet. The number of the dictionary reflects the co-occurrence frequency of two adjacent words in Chinese language. It is used to present the CD of the two words in our algorithms. Therefore, we can calculate word's CSD by the number.

Here are the steps that we apply to improve the three dictionaries.

1) Make sure a word not appear more than once in synonym dictionary. If not, it is difficult to choose which synonym set to be used when encounters the words.
2) Check words in sets of synonym dictionary are all in collocation dictionary. If not, delete the word in the set because it never be used for its CSD is 0 in any context.
3) To make the sets of synonyms more interchangeable, we divide every set by the following rules:

(a) Keep the set if the words have the same N parts of speech. In our experiment, N is 1, 2 or more. We regroup the words if they have single part of speech, and regroup the words if they have double part of speech, and regroup the words left. Then, we get a new synonym dictionary.

(b) Then, keep a synonym set if all the words in the set share at least one rational meaning; or else divide the set to make any set in synonym dictionary satisfy the condition.

4) Delete the synonym set that contains one word.

5) We dispose collocation dictionary next. Reserve a line if and only if one of the two words in the line of collocation dictionary is a synonym.

6) Extract the context words which are in collocation dictionary and not in synonym dictionary. Now we get the context dictionary and it has no intersection with synonym dictionary. Otherwise, when a word appears in the context, we cannot decide whether it is a synonym or a context word, it is confused.

3 Context-Based Synonym Substitution Information Hiding Method

As we know, all algorithms put forward previously do not consider the context to some extent. Ours take the context into account at every replaceable word. Section 3.1 describes both the hiding and recovering algorithms. Because some special problems exist in Chinese language, we improve our algorithms in Section 3.2.

3.1 The Algorithms of Hiding and Recovering

As it is introduced in Section 2.2, in our method, we find n context words which are closest to the current synonym word in the context. A word to be a candidate should satisfy that its CSD is larger than the qualifying threshold α. Because in different context, the context words are not the same and the co-occurrence frequencies of the same synonym and different context words are different, so the candidates are different. Therefore, both of the synonym set and the encoding are dynamic, which makes the stego-texts look much more natural. The hiding algorithm is described as:

1) Set the value of α, and set the max length of the words as 4.

2) Read the cover text paragraph by paragraph, and use the maximum matching algorithm to segment the sentences.

3) Find out the words in synonym dictionary and these words that can be replaced by their candidates in the current context. Dispose these synonyms one by one until all of them are done. First of all, find n context words closest to the current synonym. Then find out all the candidates of the current synonym if the candidates' CSD are all more than the qualifying threshold α. The candidates are arranged in an array by their CSDs.

4) Count the number of candidates and pull the log (base 2) of this number of bits. Choose the right one according to the bits to be hidden and the number of candidates. Then substitute the candidate for the original synonym.
5) (a) If the bits are not finished and the cover text is not over, turn to a).
   (b) If all bits are hidden, then the algorithm is over and success.
   (c) Otherwise, if the text is over, then the algorithm is failed.

The recovering algorithm is similar to the hiding algorithm, just find out the number of candidates and the synonym's position in the array in step 3) of the hiding algorithm. The algorithms run well most of time. However, sometimes it fails because of the failure of the segmentation algorithm in our method. To solve this problem, we improve our algorithms in next section.

3.2   Improvement of Algorithms

In Chinese language, words are not separated by white spaces, so we use the maximum matching algorithm to segment words in cover texts or stego-texts. Because of the substitution of some words in cover text, the stego-text is different from the cover text and the context is changed sometimes. Therefore, it may happen that the context words of a synonym are changed and the current CSD is different from the previous one. Simultaneously, its synonyms' CSD are changed so its candidates are changed too. In addition, the failure of maximum matching algorithm makes this problem more serious, since it may segment a synonym into two parts in recovering algorithm. There is an example in Fig. 2 in our previous experiment.

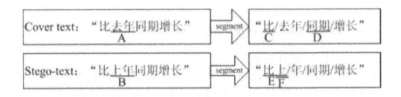

Fig. 2. An example of exception

In the cover text of Fig. 2, the synonym is word A (last year). In this context, its two context words are word C (compare to) and word D (the corresponding period). Under the judgment of our algorithm, the word A (last year) is substituted by word B (last year). But it is unfortunate that, in recovering algorithm, after the segmentation, the word word B is separated and the word F is a part of the new word E(compare to), so the synonym word B (last year) does not exist anymore. As a result, the recovering algorithm fails.

Consequently, a word to be a candidate must satisfy the condition in Fig. 3. This condition is added in the third step of our algorithm in Section 3.2.

Now, make sure that the segmentation of stego-text is always the same as the segmentation of cover-text. In other words, all context words for the same synonym set in the exact position of cover text and stego-text are the same. Therefore, the

$$S = c_1c_2\cdots c_iW_j(=c_{i+1}c_{i+2}\cdots c_{i+j})c_{i+j+1}c_{i+j+2}\cdots$$

A) for $m=i$-MSL+1 to i
    for $n=i+1$ to m+MSL-1
       $W_{new}=c_m, \cdots, c_n,$
        not $W_{new} \in SD$ and not $W_{new} \in CD$
B) for $m=i+j+1$ to $i+j$+MSL-1
    for $n=i+j$ to m-MSL+1
       $W_{new}=c_n, \cdots, c_m,$
        not $W_{new} \in SD$ and not $W_{new} \in CD$

Fig. 3. The condition of improved algorithms. c_i is the ith character in sentence S and j presents the length of W_j. SD and CD present synonym dictionary and context dictionary respectively.

candidates are the same and after improving our algorithm, the recovering algorithm works well all the time.

4   The Results and Discussion

In our experiments, we process the three dictionaries to make synonym sets much more interchangeable. Moreover, we select candidates according to the context, which is different from the algorithms that have been proposed. Finally, in some special condition, we do not replace a synonym because no other words are suitable in the context. So we can see that our algorithms are more secure and the stego-text (Fig. 4) looks more natural.

[4] used the Blind test and Non-Blind test to measure the perceptual transparency. In our experiment, we use only Non-Blind test to measure the perceptual transparency. Non-Blinded test, where human subjects are presented with protected text with original text. The PSNR [4] is used to measure the perceptual transparency. Here we use Error Rate (ER) instead of PSNR. $ER = \frac{\sum U_i}{\sum S_i}$, where $\sum U_i$ is the total number of unsuitable words and $\sum S_i$ is the total number of substituted words.

In our experiments, we only use two words which are nearest to the synonym word as context words. We set the qualifying threshold $\alpha = 0$. We compare our result with the result of [13] (LYL). We also get the result of the method that replaces synonyms according to the synonym dictionary (Primitive).

From Table 1, we can see that the total number of substituted words in Context-Based method is most, because Context-Based method does not use the words that are unsuitable under the judgement of the algorithms. The result of Context-Based method is much better than that of another two methods. In fact, if we set the qualifying threshold $\alpha > 0$, the result will be better.

You can get more information from http://home.ustc.edu.cn/~zxlcc/synonym-substitution/result.html, where the stego-texts of the three methods are available.

Cover text

他的坚定使我<u>疑惑</u>起来，<u>疑惑</u>自己<u>昨夜</u>是否睡错
了<u>地方</u>。我<u>赶紧</u>从床上跳起来，跑到门外去看门
牌号码。可我的门牌<u>此刻</u>却躺在屋内。我又重新
跑进来，在那倒在地上的门上找了门牌。<u>上面</u>写
着——虹桥新村２６号３室我问他："这是不是
你刚才踢倒的门？"

Stego-text

他的坚定使我<u>困惑</u>[11]起来，<u>纳闷</u>[01]自己昨夜
[0]是否睡错了<u>地方</u>[0]。我<u>赶紧</u>[null]从床上跳
起来，跑到门外去看门牌号码。可我的门牌<u>此刻</u>
[null]却躺在屋内。我又重新跑进来，在那倒在
地上的门上找了门牌。<u>上边</u>[1]写着——虹桥新村
２６号３室我问他："这是不是你刚才踢倒的
门？"

Fig. 4. The secrete bit string is "1101001". The bit string in the bracket after a synonym is the bit string that has been hidden here. Some synonyms are reserved because no other words suitable in the context, so the bit string is *null*. However, some synonyms are not replaced but they are used to hide information for they are chosen to hide information.

Table 1. Comparison of three methods

	Primitive	LYL	Context-Based
The total number of substituted words	439	467	579
The total number of unsuitable words	90	102	65
The ER	20.50%	21.84%	11.23%

5   Conclusion and Future Work

We have presents a novel and effective method of synonym-substitution information hiding. We consider the contexts of words to be replaced and propose a proper way to evaluate the context suitability of words in cover texts or stego-texts. In our method, both of the synonym set and the encoding are dynamic, which is brand-new for synonym-substitution information hiding. In our experiment, we use Chinese language to implement our method. The experimental results show that the text seems innocuous to human readers after being hidden information. Our method is high secure in some extent and its security can be adjusted according to requirement.

In the further work, we can improve word segmentation algorithm to make it more effective and our results will be improved at the same time. Moreover, we can change the current simple hiding algorithm for a more efficient one to make use of all the synonyms.

Acknowledgements

This work was supported by the Major Research Plan of the National Natural Science Foundation of China (No. 90818005), the National Natural Science Foundation of China (Nos. 60773032 and 60703071), and the Ph.D. Program Foundation of Ministry of Education of China (No. 20060358014).

References

1. Bennett, K.: Linguistic steganography: Survey, analysis, and robustness concerns for hiding information in text. Purdue University, CERIAS Tech. Report, 13:2004 (2004)
2. Bolshakov, I.A.: A method of linguistic steganography based on collocationally-verified synonymy. In: Fridrich, J. (ed.) IH 2004. LNCS, vol. 3200, pp. 180–191. Springer, Heidelberg (2004)
3. Chapman, M., Davida, G.I., Rennhard, M.: A practical and effective approach to large-scale automated linguistic steganography. In: Davida, G.I., Frankel, Y. (eds.) ISC 2001. LNCS, vol. 2200, pp. 156–165. Springer, Heidelberg (2001)
4. Chiang, Y.L., Chang, L.P., Hsieh, W.T., Chen, W.C.: Natural language watermarking using semantic substitution for chinese text. In: Kalker, T., Cox, I., Ro, Y.M. (eds.) IWDW 2003. LNCS, vol. 2939, pp. 129–140. Springer, Heidelberg (2004)
5. Sougou Labs. SogouR, http://www.sogou.com/labs/dl/r.html
6. Hui, W.: The statistical study of Chinese vocabulary. Date of publication unknown from the online source, http://www.huayuqiao.org/articles/wanghui/wanghui06 (doc. Last checked: 2005-06-20)
7. HIT IR Lab. Chilin-Thesaurus of Chinese Words
8. Low, S.H., Maxemchuk, N.F., Brassil, J.T., O'Gorman, L.: Document marking and identification using both line and wordshifting. In: IEEE INFOCOM 1995. Fourteenth Annual Joint Conference of the IEEE Computer and Communications Societies. Bringing Information to People. Proceedings, pp. 853–860 (1995)
9. Miller, G.A.: WordNet: a lexical database for English. Communications of the ACM 38(11), 39–41 (1995)
10. Topkara, M., Taskiran, C.M., Delp III, E.J., et al.: Natural language watermarking. In: Proc. SPIE, vol. 5681, pp. 441–452 (2005)
11. Wayner, P.: Disappearing cryptography: information hiding: steganography & watermarking. Morgan Kaufmann, San Francisco (2002)
12. Winstein, K.: Lexical steganography through adaptive modulation of the word choice hash
13. Yuling, L., Xingming, S., Can, G., Hong, W.: An Efficient Linguistic Steganography for Chinese Text. In: 2007 IEEE International Conference on Multimedia and Expo, pp. 2094–2097 (2007)
14. Zhang, H.P., Yu, H.K., Xiong, D.Y., Liu, Q.: HHMM-based Chinese lexical analyzer ICTCLAS. In: Proceedings of Second SIGHAN Workshop on Chinese Language Processing, pp. 184–187 (2003)

A Statistical and Iterative Method for Data Hiding in Palette-Based Images

Semin Kim, Wesley De Neve, and Yong Man Ro

Image and Video Systems Lab, Korea Advanced Institute of Science and Technology,
Research Wing R304, 103-6 Munji-dong, Yuseong-gu, Daejeon 305-732, Republic of Korea
{resemin,wesley.deneve}@kaist.ac.kr, ymro@ee.kaist.ac.kr

Abstract. This paper proposes an improved iterative method for data hiding in palette-based images, taking into account the statistics of the data that need to be embedded in an image. In particular, the proposed method considers the distribution of the number of zeroes and ones in the input message, as well as how the message bits are distributed over the colors in the image palette. First, according to the statistics of the input message, the proposed method modifies the pixel indexes and the color palette using an enhanced version of an iterative image pre-processing method, replacing less frequent colors by colors that are close to frequently used colors. In a next step, the actual message bits are embedded into the parity bits of the remaining colors. Finally, the proposed method applies a post-processing step, adjusting particular colors in order to further reduce the amount of image distortion. Experimental results show that the proposed method preserves image quality better than previously proposed techniques for data hiding in palette-based images.

Keywords: data hiding, information hiding, palette-based images, steganography.

1 Introduction

Thanks to the rapid growth of the Internet, people can easily exchange information. During recent years, several methods have been proposed to communicate secret data in a safe way, protecting the data from interception by attackers. One such method consists of hiding secret data in images.

Traditional approaches to embed secret data in images can be categorized into two types: methods operating in the spatial domain and methods functioning in the frequency domain. Methods working in the frequency domain first transform the image data from the spatial domain to the frequency domain, and subsequently embed message bits in the transformed coefficients. They are characterized by a high robustness against attacks (such as blurring and cropping). However, the capacity for data hiding is typically low. Frequency-domain methods have often been used for watermarking [1]-[3]. Methods working in the spatial domain store message bits directly into the pixel data. In general, spatial-domain methods have a higher capacity for data hiding than methods operating in the frequency domain [4]–[11]. However, the robustness of spatial-domain methods against attacks can be considered weak.

A.T.S. Ho et al. (Eds.): IWDW 2009, LNCS 5703, pp. 170–183, 2009.

Methods operating in the spatial domain can also be categorized into two types: on the one hand, methods that are focusing on grayscale images and images with multiple color components, and on the other hand, methods that are targeting palette-based images. A well-known method for data hiding in grayscale images consists of replacing the least significant bits (LSBs) with message bits [4]-[9]. Also, methods using pixel-value differencing were proposed in [10] and [11]. These methods compute the difference between two adjacent pixels, and subsequently embed message bits according to the measured difference.

This paper focuses on improving a data hiding technique for palette-based images. This type of images is still widely used on the Internet (cf. the popularity of the GIF image format). An important technique for data hiding in palette-based images is EZ *Stego* [12]. This method first sorts the palette colors by luminance, and subsequently embeds message bits into the LSB bits of color indexes. The message bits can be retrieved by simply collecting the LSB bits of all indices in the image. Another method for data hiding in palette-based images was proposed by Fridrich [13]. This method takes into account information about the parity bits of colors in the image palette. The parity bit of a particular color can be determined as $(R + G + B)$ mod 2, where R, G, and B respectively represent the colors red, green, and blue. If the parity bit of the color referred to by the current pixel index matches the message bit, then the index and the corresponding color are kept. Otherwise, the index of the current pixel is replaced with the index of the closest color having a parity bit matching the message bit.

Wu *et al.* proposed an iterative method for data hiding in palette-based images, minimizing the root mean square (RMS) error between the original image and the *stego image* [14]. The core idea behind the iterative method is to replace the less frequent colors in the image with the neighboring colors of the frequently used colors. This allows generating more space for secret data, while also reducing the overall image distortion. Further, the iterative method for data hiding is complementary to the EZ *Stego* technique and the method proposed by Fridrich. Indeed, the iterative method can be seen as a pre-processing step, where the actual embedding of the message bits is done using EZ *Stego* or the method of Fridrich.

The authors of the iterative method for data hiding assume that the message to be embedded has an equal number of zeroes and ones. Also, the authors assume that half of the color occurrences need to be replaced during the embedding process. However, in practice, the distribution of the number of zeroes and ones in the message data is often not even. Further, in practice, the assumption that half of the color occurrences need to be replaced when embedding message data often does not hold true. Therefore, in this paper, we propose an improved version of the iterative method for data hiding.

The proposed method takes into account the actual number of "0"s and "1"s in the message data, as well as how the message bits are assigned to the different colors in the image palette. First, according to the statistics of the input message, the proposed method modifies the pixel indexes and the color palette using an enhanced version of Wu's iterative image pre-processing method, replacing less frequent colors by colors that are close to frequently used colors. In a next step, the actual message bits are embedded into the parity bits of the remaining colors using Fridrich's method. Finally, the proposed method applies a post-processing step, adjusting particular colors in order to further reduce the amount of image distortion. We compared the performance of the proposed method with the performance of the method of Fridrich and the method of Wu. Our experimental results show that the proposed method preserves image quality better than previously proposed techniques for data hiding in palette-based images.

The remainder of this paper is organized as follows. Section 2 briefly describes the method of Fridrich and the iterative method of Wu. Our approach is explained in Section 3, while experimental results are provided in Section 4. Finally, our conclusions are presented in Section 5.

2 Related Work

2.1 Fridrich's Method

An important method for hiding secret data in palette-based images was proposed by Fridrich. Fridrich's method embeds message bits into the parity bit of close colors. The message is first converted into a binary stream of length M. Then, a user-defined seed is employed to randomly select M pixels in the image. For each pixel, the set of the closest colors is calculated (this is done by calculating the Euclidean distance between the color of the pixel from each palette entry and sorting the result). The distance between two colors in a palette is defined below [13].

Definition 1. Let i, j be two color entries in palette P with $C_i = (r_i, g_i, b_i)$ and $C_i = (r_j, g_j, b_j)$, then the color distance between C_i and C_j in Euclidean norm is represented as

$$d(i, j) = \sqrt{\left(r_i - r_j\right)^2 + \left(g_i - g_j\right)^2 + \left(b_i - b_j\right)^2}. \qquad (1)$$

Starting with the closest color (note that the closest color is the one corresponding to the same pixel), we proceed to the next closest color till we find a match between the bit to be encoded and the parity of the color. The parity of a color is defined as $R + G + B$ mod 2. To extract the message, M pixels are selected using a pseudo-random number generator (PRNG), taking as input a user-defined seed. The message is simply read by extracting the parity bits from the colors of selected pixels. For more details regarding Fridrich's method, we would like to refer the reader to [13].

2.2 Wu's Method

Wu *et al.* proposed an iterative data hiding method for palette-based images, minimizing the RMS error between the original image and the *stego* image. The method iteratively modifies both the content of the palette and the image data in the original palette-based image. The iterative algorithm relies on a COST and BENEFIT parameter: COST represents the distortion when a less frequent color is removed from the palette, while BENEFIT represents the gain that comes with creating a new color that is close to a frequently referenced color in the palette (i.e., benefit is expressed in terms of space created for embedding message data, as well as in terms of reduced image distortion). After pre-processing, the method of Fridrich can be used to embed message bits into the modified image, generating a *stego* image with less distortion (compared to an approach where for instance only the method of Fridrich is applied). Wu's method can be summarized as follows.

Step 1:   Compute the occurrence frequency of each color in the image.
Step 2:   Compute the closest colors, the first closest colors having different parity bits, and the second closest colors having different parity bits.
Step 3:   Compute the COST and BENEFIT parameters.
Step 4:   If $BENEFIT_{max} > COST_{min}$, then go to Step 5. Otherwise, go to Step 6.
Step 5:   Modify the palette and the indexes, and update the occurrence frequencies. Proceed to Step 2.
Step 6:   Apply Fridrich's method to embed message bits.
Step 7:   Stop.

For more details regarding Wu's method, we would like to refer the reader to [14].

2.3 Matching Problem in Wu's Method

Wu *et al.* assume that the embedded data are encrypted by a traditional encryption algorithm. Also, the authors assume that the resulting random pattern has approximately an equal number of "0"s and "1"s, and that an equal number of "0"s and "1"s is assigned to all colors in the image. However, in practical applications, even if the resulting random pattern has a perfectly equal number of "0"s and "1"s, it is not possible to guarantee that an equal number of "0"s and "1"s is assigned to all colors in the image. Fig. 1 illustrates this observation. Let C be a 4×4 palette-based image and let S be a secret message consisting of 16 bits. Also, suppose that S consists of an equal number of "0"s and "1"s occurring in a random pattern. However, if we compute the number of "0"s and "1"s that are assigned to each color in the palette, then the resulting numbers are not equal to each other, as shown by the third table in Fig. 1.

Color Index	Number of Assigned Secret Bits	
	0	1
0	3	1
1	1	3
2	3	1
3	1	3

Fig. 1. Example illustrating the assignment of "0"s and "1"s to colors in the image palette. The frequency table to the right shows the number of "0" and "1" message bits assigned to each palette color.

3   Proposed Method for Data Hiding

If the frequency of "0"s and "1"s is taken into account during the embedding of message bits, then the quality of the *stego* image can be improved. As such, we propose a new method that considers the frequency of "0"s and "1"s in the message bits. The proposed method enhances Wu's iterative method for data hiding in palette-based images. In particular, we modified a number of definitions and equations used by Wu's method (discussed in Section 3.1 and Section 3.2). After applying Wu's method, Fridrich's method is used to embed the actual message bits (discussed in

Section 3.3). We also introduce an additional post-processing step that further adjusts particular colors in order to minimize the amount of distortion between the original image and the *stego* image (Section 3.4).

3.1 Definitions

For each color in the image palette, the proposed method calculates the number of "0" and "1" message bits that are assigned to that particular color. Then, COST and BENE-FIT parameters are computed using the modified equations originally proposed by Wu. If BENEFIT_{max} is higher than COST_{min}, then the (less important) color associated with COST_{min} is discarded and the color associated with BENEFIT_{max} is created (i.e., a color close to a frequently used color). At this time, the indexes and the frequencies also are updated. The above process continues until BENEFIT_{max} is lower than COST_{min}. Message bits are subsequently embedded by Fridrich's method in the parity bits of the remaining colors. Afterwards, the proposed method applies a post-processing step that adjusts particular colors in order to further reduce the distortion in the *stego* image.

In order to compute the frequency of the "0" and "1" message bits, we need to modify a number of definitions and equations used by Wu's method. Some of these definitions can be found below, while the modified computation of the COST and BENEFIT parameters can be found in Section 3.2. Note that Definition 3, Definition 4, and Definition 5 can also be found in [14]. These definitions are listed below in order to make our paper more self-containing.

Let C be an $M \times N$ palette-based image with a palette size of L, where M and N represent the width and the height of C. Each pixel of C can be written as $C(m, n)$, where $0 \leq m \leq M$ and where $0 \leq n \leq N$. The secret message S consists of a bit pattern taking the form of $s_{0,0}, s_{0,1}, \ldots, s_{M-1,N-1}$. Further, each color in the palette can be written as $P(i)$, where $0 \leq i \leq L - 1$.

Definition 2. The number of "0"s and "1"s assigned to each color in the palette is computed using the equation below. This information is stored into a 256×2 frequency table $N(i, j)$, with $0 \leq i \leq L - 1$ and $0 \leq j \leq 1$ (see the table to the right in Fig. 1).

$$N(i, j) = \sum_{n=0}^{N-1} \sum_{m=0}^{M-1} \delta(m, n),$$

$$\text{where } \delta(m, n) = \begin{cases} 1 & \text{if } C(m, n) = i \text{ and } s_{m,n} = j, \\ 0 & \text{otherwise} \end{cases}$$

(2)

Definition 3. In a palette P, C_x is the closest color to C_y if index x satisfies the following equation:

$$d(x, y) = \text{Min}\{d(n, y) : n = 0, 1, \ldots, L - 1 \text{ and } n \neq y\}. \tag{3}$$

x is said to be the first index referenced by y in P and is denoted as

$$x = R^{\text{first}}(y).$$

Definition 4. In a palette P, C_x is the closest color to C_y that has different parity (given that the parity bit of the color $C_x(r_x, g_x, b_x)$ is $r_x + g_x + b_x \bmod 2$), if index x satisfies the following equation:

$$d(x, y) = \text{Min}\{d(n, y) : n = 0, 1,\ldots, L-1$$
$$\text{and } (r_y + r_n + g_y + g_n + b_y + b_n) \bmod 2 = 1\}. \quad (4)$$

x is said to be the first index referenced by y with different parity in P and is represented as

$$x = R_{DP}^{\text{first}}(y).$$

Definition 5. In a palette P, if C_x is the first closest color to C_y that has different parity, then the second closest color C_z to color C_y is defined as follows:

$$d(z, y) = \text{Min}\{d(n, y) : n = 0, 1,\ldots, L-1\, n \neq x$$
$$\text{and } (r_y + r_n + g_y + g_n + b_y + b_n) \bmod 2 = 1\}. \quad (5)$$

z is said to be the second index referenced by y with different parity in P, and is denoted as

$$z = R_{DP}^{\text{second}}(y).$$

3.2 Computation of COST and BENEFIT

In Wu's method, when computing values for COST and BENEFIT, it is assumed that all colors in the palette are assigned an equal number of "0" and "1" message bits. However, in our proposed method, the actual number of "0"s and "1"s is used when embedding secret bits. Thus, we modified and added some equations to Wu's method. First, the proposed method computes the current parity bit using equation (6).

$$parity = (r_i + g_i + b_i) \bmod 2, \text{ where } r_i, g_i, \text{ and } b_i \text{ constitute a color in } P \quad (6)$$

Next, three COST items are computed using the equations (7), (8), and (9). $\text{COST}_{\text{Fridrich}}(i)$ measures the distortion caused when only using Fridrich's method. $\text{COST}_{\text{Self}}(i)$ represents the replacement distortion when $P(i)$ is discarded. $\text{COST}_{\text{Ref}}(i)$ is the reference distortion. This type of distortion is caused when other indexes in the palette select index i as their closest color. Finally, the total COST(i) of removing a less frequent color from the palette can be computed using equation (10).

$$\text{COST}_{\text{Fridrich}}(i) = N(i, 1 - parity) \times d(i, R_{DP}^{\text{first}}(y)) \quad (7)$$

$$\text{COST}_{\text{self}}(i) = (N(i, 0) + N(i, 1)) \times d(i, R^{\text{first}}(i))$$
$$+ N(i, 1 - parity) \times d(R^{\text{first}}(i), R_{DP}^{\text{first}}(R^{\text{first}}(i))) \quad (8)$$

$$\text{COST}_{\text{ref}}(i) = \sum_{k=0}^{L-1} \delta(i, R_{DP}^{\text{first}}(k)) \times N(k, 1 - parity) \times \left| d(k, R_{DP}^{\text{second}}(k)) - d(k, R_{DP}^{\text{first}}(k)) \right| \quad (9)$$

$$, \text{where } \delta(i, R_{DP}^{\text{first}}(k)) \begin{cases} 1 & \text{if } i = R_{DP}^{\text{first}}(k) \\ 0 & \text{otherwise} \end{cases}$$

$$\Delta\text{COST}(i) = \text{COST}_{\text{self}}(i) + \text{COST}_{\text{ref}}(i) - \text{COST}_{\text{Fridrich}}(i) \quad (10)$$

In Wu's method, for each index i in the palette referencing color r_i, g_i, b_i, a new entry j is created to make a referenced pair. This is done in order to reduce the embedding error to a distance of one. In order to measure the benefit of doing so, we modified the corresponding equation in Wu's method as follows:

$$\text{Benefit}(i) = N(i, 1 - parity) \times \left| d(i, R_{DP}^{\text{first}}(i)) - 1 \right|. \tag{11}$$

3.3 Pre-processing

Our pre-processing algorithm is a modified version of Wu's method, using the definitions and equations presented in the previous sections. Our algorithm can be found below.

Algorithm 1. Pre-processing
Input: a palette-based image C, an index set $E = \varphi$
Output: a pre-processed image C_{pre}
Step 1: Compute the number of "0"s and "1"s assigned to each color in the color palette (i.e., compute $N(i, j)$)
Step 2: Compute COST and BENEFIT
Step 3: For p and $q \notin E$, find the maximum BENEFIT(q) and the minimum ΔCOST(p)
Step 4: If BENEFIT(q) > ΔCOST(p), then go to Step 5. Otherwise, go to Step 8
Step 5: Replace the palette color $P(q)$ with $P(p)$:

$$r_p = r_q$$

$$g_p = g_q$$

$$b_p = \begin{cases} 1 & \text{if } b_q = 0 \\ b_q - 1 & \text{otherwise} \end{cases}$$

Step 6: Update the pixels of image C:

$$parity = (r_q + g_q + b_q) \bmod 2$$

$$\text{if } C(m, n) = p$$

$$\text{then } C(m, n) = R^{\text{first}}(p)$$

else

$$\text{if } s_{m,n} \neq parity$$

$$C(m, n) = p$$

Step 7: Add p and q to E, and update the frequencies:

$$N(R^{\text{first}}(p), 0) = N(R^{\text{first}}(p), 0) + N(p, 0)$$

$$N(R^{\text{first}}(p), 1) = N(R^{\text{first}}(p), 1) + N(p, 1)$$

$$N(p, parity) = 0$$

$$N(p, 1 - parity) = N(q, 1 - parity)$$

$$N(q, 1 - parity) = 0$$

Step 8: Return $C_{\text{pre}} = C$

3.4 Embedding Message Bits

In our proposed method, the message bits are embedded using Fridrich's method. The embedding algorithm is presented below.

Algorithm 2. Embedding message bits
Input: the pre-processed image C_{pre} and a message S
Output: the *stego* image C_s
Step1:   Update the pixels of the pre-processed image C_{pre}
          For n ← 0 to $N-1$
                For m ← 0 to $M-1$
                    $parity = (r_{C(m,n)} + g_{C(m,n)} + b_{C(m,n)}) \bmod 2$
                If $parity \neq s_{m,n}$
                    $$C_{\text{pre}}(m,n) = R_{DP}^{\text{first}}(C_{\text{pre}}(m,n))$$
Step 2:   Return $C_s = C_{\text{pre}}$

3.5 Optimizing the *Stego* Color Palette

Unlike Wu's method, after embedding message bits, we apply a post-processing step that aims at adjusting particular colors in order to further reduce the distortion in the *stego* image C_s. The idea behind the post-processing step is to investigate which colors in the palette P_s of the *stego* image C_s are referenced by colors in the palette P_o of the original image C_o. Indeed, the distance between colors in P_o and P_s is responsible for the distortion between C_o and C_s. As such, by adjusting the value of a particular color in the palette P_s, taking into account the values of corresponding colors in P_o, we can further reduce the distortion between C_o and C_s.

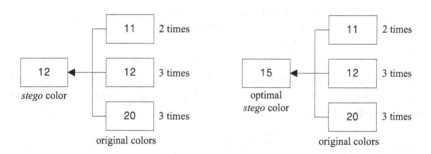

Fig. 2. Example illustrating the smoothing effect of post-processing

Fig. 2 illustrates the aforementioned idea with an example. Suppose that the R or red component of color $P_s(i)$ has a value of 12, and that color $P_s(i)$ is referenced by three other colors in P_o, having values of 11, 12, and 20 for their respective R components. Also, suppose that $P_s(i)$ is respectively referenced two times, three times, and three times. Then, the sum of square errors (SSE) for the R component is $194 = 2 \times (11 - 12)^2 + 3 \times (12 - 12)^2 + 3 \times (20 - 12)^2$. In order to find a better value for the R component of $P_s(i)$, we determine the R components with the lowest and the highest value.

In this example, these values are respectively equal to 11 and 20. As such, let c be a color component value that belongs to the interval $[11, 20]$. Then, we compute a value for c that minimizes the SSE: $2{\times}(11 - c)^2 + 3{\times}(12 - c)^2 + 3{\times}(20 - c)^2$. In this example, 15 is selected as the optimal value for c, resulting in an SSE for the R components that is equal to $134 = 2{\times}(11 - 15)^2 + 3{\times}(12 - 15)^2 + 3{\times}(20 - 15)^2$. A similar strategy can be applied to compute adjusted values for the G and B component of color $P_s(i)$.

In order to compute colors that are suitable for adjustment, for each color in the *stego* palette P_s, we have to determine and count the colors in the original color palette P_o referencing a particular color in the *stego* palette P_s. The following definitions are presented in order to allow computing the colors in P_s that are suitable for smoothing.

Definition 6. Let *PaletteCount(i)* be the number of indexes in the original palette P_o that are referencing the *stego* palette $P_s(i)$, where $0 \leq i \leq L - 1$ and where L represents the number of colors in P_s. Also, let *PaletteIndex(i, j)* be an index in P_o that is referencing $P_s(i)$ and where $0 \leq j \leq PaletteCount(i)$. Using the previous definitions, *PaletteCount(i)* and *PaletteIndex(i, j)* can be computed using Algorithm 3.

Algorithm 3. Computing *PaletteCount(i)* and *PaletteIndex(i, j)*
Input: *stego* image C_s, original image C_O
Output: *PaletteCount(i)* and *PaletteIndex(i, j)*
Step 1: Initialize *PaletteCount(i)*
　　　PaletteCount(i) ← 0
　　　Check(k) ← 0, where $0 \leq k \leq L - 1$
Step 2: Compute *PaletteCount(i)*
　　　For $n \leftarrow 0$ to $N - 1$
　　　　For $m \leftarrow 0$ to $M - 1$
　　　　　If $C_s(m, n) = i$ and $Check(C_o(m, n)) = 0$
　　　　　　PaletteIndex(i, PaletteCount(i)) ← $C_o(m, n)$
　　　　　　PaletteCount(i) ← *PaletteCount(i)* + 1
　　　　　　$Check(C_o(m, n))$ ← 1
Step 3: *PaletteCount(i)* and *PaletteIndex(i, j)*

Definition 7. Let *PaletteFrequency(i, j)* be the number of indexes in P_o that are referencing $P_s(i)$, and with $C_o(m, n) = PaletteIndex(i, j)$. *PaletteFrequency(i, j)* can then be computed by equation (12).

$$PaletteFrequency(i, j) = \sum_{n=0}^{N-1}\sum_{m=0}^{M-1} \delta(m, n), \tag{12}$$

$$\text{where } \delta(m, n) = \begin{cases} 1 & \text{if } C_s(m, n) = i \text{ and } C_o(m, n) = PaletteIndex(i, j) \\ 0 & \text{otherwise} \end{cases}$$

Fig. 3 illustrates the computation of *PaletteCount*, *PaletteIndex*, and *PaletteFrequency*. Suppose that the *stego* image has a size of 4×4 pixels. The values of the pixels denote the colors in the *stego* palette P_s. The *stego* image references the color $P_s(12)$ eight times. Comparing the original image and the *stego* image, we can observe that three colors in the original image are referencing $P_s(12)$. Consequently, *PaletteCount(12)* is equal to three. The three colors are respectively stored into

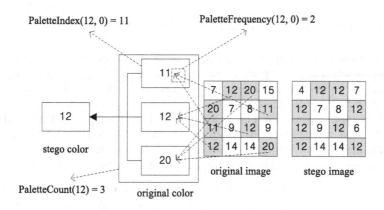

Fig. 3. Computation of *PaletteCount*, *PaletteIndex*, and *PaletteFrequency*

PaletteIndex(12, 0), *PaletteIndex*(12, 1), and *PaletteIndex*(12, 2). The number of times the three colors are used in the original palette is respectively stored into *PaletteFrequency*(12, 0), *PaletteFrequency*(12, 1), and *PaletteFrequency*(12, 2). As shown in Fig. 3, the value of *PaletteIndex*(12, 0) is equal to 11, and the value of *PaletteFrequency*(12, 0) is equal to 2.

Using the previous definitions, the adjusted color values for the *stego* image C_s can be computed by Algorithm 4. Then, we replace corresponding colors in C_s with the color values computed by Algorithm 4, resulting in the creation of an optimized *stego* image C_{os}.

Algorithm 4. Optimizing the *stego* color palette
Input: *stego* image C_s, original image C_0
Output: optimized *stego* image C_{os}
Step 1: Find the lowest and highest color values for each channel
         $low(i) \leftarrow \min\{P_o(PaletteIndex(i, k))$ of C_0 | where $0 \leq k \leq PaletteCount(i)\}$
         $high(i) \leftarrow \max\{P_0(PaletteIndex(i, k))$ of C_0 | where $0 \leq k \leq PaletteCount(i)\}$
Step 2: Compute the minimum distortion for each channel
         $parity_s(i) = (r_{si} + g_{si} + b_{si}) \bmod 2$
         $MinDistortion \leftarrow$ max value
         For $j \leftarrow low(i)$ to $high(i)$
         $sum \leftarrow 0$
         For $a \leftarrow 0$ to $PaletteCount(i)$
            $sum \leftarrow sum + (j - P_o(PaletteIndex(i, a)))^2 \times PaletteFrequency(i, a)$
         If $sum < MinDistortion$
         $OptimalColor \leftarrow j$
         $MinDistortion \leftarrow sum$
Step 3: Check *parity*
         $P_s(i)$ of $C_s \leftarrow OptimalColor$
         If $parity_s(i) \neq (r_i + g_i + b_i) \bmod 2$
         $b_i \leftarrow b_i - 1$
Step 3: Return $C_{os} \leftarrow C_s$

4 Experimental Results and Security Considerations

In this chapter, we compare the proposed method with Fridrich's method and Wu's method in terms of PSNR performance. The three data hiding methods were tested for three cases: equal case, random case, worst case (see further in this section). We used four 512×512 palette-based images: Airplane(F-16), Baboon, Lena, and Pepper. These images are shown in Fig. 4. Random data originating from the so-called "die-hard" test suite were used to create the secret messages [15]. Since the proposed method makes use of all RGB channels, we needed to average the PSNR results for each color channel. As such, the average PSNR was computed using equation (13):

$$R\_C(m,n) = Red\ Color\ in\ Palette(C(m,n))$$

$$G\_C(m,n) = Green\ Color\ in\ Palette(C(m,n))$$

$$B\_C(m,n) = Blue\ Color\ in\ Palette(C(m,n))$$

$$Aver\_MSE = \frac{1}{3 \times MN} \sum_{m=0}^{M-1} \sum_{n=0}^{N-1} \left(\begin{array}{c} \left(R\_C(m,n) - R(m,n)\right)^2 \\ + \left(G\_C(m,n) - G(m,n)\right)^2 \\ + \left(B\_C(m,n) - B(m,n)\right)^2 \end{array} \right)$$

$$PSNR = 10 \times \log_{10} \left(\frac{255^2}{Aver\_MSE} \right) \tag{13}$$

Fig. 4. Test images used (having a resolution of 512×512 pixels)

4.1 Experimental Results

First, pre-processed images were generated using Wu's method and our method. Next, Fridrich's method was applied to the original and pre-processed images in order to embed the secret message bits. Finally, for the images pre-processed using our method and containing message bits embedded using Fridrich's method, post-processing was also done using our method. Table 1 shows the PSNR results for the equal case, in which the message has an equal numbers of zeroes and ones, and where each color in the palette is assigned an equal number of zeroes and ones as well. As shown in Table 1, our proposed method produces PSNR values that are consistently higher than the PSNR values produced by Wu's method.

Table 1. PSNR results for the equal case

Images	Fridrich	Wu	Proposed
Airplane	32.9	41.8	43.2
Baboon	29.1	32.7	34.3
Lena	34.4	39.1	40.4
Pepper	28.6	36.3	37.0

The next case investigated is the random case. For each image, we computed 80 PSNR values using the random data from the "diehard" test suite. These values were subsequently averaged. Table 2 displays the PSNR values for the random case, showing that the proposed method is better than Wu's method in terms of PSNR.

Table 2. PSNR results for the random case

Images	Fridrich	Wu	Proposed
Airplane	32.9	42.1	43.1
Baboon	29.1	32.8	34.3
Lena	34.4	39.1	40.4
Pepper	28.6	35.9	37.0

Table 3 and Table 4 show the special cases in which all message bits have the same value or consist of 1/4 "0"s and 3.4 "1"s. Our proposed method again shows PSNR values that are consistently higher than the values produced by Wu's method.

Table 3. PSNR results for a message containing all zero-valued bits

Images	Fridrich	Wu	Proposed
Airplane	36.6	42.1	47.8
Baboon	31.1	33.0	40.6
Lena	35.1	39.0	45.3
Pepper	34.3	36.2	44.1

Table 4. PSNR results for a message containing 1/4 "0"s and 3/4 "1"s

Images	Fridrich	Wu	Proposed
Airplane	31.9	41.9	43.9
Baboon	28.4	32.9	34.8
Lena	35.4	39.0	40.5
Pepper	27.3	35.9	37.4

4.2 Security Considerations

In our proposed method, the optimized palette of C_{os} has colors that may often be very similar, which is also a weakness of Wu's method. This weakness could be exploited by methods that check whether palette-based images may contain secret messages. As such, in order to improve the security of a *stego* image, a technique is required to hide the existence of secret message data in a palette-based image. Such a technique can be constructed using various approaches. We define a threshold value T that represents the smallest distance between two colors in the original mage C_o. This value can be computed using equation (14):

$$T = \min\{d(i, j) \mid i \neq j\} \tag{14}$$

where $0 \leq i \leq L - 1$, $0 \leq j \leq L - 1$, and with L the number of colors in C_{os}. If the distance between two colors is smaller than T, then the two colors can be adjusted by equation (15):

$$r_i = r_i - r_t, \; g_i = g_i - g_t, \; and \; g_i = g_i - g_t$$
$$r_j = r_j + r_t, \; g_j = g_j + g_t, \; and \; g_j = g_j + g_t \tag{15}$$

where r_t, g_t, and b_t are randomly selected, while satisfying the following constraint:

$$T = \sqrt{\left(\frac{r}{2}\right)_t^2 + \left(\frac{g}{2}\right)_t^2 + \left(\frac{b}{2}\right)_t^2}.$$

5   Conclusions

In this paper, we discussed an input-adaptive and iterative method for data hiding in palette-based images, taking into account the statistics of the data that are to be embedded. In particular, our method considers the number of zeroes and ones in the message, as well as how the message bits are distributed over the colors in the image palette. First, according to the statistics of the input message, the proposed method modifies the pixel indexes and the color palette of an image using an enhanced version of Wu's iterative pre-processing method. Then, the actual message bits are embedded into the image by Fridrich's method. Finally, the proposed method applies a post-processing step, adjusting particular colors in the *stego* image in order to further reduce the amount of image distortion. We compared the PSNR performance of the proposed method with the PSNR performance of Fridrich's method and Wu's method. For all test cases used, the proposed method consistently allowed better reducing the amount of image distortion, compared to Fridrich's method and Wu's iterative method for data hiding in palette-based images.

References

[1] Yu, Y.H., Chang, C.C., Hu, Y.C.: Hiding secret data in images via predictive coding. Pattern Recognition 38, 691–705 (2005)

[2] Ashourian, M., Moallem, P., Ho, Y.S.: A Robust Method for Data Hiding in Color Images. LNCS, vol. 3786, pp. 258–269. Springer, Heidelberg (2005)

[3] Iwata, M., Miyake, K., Shiozaki, A.: Digital Steganography Utilizing Features of JPEG Images. IEICE Trans. Fundamentals E87-A(4), 929–936 (2004)

[4] Katzenbeisser, S., Petitcolas, F.A.P.: Information Hiding Techniques for Steganography and Digital Watermarking. Artech House, Boston (2000)

[5] Bender, W., Gruhl, D., Morimoto, N.: Techniques for data hiding. IBM Systems Journal 35(3), 314–336 (1996)

[6] Chan, C.K., Cheng, L.M.: Hiding data in images by simple substitution. Pattern Recognition 37(3), 489–494 (2004)

[7] Thien, C.C., Lin, J.C.: A simple and high-hiding capacity method for hiding digit-by-digit data in images based on modulus function. Pattern Recognition 36(11), 2875–2881 (2003)

[8] Wang, S.J.: Steganography of capacity required using modulo operator for embedding secret image. Applied Mathematics and Computation 164, 99–116 (2005)

[9] Yang, C.H.: Inverted pattern approach to improve image quality of information hiding by LSB substitution. Pattern Recognition 41, 2674–2683 (2008)

[10] Wu, D.C., Tsai, W.H.: A steganographic method for images by pixel-value differencing. Pattern Recognition 24, 1613–1626 (2003)

[11] Wu, H.C., Wu, N.I., Tsai, C.S., Hwang, M.S.: Image steganographic scheme based on pixel-value differencing and LSB replacement methods. IEE Proc. Vision Image Signal Process 152(5), 611–615 (2005)

[12] Machado, R.: EzStego, Stego Online, http://www.fqa.com/stego_com/

[13] Fridrich, J.: A new steganographic method for palette-based images. In: PICS 1999: Image Processing, Image Quality, Image Capture System Conference, Savannah, Georgia, USA, vol. II, pp. 285–289 (1999)

[14] Wu, M.Y., Ho, Y.K., Lee, J.H.: An iterative method of palette-based image steganography. Pattern Recognition Letters 25, 301–309 (2004)

[15] Diehard Battery of Tests of Randomness, http://www.stat.fsu.edu/pub/diehard/

Estimating the Information Theoretic Optimal Stego Noise

Andrew D. Ker

Oxford University Computing Laboratory, Parks Road, Oxford OX1 3QD, England
adk@comlab.ox.ac.uk

Abstract. We recently developed a new benchmark for steganography, underpinned by the *square root law of capacity*, called *Steganographic Fisher Information* (SFI). It is related to the multiplicative constant for the square root capacity rate and represents a truly information theoretic measure of asymptotic evidence. Given a very large corpus of covers from which the joint histograms can be estimated, an estimator for SFI was derived in [1], and certain aspects of embedding and detection were compared using this benchmark.

In this paper we concentrate on the evidence presented by various spatial-domain embedding operations. We extend the technology of [1] in two ways, to convex combinations of arbitrary so-called *independent embedding functions*. We then apply the new techniques to estimate, in genuine sets of cover images, the spatial-domain stego noise shape which optimally trades evidence – in terms of asymptotic KL divergence – for capacity. The results suggest that smallest embedding changes are optimal for cover images not exhibiting much noise, and also for cover images with significant saturation, but in noisy images it is superior to embed with more stego noise in fewer locations.

1 Introduction

A particular challenge, for the design of better steganographic embedding algorithms, is the lack of universal benchmarks. When a new method is proposed, just about the best that can be done is to test it against leading steganalysis algorithms, and if their detection accuracy is diminished then the steganography method is considered an advance. In practice, new embedding methods usually turn out to be easily broken by a modified detector. The root of the problem is that the metric was really one for novelty, not security.

Information theoretic models of stego systems [2] provide the foundation for an alternative: the Kullback-Leibler (KL) divergence between cover and stego distributions can bound secure embedding capacity, but such distributions are arguably incognisable [3] and certainly infeasible to estimate in full. However, in [1] we argued that the *asymptotic* KL divergence is sufficient, and that this is determined by so-called *Steganographic Fisher Information* (SFI). Furthermore, SFI can indeed be estimated for small groups of pixels, and it was argued that this is highly relevant for practical steganalysis which almost inevitably takes

A.T.S. Ho et al. (Eds.): IWDW 2009, LNCS 5703, pp. 184–198, 2009.

evidence from small groups. Some experimental results, in [1], used the estimator to compare a few simple embedding functions' security, but mainly focused on lessons for steganalysis.

This is a sequel to [1], using SFI to evaluate spatial-domain embedding functions. We extend the SFI estimator to remove some of the limitations in [1] and to *convex combinations* of different embedding functions. Then we apply the new estimator to find the *optimal* combination of certain simple spatial-domain embedding functions. We may have confidence in the true optimality of these combinations because the metric has well-founded information theoretic roots. Our results are not surprising – in noisy covers it is better to embed with larger stego noise – but allow, for the first time, calculation of an optimized embedding function for real-world cover sources.

This paper contains: (Sect. 2) a brief recapitulation of the argument and results of [1], and an explanation of why slightly different notation must be adopted for the present work; (Sect. 3) an extension of the estimator of [1], both to arbitrary embedding functions and to convex combinations thereof; (Sect. 4) some experiments using the SFI estimate to choose optimal combinations of embedding functions, thereby deriving optimally-shaped stego noise for simple variable-base (mod k)-matching embedding; (Sect. 5) a conclusion.

Some notational conventions: random variables and distributions will be denoted by upper-case letters, and realizations of random variables the corresponding lower case. Vectors of either random variables or realizations will be boldface $\boldsymbol{x} = (x_1, \ldots . x_n)$, with n implicit. All logs will be to natural base.

2 Steganographic Fisher Information

We model stego objects as random variables with distribution $P(\lambda)$, where λ indicates the payload size (how the size is measured is important and we will return to this momentarily), so that $P(0)$ is the distribution of covers. KL divergence cannot be increased by processing, and thus we reach the well-known limit on the accuracy of *any* detector for the presence of steganography, in terms of $D_{\mathrm{KL}}(P(0) \| P(\lambda))$ [2]. This justifies using KL divergence as a measure of *evidence*. In [4] it is argued that we should focus on *asymptotic* capacity, as relative payload size tends to zero, because repeated communication must reduce the embedding rate or face eventual certain detection. So in order to make an asymptotic judgement about secure capacity it is sufficient to consider the asymptotic behaviour of $D_{\mathrm{KL}}(P(0) \| P(\lambda))$ as $\lambda \to 0$, and usually (see [5]), this is locally quadratic in λ, i.e.

$$D_{\mathrm{KL}}(P(0) \| P(\lambda)) \sim \tfrac{1}{2} I \lambda^2 + O(\lambda^3).$$

I is called, in this setting, *Steganographic Fisher's Information*. Unlike most other benchmarks, SFI is a single figure which can be used to compare the asymptotic performance of embedding methods or, by considering SFI of projections of the stego object space, the evidence available to various feature sets. It also seems to be easier to estimate SFI than KL divergence directly.

We suppose that stego objects are made up of n *locations* – pixel values, transform coefficients, or suchlike – and that embedding alters some locations. How λ measures payload size is critical to the interpretation of SFI. If we define λ to be the relative number of embedding changes – the proportion of cover locations changed by embedding – then we call it *SFI with respect to change rate* and write I_c. But this does not correctly take account of the cover size n, nor does it correctly compare embedding methods with different *embedding efficiency* – usually defined as the average number of covert payload bits conveyed per embedding change [6], and denoted e – so [1] defined *SFI with respect to payload rate*

$$I_p = \frac{I_c}{ne^2}.$$

It was I_c which was directly estimated in [1], and converted to I_p as above for proper comparison of embedding and detection methods. I_p has the following interpretation, to connect it with the square root law of steganographic capacity [7,8]: if one embeds a small m bit payload into a cover with n locations, using an embedding method with SFI I_p, one expects to produce a KL divergence of approximately $I_p(m^2/n)$ nats of evidence.

Here, we find it more convenient to use a different parameterization for λ. Let us measure payload as the relative number of payload locations used for embedding, whether changed or not. In the case of embedding one bit per symbol, this is exactly the relative payload size, but if embedding k-ary symbols in m locations the total payload transmitted is $m \log_2 k$ bits. This measure is convenient because different embedding methods have different probabilities of changing a location, which is otherwise an algebraic nuisance. We call the SFI thus derived *SFI with respect to location rate* and denote it I_l; it is I_l which will be estimated in Sect. 3. Then I_p can be recovered as

$$I_p = \frac{I_l}{ne'^2}, \tag{1}$$

where e' denotes the number of covert bits transmitted per location used. We will later consider (mod k)-matching embedding, for which $e' = \log_2 k$.

2.1   Estimating SFI

The dimensionality of the space of digital images is outrageously large, so it is not possible to estimate true SFI for entire images. In [1] we advocated the following lower-dimensional model: imagine that an image is made up of many independent pixel *groups*, where the groups are of fixed size such as 1×2 pixels, 2×2, 3×3, etc. Thus we reduce each image to its histogram of groups: in the case of 1×1 groups this is the standard histogram, in the case of 1×2 groups it is the *co-occurrence matrix*, and so on. We argued that, although this certainly destroys information, it is a fact that most leading steganalysis methods do exactly the same: they base their decision on information extracted from histograms, adjacency histograms, or (in the case of JPEG images) 8×8

blocks. (This is no surprise because models of digital media are usually local.) So, if we do likewise, computing SFI for small pixel groups gives us asymptotic bounds on the performance of these steganalysis methods. Indeed, the main focus of [1] was the comparison of evidence in different pixel groups.

Having reduced an image to independently-considered groups of pixels, we obtained the SFI as a function of the group frequencies and embedding function, via a Taylor expansion of KL divergence in change rate, but only for a particular type of embedding operation which changes cover samples to one of a fixed number of alternatives, equiprobably: this is suitable for LSB embedding, but not for more complex examples such as the convex combinations we explore later in this paper. An estimator for SFI was obtained by plugging the empirical group histogram, obtained from a corpus of genuine covers, into the SFI formula. This estimator has limitations – we need a very large corpus from which to estimate the histogram, particularly for larger groups of pixels where the histogram itself has very many bins – but does converge in probability to the true value as the corpus size tends to infinity.

We performed some experiments, mostly with just one corpus of covers, to compare the SFI found in different types of pixel groups in grayscale images. Some brief experiments compared the relative security of LSB replacement and 2LSB replacement (where each pixel carries two bits of payload, at the cost of higher embedding noise), motivated by an observation in [9] that 2LSB embedding was, on a per-payload basis, slightly less sensitively detected by structural detectors. Our experiments in a set of very well-regulated cover images contradicted this hypothesis, but brief experiments on noisier image sets were consistent with it. This raises the questions addressed in this paper: given the options of embedding more payload per change with greater stego noise, or less payload with lower stego noise, which is better? And what of intermediate options?

3   Extending the SFI Estimator to Arbitrary Embedding

With weaker assumptions, but using similar techniques as in [1], we will compute I_l by expanding the KL divergence in location rate. Our model is that the cover is made up of a fixed-length sequence of symbols $(X_1, \ldots, X_n)$, each drawn from finite alphabet $\mathcal{X}$ (with arbitrary distribution: the components X_i need not be independent). The corresponding stego object is denoted $(Y_1, \ldots, Y_n)$. We are concerned with *independent embedding*, where the embedding function chooses whether to locate a payload in each cover symbol independently with probability λ, and if location X_i is chosen then it is altered randomly according to a matrix $B = (b_{ij})$, so that $P(Y_i=y \mid X_i=x) = b_{xy}$ in the chosen locations (otherwise $Y_i = X_i$). For this to be well-defined, B must be stochastic: $\sum_j b_{ij} = 1$ for all i. Most non-adaptive steganography methods are accurately described by this model, including bit replacement, (mod k)-matching, and additive noise.

We also assume that the distribution of cover sequences $P(\boldsymbol{X}=\boldsymbol{x})$ is such that $P(\boldsymbol{X}=\boldsymbol{x}) = 0 \iff P(\boldsymbol{Y}=\boldsymbol{x}) = 0$. This ensures that the KL divergence between cover and stego sequences is finite. And we assume that the embedding is not *perfect*: for at least some $\boldsymbol{x}$, $P(\boldsymbol{X}{=}\boldsymbol{x}) \neq P(\boldsymbol{Y}{=}\boldsymbol{x})$, otherwise SFI is zero and the square root law of capacity does not apply.

We begin with

$$P(\boldsymbol{Y}{=}y \,|\, \boldsymbol{X}{=}x) = (1 - \lambda)\delta_{xy} + \lambda b_{xy}$$

from which we derive

$$
\begin{aligned}
P(\boldsymbol{Y} = \boldsymbol{y}) &= \sum_{\boldsymbol{x} \in \mathcal{X}^n} P(\boldsymbol{Y}{=}\boldsymbol{y} \,|\, \boldsymbol{X}{=}\boldsymbol{x})P(\boldsymbol{X}{=}\boldsymbol{x}) \\
&= (1 - \lambda)^n P(\boldsymbol{X}{=}\boldsymbol{y}) + \lambda(1{-}\lambda)^{n-1}A(\boldsymbol{y}) + \lambda^2(1{-}\lambda)^{n-2}B(\boldsymbol{y}) + O(\lambda^3) \\
&= P(\boldsymbol{X}{=}\boldsymbol{y}) + \lambda\big[-nP(\boldsymbol{X}{=}\boldsymbol{y}) + A(\boldsymbol{y})\big] \\
&\quad + \lambda^2\big[\tfrac{n(n-1)}{2}P(\boldsymbol{X}{=}\boldsymbol{y}) - (n{-}1)A(\boldsymbol{y}) + B(\boldsymbol{y})\big] + O(\lambda^3)
\end{aligned}
$$

where

$$A(\boldsymbol{y}) = \sum_{i=1}^{n} \sum_{u \in \mathcal{X}} P(\boldsymbol{X}{=}\boldsymbol{y}[u/y_i])b_{uy_i}, \tag{2}$$

$$B(\boldsymbol{y}) = \sum_{\substack{i,j=1 \\ i<j}}^{n} \sum_{u,v \in \mathcal{X}} P(\boldsymbol{X}{=}\boldsymbol{y}[u/y_i, v/y_j])b_{uy_i}b_{vy_j},$$

and $\boldsymbol{y}[u/y_i]$ denotes the sequence $(y_1, \ldots, y_{i-1}, u, y_{i+1}, \ldots, y_n)$, $\boldsymbol{y}[u/y_i, v/y_j]$ analogously. $A(\boldsymbol{y})$, respectively $B(\boldsymbol{y})$, represents the probability of observing $\boldsymbol{y}$ in a stego object given exactly one, respectively two, locations used. Now, using $\log(1 + z) = z - \frac{z^2}{2} + O(z^3)$, we can expand the KL divergence:

$$
\begin{aligned}
D_{\mathrm{KL}}(\boldsymbol{X} \,\|\, \boldsymbol{Y}) &= - \sum_{\boldsymbol{y} \in \mathcal{X}^n} P(\boldsymbol{X}{=}\boldsymbol{y}) \log\!\left(\tfrac{P(\boldsymbol{Y}{=}\boldsymbol{y})}{P(\boldsymbol{X}{=}\boldsymbol{y})}\right) \\
&= \lambda\Big[n \sum P(\boldsymbol{X}{=}\boldsymbol{y}) - \sum A(\boldsymbol{y})\Big] \\
&\quad + \lambda^2\Big[\tfrac{n}{2} \sum P(\boldsymbol{X}{=}\boldsymbol{y}) - \sum A(\boldsymbol{y}) - \sum B(\boldsymbol{y}) + \tfrac{1}{2} \sum \tfrac{A(\boldsymbol{y})^2}{P(\boldsymbol{X}{=}\boldsymbol{y})}\Big] + O(\lambda^3) \\
&= \tfrac{\lambda^2}{2}\Big[\sum \tfrac{A(\boldsymbol{y})^2}{P(\boldsymbol{X}{=}\boldsymbol{y})} - n^2\Big] + O(\lambda^3).
\end{aligned}
\tag{3}
$$

For the final step, we use $\sum_{\boldsymbol{y}} P(\boldsymbol{X}{=}\boldsymbol{y}) = 1$, and

$$
\begin{aligned}
\sum_{\boldsymbol{y}} A(\boldsymbol{y}) &= \sum_{\boldsymbol{y}} \sum_{i=1}^{n} \sum_{u} P(\boldsymbol{X}{=}\boldsymbol{y}[u/y_i])b_{uy_i} \\
&= \sum_{i=1}^{n} \sum_{u} \sum_{\substack{\boldsymbol{y} \\ \text{except } y_i}} P(\boldsymbol{X}{=}\boldsymbol{y}[u/y_i]) \sum_{y_i} b_{uy_i} \\
&= \sum_{i=1}^{n} \sum_{\boldsymbol{y}} P(\boldsymbol{X}{=}\boldsymbol{y}) = n,
\end{aligned}
$$

similarly $\sum_{\boldsymbol{y}} B(\boldsymbol{y}) = \frac{n(n-1)}{2}$.

Thus, once we know the embedding efficiency per location for our embedding function e', we combine (3) and (1) to compute the SFI with respect to payload rate

$$I_p = \frac{\displaystyle\sum_{y \in \mathcal{X}^n} \frac{A(y)^2}{P(X=y)} - n^2}{n e_i'^2} \qquad (4)$$

as a function of the true frequencies of each symbol group in $\mathcal{X}^n$ (note that $A(y)$ is a linear combination of such frequencies). As in [1], we can estimate this quantity from a large corpus of cover objects, simply by plugging the empirical frequencies into (4). We must omit any terms where $P(X=y) = 0$, i.e. groups of n which never occur in the corpus, but if sufficiently large then this should happen never or rarely, and the missing terms should be negligible.

Considering digital images, for $n \geq 4$ it can be challenging even to compute the empirical histogram, because there are potentially 256^n histogram bins and our image corpus will consist of at least 10^{10} groups of pixels, so computer memory is soon exhausted. We solved this problem in [1], using red-black trees to create overlapping histogram chunks, shuffle-sorting the chunks, making a second pass through the histogram to adjoin the value of $A(x)$ to each $P(X=x)$, and finally summing the ratio $A(x)^2/P(X=x)$. We will not go into the detail here because the same techniques can be used, although the second stage is somewhat slower because $A(x)$ depends on potentially the entire histogram, but for the experiments we report here on (mod k)-matching it is still the case that only portions local to x need be examined. With our available computing resources (a cluster of 20 dual-core machines) it is feasible to estimate I_p for pixel groups of size up to about 9, but our image libraries are only large enough adequately to sample the histograms for $n \leq 6$.

3.1   Convex Combinations of Embedding Functions

As well as extending the estimator to arbitrary independent embedding, we will consider the combination of embedding functions. Suppose that the steganographer and recipient share k different embedding options each of which matches the hypotheses of the previous section. Let us denote the change probabilities for embedding method i by the matrix B_i, and the embedding efficiency per location as e_i'. They can construct a hybrid embedding method which, on a per-symbol basis, picks embedding method i with fixed probability π_i such that $\sum_i \pi_i = 1$ (the correspondence between symbols and embedding functions can be generated from their shared secret key). This convex combination has overall embedding efficiency per location $\sum \pi_i e_i'$ and its change matrix is $B = \sum_i \pi_i B_i$, and this allows us to vary continuously between the different options. In particular, we can vary the tradeoff between higher stego noise and higher embedding rates. Here, we examine the SFI of such a combination, and later will demonstrate that combinations can indeed provide better transmission rates, at comparable levels of risk, than any of the individual options alone.

Recall that SFI is defined in terms of $A(y)$, the probability of observing y in a stego group with exactly one embedding location used. Observe in (2) that $A(y)$

is a linear function of B. Therefore if embedding method i has corresponding function $A_i(\boldsymbol{y})$, for the convex combination we have $A(\boldsymbol{y}) = \sum_i \pi_i A_i(\boldsymbol{y})$.

Therefore, the SFI with respect to payload rate is given by

$$I_p = \frac{\sum_{\boldsymbol{y} \in \mathcal{X}^n} \dfrac{(\sum_i \pi_i A_i(\boldsymbol{y}))^2}{P(\boldsymbol{X}=\boldsymbol{y})} - n^2}{n(\sum_i \pi_i e_i')^2} = \frac{\sum_{i,j} c_{ij} \pi_i \pi_j - n^2}{n(\sum_i \pi_i e_i')^2} \tag{5}$$

where

$$c_{ij} = \sum_{\boldsymbol{y} \in \mathcal{X}^n} \frac{A_i(\boldsymbol{y}) A_j(\boldsymbol{y})}{P(\boldsymbol{X}=\boldsymbol{y})}. \tag{6}$$

The optimal convex combination is the probability vector π which minimizes (5): lower SFI means lower KL divergence – less accurate detection – or alternatively a greater secure capacity for equivalent risk. SFI is inversely proportional to the square of the "root rate", the asymptotic constant in secure capacity $r\sqrt{n}$ where n denotes cover size [7,8].

Equation (5) is a ratio between two quadratic forms and there does not seem to be an easy analytic form for the minimum, but the optimization can be performed very efficiently by numerical methods because all c_{ij} and e_i' must be positive, and I_l must also positive, so both $\sum_{i,j} c_{ij} \pi_i \pi_j$ and $(\sum_i \pi_i e_i')^{-1}$ are positive and convex in $\boldsymbol{\pi}$. So (5) can be written as the product of positive convex functions, and therefore is a convex function. Thus, given c_{ij} and e_i', numerical optimization of (5), subject to $\sum \pi_i = 1$, can be performed using standard convex programming methods.

4   Results

We now apply the extended estimator to find the optimal convex combinations of some simple embedding functions. Of course, the results depend on the cover source: there is no universally-optimal embedding function, and we expect different results for different sources. We will restrict our attention to spatial-domain **(mod k)-matching** embedding in grayscale digital images: each selected pixel conveys one k-ary symbol ($\log_2 k$ bits) of information in its remainder (mod k), and the embedding function alters the cover pixel to the nearest value with the correct remainder. We consider only odd $k = 2j + 1$, so that the embedding is symmetric. Most of the time, this results in additive noise uniformly distributed from the range $-j, \ldots, j$, but for pixels near to saturation at 0 or 255 the absolute value of the noise could reach $2j$. (Although it was LSB and 2LSB embedding which was briefly considered in [1], here we have excluded bit replacement and (mod $2k$)-matching embedding because it has been demonstrated, time and again, that asymmetrical embedding causes additional weaknesses [9,10].)

The case of (mod 3)-matching is also sometimes known as ± 1 embedding, and $k = 5, 7$ can be called $\pm 2, \pm 3$ embedding, respectively. However, we eschew this terminology for two reasons. First, ±1 more accurately describes the effect of LSB *replacement* while (mod 3)-matching can cause stego noise of ±2 when applied to saturated pixels. Second, there is some confusion in the literature as to exactly what shape stego noise ±2 denotes: uniform distortions of ±2, or including ±1 noise as well, or some other shape? Our preferred terminology is *ternary embedding* for (mod 3)-matching, *quinary embedding* for (mod 5)-matching, *septenary embedding* for (mod 7)-matching, and so on.

Our experiments will involve four sets of cover images, chosen for different levels of noise, to test the hypothesis that greater stego noise is optimal for noisy covers.

Set A: 2121 grayscale images taken with a single digital camera, all sized approximately 4.7 Mpixels. The histograms were computed from the images in each of four orientations, to boost the evidential base, so that a total of just over $4 \cdot 10^{10}$ pixel groups were used to estimate the joint histograms. The images had never been subject to JPEG compression, but as part of their conversion from RAW format were substantially denoised; also, images with significant areas of saturation were removed. This set of images is extremely well-behaved and it is the main corpus used for the results in [1].

Set B: 1040 grayscale images taken with a mixture of digital cameras, all sized approximately 1.5 Mpixels, for a total of over $6 \cdot 10^9$ pixel groups. Again, the images were never JPEG compressed and had been denoised in conversion from RAW format, but the denoising is not as aggressive as in set A.

Set C: 3200 grayscale images taken with the same camera as set A (in fact, the parent RAW files for set A are a subset of these), for a total of about $1.5 \cdot 10^{10}$ pixel groups. In conversion from RAW format, all optional denoising was disabled, so these images are visibly more noisy than those of sets A or B. Note that, unlike in set A, images with saturated areas (typically over-exposed highlights) have not been excluded.

Set D: 10000 grayscale decompressed JPEG images from a photo library CD, all sized about 900 × 600. Like set A, the images were re-used in each of four orientations, for a total of about $2 \cdot 10^{10}$ pixel groups. These images are certainly noisy, but feature quantization noise rather than sensor noise.

In each case we use the technology of [1] to estimate the histograms of individual pixels, and pixel groups of shapes 1 × 2, 1 × 3, 1 × 4, 2 × 2 (we will not follow [1] to even larger group sizes, to be sure that the histograms are not undersampled). For ternary, quinary, and (sometimes) septenary embedding, the coefficients c_{ij} (6) are computed and (5) minimized numerically to find the optimal combination.

4.1 Combination of Ternary and Quinary Embedding

We begin by considering combinations of ternary and quinary embedding: this allows stego noise up to level ± 2 (except at saturated cover locations). The embedding matrices are

$$B_1 = \begin{pmatrix} \frac{1}{3} & \frac{1}{3} & \frac{1}{3} & 0 & 0 & 0 & \cdots & 0 & 0 & 0 & 0 & 0 & 0 \\ \frac{1}{3} & \frac{1}{3} & \frac{1}{3} & 0 & 0 & 0 & \cdots & 0 & 0 & 0 & 0 & 0 & 0 \\ 0 & \frac{1}{3} & \frac{1}{3} & \frac{1}{3} & 0 & 0 & \cdots & 0 & 0 & 0 & 0 & 0 & 0 \\ 0 & 0 & \frac{1}{3} & \frac{1}{3} & \frac{1}{3} & 0 & \cdots & 0 & 0 & 0 & 0 & 0 & 0 \\ & & & & & & \ddots & & & & & & \\ 0 & 0 & 0 & 0 & 0 & 0 & \cdots & 0 & \frac{1}{3} & \frac{1}{3} & \frac{1}{3} & 0 & 0 \\ 0 & 0 & 0 & 0 & 0 & 0 & \cdots & 0 & 0 & \frac{1}{3} & \frac{1}{3} & \frac{1}{3} & 0 \\ 0 & 0 & 0 & 0 & 0 & 0 & \cdots & 0 & 0 & 0 & \frac{1}{3} & \frac{1}{3} & \frac{1}{3} \\ 0 & 0 & 0 & 0 & 0 & 0 & \cdots & 0 & 0 & 0 & \frac{1}{3} & \frac{1}{3} & \frac{1}{3} \end{pmatrix}$$

$$B_2 = \begin{pmatrix} \frac{1}{5} & \frac{1}{5} & \frac{1}{5} & \frac{1}{5} & \frac{1}{5} & 0 & \cdots & 0 & 0 & 0 & 0 & 0 & 0 \\ \frac{1}{5} & \frac{1}{5} & \frac{1}{5} & \frac{1}{5} & \frac{1}{5} & 0 & \cdots & 0 & 0 & 0 & 0 & 0 & 0 \\ \frac{1}{5} & \frac{1}{5} & \frac{1}{5} & \frac{1}{5} & \frac{1}{5} & 0 & \cdots & 0 & 0 & 0 & 0 & 0 & 0 \\ 0 & \frac{1}{5} & \frac{1}{5} & \frac{1}{5} & \frac{1}{5} & \frac{1}{5} & \cdots & 0 & 0 & 0 & 0 & 0 & 0 \\ & & & & & & \ddots & & & & & & \\ 0 & 0 & 0 & 0 & 0 & 0 & \cdots & \frac{1}{5} & \frac{1}{5} & \frac{1}{5} & \frac{1}{5} & \frac{1}{5} & 0 \\ 0 & 0 & 0 & 0 & 0 & 0 & \cdots & 0 & \frac{1}{5} & \frac{1}{5} & \frac{1}{5} & \frac{1}{5} & \frac{1}{5} \\ 0 & 0 & 0 & 0 & 0 & 0 & \cdots & 0 & \frac{1}{5} & \frac{1}{5} & \frac{1}{5} & \frac{1}{5} & \frac{1}{5} \\ 0 & 0 & 0 & 0 & 0 & 0 & \cdots & 0 & \frac{1}{5} & \frac{1}{5} & \frac{1}{5} & \frac{1}{5} & \frac{1}{5} \end{pmatrix}$$

and we consider the mixture $B = \pi_1 B_1 + \pi_2 B_2$, where $\pi_1 + \pi_2 = 1$, i.e. the embedding will use proportion π_1 ternary symbols and π_2 quinary symbols. (The embedder and recipient may need to transcode the payload via a variable-base format, but we will not concern ourselves with the technicalities of doing so.)

Figure 1 shows the results of SFI estimation, considering both 1×2 and 1×4 blocks (most other shapes were similar; we shall see shortly that 1×1 groups are anomalous). For each image set we first plot the SFI with respect to location rate I_l, as a function of π_2: for most image sets, the graphs are rising, indicating that the greater the proportion of quinary symbols, the greater the evidence of payload. This is no surprise, because quinary embedding causes greater stego noise. (However, the slight decrease for small values of π_2 in set B, and the significant U-shape in set D, means that it can be less suspicious to embed with more noise, a paradox which probably deserves further study.)

The second column in Fig. 1 shows how the embedding efficiency e', measured in bits per payload location, increases as we increase the proportion of quinary symbols (which carry more bits each). This linear function is the same for all image sets, of course. The final column computes the trade-off between these functions, showing SFI per payload: for a given (small) payload, this indicates how much evidence is available to the opponent for each combination of ternary and quinary embedding. For cover image set A, which contains little noise, pure ternary embedding is best. For set B, which is more noisy, the optimum is about 1/3 ternary and 2/3 quinary embedding: the exact minimum does depend on whether we look at 1×2 or 1×4 pixel groups. For set C, which is very noisy, we might have expected an even higher proportion of quinary embedding, but in fact observe the opposite: we attribute this to the saturated areas in some of the images, because the embedding noise is exaggerated for saturated pixels. For set D, which has quantization noise, the optimum is almost pure quinary embedding for 1×2 pixel groups, but nearer to an even mixture for 1×4 groups.

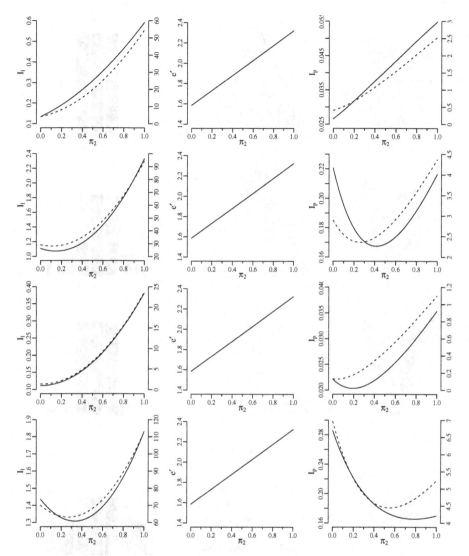

Fig. 1. SFI for varying combinations of ternary and quinary embedding. In each case the x-axis represents the proportion of quinary locations, so that leftmost points correspond to entirely ternary and rightmost entirely quinary embedding. Left graphs, SFI with respect to location rate I_l; middle, embedding efficiency e'; right, SFI with respect to payload I_p. For SFI measures, the solid line is derived from pixel pairs and is denoted on the left axis, the dotted line from 1×4 groups on the right axis. From top to bottom, image sets A to D.

4.2   Optimal Embedding Noise Up to ±3

We can extend the analysis further, but we will go only as far as mixtures of ternary, quinary, and septenary embedding. Such a mixture is specified by

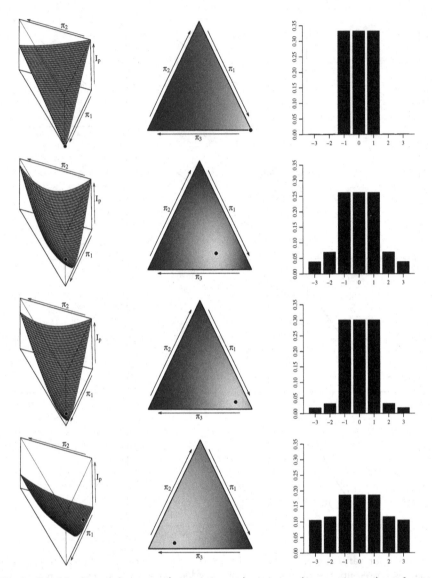

Fig. 2. Combinations of ternary (proportion π_1), quinary (proportion π_2), and septenary (proportion π_3) embedding. Left, a three-dimensional depiction of the surface I_p, as it depends on π_1 and π_2. Centre, the same information in two dimensions, where lighter shading indicates lower SFI. In both cases the location of the minimum is marked. Right, the shape of optimal stego noise, at the SFI minimum. In all cases 1×2 pixel groups have been used to estimate SFI. From top to bottom, image sets A to D.

respective probabilities π_1, π_2, π_3. The matrix for septenary embedding, B_3, is analogous to B_1 and B_2 in Subsect. 4.1 and the same procedure, albeit more computationally expensive, can be used to determine the coefficients c_{ij} for $1 \leq i,j \leq 3$. With two degrees of freedom, the result can be visualised as

Table 1. The optimal mixture of ternary (π_1), quinary (π_2), and septenary (π_3) embedding, for each image set and considering joint histograms from five different pixel group shapes. The final column indicates the relative SFI for the optimum, compared with pure ternary embedding.

Image Set	Group Size	π_1	π_2	π_3	$\frac{I_p(\pi_1,\pi_2,\pi_3)}{I_p(1,0,0)}$
A	1×1	1.000	0.000	0.000	1.000
A	1×2	1.000	0.000	0.000	1.000
A	1×3	1.000	0.000	0.000	1.000
A	1×4	1.000	0.000	0.000	1.000
A	2×2	1.000	0.000	0.000	1.000
B	1×1	0.130	0.115	0.755	0.346
B	1×2	0.576	0.152	0.272	0.684
B	1×3	0.684	0.099	0.216	0.707
B	1×4	0.718	0.119	0.163	0.749
B	2×2	0.707	0.157	0.136	0.792
C	1×1	0.434	0.071	0.495	0.576
C	1×2	0.805	0.067	0.128	0.883
C	1×3	0.921	0.041	0.038	0.944
C	1×4	0.961	0.024	0.015	0.971
C	2×2	1.000	0.000	0.000	1.000
D	1×1	0.000	0.987	0.013	0.181
D	1×2	0.210	0.053	0.736	0.444
D	1×3	0.187	0.346	0.467	0.437
D	1×4	0.408	0.228	0.364	0.522
D	2×2	0.487	0.291	0.222	0.594

either a three-dimensional surface, or a two-dimensional "heatmap"; both types of graphic are displayed in Fig. 2, for SFI in pixel pairs.

In the first row, corresponding to image set A, the I_p surface slants sharply down towards the point where $\pi_1 = 1$: pure ternary embedding is clearly optimal. For image set B the surface is curved, and at the optimum a majority of ternary embedding is mixed with smaller amounts of both quinary and septenary symbols. Set C is similar but with a lower proportion of quinary and septenary symbols, despite the extra noise in the covers: again, we attribute this to saturation. Finally, for set D the mixture features a majority of septenary embedding: these covers are so noisy that, had we extended our analysis to nonary embedding and beyond, it is likely that we would have seen even larger stego noise in the mixture as well. (Of course, there exist other detectors for steganography in previously JPEG-compressed images, which make use of the 8×8 JPEG block structure and can be extremely sensitive [11]. Such detectors are not accounted for in our analysis, which only covers smaller pixel groups.)

To examine other pixel groups, we show how the location of the minimum depends on the group size and shape in Tab. 1. Although there is certainly variation with pixel group size, most of the results are broadly similar as the group size changes. Further examination (not included here) shows that the surface slopes rather gently near the optimum so that the optimum for, say, 1×2 pixel groups is quite close to optimal for the others. The notable exceptions are the results for 1×1 groups, which have markedly different optima in all cases except set A. There is no contradiction here, and it underlines an important lesson: optimizing embedding to best preserve image histograms is far from optimal when inter-pixel dependencies are considered. This is a familiar pattern from steganalysis literature.

How much difference does it make, to use the optimal combination of embedding functions instead of, say, pure ternary embedding? The final column of Tab. 1 shows the ratio between the SFI I_p of optimally-mixed and pure ternary embedding. For example, looking at set B, we see that the SFI is about 30% lower with a suitable mixture of embedding functions, and this means that a payload of about $(1/0.7)^{1/2} \approx 1.2$ times as large can be carried with equivalent asymptotic KL divergence.

5   Conclusions

Steganographic Fisher Information can be estimated from a large corpus of covers, and we have demonstrated that the technology of SFI estimation can be used to examine convex combinations of embedding functions. It is then simple to find the optimal embedding function combination for a given cover source, though of course the results vary depending on the nature of the cover objects. Optimal SFI is a true information theoretic optimality, indicating lowest asymptotic KL divergence and therefore best security again detection. Except in the image set subject to heavy denoising, combinations of ternary, quinary, and septenary embedding outperform any single embedding method.

Of course, true optimality happens if the embedding method is perfect (preserves the distribution of covers exactly), in which case the SFI is zero and secret payload can be conveyed at a linear, not square root, rate. But constructing such an embedding is difficult and requires perfect knowledge of the cover source, whereas a pseudorandom combination between ternary, quinary, etc, embedding is very simple to implement at both embedder and receiver (though we have not considered the difficulty of transcoding the payload into variable-base). We could take this work further, into quasi-adaptive embedding where the rows of the matrix B are not regular, and find the optimal matrix, but again this asks a lot of the sender and recipient. For the same reasons, we have assumed that the embedder does make use of source coding [6], which usually requires solving systems of linear equations. We must acknowledge that the presence of source coding can complicate the analysis, and may lead to different conclusions.

This paper has a number of limitations. First, our model for covers is of independent groups of pixels. We have argued that, although the model is certainly not accurate for digital images, it mirrors the practice of steganalysis methods which inevitably base their decisions on joint histograms of pixel groups (although the group size might be larger than we are able to examine here), and therefore SFI is properly connected with the security against such detectors. One difficulty in selecting an optimal embedding combination is that the optimum depends on the size of the pixel groups examined: there is no easy solution to this conundrum, but it makes sense to base decisions on the largest possible group size, since the evidence in large groups subsumes that in small groups. Thankfully, roughly similar results seem to appear in most pixel group shapes with the notable exception of 1×1 groups. We re-iterate this observation: selecting an embedding method to preserve, as best as possible, the histogram of image pixels is a poor strategy. This lesson has been observed a number of times in the literature, with steganography methods touted as "perfect" because of histogram preservation soon falling to steganalysis which considers pairs of pixels or other higher-order information. Nonetheless, a number of authors continue to advance ad hoc embedding methods to preserve cover histograms.

We note that we make the implicit assumption, when using SFI as a benchmark, that the enemy steganalyst has complete knowledge of both the cover source and the chosen embedding function. This is in keeping with Kerckhoffs' Principle but could be argued too pessimistic. However, any other scenario is difficult to examine using KL divergence.

Our experiments were carried out using four sets of cover images, which happened to be conveniently available to the author. In some respects the choice was unfortunate, because they differ in both noise levels and saturation, and there appears to be some interplay between these factors regarding the optimal embedding function. In future work we could examine systematically the effects of noise, saturation, prior JPEG compression, or other macroscopic properties, in isolation, though the computational demands may be considerable.

We should contrast SFI, as an information theoretic measure of asymptotic evidence, with Maximum Mean Discrepancy (MMD), applied to information hiding in [12]. MMD is now quite well-studied though its application in information hiding is still in infancy, and there are efficient estimators allowing MMD to be computed for large-dimensional feature sets. However, although there is some connection between MMD and the performance of kernelized support vector machines, it is not a truly entropic measure and we know no analogue of the connection between KL divergence and maximum hypothesis test performance. Nonetheless, it would be interesting to derive an estimator for asymptotic MMD, and repeat these experiments with that metric to see whether similar results arise.

We may also contrast the SFI estimator here and in [1] with an independent approach to the same problem by Filler & Fridrich [13]. Their estimator differs significantly, modelling the images as a Markov chain with a parameterised transition matrix. They also examine convex combinations, but only of LSB replacement and ternary embedding. Hopefully there will be a confluence of ideas in the area of Fisher Information estimation, which only recently emerged as the true asymptotic benchmark for steganography [4].

Acknowledgements

The author is a Royal Society University Research Fellow. Thanks are due to Tomáš Filler and Rainer Böhme, who both suggested that SFI can be used to optimize embedding functions.

References

1. Ker, A.: Estimating Steganographic Fisher Information in real images. In: Proc. 11th Information Hiding Workshop (to appear, 2009)
2. Cachin, C.: An information-theoretic model for steganography. Information and Computation 192(1), 41–56 (2004)
3. Böhme, R.: Improved Statistical Steganalysis using Models of Heterogeneous Cover Signals. PhD thesis, Technische Universität Dresden (2008)
4. Ker, A.: The ultimate steganalysis benchmark? In: Proc. 9th ACM Workshop on Multimedia and Security, pp. 141–148 (2007)
5. Kullback, S.: Information Theory and Statistics. Dover, New York (1968)
6. Fridrich, J., Soukal, D.: Matrix embedding for large payloads. IEEE Transactions on Information Forensics and Security 1(3), 390–394 (2006)
7. Ker, A., Pevný, T., Kodovský, J., Fridrich, J.: The square root law of steganographic capacity. In: Proc. 10th ACM Workshop on Multimedia and Security, pp. 107–116 (2008)
8. Filler, T., Ker, A., Fridrich, J.: The square root law of steganographic capacity for Markov covers. In: Proc. SPIE. Media Forensics and Security XI, vol. 7254, pp. 801–811 (2009)
9. Ker, A.: Steganalysis of embedding in two least significant bits. IEEE Transactions on Information Forensics and Security 2(1), 46–54 (2007)
10. Ker, A.: A general framework for the structural steganalysis of LSB replacement. In: Barni, M., Herrera-Joancomartí, J., Katzenbeisser, S., Pérez-González, F. (eds.) IH 2005. LNCS, vol. 3727, pp. 296–311. Springer, Heidelberg (2005)
11. Böhme, R.: Weighted stego-image steganalysis for JPEG covers. In: Solanki, K., Sullivan, K., Madhow, U. (eds.) IH 2008. LNCS, vol. 5284, pp. 178–194. Springer, Heidelberg (2008)
12. Pevný, T., Fridrich, J.: Benchmarking for steganography. In: Solanki, K., Sullivan, K., Madhow, U. (eds.) IH 2008. LNCS, vol. 5284, pp. 251–267. Springer, Heidelberg (2008)
13. Filler, T., Fridrich, J.: Fisher Information determines capacity of ϵ-secure steganography. In: Proc. 11th Information Hiding Workshop (to appear, 2009)

Multi-class Blind Steganalysis Based on Image Run-Length Analysis

Jing Dong, Wei Wang, and Tieniu Tan

National Laboratory of Pattern Recognition, Institute of Automation,
Chinese Academy of Sciences, P.O. Box 2728, Beijing

Abstract. In this paper, we investigate our previously developed run-length based features for multi-class blind image steganalysis. We construct a Support Vector Machine classifier for multi-class recognition for both spatial and frequency domain based steganographic algorithms. We also study hierarchical and non-hierarchical multi-class schemes and compare their performance for steganalysis. Experimental results demonstrate that our approach is able to classify different stego images according to their embedding techniques based on appropriate supervised learning. It is also shown that the hierarchical scheme performs better in our experiments.

Keywords: blind steganalysis, multi-class, image steganalysis, run-length analysis.

1 Introduction

Steganography aims at concealing information communication by means of cover medium transmission. It has been a hot topic in information security and has drawn much attention in recent years. On the other hand, steganalysis, which is the counter-technology of steganography aiming at detecting the very presence of secret message in cover medium, serves the urgent needs of network security to block covert communication with illegal or undesirable information.

Various steganalysis techniques have been proposed for tackling steganographic algorithms. These techniques can be roughly ascribed to two categories. One is called specific steganalysis[1] [2] [3] and the other is named blind steganalysis [4] [5] [6] [7] [8]. Specific steganalysis is targeted at a particular known steganographic algorithm, whereas blind steganalysis can detect the presence of hidden data without knowing its embedding method. Since there are a variety of steganographic methods and it is often difficult to assume the knowledge about which embedding methods have been used in real application, blind steganalysis is gaining more attention from researchers.

Usually, blind steganalyzer only makes a binary decision regarding the presence of the hidden message while specific steganalyzer could provide more information with better reliability and accuracy such as estimating the message length or even retrievaling the message content for a targeted steganographic

A.T.S. Ho et al. (Eds.): IWDW 2009, LNCS 5703, pp. 199–210, 2009.

algorithm. The disadvantage of specific steganalysis is that it can not automatically recognize which embedding algorithm is used and can not cope with new algorithms. On the other hand, blind steganalysis has good generality to detect various embedding algorithms, even an unknown algorithm. In a sense, specific steganalysis and blind steganalysis complement each other under a certain framework, that is, multi-class steganalysis. The goal of multi-class steganalysis is to construct a steganalyzer for images capable of not only discriminating cover and stego images but also recognizing the steganographic algorithms used. One can then use this recognition result and apply a specific steganalyzer for further analysis. Also, the detection accuracy of blind steganalyzer could be verified by multi-class steganalyzer by providing a probability of known and unknown steganographic algorithms. Fig.1 shows such an image steganalysis framework by combining the blind, specific and multi-class steganalysis.

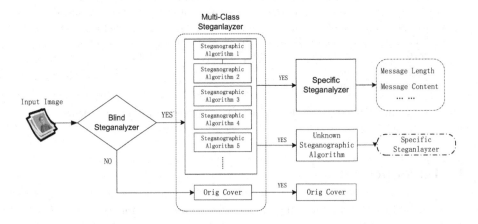

Fig. 1. Framework of hierarchical image steganalysis

The goal of this paper is to investigate multi-class blind image steganalysis according to our proposed run-length based image features [8]. The remainder of this paper is organized as follows. In the next section, we briefly introduce previous work in multi-class steganalysis. Section 3 describes the proposed approach. In Section 4, we carry out some experiments and analyze the performance of both binary detection and multi-class detection results of our proposed scheme. Discussions and conclusions are presented in Section 5.

2   Related Work

There are only a few methods about multi-class steganalysis in the open literature. For JPEG image steganalysis, Pevny and Fridrich [9] used their previously proposed calibrated DCT features for both binary classification and multi-classification for four steganographic techniques (namely F5, OutGuess,

MB [10] and JP Hide&Seek). They presented a multi-class steganalyzer using a set of SVM classifiers and studied the parameters for each binary classifier construction. Although there are some misclassifications in their experimental results, their proposed scheme is capable of not only detecting stego images but also classifying them to appropriate stego algorithms at a high embedding rate. In their subsequent work [11], they made a more detailed analysis on multi-classification of JPEG images for their single and double JPEG compression estimation. Also, they combined their DCT-based steganlaysis features with the Markov features proposed by Shi et al.[12] and used these features for multi-classification by a SVM-based multi-classifier. The experimental results showed the detection accuracy of the proposed method is very good although it suffers from an increased false positive rate. Though their study is only focused on JPEG format and also a preliminary study for multi-class steganalysis, they identified several principles for designing the multi-class steganalysis schemes.

Later in the work of [13], Savoldi and Gubian considered a blind multi-class steganalysis system using wavelet statistics. This multi-class system is based on high-order wavelet statistics to recognize four popular frequency domain steganographic algorithms, namely F5 [14], OutGuess[15], JP Hide&Seek [16] and Steghide [17]. In their work, they used soft-margin Support Vector Machine (SVM) with Gaussian kernel and used a 360-D feature vector extracted from image decomposition coefficients based on separable quadrature mirror filters (QMFs). Another work is presented by Wang et al. in [18]. In this paper, they explored two hieratical multi-class steganalysis schemes to recognize popular stego algorithms used for JPEG images and compared the two schemes in terms of accuracy, reliability and computational cost.

The multi-class steganalysis methods mentioned above are all designed for JPEG format and constrained to a few trained popular embedding algorithms. However, since there are many steganographic techniques for BMP images and new embedding algorithms continue to be developed, a more general multi-class steganalysis scheme is highly desirable. This is the main motivation of this paper. In the next section, we will describe our proposed multi-class steganalyzer based on image run-length statistics and a support vector machine.

3   Proposed Approach for Multi-class Steganalysis

There are two key issues in designing a proper multi-class steganalyzer. The first is the extraction of effective features which should be sensitive to various image steganographic techniques. These features should be capable of distinguishing cover and stego images as well as capable of distinguishing different stego techniques. In other words, the ideal distribution of the steganalysis feature space should be something as shown in Fig.2. In this feature space, not only the cover images and stego images can be distinguished, but also the stego images generated by different steganographic schemes form separable clusters. Such image steganalysis features are considered as very effective and powerful for multi-class steganalysis.

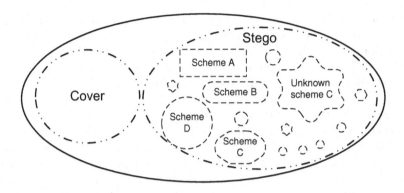

Fig. 2. Illustration of ideal steganalysis feature space

In order to detect different steganographic techniques as much as possible, the proposed feature set should have a good generality. Here, we apply the previously proposed effective run-length based statistic moments as basic features [8]. These features are extracted from image run-length histograms and are very sensitive to data embedding both in spatial domain and in frequency domain.

3.1   Run-Length Based Statistic Moments

Our previously proposed features for steganlaysis in [8] are inspired by the concept of run-length, which was proposed for bitmap-file coding and compression standard in fax transmissions [19]. Normally, a run is defined as a string of consecutive pixels which have the same gray level intensity along a specific linear orientation θ (typically $0°$, $45°$, $90°$, and $135°$). The length of the run is defined as the number of repeating pixels in this run. For a given image, a run-length matrix $p(i, j)$ is considered as the number of runs with pixels of gray level i and run length j. For a run-length matrix $p_\theta(i, j)$, let M be the number of gray levels and N be the maximum run length. We can define the image run-length histogram (RLH) as a vector:

$$H_\theta(j) = \sum_{i=1}^{M} p_\theta(i, j), \qquad 1 < j < N \qquad (1)$$

This vector represents the sum distribution of the number of runs with run length j in the corresponding image. In order to reduce the effect of different image sizes, the RLH may be normalized by the maximal value of the histogram. Short runs (with smaller j) refer to those runs with a small number of pixels, while long runs (with larger j) imply those runs with a large number of pixels.

For most steganographic algorithms, once a bit of message is embedded in the cover image, one or several corresponding image pixel would be changed slightly to "hide" data, regardless the change is directly caused in spatial domain or reflected by frequency domain, since the data hidden in DCT domain also cause changes of image intensity in the spatial domain. Such attributes of data embedding process would directly affect the local intensity variations of the image. As the image intensity has been changed, the original distribution of image run-length would be altered. That is to say, the original consecutive pixels with identical gray level in a run may turn to different shorter runs. More specifically, the tendency of long runs turning into shorter runs could be due to data embedding. Based on this observation, we proposed a 36-D feature vector for image steganalysis in [8]. Here in this paper, we also take a similar feature set which is slightly modified and improved from the previous feature set. Instead of calculating the Characteristic Function of image run-length histograms, we directly extracted the higher order moments of image run-length histograms according to the following function as our features for multi-class steganalysis. $H(\theta, i)$ represents different run-length histograms along direction θ. More details about the feature extraction may be found in [8].

$$M_n = \sum_{j=1}^{L/2} j^n |H_{(\theta,i)}(j)| / \sum_{j=1}^{L/2} |H_{(\theta,i)}(j)|. \quad 1 < j < N, \quad i = 1, 2, 3; \quad (2)$$

The run-length based feature set has shown very effective performance for blind image steganlaysis not only for detection accuracy but also for computational complexity [8]. Besides, these features are also considered as sensitive features for blind image steganalysis of BMP images as well as JPEG format. Although these features are extracted from spatial domain, they represent the changes in inter-pixel correlation which either steganographic process would cause. Hence we also apply these features for the following multi-class steganalysis schemes. It should be pointed out that the focus of this paper is on the study of the feasibility of run-length analysis for multi-class steganalysis, not on the design of new features per se.

3.2   Multi-class Detector

Another key issue for multi-class steganalysis is the design of proper classifiers. SVM (Support Vector Machine) [20] is a useful technique that provides state-of-the-art performance in a wide variety of application domains. The goal of SVM is to produce a model which could predict class labels of data instances in the testing set which is given only the sensitive features. It performs pattern recognition for two-class problems by determining the separating hyperplane that has maximum distance to the closest points of the training samples. The key issues for SVM is to decide which kernel function is to be used (such as linear, polynomial, radial basis function (RBF), sigmoid etc.) and find the best parameters to construct the training model. Since SVM has shown its optimal and efficient classification performance for large scale learning, it was considered as a popular choice for steganalysis classifiers [4] [12] [21] [22]. For its powerful classification performance and its popularity in use of pattern recognition, we also consider our multi-class detector based on SVM. In this paper the SVM method used is Lib-SVM with a RBF kernel [20].

SVM was originally designed for binary classification. How to effectively ex-tend it for multi-class classification is still under research. There are two ways for multi-class classification. One is a hierarchical multi-classifier which can be realized by constructing and combining several binary classifiers. The other is to consider all data in one optimization formulation and perform multi-classification by one classifier (for example, by regression methods). The formulation to solve multi-class SVM problems depends on the number of classes and is very sensitive to the training data, especially sensitive to outliers. In general it is computation-ally more expensive to solve a multi-class problem than a binary problem with the same number of data. A comparison between several SVM based multi-classification schemes are described in [23]. Generally speaking, there are three strategies called one-against-all, one-against-one, and directed acyclic graph SVM (DAGSVM) which are designed for solving several binary classification problems for multi-classification. However, for limited data sets, it is believed and suggested in [23] that the one-against-one method is more suitable for prac-tical use than the other methods for multi-classification based on binary classi-fiers. In this method, training is accomplished by comparing one class against each of the other classes. The goal is to train the multi-class rule based on the majority voting strategy.

As a preliminary study for multi-class steganalysis, we test our proposed run-length based statistics using the "one-against-one" strategy under the following two slightly different schemes.

- Scheme One (S1):We construct the multi-class SVM to classify cover images from different stego images at one time. In this scheme, we simply apply the SVM based multi-classifier to categorize cover images as well as stego images generated by n different embedding algorithms. The number of binary classifiers we used in this scheme is $n(n+1)/2$ (n is the number of known categories of steganographic techniques).

- Scheme Two (S2): In this scheme, we firstly apply a binary SVM as for blind steganalysis to classify cover and stego images. Then we construct a multi-class SVM to classify stego images generated by different known steganographic algorithms. As the primary objective for image steganalysis is to detect whether there are data hidden in cover images, detecting the stego image from clean cover image is the top priority in designing the classifier. Hence, we use a binary SVM classifier for all samples to classify cover and stego images at the first step. Afterwards, we apply a multi-classifier for all labeled stego samples by using a trained multi-classification model to classify images generated by known steganographic algorithms.The number of binary classifiers we used in this scheme is $n(n-1)/2+1$ (n is the number of known categories of of steganographic techniques).

The above two schemes can be considered as one scheme if the feature space of cover and different categories of stego images are well separated from each other. By comparing S1 with S2, the only difference is the number of classes. Since we believe that the distance between cover images and all stego images in the feature space should be larger than the distance among stego algorithms in the feature space (as shown in Figure 2), the optimization problem for SVM to get the best classification curve would be more efficient in S2 than in S1 as the number of classes in S2 is smaller hence the number of binary classifiers used in S2 is fewer. We will investigate this issue in the following experiments in details.

4 Experimental Results

4.1 Database Description

For our experiments, we use the 1338 images downloaded from the Uncompressed Color Image Database (UCID) constructed by Schaefer and Stich [24], available at [25]. All the images in UCID are high resolution uncompressed digital TIFF files with size of 512×384 or 384×512. This database contains various images captured from indoor and outdoor, daylight and night, event and natural scenes, and provides a real and challenging environment for a steganalysis problem. All images were then converted to gray level BMP or JPEG at 75% quality for our experiments. Then, we generated five sets of stego images using the following embedding algorithms. In order to test the effectiveness of our proposed scheme, we only embedded a small amount of messages in our experiments. The embedding rate is below 0.3bpp for BMP images and around 25% message for JPEG image embedding.

#1: Generic LSB embedding method at 0.3bpp;
#2: Non-blind spread spectrum (SS)method [26] at 0.15bpp;
#3: F5 method [14] at 0.25bpnc;
#4: Model Based steganographic method [10] at 0.25bpnc;
#5: Yet Another Steganographic Scheme (YASS) embedding method [27] at 0.15bpnc.

We totally get 6 classes (including cover images) for multi-classification in our experiments. The total number of images we used in our experiments is $1338 \times 6 = 8028$. For each experiment, we divided the images into training and testing sets. There is no overlap between training and testing sets for each experiment. The feature set used in all experiments is obtained from image gray level run-length histograms as mentioned in Section 3.1.

4.2 Detection Performance

Experiments for 2-class Steganalysis. In this experiment, we intend to test the effectiveness of the run-length based features for JPEG image steganalysis as well as for BMP images. We first design some tests for blind steganalysis. Blind means the classifier is able to classify all images into two classes: cover and stego images. The SVM was trained using multiplicative grid search. We compared the detection results for distinguishing the cover images from stego images embedded with each and all specific embedding algorithms in Table 1.

For the first five rows, the training sets and testing sets equally contain 669 cover images and 669 stego images corresponding to the algorithm index. The column of 'Cover'and 'Stego' represents the number of images that were classified as cover or stego under each test. The detection accuracy is calculated by counting the number of images whose cover images are correctly classified as cover and stego images are classified as stego at a 3.5% false positives rate. From this table, we see that the run-length based statistic features are effective to all listed embedding algorithms regardless embedding is performed in the spatial or the frequency domain.

Also, in the last row of this table, which we call 'Cover vs. Mixed' mode, the cover images are the same as in previous tests but the stego images consist of randomly selected 1338 images from all stego image sets (1338×5) and are also divided equally into training and testing sets. Hence, in this mode, it is a real blind mode for image steganalysis. We can also see a good detection performance.

Table 1. Blind detection results for trained binary SVM using run-length based features

Embedding Algorithm	Cover	Stego	Accuracy
Cover vs. LSB	608 (90.88%)	641 (95.81%)	93.35%
Cover vs. SS	583 (87.14%)	610 (94.18%)	89.16%
Cover vs. F5	658 (98.36%)	648 (96.86%)	97.61%
Cover vs. MB1	652 (97.46%)	642 (95.96%)	96.71%
Cover vs. YASS	648 (96.86%)	640 (95.67%)	96.26%
Cover vs. Mixed	628 (93.87%)	646 (96.56%)	95.2167%

As shown in Table 1, the run-length based features are able to classify cover images from all stego images generated by either spatial or frequency based embedding algorithms. The trained SVM classifier also serves as a good classifier for universal image steganlysis.

Experiments for Multi-class Steganalysis. Here for multi-class steganalysis, we designed our experiments for two schemes. One was to consider the cover images as one of the classes for multi-classification while the other excluded the cover image as one candidate class since we can perform a blind classification at the first step. The blind detection has already shown a high confidence for cover and stego image classification results in our previous test shown in Table 1. Hence, in order to investigate the multi-class problem among stego images as well as cover and different stego images, here we just design the following two schemes by considering cover as or not as one of the classes for multi-classifier construction.

The training and testing process for multi-classifier is the same for both schemes though the total number of classes is 6 in S1 while 5 in S2 (the cover images are not considered as one class in S2). However, the binary classifier needed for the two schemes are quite different. In S1, we totally need to construct $5(5 + 1)/2 = 15$ classifiers while in S2 we need $5(5 - 1)/2 + 1 = 11$. If we

Table 2. Confusion matrix of the detection accuracy for Scheme One (cover included as one class)

Embedding	Classified as					
Algorithm	Cover	LSB	SS	F5	MB1	YASS
Cover	493(73.7%)	30(4.5%)	126(18.8%)	0(0%)	9(1.3%)	11(1.6%))
LSB	33(4.9%)	609(91%)	20(3%)	0(0%)	6(0.9%)	1(0.1%)
SS	56(8.4%)	6(0.9%)	588(87.9%)	3(0.5%)	13(2%)	3(0.5%)
F5	0(0%)	3(0.5%)	3(0.5%)	571(85.35%)	80(12%)	12(1.8%)
MB1	1(0.1%)	19(2.8%)	126(18.8%)	74(11%)	514(76.8%)	58(8.6%)
YASS	5(0.7%)	2(0.3%)	25(3.7%)	21(3.1%	105(15.7%)	511(76.4%)

Table 3. Confusion matrix of the detection accuracy for Scheme Two (cover excluded as one class)

Embedding	Classified as				
Algorithm	LSB	SS	F5	MB1	YASS
LSB	639(95.5%)	28(4.2%)	2(0.3%)	0(0%)	0(0%)
SS	19(2.8%)	638(95.4%)	14 (2.1%)	8(1.2%)	3(0.5%)
F5	0(0%)	5(0.7%)	586(87.6%)	52(7.8%)	26(3.9%)
MB1	1(0.1%)	23(3.4%)	68 (10.1%)	508(75.9%)	70(10.4%)
YASS	2(0.3%)	24(3.6%)	15(2.2%)	111(16.6%)	517(77.3%)

have more classes for classification, the difference of constructing binary classifier for the two schemes would be larger, which would result in higher complexity for both training and testing.

Table 2 shows the confusion matrix of the detection accuracy for S1 (consider the cover images as one class) and Table 3 presents the confusion matrix of the detection accuracy for S2 (without considering the cover images as one class). Both schemes are based on the SVM multi-classifier with default thresholds and the detection results are obtained at a 3.5% false positive rate. Each class in our experiment contains 669 samples for both training and testing. In S1, we classified totally six classes while in S2 we classified five classes in total. Each row in the tables presents the classification results by counting the number of images being labeled. For example, in Row 2, for the testing sets which consist of 669 stego images generated using the LSB embedding method, there are 33 images classified as cover class and 609 images labeled as LSB class. From Table 2 and Table 3, we can see the two multi-classification schemes based on the SVM classifier achieved good detection performance although there are some misclassifications. Moreover, for S2, the classification accuracy is better than S1 since we excluded the cover images as a class to classifier. We think that the better classification results in S2 may be due to the distribution of steganalysis feature space.

Moreover, we also notice that the multi-classification schemes have a good classification performance on embedding methods for spatial domain as well as frequency domain. Besides, even there are some misclassifications between classes, the misclassification rate between frequency domain methods and spatial domain methods is much lower than that among frequency domain methods or spatial domain methods. That is to say, both of our schemes have a promising detection performance on classifying at least two different categories of stego images (say spatial domain and frequency domain).

5   Conclusion

In this paper, we have investigated a novel multi-class system for image steganlaysis. We have designed two multi-class schemes which are capable of not only detecting stego images but also classifying them into appropriate stego techniques based on the modification of our previously developed features of image run-length statistics. We have constructed a Support Vector Machine (SVM) based multi-classifier to recognize various steganographic algorithms designed for spatial domain as well as for frequency domain. We have also described an evaluation of the generality of the proposed features which are extracted from image run-length histograms for universal image steganalysis. Our feature set shows good distinguishability for JPEG images as well as for BMP images. In order to decrease the computing complexity for multi-classifier construction, we have designed a hierarchical multi-classifier in which the classification of cover and all stego images is performed in advance. Then, the multi-class recognition is done among stego algorithms. Our experimental results have demonstrated that this scheme is more reliable and efficient than the other one which considers the cover and all stego algorithms in one pool for multi-class recognition. Since our approach is able to classify stego images to their embedding techniques under proper supervised learning, we will consider to combine different effective features sets (such as the Markov feature in [12], DCT based feature [22], etc.) for multi-class recognition in order to get more reliable and powerful detection performance in the future.

Acknowledgments. The work presented in this paper was supported by Nature Science Foundation of China (Grant No.60603011).

References

1. Fridrich, J., Goljan, M., Hogea, D., Soukal, D.: Quantitative steganalysis: Estimating secret message length. ACM Multimedia Systems Journal. Special issue on Multimedia Securrity 9(3), 288–302 (2003)
2. Dumitrescu, S., Xiaolin, W., Wang, Z.: Detection of lsb steganography via sample pair analysis. In: Petitcolas, F.A.P. (ed.) IH 2002. LNCS, vol. 2578, pp. 355–374. Springer, Heidelberg (2003)
3. Ker, A.: Resampling and the detection of lsb matching in colour bitmaps. In: Proceedings of SPIE Electronic Imaging, Security, Steganography and Watermarking of Multimedia Contents VII (2005)

4. Farid, H., Siwei, L.: Detecting hidden messages using higher-order statistics and support vector machines. In: Petitcolas, F.A.P. (ed.) IH 2002. LNCS, vol. 2578, pp. 340–354. Springer, Heidelberg (2003)
5. Fridrich, J., Goljan, M.: Practical steganalysis of digital images — state of the art. In: Security and Watermarking of Multimedia Contents. SPIE, vol. 4675, pp. 1–13 (2002)
6. Harmsen, J.J., Pearlman, W.A.: Steganalysis of additive noise modelable information hiding. In: Proc. SPIE, Security, Steganography, and Watermarking of Multimedia Contents VI, pp. 131–142 (2003)
7. Shi, Y.Q., et al.: Image steganalysis based on moments of characteristic functions using wavelet decomposition, prediction-error image, andneural network. In: ICME 2005, pp. 269–272 (2005)
8. Dong, J., Tan, T.N.: Blind image steganalysis based on run-length histogram analysis. In: 15th International Conference of Image Processing 2008 (ICIP 2008), pp. 2064–2067 (2008)
9. Pevny, T., Fridrich, J.: Towards muti-class steganalyzer for jpeg images. In: Barni, M., Cox, I., Kalker, T., Kim, H.-J. (eds.) IWDW 2005. LNCS, vol. 3710, pp. 39–53. Springer, Heidelberg (2005)
10. Salle, P.: Model based steganography. In: Kalker, T., Cox, I., Ro, Y.M. (eds.) IWDW 2003. LNCS, vol. 2939, pp. 154–167. Springer, Heidelberg (2004)
11. Pevny, T., Fridrich, J.: Determining the stego algorithm for jpeg images. In: Proceddings of Information Security, vol. 153, pp. 77–86 (2006)
12. Shi, Y.Q., Chen, C., Chen, W.: A markov process based approach to effective attacking jpeg steganography. In: Camenisch, J.L., Collberg, C.S., Johnson, N.F., Sallee, P. (eds.) IH 2006. LNCS, vol. 4437, pp. 249–264. Springer, Heidelberg (2006)
13. Savoldi, A., Gubian, P.: A markov process based approach to effective attacking jpeg steganography. In: Proceedings of the Third International Conference on International Information Hiding and Multimedia Signal Processing, vol. 2, pp. 93–96 (2007)
14. Westfeld, A.: High capacity despite better steganalysis(f5). In: Moskowitz, I.S. (ed.) IH 2001. LNCS, vol. 2137, pp. 289–302. Springer, Heidelberg (2001)
15. Provos, N.: Software, http://www.outguess.org
16. Latham, A.: Software, http://linux01.gwdg.de/~alatham/stego.html
17. Hetzl, S.: Software, http://steghide.sourceforge.net
18. Wang, P., Liu, F., Wang, G., Sun, Y., Gong, D.: Multi-class steganalysis for jpeg stego algorithms. In: Proceedings of the 15th International Conference on Image Processing, pp. 2076–2079 (2008)
19. Galloway, M.M.: Texture analysis using gray level run lengths. In: Cornput. Graph. Image Proc., vol. 4, pp. 171–179 (1975)
20. Cortes, C., Vapnik, V.: Support-vector network. In: Proceedings of SPIE Electronic Imageing, Security, Steganography and Watermarking of Nultimedia Contents VII, vol. 20, pp. 273–297 (1995)
21. Kharrazi, M., Sencar, H.T., Memon, N.: Benchmarking steganographic and steganalysis techniques. In: Proceedings of SPIE Electronic Imaging, Security, Steganography and Watermarking of Multimedia Contents VII (2005)
22. Fridrich, J.: Feature-based steganalysis for JPEG images and its implications for future design of steganographic schemes. In: Fridrich, J. (ed.) IH 2004. LNCS, vol. 3200, pp. 67–81. Springer, Heidelberg (2004)

23. Hsu, C., Kin, C.: A comparision of methods for multi-class support vector machines. Technical Report, Department of Computer Science and Information Engineering, National Taiwan University,
    http://citeseer.ist.psu.edu/hsu01comparision.html
24. Schaefer, G., Stich, M.: Ucid - an uncompressed colour image database. In: Proc. SPIE, Storage and Retrieval Methods and Applications for Multimedia, pp. 472–480 (2004)
25. Database, U.C.I.: http://vision.cs.aston.ac.uk/datasets/ucid/ucid.html
26. Cox, I.J., Kilian, J., Leighton, F.T., Shamoon, T.: Secure spread spectru, watermarking for multimedia. IEEE Trans.Image Process. 6(12), 1673–1687 (1997)
27. Solanki, K., Sarkar, A., Manjunath, B.S.: YASS: Yet another steganographic scheme that resists blind steganalysis. In: Furon, T., Cayre, F., Doërr, G., Bas, P. (eds.) IH 2007. LNCS, vol. 4567, pp. 16–31. Springer, Heidelberg (2008)

Local Patch Blind Spectral Watermarking Method for 3D Graphics

Ming Luo[1], Kai Wang[2], Adrian G. Bors[1], and Guillaume Lavoué[2]

[1] Department of Computer Science, University of York, York YO10 5DD, UK
[2] Université de Lyon, CNRS, INSA-Lyon, LIRIS, UMR5205, F-69621, France

Abstract. In this paper, we propose a blind watermarking algorithm for 3D meshes. The proposed algorithm embeds spectral domain constraints in segmented patches. After aligning the 3D object using volumetric moments, the patches are extracted using a robust segmentation method which ensures that they have equal areas. One bit is then embedded in each patch by enforcing specific constraints in the distribution of its spectral coefficients by using Principal Component Analysis (PCA). A series of experiments and comparisons with state-of-the-art in 3D graphics watermarking have been performed; they show that the proposed scheme provides a very good robustness against both geometry and connectivity attacks, while introducing a low level of dis torsion.

1 Introduction

During the last decade, various 3-D watermarking methods have been developed. Watermarking algorithms can be classified as being in the spatial domain [1,2,3] or the frequency domain [4,5]; they also can be classified as relying on local constraints [1] or as being statistical in nature [2,3]. A survey of existing 3D watermarking algorithms was carried out in [6]. Most of the robust blind methods developed so far are in the spatial domain. Methods in the frequency domain include those using wavelets as well as those using spectral decomposition [4,5]. The spectral transform consists of the eigen-decomposition of the Laplacian matrix for a given mesh. The resulting spectral coefficients consist of a unique representation. The spectral decomposition is reversible and the graphical object mesh can be entirely reconstructed from the spectral coefficients. Spectral methods were firstly introduced in graphics by Karni and Gotsman [7] for the purpose of mesh compression. Ohbuchi [4] proposed a non-blind method to embed watermarks in the spectral domain based on Karni's analysis. Lavoué et al. [8] and Cotting et al. [9] improved Ohbuchi's algorithm for subdivision mesh and point sampling distributions, respectively. All these algorithms use the low-frequency coefficients as the message carrier and are non-blind. Blind and robust spectral domain watermarking have been proposed in [5,10,11]. The algorithm described in [10] has a very low bit-capacity while a set of specific constraints are enforced onto the distributions of spectral coefficients for information embedding in [11].

The advantage of the spectral domain mainly relies in the fact that the watermark information is spread over the object in such a way that it is very hard to

A.T.S. Ho et al. (Eds.): IWDW 2009, LNCS 5703, pp. 211–226, 2009.
© Springer-Verlag Berlin Heidelberg 2009

determine its presence, thus increasing its security. Usually, existing spectral domain algorithms are not that robust as the spatial domain algorithms. Another disadvantage for spectral domain watermarking is the computational complexity required for the eigendecomposition of the Laplacian matrix corresponding to meshes containing a large number of vertices, which is actually the case with most graphical objects [11].

In this paper we propose a novel robust blind spectral watermarking method which consists of applying spectral decomposition locally, in well defined patches of the graphical object. The proposed methodology has the following stages. Firstly, the object is robustly aligned along the principal axis calculated using the analytic volumetric moments. Then the object is decomposed into patches (*i.e.* connected spatial regions) of equal areas defined along the first and second principal axes. Lastly, the spectral analysis is performed on each patch and the spectral coefficients are extracted. The watermark insertion is done by embedding specific constraints in the distribution of the spectral coefficients. The constraints are enforced by an embedding function which relies on the principal component analysis (PCA) of the spectral coefficients. The distribution of the spectral coefficients is constrained to a sphere when embedding a bit of zero and to a squashed ellipsoid when embedding a bit of one. The reminder of this paper is organized as follows. In Section 2 we describe the volumetric method for aligning the 3D graphical object, while in Section 3 we describe the algorithm for generating the equal area patches. In Section 4 the spectral graph theory is briefly introduced, while Section 5 gives the details of the proposed watermark insertion and extraction based on spectral coefficients analysis. The experimental results and comparison with the state of the art are provided in Section 6, while the conclusions of this study are drawn in Section 7.

2   Robust Object Alignment

We propose to use a robust alignment scheme called volume moment alignment which was proposed in [12]. The volume moments of a 3D object are defined as:

$$M_{pqr} = \int \int \int x^p y^q z^r \rho(x, y, z) d_x d_y d_z \tag{1}$$

where p, q, r are moment orders, and $\rho(x, y, z)$ is the volume indicator function (it equals to 1 if (x, y, z) is inside the mesh and to 0 otherwise). For a triangular face $f_i = \{\mathbf{v}_{i1}, \mathbf{v}_{i2}, \mathbf{v}_{i3}\} = \{(x_{i1}, y_{i1}, z_{i1}), (x_{i2}, y_{i2}, z_{i2}), (x_{i3}, y_{i3}, z_{i3})\}$ on a mesh object, the moments are defined as :

$$M_{000}^{f_i} = \frac{1}{6}|x_{i1}y_{i2}z_{i3} - x_{i1}y_{i3}z_{i2} - y_{i1}x_{i2}z_{i3} + y_{i1}x_{i3}z_{i2} + z_{i1}x_{i2}y_{i3} - z_{i1}x_{i3}y_{i2}|$$
$$M_{100}^{f_i} = \frac{1}{4}(x_{i1} + x_{i2} + x_{i3}) \cdot M_{000}^{f_i}$$
$$M_{200}^{f_i} = \frac{1}{10}(x_{i1}^2 + x_{i2}^2 + x_{i3}^2 + x_{i1}x_{i2} + x_{i1}x_{i3} + x_{i2}x_{i3}) \cdot M_{000}^{f_i}$$
$$M_{110}^{f_i} = \frac{1}{10}(x_{i1}y_{i1} + x_{i2}y_{i2} + x_{i3}y_{i3} + \frac{x_{i1}y_{i2} + x_{i1}y_{i3} + x_{i2}y_{i1} + x_{i2}y_{i3} + x_{i3}y_{i1} + x_{i3}y_{i2}}{2}) \cdot M_{000}^{f_i} \tag{2}$$

In fact it corresponds to the moment of the tetrahedron linking this face to the coordinate system origin. The global moments of a mesh are obtained by summing these elementary moments over all the facets (with the appropriate contribution sign). The complete set of explicit volume moment functions can be found in [13]. The object centre is defined as $\mu = (M_{100}/M_{000}, M_{010}/M_{000}, M_{001}/M_{000})$, and the 3×3 matrix of the second order moments of the 3D object is constructed as:

$$\mathbf{\Psi} = \begin{pmatrix} M_{200} & M_{110} & M_{101} \\ M_{110} & M_{020} & M_{011} \\ M_{101} & M_{011} & M_{002} \end{pmatrix} \tag{3}$$

The principal axes of the object are the eigenvectors obtained by applying eigen-decomposition to the covariance matrix $\mathbf{\Psi}$:

$$\mathbf{\Psi} = \mathbf{W}^T \mathbf{\Delta} \mathbf{W} \tag{4}$$

where $\mathbf{\Delta} = \{\delta_1, \delta_2, \delta_3\}$ is the diagonal matrix containing the eigenvalues assuming $\delta_1 > \delta_2 > \delta_3$ and $\mathbf{W} = [\mathbf{w}_1 \ \mathbf{w}_2 \ \mathbf{w}_3]^T$ is the matrix whose columns are the eigenvectors of $\mathbf{\Psi}$. The eigenvalues $\{\delta_1, \delta_2, \delta_3\}$ characterize the extension of the object along its principal axes whose directions are defined by the corresponding eigenvectors. In order to define a unique alignment, we propose two constraints. Firstly, the three axes must conform the right hand rule such that the direction of the third axis will be well defined as the cross product of the first two. Furthermore, the valid alignment satisfies the condition that the third order moments M_{300} and M_{030} of the rotated object are positive. By following these constraints the principal axis alignment is unique [12] and much more robust than the alignment produced by the moments using the vertex coordinates.

3   Object Patch Generation

Watermarking in spectral domain owns a series of advantages including increased watermark key security and good watermark imperceptibility. However, as shown in [11], the application of blind spectral watermarking is limited to rather small graphical objects due to the high computational complexity requirements of spectral decomposition for large meshes. In this study in order to apply the spectral algorithm to a large 3D object, we propose to split it into segments (*i.e.* spatial regions) so that each segment is used for carrying one bit of message. Note that one segment can be used to embed more than one bit, but in this paper, we only embed one bit for the sake of aiming for the highest robustness. After aligning the graphical object as described in Section 2 we trim away, for the further watermark embedding usage, the ends of the object as defined along its principal axis $\mathbf{w}_1$. In this way we increase the watermark security. Then the trimmed object is split into layers which are defined by planes perpendicular to $\mathbf{w}_2$, the second principal axis. Finally, the vertices and triangles in each layer are divided into connected patches of equal area in a direction along the first principal axis $\mathbf{w}_1$. All these steps are detailed below.

Let us consider x_{max} and x_{min} the maximum and minimum value along the first principal axis $\mathbf{w}_1$. $\alpha \in [0, 1/2]$ is a value generated by the secret key which is used for trimming the extremities of the object. We define two boundary values

x_1 and x_2 on the line, passing through the object center and in the direction of the first principal axis $\mathbf{w}_1$, such that:

$$\begin{cases} B_{min} = (x_{max} - x_{min}) \cdot \alpha + x_{min} \\ B_{max} = (x_{max} - x_{min}) \cdot (1 - \alpha) + x_{min} \end{cases} \tag{5}$$

All the vertices whose x coordinates are outside this range, i.e., $v_x < B_{min}$ and $v_x > B_{max}$ will be excluded from the watermark embedding process. Let us define the trimmed object $\mathcal{O}_T$ as:

$$\mathcal{O}_T = \{\mathbf{v} | B_{min} \leq v_x < B_{max}, \ \forall \mathbf{v} \in \mathcal{O}\} \tag{6}$$

The trimmed object area considered for watermarking, denoted as A_t, is defined as the sum of all polygons, usually triangles, which are located on the surface of the trimmed object $\mathcal{O}_T$.

$\mathcal{O}_T$ is then split into κ layers defined by planes perpendicular on the second principal axis, i.e. $\mathbf{w}_2$. κ is chosen as a function depending on the number of bits M to be embedded and on the geometrical characteristics of the graphical object such as its aspect ratio given by δ_1/δ_2 obtained from (4). Thus, there are $\kappa + 1$ boundary values defined as:

$$y_i = y_{min} + \frac{y_{max} - y_{min}}{\kappa} \cdot i \tag{7}$$

where $i = 0, \ldots, \kappa$. The vertices of the trimmed object are thus split into κ layers and for each layer we have:

$$L_i = \{\mathbf{v} | y_{i-1} \leq \mathbf{v}_y < y_i, \ \forall \mathbf{v} \in \mathcal{O}_T\} \tag{8}$$

where $i = 1, \ldots, \kappa$. These layers are then divided such that to obtain a set of N patches of equal areas.

The desired area for each patch is calculated according to the following:

$$A_p = \frac{A_t}{N} \tag{9}$$

where $N > M$ and M is the number of bits to be embedded in the object. The reason for which more patches are generated than the number of bits to embed is because a segment may be eliminated if its area is smaller than a pre-defined threshold while we also aim to increase the watermark security by deliberately excluding certain patches. For example, the last patch of each layer is likely to have an area smaller than A_p and thus if watermarked it may result into a skewed distributed embedding capacity onto the 3D object surface.

Next, we sort all vertices of all layers L_i in ascending order of their x coordinates, i.e. along the first principal axis $\mathbf{w}_1$. Vertices are then iteratively added into a patch from left to right of the sorted sequence; when the area A_p is achieved for the current growing patch, a new patch is initiated. Let us denote $\mathcal{P}_j$ as the jth patch generated, where $j = 1, \ldots, N$. The first M patches $\mathcal{P}_1, \ldots, \mathcal{P}_M$ are used for watermarking. The patches to be watermarked can be picked up randomly according to the watermark key. This patch segmentation mechanism is summarized in the Algorithm 1.

Algorithm 1. Patch Segmentation Algorithm

1: $seg = 0$; // Patch index
2: **for** $i = 1$ to κ **do**
3:     Let $\mathbf{V}$ be the sorted sequence of $\forall \mathbf{v} \in L_i$ in ascending order of the x coordinate
4:     $A = 0$;
5:     **for** $j = 1$ to $|L_i|$ **do**
6:         $\mathbf{v}_j = \mathbf{V}[j]$;
7:         Add $\mathbf{v}_j$ into patch $\mathcal{P}_{seg}$;
8:         **for all** Neighbouring face f incident to $\mathbf{v}_j$ **do**
9:             **if** f is not processed and each vertex of f has been assigned to a patch **then**
10:                Calculate the area A_{in} inside the layer L_i;
11:                Increment the area accumulator $A+ = A_{in}$;
12:                **if** $A > A_P$ **then**
13:                    $seg + +$; // Move to the next patch;
14:                    Move $\mathbf{v}_j$ to patch P_{seg}
15:                    $A = A - A_p$ // Residue area is assigned to the next patch
16:                **end if**
17:            **end if**
18:        **end for**
19:    **end for**
20:    Mark all $\mathbf{v}$ in the last patch of the layer L_i as -1.
21: **end for**

When one triangle is crossing several boundaries of layer planes, that triangle will be split and only the area of its section which is within the layer L_i will be accounted into the current patch area. For example, as shown in Fig. 1, triangle $\triangle ABC$ is located at the intersection of two different layers; B_{max} indicates the trimming boundary value. Only the area of the red region, i.e. polygon $ADEF$ is accumulated in the current patch area. Ideally, one segment should contain only one compact 3D patch surface. However, if an object has a complex topology, e.g. the graphical object contains many holes, one segment may include several small and isolated patches. Watermarking such discontinuous patches will result into visible distortions and may cause visible artifacts on the graphical object surface following spectral watermarking. Therefore, those patches which contain discontinuous areas that are smaller than a predefined threshold, resulting after segmentation, are removed from the further watermark embedding process.

There are several advantages for the proposed layer segmentation algorithm. Firstly, the patches generated using this algorithm are highly secure. As it can be observed the percentage of the trimmed extremities is generated according to a secret key and it is therefore impossible to recover the patches without the knowledge of this secret key. By increasing the number of layers we are more likely to achieve a superior patch compactness. Patches which are closer to a square-like shape are more appropriate for spectral watermarking since they provide higher area compactness and an increased connectivity which are both

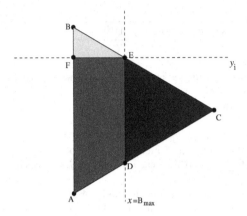

Fig. 1. An example of a mesh triangle splitting over different patches

desired by a watermark embedding procedure. On the contrary, if only one layer is used, the algorithm splits the object into narrow strips which contain a lower level of mesh connectivity. By adjusting the parameter κ, we therefore have the flexibility to adjust the size and the shape of the patches.

According to the experimental results the proposed patch segmentation algorithm is robust against most of the mesh attacks including additive noise, mesh simplification and Laplacian smoothing. Moreover, the process of watermarking the 3D object will have no influence on the graphical object segmentation procedure in the detection stage. Such a robustness is a very strong asset for a graphical object watermarking application. The proposed algorithm produces patches with equal areas and each patch will carry only one watermark bit, resulting into a high robustness. Two examples of patch segmentation for the Venus head graphical object are illustrated in Figs 2(a) and 2(b), for one layer and three layers, respectively. From these figures it is clear that three layers segmentation produces more compact patches than a single layer segmentation.

4   Spectral Decomposition of Mesh Patches

A patch $\mathcal{P}_i$ consists of a set of vertices $\{\mathbf{v}_j, j = 1, \ldots, |\mathcal{P}_i|\}$ where $|\mathcal{P}_i|$ is the number of the vertices within the patch $\mathcal{P}_i$, and a set of edges characterizing the connectivity information. The Laplacian matrix $\mathbf{L}^i$ is calculated as the difference between the degree matrix and the adjacency matrix and has the following entries:

$$L^i_{j,k} = \begin{cases} |\mathcal{N}(\mathbf{v}_j)| & \text{if } j = k \\ -1 & \text{if } j \neq k \text{ and } \mathbf{v}_j \text{ adjacent to } \mathbf{v}_k \\ 0 & \text{otherwise} \end{cases} \tag{10}$$

where $|\mathcal{N}(\mathbf{v}_j)|$ represents the degree of the vertex $\mathbf{v}_j$ (the number of neighbouring vertices $\mathbf{v}_k \in \mathcal{N}(\mathbf{v}_j)$). Then the Laplacian matrix is eigen-decomposed as:

$$\mathbf{L}^i = \mathbf{q}_i^T \, \Omega_i \mathbf{q}_i \tag{11}$$

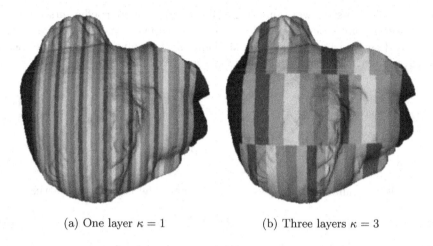

(a) One layer $\kappa = 1$ (b) Three layers $\kappa = 3$

Fig. 2. Patch segmentation of the Venus head graphical object. The blue regions represent the trimmed extremities along the first principal axis $\mathbf{w}_1$.

where Ω_i is a diagonal matrix containing the eigenvalues of the Laplacian, and $\mathbf{q}_i$ is a matrix containing its eigenvectors. The eigenvectors of $\mathbf{L}^i$ represent an orthogonal basis and the associated eigenvalues are considered as frequencies. In the following we assume that $\mathbf{q}_i$ are sorted according to the ascending order of their corresponding eigenvalues from the diagonal matrix Ω_i. The spectrum is provided by the projections of each vertex coordinate on the directions defined by the basis function $\mathbf{q}_i$. The spectral coefficients $\mathbf{C}_i$ are calculated as:

$$\mathbf{C}_i = \mathbf{q}_i \mathbf{V}_i \tag{12}$$

where $\mathbf{V}_i$ is the set of spatial coordinates of the vertices of the patch.

The transformation is reversible and the patch vertices can be recovered as:

$$\mathbf{V}_i = \mathbf{q}_i^T \mathbf{C}_i \tag{13}$$

5   Watermarking Using PCA of the Spectral Coefficients

5.1   Watermark Embedding

The spectral coefficients can be divided into "low frequency" and "high frequency". The low frequency reflects the large scale information of the 3D object while the high frequency corresponds to the details of the object. Changing the low frequency coefficients may result in severe deformation and the shearing of the object. In contrast, changing the high frequency could introduce noisy effects on the object surface. In this paper, we propose to embed the watermark in the high frequency coefficients so as to minimize the resulting object distortion. In the following we consider the distribution of the highest 70% of the spectral coefficients for watermarking. The high frequency coefficients for each patch form a point cloud in the 3D space. The shape of this point cloud distribution is described by using Principal Component Analysis (PCA). The mean and covariance matrix of each set of points are calculated as:

$$\mu_i = \frac{\sum_{j=1}^{n} \mathbf{C}_{i,j}}{n} \tag{14}$$

$$\Sigma_i = \frac{1}{n} \sum_{j=1}^{n} (\mathbf{C}_{i,j} - \mu_i)^T (\mathbf{C}_{i,j} - \mu_i) \tag{15}$$

where n is the number of frequency coefficients. The covariance matrix Σ_i is decomposed as:

$$\Sigma_i = \mathbf{U}_i^T \Lambda_i \mathbf{U}_i \tag{16}$$

where Λ is the diagonal matrix containing the eigenvalues $\{\lambda_1, \lambda_2, \lambda_3\}$ where we assume $\lambda_1 > \lambda_2 > \lambda_3$. $\mathbf{U}_i$ is the transformation matrix whose columns are the eigenvectors of Σ_i. The eigenvalues $\{\lambda_1, \lambda_2, \lambda_3\}$ determine the extension (variance) of the point cloud along the axes defined by the eigenvectors. The spectral coefficients of a patch are shown as a signal for the x axis in Fig. 3(a) and as a 3D distribution in Fig. 3(b).

The watermark embedding method has three steps. Firstly, the point cloud of spectral coefficients $\mathbf{C}_i$ is rotated such that its axes coincide with the orthogonal axes defined by the eigenvectors:

$$\mathbf{D}_i = \mathbf{C}_i \mathbf{U}_i \tag{17}$$

In this case the variances along the three axes are not correlated with each other.

The cloud of 3-D points of $\mathbf{C}_i$ is then "squashed" for embedding a bit of 1 and "inflated" to a sphere for embedding a bit of 0, by using the ratio between the eigenvalues :

$$\frac{\lambda_1}{\lambda_k} = K \quad \begin{cases} K > 1 \text{ for a bit of 1} \\ K = 1 \text{ for a bit of 0} \end{cases} \tag{18}$$

where $k \in \{2, 3\}$. In order to enforce these constraints, the variance along the second and third axis is changed without affecting the variance corresponding to the largest eigenvalue :

$$\hat{D}_{i,k} = D_{i,k} \sqrt{\frac{\lambda_1}{K \lambda_k}} \tag{19}$$

where $k \in \{2, 3\}$, λ_1 is the highest variance, corresponding to the cloud principal axis, and $\hat{D}_{i,k}$ represents the modified k component of the coefficient vector after embedding the watermark. For embedding a '1' bit, K is set to be larger than 1, and for embedding a '0' bit, K is set to be 1. Figs. 3(c) and 3(d), illustrate the shape of the coefficients cloud after embedding a bit of 0 and 1, respectively.

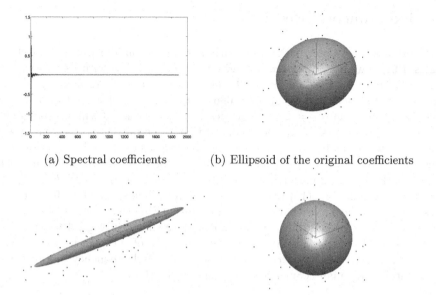

(a) Spectral coefficients   (b) Ellipsoid of the original coefficients

(c) Ellipsoid with a bit of 1 embedded (d) Ellipsoid with a bit of 0 embedded

Fig. 3. Enforcing constraints into spectral coefficients of meshes

The watermarked spectral coefficients of high frequency are reconstructed as:

$$\hat{\mathbf{C}}_i = \hat{\mathbf{D}}_i \mathbf{U}_i^T \qquad (20)$$

Finally, we enforce the changes back to the watermarked coefficients $\hat{\mathbf{C}}_i$. The reverse transformation of equation (13), using the watermarked coefficients $\hat{\mathbf{C}}_i$, is used for recovering the geometry of each individual patch. The entire watermarked graphical object is reconstructed by connecting back the patches with each other in the reversal of the procedure from Section 3.

5.2   Watermark Extraction

The proposed spectral PCA watermarking detection stage does not require the original object for retrieving the watermark. First of all, the mesh object is aligned and segmented as explained in Sections 2 and 3 Then, we apply the spectral analysis on each patch and extract the spectral coefficients in the same way as proposed in Section 4. Finally, we calculate the ratio between the largest and the smallest eigenvalues of the point cloud formed by the watermarked coefficients and retrieve the information bit as :

$$\begin{aligned} &\text{if } \frac{\hat{\lambda}_1}{\hat{\lambda}_3} > T \quad \text{then } bit = 1 \\ &\text{otherwise} \quad \text{then } bit = 0 \end{aligned} \qquad (21)$$

where T is a threshold which depends on the embedding level K.

6   Experimental Results

The proposed 3D watermarking algorithm is applied on four different mesh objects: Bunny with $34,835$ vertices and $69,666$ faces, Horse with $67,583$ vertices and $135,162$ faces, Buddha with $89,544$ vertices and $179,222$ faces and Venus head with $134,345$ vertices and $268,686$ faces. Each object is split into $N = 70$ patches grouped into $\kappa = 2$ layers as described in Section 3 while embedding a total of $M = 64$ bits. It can be observed that these objects contain many vertices and faces but by splitting them into patches as explained in Section 3 we reduce the required computational complexity for spectral watermarking. The watermark algorithm parameters are set as: $\alpha = 0.1$, $K = 15$ and $T = 2.25$, as used in equations (5), (18) and (21), respectively. The spectral coefficients corresponding to the y axis coordinate, $i.e.$ corresponding to the second component eigen-vector, before and after watermarking are shown in Figs. 4(a) and 4(b), respectively. It can be observed that the amplitude of the high frequency coefficients is shrunk after watermarking a bit of '1'. High frequency modifications only introduces small geometric distortions to the shape.

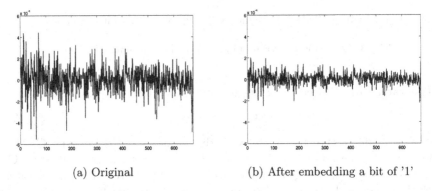

(a) Original   (b) After embedding a bit of '1'

Fig. 4. Spectral coefficients corresponding to the y axis component

In Fig. 5 we experimentally examine the robustness of the equal area segmentation method proposed in Section 3. The segmentation result on the original object is shown in Fig. 5(a). The results obtained after considering additive noise, mesh simplification and Laplacian smoothing are shown in Figs. 5(b), 5(c) and 5(d), respectively. For the simplification, we used the quadric error metric software described in [14], while for the mesh smoothing we employed the Laplacian filter proposed in [15] with a parameter $\lambda = 0.2$ and for 10 iterations. The segmentation is consistent almost perfectly under the simplification and the Laplacian smoothing. Some errors emerge at the leg of the horse under the additive noise attack however most of the segments remain identical with the original ones.

The proposed 3D graphics watermarking algorithm is compared with the state-of-art robust algorithm proposed by Cho et $al.$ in [3]. We denote by

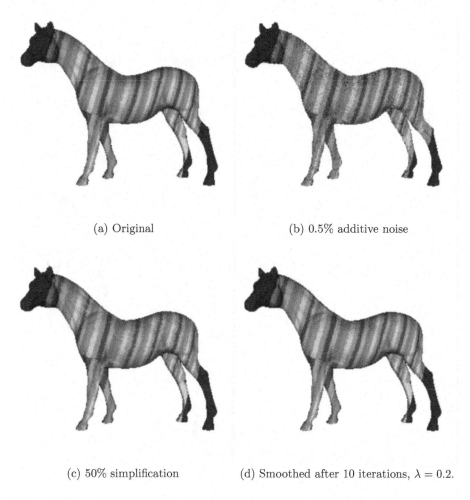

(a) Original

(b) 0.5% additive noise

(c) 50% simplification

(d) Smoothed after 10 iterations, $\lambda = 0.2$.

Fig. 5. Robustness of the segmentation method

ChoMean and ChoVar, the mean change and the variance change algorithms, described in [3]. We set the watermark parameter $\alpha = 0.05$ for the ChoMean and ChoVar methods according to their embedding algorithm from [3].

The distortion introduced by our spectral watermarking algorithm is compared objectively and visually. As the numerical objective comparison measure, we use the MRMS proposed in [16]. The comparison of the visual distortions is shown in Fig. 6, while the numerical results are listed in Table 1. From these results it is clear that the algorithm proposed in this paper introduces less distortion than Cho's algorithms for all four objects from both geometric and visual points of view.

The robustness comparison results of the three algorithms against various attacks such as additive noise, mesh simplification, quantization and Laplacian smoothing are shown in Figs. 7 and 8, respectively. For smoothing, the robustness

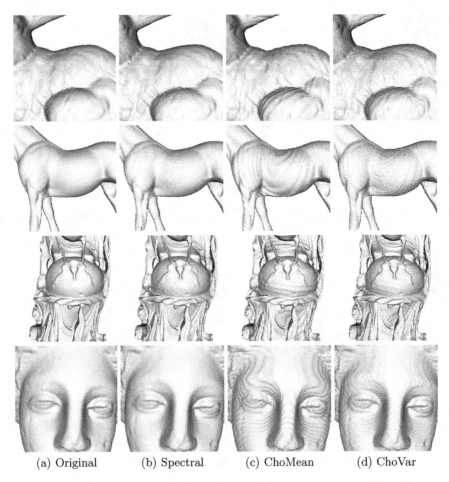

(a) Original   (b) Spectral   (c) ChoMean   (d) ChoVar

Fig. 6. Visual distortions introduced by different watermarking algorithms

Table 1. Geometric distortions measured by MRMS ($\times 10^{-4}$)

Object	Spectral	ChoMean	ChoVar
Bunny	1.91	4.95	2.29
Horse	0.43	0.87	0.54
Buddha	0.39	0.78	0.47
Head	0.10	0.25	0.15

results are basically similar for all three methods; our algorithm produces slightly better results when using fewer smoothing iterations. Our algorithm is also better than Cho's algorithms for quantization attacks. However, the Cho's results are better when considering mesh simplification. Finally for additive noise, the results are basically similar for all three methods for Buddha and Head objects,

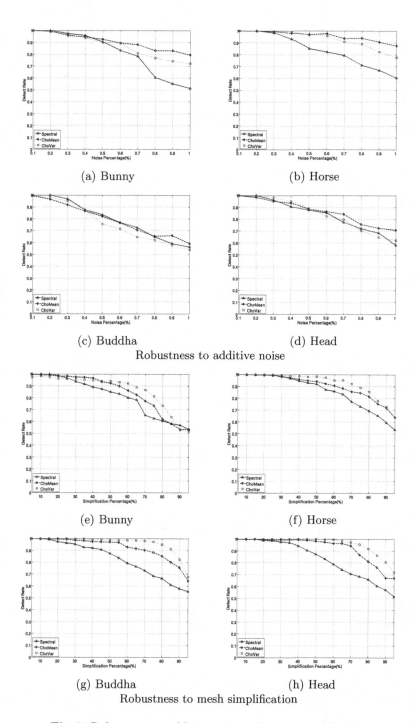

(a) Bunny

(b) Horse

(c) Buddha

(d) Head

Robustness to additive noise

(e) Bunny

(f) Horse

(g) Buddha

(h) Head

Robustness to mesh simplification

Fig. 7. Robustness to additive noise and mesh simplification

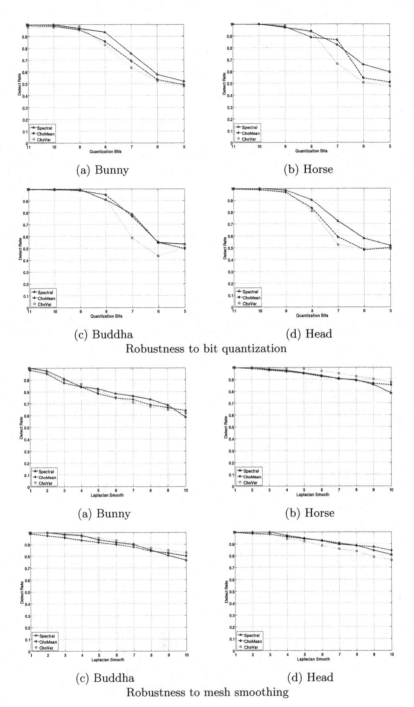

(a) Bunny   (b) Horse

(c) Buddha   (d) Head

Robustness to bit quantization

(a) Bunny   (b) Horse

(c) Buddha   (d) Head

Robustness to mesh smoothing

Fig. 8. Robustness to quantization and mesh smoothing

while Cho's algorithms demonstrate a higher robustness in the case of Bunny and Horse objects. This comparison demonstrates the good trade-off of the proposed method between the watermark robustness and the distortion. The proposed algorithm introduces a lower distortion, both geometrically and visually, when compared to the Cho's methods at the price of a lower robustness for certain attacks, while maintaining the same robustness for others.

7 Conclusion

In this paper we propose a local blind spectral watermarking method for 3D meshes. The 3D object is split into patches in order to minimize the required computational complexity of the spectral decomposition. This segmentation algorithm produces equal area regions and is robust to both geometry and connectivity attacks. The watermark is then embedded by enforcing constraints on the spectral coefficients corresponding to each patch. The spectral coefficient distribution corresponds to an ellipsoid when embedding a bit of 1 and to a sphere when embedding a bit of 0. The proposed methodology provides increased watermark security and was shown to produce minimal distortion in the object shape, both from geometric and visual points of view. Extensive experiments have shown that the proposed method provides a good trade-off between distortion and robustness when compared with state-of-the-art spatial domain methods.

References

1. Bors, A.G.: Watermarking mesh-based representations of 3-D objects using local moments. IEEE Trans. on Image Processing 15(3), 687–701 (2006)
2. Zafeiriou, S., Tefas, A., Pitas, I.: Blind robust watermarking schemes for copyright protection of 3D mesh objects. IEEE Trans. on Visualization and Computer Graphics 11(5), 496–607 (2005)
3. Cho, J.W., Prost, R., Jung, H.Y.: An oblivious watermarking for 3-D polygonal meshes using distribution of vertex norms. IEEE Trans. on Signal Processing 55(1), 142–155 (2007)
4. Ohbuchi, R., Mukaiyama, A., Takahashi, S.: A frequency-domain approach to watermarking 3-D shapes. In: Proc. of Eurographics, Computer Graphics Forum, vol. 21, pp. 373–382 (2002)
5. Cayre, F., Alface, P.R., Schmitt, F., Macq, B., Maître, H.: Application of spectral decomposition to compression and watermarking of 3D triangle mesh geometry. Signal Processing: Image Communication 18(4), 309–319 (2003)
6. Wang, K., Lavoué, G., Denis, F., Baskurt, A.: A comprehensive survey on three-dimensional mesh watermarking. IEEE Trans. on Multimedia 10(8), 1513–1527 (2008)
7. Karni, Z., Gotsman, C.: Spectral compression of mesh geometry. In: Proc. of SIGGRAPH, Computer Graphics Proceedings, pp. 279–286 (2000)
8. Lavoué, G., Denis, F., Dupont, F.: Subdivision surface watermarking. Computers & Graphics 31(3), 480–492 (2007)

9. Cotting, A., Weyrich, T., Pauly, M., Gross, M.: Robust watermarking of point-sampled geometry. In: Proc. of Int. Conf. on Shape Modeling and Applications, pp. 233–242 (2004)
10. Liu, Y., Prabhakaran, B., Guo, X.: A robust spectral approach for blind watermarking of manifold surfaces. In: Proc. of ACM Multimedia and Security Workshop, pp. 43–52 (2008)
11. Luo, M., Bors, A.G.: Principal component analysis of spectral coefficients for mesh watermarking. In: Proc. of IEEE Int. Conf. on Image Processing, pp. 441–444 (2008)
12. Zhang, C., Chen, T.: Efficient feature extraction for 2D/3D objects in mesh representation. In: Proc. of IEEE Int. Conf. on Image Processing, pp. 935–938 (2001)
13. Tuzikov, A., Sheynin, S., Vasiliev, P.: Computation of volume and surface body moments. Pattern Recognition 36(11), 2521–2529 (2003)
14. Garland, M., Heckbert, P.: Surface simplification using quadric error metrics. In: Proc. SIGGRAPH, Graphical Models, vol. 66(6), pp. 370–397 (1997)
15. Taubin, G.: Geometric signal processing on polygonal meshes. In: Eurographics state of the art report (2000)
16. Cignoni, P., Rocchini, C., Scopigno, R.: Metro: Measuring error on simplified surfaces. Computer Graphics Forum 17(2), 167–174 (1998)

Reading Watermarks from Printed Binary Images with a Camera Phone

Anu Pramila, Anja Keskinarkaus, and Tapio Seppänen

MediaTeam Oulu group,
Department of electrical and information engineering,
University of Oulu, P.O. Box 4500
FIN-90014 University of Oulu, Finland
{Anu.Pramila,Anja.Keskinarkaus,Tapio.Seppanen}@ee.oulu.fi

Abstract. In this paper, we propose a method for reading a watermark from a printed binary image with a camera phone. The watermark is a small binary image which is protected with (15, 11) Hamming error coding and embedded in the binary image by utilizing flippability scores of the pixels and block based relationships. The binary image is divided into blocks and fixed number of bits is embedded in each block. A frame is added around the image in order to overcome 3D distortions and lens distortions are corrected by calibrating the camera. The results obtained are encouraging and when the images were captured freehandedly by rotating the camera approximately -2 - 2 degrees, the amount of fully recovered watermarks was 96.3%.

Keywords: Binary image watermarking, print-cam, camera phone.

1 Introduction

More and more people are carrying with them a mobile device, many of which include a camera. Possibility to connect to internet, share content and thoughts with others, is no longer tied to a time and place.

In this paper, we propose a method for reading a watermark from a printed binary image with a camera phone. To our knowledge, this is the first paper to propose a print-cam robust watermarking system for binary images. In the print-cam process the image is watermarked and printed and then the printed image is captured with a camera phone in order to read the watermark.

Traditionally, different kinds of barcodes have been used as a way to link physical world to the digital. Kato and Tan [1] indentified the most suitable 2D barcodes for mobile phones and selected some features desirable for standard 2D barcode optimized for the mobile phone platform. Rohs [2] designed a barcode technique especially for camera phones. The system included a code coordinate system, detected camera movements, and inverted rotation and amount of tilting of the optical axis.

However, usage of barcodes is not always desired. They are highly visible markings by nature and the linkage needs not always be so obvious or a more aesthetically appealing method is required. Watermarking has been used in digital world mostly as

A.T.S. Ho et al. (Eds.): IWDW 2009, LNCS 5703, pp. 227–240, 2009.

a copy- and copyright protection for different kinds of images. Nevertheless, some watermarking methods have been already proposed in which the watermark can be read with a digital camera or a camera phone from a printed color image. [3, 4, 5]

In this paper, we show that a binary watermarking method can survive the print-cam process. An example use scenario is presented in Fig. 1. Instead of using a bar-code, a small binary image, representing a company logo, is watermarked and placed on a catalog. The watermarked logo can contain, for example, a link to company's website, information about the product on the catalog page, up-to-date price information and offers etc. The logo can then be captured with a camera phone and after a short processing time the content of the watermark is shown to the user.

Fig. 1. An example use scenario where the watermark contains a link to the company website

Another use scenario is illustrated in Fig. 2. Here the logo contains a product code and the logo is placed on a side of a product container. This code can be used for comparison of the code in the watermark and in the container itself in order to verify the genuinity of the product package. The code can be in visual form or as a bit sequence and respectively the evaluation of the result can be done either visually or through a program.

Reading watermarks with a digital camera or a camera phone has its own difficulties as explained in [6] and [5]. Mobile phones lack processing power and the captured images appear tilted, scaled and rotated in the camera images. The attacks against the watermark of the image are mostly unintentional, such as DA/AD transform, rotation, scale, translation and tilt of the optical axis. Effects of the printing, paper properties, light variations and lens distortions need also be taken into account. In this paper we focus on lens distortions, rotation, translation, scale and the tilt of the optical axis as they will be the most severe of the attacks.

Fig. 2. An example scenario in which the watermark contains a verification code

The tilting of the optical axis leads to uneven sampling frequency over the image and consequently the synchronization of the watermark is lost. It is practically impossible to place the camera directly over the watermarked image freehandedly so that they are perpendicular to each other and thus the picture taken appears to be slanted as shown in Fig. 3. The image is rotated towards or away from the camera and, therefore, some parts of the image are closer to the camera than the other. In the captured image, the parts that are close are presented with a high resolution but parts that are further away are presented with a lower resolution. As a result, the resolution can be too low in some parts of the captured image and the watermark cannot be extracted correctly. [5]. This results also to some difficulties to focus the camera correctly to the image as all parts of the image cannot be in the focus all the time.

In binary image watermarking, the watermark can be embedded with many ways. It can be embedded in the transform domain [7] or it can be embedded directly by flipping pixels [8, 9, 10]. These methods referred here focus on authentication or on enhancing the security of the watermark in the binary images in digital form. However, none of these methods are designed to be robust against any 3D distortions. Wu and Liu [11] added some small synchronization dots into the image background in order to make the method robust against print-scan. Unfortunately, such an approach would not work here, because such dots would be difficult to locate in a distorted image captured with a digital camera.

In our earlier work [5], we have shown that ordinary, non-robust, watermarks can be used in print-cam applications of color images. In order to extract the watermark a way to compensate distortions inflicted by the print-cam process [6] to the image is required. It can be expected that these results work also to some extent in the case of binary images.

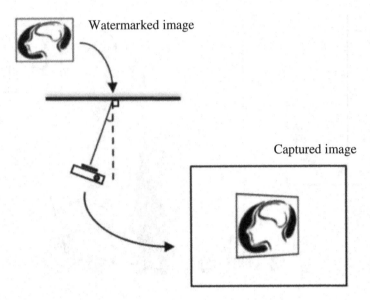

Fig. 3. Tilt of the optical axis and how it affects the captured image

However, binary images are more sensitive when the original image is reconstructed after print-cam process. Each of the pixels needs to be found correctly in order to read the watermark message without errors and thresholding back to binary form must be done carefully.

There is an abundance of methods for reading barcodes with a camera phone and many proposals for watermarking binary images but combining these two is rare. In this paper, we focus on the robustness of the binary image watermarking system and leave the verification of the security for the future. In the first chapter, the method is explained in detail and in the following chapters the robustness of the method is shown and the results discussed.

2   Binary Image Watermarking Algorithm

2.1   Embedding Watermark

Here, we use a blind binary image watermarking method by Wu and Liu [11]. In the method, the binary image is divided into blocks and fixed number of bits is embedded in each block. The method was chosen because it is a simple yet effective binary image watermarking method with visually appealing results.

In order to select the pixels for modification so as to introduce as little visual artifacts as possible, Wu and Liu studied each pixel and its immediate neighbors and assigned each of the pixels a flippability score of how unnoticeable a change on that pixel would cause. The scores, between 0 and 1 with 0 indicating no flipping, were determined dynamically by observing smoothness and connectivity in the neighborhood of the pixel. The smoothness was calculated by measuring horizontal, vertical and diagonal transitions in local window. Connectivity was measured as a number of black and white clusters in the local window. Here a 3x3 window was applied. [11]

The pixels with high flippability scores were chosen for manipulation. After the flippability scores were determined the image was divided into blocks. Here 10x10 block size was applied. However, Wu and Liu noted that the distribution of flippable pixels may vary dramatically from block to block. In spite of this, constant embedding rate was chosen in the method, but shuffling of the pixels with an encryption key was applied in order to equalize the uneven embedding capacity and increasing the security. The shuffling dynamically assigned the flippable pixels in active regions and boundaries to carry more data than less active regions. [11]

In order to determine if one or zero was embedded, the total number of black pixels in a block was used as a feature. To embed a 0 in a block, a number of pixels are changed according to the flippability scores so that the total number of black pixels in that block is an even number. Similarly, if 1 is embedded, a number of pixels are changed so that the total number of black pixels is an odd number. The watermark could later be easily read by observing the amount of black pixels in a block. [11]

The method is not robust against tilt of the optical axis. Only few print-cam robust watermarking methods have been proposed and those methods are designed for color images. Katayama *et al.* [4] and Takeuchi *et al.* [12] relied on a frame around the image. In order to compensate the geometrical distortions the frame can later be found and by using the corner point of the frame, the geometrical distortions can be corrected. Unlike the method by Katayama *et al.* [4], the method by Takeuchi *et al.* compensated also the radial distortions by assuming that the parameters of the radial distortions correction model would not change between phones of the same model and creating a database for the parameters.

Kim *et al.* [13] proposed a print-cam robust fingerprinting system which did not require the frame. The fingerprint was embedded in their method as a pseudorandom sequence to the image repeatedly and it was extracted with autocorrelation afterwards. Unfortunately, their method showed only some success as it required lot of work done by hand before the fingerprint could be extracted. In addition, they used a tripod while taking the pictures, the use of which lessens the distortions significantly in the captured image but decreases the usability of the method. In general, self-referencing, auto-correlation based methods are not necessarily suitable for print-cam process because they give no information about the location of the watermarked image in the captured image. Finding the location of the watermarked image in the captured image requires either full search which is time consuming or some other more sophisticated way of locating the watermarked image.

Here, a frame is added around the watermarked binary image. This is the only acknowledged and fully working way to deal with the 3D distortions in digital image watermarking and thus this approach has been chosen, also in here. The frame extraction algorithm applied here differs from the method by Katayama *et al.* [3] in that no thresholding is used for locating the corner points. This is an advantage when different kinds of images in variable light are used. The frame may not be necessary if the borders of the image are visible with some other way. For example, in the case of self-referencing in id-cards, the edge of the card could work as a reference frame. In this case, the frame is a black line as illustrated in Fig. 4.

Fig. 4. The original and a framed and watermarked image

In the print-cam process the attacks against watermark are heavy. Some errors are bound to occur. Here we embed a small 12x10 binary image into the image. The image watermark is protected with Hamming (15, 11) error coding which is capable of correcting 1 bit. Few errors in watermark extraction are not necessarily crucial as the image can still be recognizable after relatively small amount of errors although each of the errors makes the recognition of the image more difficult. A small image can be used for visual verification as illustrated in the scenario in Fig. 2.

If the embedded data was a pointer, the data could be protected with a stronger error correction or repetition because the payload is often smaller for pointers than for images. Here we embed 120 bits excluding the bits required for Hamming error correction.

2.2 Image Correction after Capturing the Image

The camera is calibrated prior handling the captured image with Camera Calibration Toolbox [14, 15] by Kannala *et al.* developed in our laboratory. The Calibration Toolbox is based on a generic camera model and the calibration of a camera is performed with a calibration plane with white circles on black background. Here the camera was calibrated with a calibration image shown on an LCD computer screen. The calibration was performed by taking several images of the calibration plane and analyzing the captured images. The calibration is needed in order to correct the pincushion and barrel distortions inflicted by the lens but it needs to be done only once for each camera. After calibration, the obtained calibration parameters can be used repeatedly to invert lens distortions from captured images.

When reading the watermark image, the image is captured with a camera phone and the resulting image is turned into a grayscale image. The frame is found from the grayscale image and distortions corrected with a slightly modified method of the method described in [5]. The algorithm for the extracting the corner points is as follows:

1. Determine a frame detection filter. Here the filter is a simple edge detection filter of length n with n/2 1's in the beginning and -1's in the end;
2. Locate the corner points with the frame detection filter;
   2.1. Start from the middle of the left side of the image;
   2.2. Find all the sides of the frame;
      2.2.1. Advance to the right until a side of the frame has been found, i.e., a large local maximum indicating an edge;

2.2.2. Trace the frame up and downwards and examine also the points one pixel to the left and right of the current side position; Select maximum of the three points to be part of the frame;

2.2.3. Rotate the image to find other sides and go back to 2.2.1 until all the sides of the frame have been found;

2.3. Approximate the points with straight lines;

2.4. Calculate the intersections of the lines. These intersections work as an approximation of the location of the corner;

3. Refine corner locations, i.e., utilize a pattern matching algorithm;

3.1 Select a small area around the approximated location of a corner point and Correlate this small area with a pattern representing a corner and search for the maximum.

After the corner points have been extracted, the effects of the tilting of the optical axis, rotation, translation and scale are corrected with the following equations:

$$
x' = \frac{a_1 x + b_1 y + c_1}{a_0 x + b_0 y + 1} , \qquad (1)
$$
$$
y' = \frac{a_2 x + b_2 y + c_2}{a_0 x + b_0 y + 1}
$$

where (x', y') are the original picture positions, (x, y) are the camera picture positions and a, b and c are coefficients for the transform. Bilinear interpolation is applied while scaling the image to its original dimensions.

After the distortions have been corrected, the image needs to be thresholded in order to obtain a binary image. The image is thresholded by calculating an image

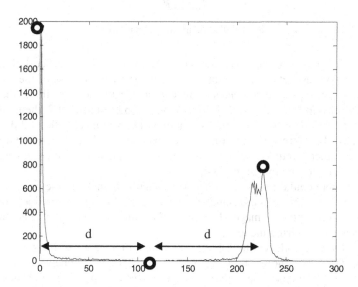

Fig. 5. Thresholding with the image histogram

histogram and finding the middle point between the two maximums which are formed by the variations of the light and dark pixels. This process is show in Fig. 5. When the image is back in the binary form, the watermark is read by dividing the image into blocks and calculating the number of black pixels in a block. Even number corresponds to 0 and uneven to 1. Error correction is applied and the obtained watermark sequence is reshaped into an image.

3   Experimental Results

If the tilt of the optical axis, rotation and scale were the only distortions occurring the experiments could be done by simulating. Unfortunately, this is not possible, because, for example, lighting and camera affect the watermark extraction. In addition to this, simulations require interpolations and in the case of black and white binary images the interpolation would not correspond perfectly to the real life situations.

The experiments were conducted with six images with resolutions of 164x117. Each image was watermarked with a 12x10 pixel image containing letters 2D and a frame was added around the image. In the following, one bit corresponds to one pixel. The watermark image used is shown in Fig. 6. and the resulting images are shown in Fig. 7. The images were printed with Canon HP Color LaserJet 4650 and placed on a wall. The physical sizes of the images were 4.7x3.4 cm. The camera phone used in the experiments was Nokia N82 with 5 megapixel camera but only 2 megapixel resolution was used in order to keep the processing speed at a comfortable level.

Fig. 6. Watermark image magnified

The test images were captured free-handedly in an ordinary office lighting. Two non-overlapping test sets were captured in order to test robustness of the method: In the first test set, set 1, the images were captured 50 times by tilting the camera randomly approximately -2 – +2 degrees. In the second test set, set 2, the images were captured 50 times by tilting the camera randomly approximately atleast 2 degrees but no more than 10 degrees around the optical axis, vertically and horizontally. At 90 degrees the camera would be at the same line as the optical axis of the image making the recognization of the image impossible.

As the camera could not focus on distances smaller than 10cm the images were not taken closer than that. At that distance the watermarked image covered approximately one third of the captured image. The camera's build-in property of auto focus was taked advantage of during the testing.

The results were collected to Table 1 and some of the captured images can be seen in Fig. 8. The table shows, how many times each of the embedded images were completely recovered, i.e., the obtained image is a exact copy of the embedded image,

Fig. 7. Watermarked images: a) Bamboo, b) Snake, c) Face, d) Logo (by courtesy of Starcke Ltd.), e) Karateka, f) Spider

Table 1. Successful watermark extractions

	Set 1		Set 2	
	Fully recovered	<5 bits incorrect	Fully recovered	<5 bits incorrect
Bamboo	48	48	43	45
Snake	49	49	44	48
Face	49	49	45	46
Logo	48	48	49	49
Karateka	50	50	35	43
Spider	48	49	40	42

and when less than 5 bits were incorrect, i.e., when the watermark could still be recovered with stronger error correction or, in the case of watermark being a binary image, visual evaluation.

Success ratios were calculated for each group of images: For the set 1 the amount of fully recovered watermarks was 96.3% and the amount of watermarks with less than 5 bits incorrect was 97.7%. When the images were captured with less care in the set 2, the amount of fully recovered watermarks was 85.3% and the amount of watermarks with less than 5 bits incorrect was 91.0%.

Fig. 9 shows the case when the binary image was reconstructed after print-cam process but three errors remained in the obtained watermark image. As can be seen form the zoomed image, the reconstructed image contains some errors, which result in errorneous watermark extraction.

Figures 10-15 illustrates the obtained BER (Bit Error Ratio) results. The y-axels of the images show the BER whereas the x-axis tells the number of the image being handled. The BER was calculated for each of the images separately.

Fig. 8. Examples of images from which the watermark was fully recovered

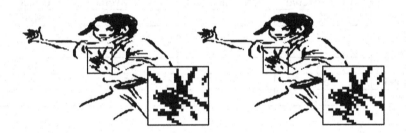

Fig. 9. A comparison of a) reconstructed image after print-cam process when the watermark was extracted with 3 errors b) the original image

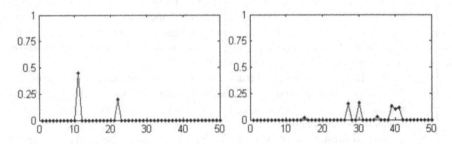

Fig. 10. BER for a) the Bamboo image rotated ±2° b) the Bamboo image rotated arbitrarily

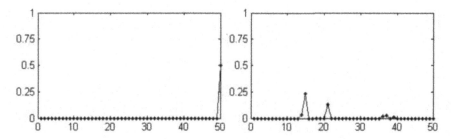

Fig. 11. BER for a) the Snake image rotated ±2° b) the Snake image rotated arbitrarily

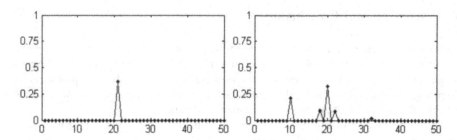

Fig. 12. BER for a) the Face image rotated ±2° b) the Face image rotated arbitrarily

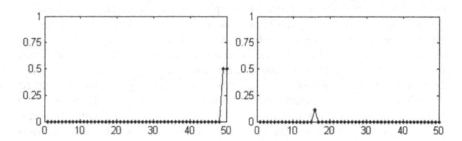

Fig. 13. BER for a) the Logo image rotated ±2° b) the Logo image rotated arbitrarily

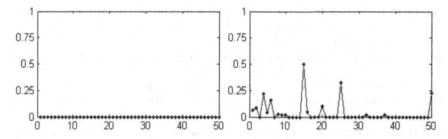

Fig. 14. BER for a) the Karateka image rotated ±2° b) the Karateka image rotated arbitrarily

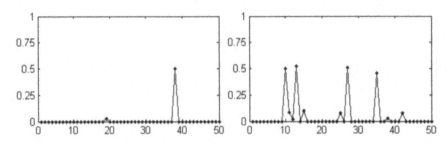

Fig. 15. BER for a) the Spider image rotated ±2° b) the Spider image rotated arbitrarily

4 Discussion and Conclusion

The results in Table 1 and success ratios show, that if the image is taken with some care, the watermark can be obtained without errors or with minimal amount of errors so that in the future, a better error correction coding would solve the problems. If the image is taken quite randomly without stressing the direction of the camera, the watermark can still be obtained with a reasonable accuracy.

As can be seen from Fig. 8. the watermarked image can be tilted and rotated and still the watermark can be read without errors. On the other hand, it can be assumed that the user wants the process to succeed and therefore makes his or her best to take the image as well as possible.

The most difficult images proved to be the spider and karateka images. One answer for the difficulties is that the spider image has very fine lined details around the legs of the spider which make the thresholding process difficult. Similarly, the karateka image contains many small details that are lost when the optical axis is tilted. These details, however, are important for watermark extraction.

The best results were obtained from the logo image. The logo image is relatively small and centered inside the frame and thus it is not so sensitive the 3D distortions as the karateka and spider images. It needs to be noted, however, that only 50 images were taken per printed image. Therefore the success ratios would most probably approach each other if more tests were made.

The illustrations of the BER values in Figures 10-15 show that not all of the information is lost during the capturing process. The BER values rarely reach 50% and thus better results could be obtained, by using a stronger error correction coding. If the same watermarking method was used, the message would need to be a bit smaller in order to fit in better error correction coding. However, 165 bits embedded here would be enough room for many applications even with efficient error correction coding.

In the print-cam process, tampering with message lengths and error correction coding is not the only option for improving the robustness. Depending on the application, the printed image can be small or large and the original image size can be varied. Unfortunately, also the attacks vary ranging from simple rotations of the image to complex light variations and problems concerning properties of the cameras. Finding the optimal selection of watermark system properties for each application is the key for a successful application.

The 2D barcodes and watermarking should not be seen as competitors but more like different solutions for different applications. Depending on the application areas, the selection between barcodes and watermark images can be made. The watermarking method can be, for example, utilized to check the genuinity of a product with company logo as well as introducing a method for linking the logo to some specific website. The advantages of using watermarking over 2D barcodes are the aesthetics and security. Watermarking need not to be visible and their existence altogether can be kept as a secret.

As a conclusion, a print-cam robust method for watermarking binary images, such as logos, is shown in this paper. The print-cam robustness requires from the watermarking method robustness against 3D distortions, such as rotations, translation and scale, as well as robustness against lens distortions. The binary image needs to be reconstructed perfectly pixel by pixel in order to be able to read the watermark. The method was based on inversion of the distortions by applying a frame around the image. The results obtained show that the method is robust against translation, rotation, scale, tilt of the optical axis and lens distortions. In the future work, the aim is to make the frame obsolete.

References

1. Kato, H., Tan, K.T.: 2D Barcodes for Mobile Phones. In: IEEE 2nd International Conference on Mobile Technology, Applications and Systems (2005)
2. Rohs, M.: Real-World Interaction with Camera Phones. In: Murakami, H., Nakashima, H., Tokuda, H., Yasumura, M. (eds.) UCS 2004. LNCS, vol. 3598, pp. 74–89. Springer, Heidelberg (2005)
3. Perry, B., MacIntosh, B., Cushman, D.: Digimarc MediaBridge – The birth of a consumer product, from concept to commercial application. In: Security and Watermarking of multimedia Contents IV. Proc SPIE, vol. 4675, pp. 118–123 (2002)
4. Katayama, A., Nakamura, T., Yamamuro, M., Sonehara, N.: New high-speed frame detection method: Side trace algorithm (STA) for i-appli on cellular phones to detect watermarks. In: Proc. of the 3rd International Conference on mobile and Ubiquitous Multimedia, pp. 109–116. ACM, New York (2004)
5. Pramila, A., Keskinarkaus, A., Seppänen, T.: Watermark robustness in the Print- Cam Process. In: IASTED International Conference on Signal Processing, Pattern and Applications, Innsbruck, Austria (2008)
6. Pramila, A., Keskinarkaus, A., Seppänen, T.: Camera based watermark extraction - Problems and examples. In: Finnish Signal Processing Symposium 2007 (FinSig 2007), Oulu, Finland, On CD (2007)
7. Lu, H., Shi, X., Shi, Y.Q., Kot, A., Chen, L.: Watermark embedding in DC components of DCT for Binary Images. In: IEEE Workshop on Multimedia Signal Processing, pp. 300–303 (2002)
8. Wu, M., Tang, E., Liu, B.: Data Hiding in Digital Binary Image. In: IEEE International Conference on Multimedia and Expo, ICME 2000, vol. 1, pp. 393–396 (2000)
9. Chen, J., Chen, T.-S., Cheng, M.-V.: A new data hiding method in binary image. In: International Symposium on Multimedia Software Engineering, ISMSE 2003, p. 88 (2003)
10. Pan, H.-K., Chen, Y.-Y., Tseng, Y.-C.: A secure data hiding scheme for two-color images. In: Fifth IEEE Symposium on computers and Communications, Proceedings, ISCC 2000, pp. 750–755 (2000)

11. Wu, M., Liu, B.: Data Hiding in Binary Image for Authentication and Annotation. IEEE Transactions on Multimedia 6(4), 528–538 (2004)
12. Takeuchi, S., Kunisa, A., Tsujita, K., Inoue, Y.: Geometric distortion compensation of printed images containing inperceptible watermarks. In: International conference on cosumer Electronics, Digest of Technical paper, pp. 411–421 (2005)
13. Kim, W.-G., Lee, S.H., Seo, Y.S.: Image fingerprinting scheme for print-and-capture model. In: Zhuang, Y.-t., Yang, S.-Q., Rui, Y., He, Q. (eds.) PCM 2006. LNCS, vol. 4261, pp. 106–113. Springer, Heidelberg (2006)
14. Camera Calibration Toolbox for Generic Lenses. Matlab version 6.5 or later with the Image Processing Toolbox and Optimization Toolbox is required, `http://www.ee.oulu.fi/~jkannala/calibration/calibration.html` (Retrieved, 12.12. 2008)
15. Kannala, J., Brandt, S.S.: A Generic Camera Model and Calibration Method for Conventional, Wide- Angle, and Fish-Eye Lenses. IEEE Transactions on pattern analysis and machine intelligence 28(8), 1335–1340 (2006)

A New Approach in Reversible Watermarking

Ahmad Mahmoudi Aznaveh, Azadeh Mansouri, and Farah Torkamani-Azar

Department of Electrical and Computer Engineering
Shahid Beheshti University, Evin, Tehran, Iran
{a_mahmoudi,a_mansouri,f-torkamani}@sbu.ac.ir

Abstract. A great number of reversible watermarking methods have been put forward in the last few years. After analysis of some recent methods, we offer a new simple transform to increase the capacity applying just one iteration. Another advantage of our method is its simplicity. Moreover, it does not need to embed a compressed location map for recovering the original host. Therefore, the computational cost of our method is reduced in comparison to similar methods. The flexibility of the proposed method, on account of selecting appropriate contribution factor, is another advantage of our algorithm.

Keywords: Reversible Watermarking, Location Map, Difference Expansion.

1 Introduction

Reversible watermarking, also called lossless data hiding, embeds the watermark data into a digital image in a reversible manner i.e. one can restore the original image without any degradation. Although the distortion introduced by non-reversible watermarking method is often quite small and imperceptible, in some applications such as military, legal, and medical imagery even a very slight change in pixel values is undesirable. Other applications including extreme magnification or iterative processing can be added to the aforementioned list.

The practical demands expedite the research on reversible watermarking. As a case in point, by using a reversible scheme, it is possible to insert the hash of an image without losing its entirety in a classical authentication algorithm. Moreover, using reversible watermarking in trustworthy camera, used in integrity protection, could be useful due to some legal problem [1].

The requirements of other watermarking methods, such as imperceptibility and capacity should be fulfilled in lossless watermarking. Regardless of the fact that the distortion is completely removable, it is important to minimize the amount of distortion resulted from embedding. To shed some more light on this matter, we remark the difference between cryptography and watermarking.

In this paper, a new transform for reversible data hiding is proposed. Through this method it is possible to achieve more capacity just in one iteration along with preserving the quality of the watermarked media. Section 2 reviews the major reversible watermarking methods. In section 3 the proposed methods is illustrated. The experimental results are presented in section.4. Finally, we conclude the paper in section 5.

A.T.S. Ho et al. (Eds.): IWDW 2009, LNCS 5703, pp. 241–251, 2009.
© Springer-Verlag Berlin Heidelberg 2009

2 Fundamental of Reversible Watermarking

In this section, we sketch out the framework of reversible schemes, and discuss about its demands. Strong correlation between components of natural images, make it possible to embed the watermark in a reversible fashion. Reversible methods put this correlation to use for embedding the payload. In order to simplify the explanation of reversible schemes, some useful expression will be defined.

It is necessary to contrive the embedding operator in such a way that after embedding, the dynamic range does not change. Otherwise, overflow and underflow cause to have the loss of information. In non reversible watermarking, however, one can easily ignore the overflows or underflows, since the resultant distortion is imperceptible in most of the cases.

The upper bound capacity is different among reversible methods. Although it is not possible to achieve this capacity, it can be consider as a suitable measure for comparing the reversible methods since this amount is independent from the host image.

Definition 1. The *raw capacity* of a method is the upper bound capacity which can be achieved in a reversible watermarking scheme. Note that this raw capacity usually is not attained practically due to some overhead.

Definition 2. The *actual capacity* is the amount of embedded data into an image. The actual capacity is usually less than the raw capacity and in addition to the method; it is dependent on the host image.

Due to the limitation of actual capacity, it is usual to embed the watermark in more iterations. In this case, the extracting phase should be done in reverse order, and using a header file to specify the number of necessary iterations. In this case, it is not possible to improve the method for tamper proofing since any problem in the first extracting iteration will make the recovering procedure impossible.

Definition 3. *Multiple-Layer Embedding*: to achieve more capacity, the algorithm is applied more than once [2]. In this case the payload should be divided to several pieces; then each part is embedded in a separate embedding phase.

After embedding, as all the image components cannot carry the watermark bit, it is required to distinguish the container element with non-container. In most of the cases a location map is used to distinguish between two groups; however, modifying some properties of these groups can lead to removing the location map. Some overhead, still, should be added to payload for restoring the original states.

Definition 4. Auxiliary Information: the extra information needed to be appended to the watermark e.g. the location map or correction data is called auxiliary data.

3 Review of Major Methods

There are some schemes considered as the pioneer of the concept of lossless data embedding. The Barton patent [3], filed in 1994, is one of them in which the bitstring is added to the compressed host signal. Mintzer *et al.* presented a reversible visible watermarking method. The watermark can be removed to recreate the unmarked image by using a "vaccine" program. Honsinger *et al.* [4] proposed a lossless data embedding using addition modulo 256.

In the last decade several different reversible watermarking scheme has been proposed. Macq [5] extended the patchwork algorithm and Fridrich *et al.* [6] defined different status for a group of pixels and embed the watermark through changing the appropriate states. The compressed states of pixel group in original host should be appended to the watermark string. De Vleeschouwer *et al.* [7] proposed a bijective transform to enhance the classical patchwork algorithm to a reversible scheme. Celik *et al.* developed a reversible algorithm compressing the quantization residue which is called Lossless Generalized-LSB Data Embedding.

Difference expansion proposed by Tian [2] is an eminent reversible data hiding which is a base for many recent methods [8-13]. As a result, we want to focus on expansion based algorithms and investigate the inner working of such methods.

3.1 Difference Expansion Based Methods

In this part, we outline the idea of difference expansion based methods from Tian's algorithm to the last developed scheme. The DE (Difference Expansion) embedding algorithm transforms the original host into a low frequency and a high frequency part through the integer Haar wavelet or S transform. If x and y represent the intensity of a pair of pixels; then the integer average, l, and the difference, h, will be defined as:

$$l = \left\lfloor \frac{x+y}{2} \right\rfloor$$

$$h = y - x \tag{1}$$

The inverse transform of (1) is given as follows:

$$y = l + \left\lfloor \frac{h+1}{2} \right\rfloor$$

$$x = l - \left\lfloor \frac{h}{2} \right\rfloor \tag{2}$$

There is a one-to-one corresponding between (x, y) and (l, h). Considering the correlation between adjacent pixels in natural images, the difference values are expected to be near zero. Based on this assumption, the watermark bit can be embedded into h by expanding its value as:

$$h' = 2 \times h + b \tag{3}$$

It is necessary to consider that the expansion procedure may cause underflow or overflow. To prevent this problem, h' should satisfy

$$|h'| \leq \min(2(255-l), 2l+1) \tag{4}$$

If the above condition is satisfied, the difference value, h, will be called expandable under the integer average l. Since some of the expandable pairs could not be recognized after embedding, the LSB replacement is also used. In this technique, the LSB of difference is replaced with a watermark bit. In fact, this embedding technique is lossy; therefore, it is necessary to store the altered LSBs to guarantee reversibility. It is noteworthy that the LSB replacement of some difference value may cause violating the dynamic range of pixels after invert back to the spatial domain. The pairs which are capable to undergo LSB replacement is called changeable. From the above definition, it can be concluded that a changeable difference value, after modification remains changeable. Furthermore, an expandable difference value, even after expansion, is changeable too.

Still, the decoder must know where the expandable pairs are. The positions of the expandable pair are provided through a location map which is appended to the payload. The size of the original location map is equal to raw capacity; therefore, the location map should be losslessly compressed to free some space for embedding the watermark string. In Tian's paper, JBIG2 compression is used for compressing the location map with an end of message symbol.

Eventually, the payload consists of the location map, original LSB of changeable pairs, and the watermark. In the embedding phase, the payload is substituted in LSBs of each difference by expanding or replacement. Therefore, in extracting phase the watermark string and the needed information for restoring the original host can be attained by extracting the LSBs of the watermarked image.

In Tian's method the raw capacity is less than 0.5 bpp. Since the introduced distortion is proportional to difference values, some distortion control strategy has been put forward, especially when the required capacity is less than the actual one. The first one is to restrict the criterion of being expandable by the absolute value of differences. In other words, when the absolute value of a difference is more than the predefined threshold, it should not be deemed as expandable due to its high imposed alternation. The other policy is based on hiding ability which is defined as follows:

For a difference value h and integer average l, the largest integer $k \geq 1$ such that

$$\left| k \times h + b \right| \leq \min(2(255 - l), 2l + 1)) \tag{5}$$

for all $0 \leq b \leq k-1$, the hiding ability of h is $\log_2 k$. In this case, the hiding ability is used for prioritizing the expandable pairs. In addition, it can be concluded that by expanding the difference more than two times, it is possible to embed more than one bit per pair of pixels.

Alattar [14] extended Tian's approach using difference expansion of vectors instead of pairs by defining a generalized integer difference expansion transform. Therefore the hiding ability can be increased due to decreasing the size of location map. Furthermore, a feedback system for controlling this size is developed. Finally, Alattar states that the spatial quad-based algorithm allows for hiding the largest amount of payload at the highest PSNR. The raw capacity in this algorithm is as high as $(n-1)/n$ bpp where n is the number of vector elements.

Kamstra et al. [15] modified DE method by sorting the pair based on the information of integer averages which do not alter during embedding process. In doing so, the compressibility of the location map increases. In addition, they proposed not to replace the LSBs of changeable pairs which are located after the position of the location map. This improves the quality of the watermarked image; however, the raw capacity remains the same as the DE method. They also removed the non-changeable pair from the location map which can increase slightly the actual capacity.

Thodi *et al.* [10], introduced a histogram shifting in order to reduce the amount of auxiliary data. To recognize the expandable difference two strategies are proposed: using an overflow map and interspersed flag bits. In addition, the prediction error expansion is proposed since a predictor better exploits the correlation inherent in the neighborhood of a pixel. In this case, the raw capacity approaches to 1 bpp; however, the restoration process still requires restoring the context of a pixel before the pixel itself can be restored. Therefore, the restoration process is sequential. Weng *et al.* [9] presented PDA method to reduce the location map which is similar to histogram shifting in [10]. Although the embedding process is a bit different form the original DE methods, we can consider both almost the same.

Lee *et al.* [16] divided an input image into non-overlapping blocks and embedded a watermark into the high frequency wavelet coefficients of each block. The raw capacity of this method is as high as 0.5 bpp.

Kim *et al.* [11] defined the concept of unambiguously expandable to simplify the location map. Therefore, embedding without compressing the location map is possible although with lower data hiding ability. Kuribayashi *et al.* [13] proposed similar terminology: absolutely expandable and absolutely changeable to decrease the size of location map. They also enhance the prediction expansion by vectorization to reduce the size of location map more.

Jin *et al.* [12] expanded the difference between the pixel intensity and the average of neighboring pixels. In their method the location map is completely removed. This technique, however, suffer from the unsolved issue to communicate some information separately. Therefore, the quality-distortion ratio is improved for low capacity embedding; the raw capacity is less than 0.25 bpp. Han *et al.* [17] utilized the Jin *et al.* method to provide a coarse-to-fine tamper localization.

Lu *et al.* [18] extend the DE method for nibble pairs. In this scheme, every pixel in a host image is divided into two nibbles and each nibble pair between two adjacent pixels can be used to hide a secret message through DE methods.

Finally, Coltuc *et al.* proposed a different reversible watermarking. Although they did not use the DE directly, they expanded the difference between a pair of pixels in another way. In [8] they defined the forward RCM (Reversible Contrast Mapping) as follows:

$$\begin{aligned} x' &= 2x - y \\ y' &= 2y - x \end{aligned} \tag{6}$$

Where the difference between two pixels is doubled (expanded). In doing so, it is possible to embed more than one bit per pair of pixels, however, Coltuc sacrificed this amount to completely remove the location map. Some auxiliary data should, still, intersperse among the pixel pairs to ensure reversibility. It is needless to say that only those pairs can be transformed that does not trespass the dynamic range. The inverse transform is defined as

$$\begin{aligned} x &= \left\lceil \frac{2x' + y'}{3} \right\rceil \\ y &= \left\lceil \frac{2y' + x'}{3} \right\rceil \end{aligned} \tag{7}$$

Except when both LSBs are odd, the inverse transform perform exactly. In this case, the LSBs can be replaced with desired information. The first LSB serves as an indicator showing the pair containing any information or not. Here the raw capacity is 0.5 bpp. In [19], they generalized this work by expanding the difference n times. In this case, the data embedding capacity is increased; the raw capacity is $\log_2(2n)/2$ bpp. To achieve more embedding ability it is possible to chose the pixel pairs throw an overlapping window [20] in which the raw capacity is $\log_2(n)$ bpp. However, the extracting should be done in a sequential manner.

4   The Proposed Method

In this section, we introduce a method to enhance the raw capacity in a single iteration to be more than 1 bpp. In this scheme, a new integer transform is proposed in which the spatial correlation among neighboring pixels is exploited. Needless to say, after applying the proposed transform, there are some pixel groups which trespass the dynamic range of pixel intensity. To specify such pixels, different mechanism can be utilized: embedding location map or distinguishing the data container pixel groups at expense of one symbol per group.

Consider the pixel P and its neighboring pixels as a "pixel group" which is depicted in Fig. 1. Due to high spatial correlation in natural images, it is expected that differences between P and its neighborhoods will be small (which is the basic assumption in difference based methods).

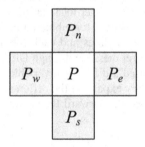

Fig. 1. The utilized neighboring pixels in north, south, east and west

Therefore, the sum of these differences is extremely small in smooth areas. In addition, these differences may attenuate the effect of each other in some parts of image. Based on these facts, the following transform is defined to embed the watermark symbol

$$P_{wkd} = P + (A_n h_n + A_s h_s + A_e h_e + A_w h_w) + [w]$$
$$where \ h_* = P - P_* \ and \ * \in \{n,s,e,w\}$$

(8)

in which A_n, A_s, A_e and A_w indicate the contribution factors of corresponding neighbors. For example, as a special case, it is possible to consider equal participations as $A_n = A_s = A_e = A_w = 1$.

In extraction phase, it is sufficient to compute the sum of the pixel group which leads to the following equation:

$$\bar{P} = M \times P + [w]$$
$$where \quad M = (A_n + A_s + A_e + A_w + 1) \tag{9}$$

Consequently, it can be concluded from equation (9) that M symbols can be embedded in each pixel group in a reversible manner. As mentioned before, the sum of differences is often extremely small; however, in some cases it is possible to cause overflow or underflow. As a result, the transform can be applied only when do not change the intensity interval:

$$0 \le P + (A_n h_n + A_s h_s + A_e h_e + A_w h_w) + [w] \le 255 \tag{10}$$

In the proposed scheme, the sum of adjacent pixels should be remained intact so that the watermark extraction and recovery of the original host become possible. In this case, by using a checkerboard structure, it is possible to embed at most M symbols per pair of pixels; as a result, the raw capacity is $(\log_2 M)/2$ bpp with the first order difference expansion. In this case, the achieved actual capacity will be the highest among previous methods.

In order to remove the location map, we assign one symbol to distinguish between the container elements and non containers. After transforming a pixel, the sum of its intensity and its northern, southern, eastern and western neighbors will be multiple of M. Therefore, one can embed M symbols $[0, M-1]$ with keeping the ability of recovering the original value. We reserve the symbol '0' for non container elements, hence, the watermark symbol can be chosen from $[1, M]$. The pixels which do not satisfy the equation (10) are changed in such a way that the sum of their pixels in group will be multiple of M. The modification done in this step is not invertible; as a result, the applied changes should be saved to ensure the reversibility.

5   Experimental Results

As stated in previous section, with a single iteration of embedding, the raw capacity can exceed 1 bpp. One of the advantages of our method is its low computational cost owing to the simple integer transform. Moreover, it is not needed to store the compressed location map. Image structure has a strong effect on capacity in various methods. Selecting the suitable pixel group with appropriate contribution factors can enhance the amount of capacity. Thus, the flexibility on applying the integer transform based on image structure is one of major advantage of our method. As an illustration, Table 1 shows the capacity distortion results using different contribution factors for "Lena" of size 256×256.

As can be seen, using different values for contribution factors would lead to getting a wide range of capacity/distortion results. It is obvious that the better results could be achieved if the selected contribution factors are more compatible with the image structure. In Fig. 2 the original and watermarked image with various contribution factors, and therefore, different capacity are shown.

Table 1. The capacity distortion results for Lena using different contribution factors

Capacity (bpp)	PSNR (dB)	weights [Ae Aw An As]	execution time(sec) embedding,	extraction
0.9068	25.38	[1 1 1 1]	0.037	3
0.99	23.79	[2 1 1 1]	0.04	3.3
0.9963	23.8	[1 2 1 1]	0.05	3.8
1.02	24.34	[1 1 2 1]	0.04	3.7
1.02	24.25	[1 1 1 2]	0.04	3.7
1.1138	23.84	[1 1 2 2]	0.04	3.7
1.1745	22.55	[2 2 2 2]	0.09	2.6
1.2038	22.24	[2 2 3 2]	0.09	3.21
1.2157	21.25	[3 3 3 3]	0.19	2
1.2548	22.45	[1 1 3 4]	0.07	2.93
1.2836	22.13	[1 1 4 4]	0.116	3.1

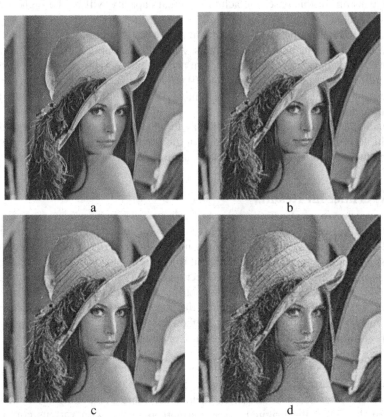

Fig. 2. a) Original image, watermarked image with contribution factors *[Ae Aw An As]*, capacity and PSNR respectively b) [1 1 1 1], 0.9bpp, 25.38dB c) [1 1 21], 1.02bpp, 24.34dB, d) [1 1 4 4], 1.28 bpp, 22.13 dB

We compare our results with Coltuc's method [19] since it has the highest capacity in a single pass of embedding. The results of this comparison are illustrated in Table 2.

It is noteworthy that the method given in [20], however, has been reached more capacity, this amount of capacity is owing to overlapped pixel pairs and sequential embedding. This technique can also be applied using the proposed method to improve the embedding capacity. Thus, we compare just the utilized transform in this paper.

Table 2. The comparison between the results of proposed method with [19]

	Capacity	PSNR	weights [Ae Aw An As]	execution time embedding, extraction		Capacity	PSNR	n	execution time embedding, extraction	
	1.02	24.34	[1 1 2 1]	0.04	3.70	0.94	24.58	2	0.40	7.67
Lena	1.17	22.56	[2 2 2 2]	0.09	2.60	1.15	22.90	3	0.36	7.60
	1.28	22.14	[1 1 4 4]	0.12	3.10	1.26	22.00	4	0.39	6.93
	0.75	20.00	[1 1 1 1]	0.10	2.65	0.80	18.71	2	0.40	5.57
Baboon	0.75	19.41	[1 2 1 1]	0.26	2.77	0.81	17.75	3	0.56	4.80
	0.74	19.10	[2 2 1 1]	0.30	2.60	0.71	17.50	4	0.75	4.50
	0.91	27.05	[1 1 1 1]	0.02	0.22	0.94	25.38	2	0.16	0.64
bird	1.01	25.58	[2 1 1 1]	0.02	0.25	1.15	24.02	3	0.16	0.53
	1.28	23.58	[2 3 2 2]	0.02	0.18	1.26	23.23	4	0.16	0.51

For comparison, we use Lena, Baboon and Bird of size 256×256. As it is clearly shown, the proposed method mostly can reach higher capacity in one iteration. In addition, with equal embedding payload, the better PSNR value can be achieved. Another advantage of our method is its low computational complexity. The exestuation time for both embedding and extracting at the same situation is depicted in Table 2. A rough comparison can demonstrate the less computational cost of the proposed method.

As it is stated before, the proposed method can reach more capacity in a single iteration. As an illustration, for Lena 256×256, the capacity of Tian's method [2] is at most 0.489 bpp, while Alatter's [14] achieves 0.72 bpp using quad vectors as the best case. Moreover, the complexity of the proposed method is considerably lower than these two methods.

5 Conclusion

In this paper, we propose an integer transform to improve the capacity of reversible embedding in a single iteration along with preserving the quality of the watermarked image. The flexibility of the proposed method, owing to selecting appropriate contribution factors, provides the capability of achieving various amount of payload for different image structure. The proposed method does not need to store the compressed location map; as a result, it reduces the computational complexity. Furthermore, due to utilizing the simple proposed integer transform, the computational cost of our method is extremely lower than the recent reversible schemes. Contriving a mechanism to select the appropriate contribution factors can enhance the capacity/distortion characteristic of the proposed algorithm. We are going to devise an adaptive embedding based on image structure as our future work.

References

1. Fridrich, J., Goljan, M., Du, R.: Lossless data embedding: new paradigm in digital watermarking. EURASIP J. Appl. Signal Process 2002, 185–196 (2002)
2. Tian, J.: Reversible data embedding using a difference expansion. IEEE Transactions on Circuits and Systems for Video Technology 13, 890–896 (2003)
3. Barton, J.M.S.A.: Method and apparatus for embedding authentication information within digital data. United States (1997)
4. Honsinger, C.W.W., Jones, P. W., Rabbani, M., Stoffel, J. C.: Lossless recovery of an original image containing embedded data. Eastman Kodak Company, United States (2001)
5. Macq, B.: Lossless Multiresolution Transform for Image Authenticating Watermarking. In: Proc. EUSIPCO, Tampere, Finland (2000)
6. Fridrich, J., Goljan, M., Rui, D.: Lossless data embedding: new paradigm in digital watermarking. EURASIP J. Appl. Signal Process 2002, 185–196 (2002)
7. De Vleeschouwer, C., Delaigle, J.F., Macq, B.: Circular interpretation of bijective transformations in lossless watermarking for media asset management. IEEE Transactions on Multimedia 5, 97–105 (2003)
8. Coltuc, D., Chassery, J.M.: Very Fast Watermarking by Reversible Contrast Mapping. Signal Processing Letters, IEEE 14, 255–258 (2007)
9. Weng, S., Zhao, Y., Pan, J.S., Ni, R.: Reversible Watermarking Based on Invariability and Adjustment on Pixel Pairs. Signal Processing Letters, IEEE 15, 721–724 (2008)
10. Thodi, D.M., Rodriguez, J.: Expansion Embedding Techniques for Reversible Watermarking. IEEE Transactions on Image Processing 16, 721–730 (2007)
11. Kim, H.J., Sachnev, V., Shi, Y.Q., Nam, J., Choo, H.-G.: A Novel Difference Expansion Transform for Reversible Data Embedding. IEEE Transactions on Information Forensics and Security 3, 456–465 (2008)
12. Jin, H.L., Fujiyoshi, M., Kiya, H.: Lossless data hiding in the spatial domain for high quality images. IEICE Transactions on Fundamentals of Electronics Communications and Computer Science E90A, 771–777 (2007)
13. Kuribayashi, M., Morii, M., Tanaka, H.: Reversible Watermark with Large Capacity Based on the Prediction Error Expansion. IEICE Trans. Fundamentals E91-A, 1780–1790 (2008)
14. Alattar, A.M.: Reversible watermark using the difference expansion of a generalized integer transform. IEEE Transactions on Image Processing 13, 1147–1156 (2004)
15. Kamstra, L., Heijmans, H.J.A.M.: Reversible data embedding into images using wavelet techniques and sorting. IEEE Transactions on Image Processing 14, 2082–2090 (2005)
16. Lee, S., Yoo, C.D., Kalker, T.: Reversible image watermarking based on integer-to-integer wavelet transform. IEEE Transactions on Information Forensics and Security 2, 321–330 (2007)

17. Han, S., Fujiyoshi, M., Kiya, H.: An Efficient Reversible Image Authentication Method. IEICE Trans. Fundamentals E91-A, 1907–1914 (2008)
18. Tzu-Chuen, L., Chin-Chen, C.: Lossless nibbled data embedding scheme based on difference expansion. Image Vision Comput. 26, 632–638 (2008)
19. Coltuc, D., Chassery, J.M.: High Capacity Reversible Watermarking. In: IEEE International Conference on Image Processing, pp. 2565–2568 (2006)
20. Coltuc, D.: Improved Capacity Reversible Watermarking. In: IEEE International Conference on Image Processing. ICIP 2007, vol. 3, pp. III-249–III-252 (2007)

Classification Framework for Fair Content Tracing Protocols

Geong Sen Poh and Keith M. Martin

Information Security Group, Royal Holloway, University of London,
Egham, Surrey, TW20 0EX, United Kingdom
{g.s.poh,keith.martin}@rhul.ac.uk

Abstract. Fair content tracing (FaCT) protocols have been proposed by many authors to allow content tracing based on digital watermarking to be performed in a manner that does not discriminate either the client who downloads content or the distributor who provides content. We propose a general design framework for fair content tracing (FaCT) protocols. This framework provides a means to address the ad hoc design issues arising for many existing protocols, several of which have been broken through poor design. We then classify existing FaCT protocols based on this framework, which allows for a more systematic approach to FaCT protocol analysis. We further provide general comparisons and evaluation criteria for FaCT protocols.

1 Introduction

Distribution of digital content, such as sharing, viewing and purchasing of songs and movies, is popular and can be performed with ease. A significant problem is that, after obtaining digital content, a client can easily make many copies and mass distribute them without the consent of the distributor. Therefore *content tracing* has been proposed to alleviate this concern.

Content tracing provides a distributor with the capability to trace the identity of a client based on a copy of content. To achieve this, the distributor generates and places a unique digital watermark into content to create a marked copy. This marked copy is given to the client. When a marked content is found, the distributor traces the identity of the client based on the detected watermark. The process of embedding and detecting the watermark is realised by digital watermarking schemes [4]. More importantly, letting clients know that there is a tracing mechanism in place may help to *deter* them from making copies and illegally distributing these copies.

However, Qiao and Nahrstedt [22], and Pfitzmann and Schunter [17] independently pointed out concerns with such an approach. In content tracing, the distributor generates and embeds a watermark into content. Hence the distributor has in his possession the original content, the watermark and the marked copy. It is clear that a client has no choice but to trust the distributor to act honestly, since the distributor can embed a watermark into any content, distribute

A.T.S. Ho et al. (Eds.): IWDW 2009, LNCS 5703, pp. 252–267, 2009.
© Springer-Verlag Berlin Heidelberg 2009

copies of this content, and frame a client for illegally distributing content. Conversely, due to this framing possibility, a dishonest client can claim that illegal copies are distributed by the distributor.

Therefore, content tracing must be performed in a way that does not discriminate either the client or the distributor. We term such techniques as *fair content tracing (FaCT)* and refer to protocols for implementing fair content tracing as *FaCT protocols*.

Motivation and Contribution: Two of the earliest FaCT protocols are the *buyer-seller watermarking (BSW) protocol* proposed by Memon and Wong [15] and the *asymmetric fingerprinting (AF) protocol* proposed by Pfitzmann and Schunter [17]. Many FaCT protocols has been proposed since then, with the majority being variants of these two ideas. Many of these protocols use different terms and different interpretations of security requirements in their construction. In many cases there is a lack of clear assumptions, threat model or appropriately defined security requirements. Furthermore, some of the newer proposals introduce new features (or "fixes") on top of existing ones, or propose an alternative approach in an ad hoc way. The result is that a protocol is either incomplete, or that additional features are not always added with a clear definition of purpose. As a consequence, these ad hoc designs are hard to analyse and many contain flaws, as shown in [5,8,21,27]. We thus extend some preliminary ideas in [19] to propose a general design framework that can be used to design and analyse FaCT protocols in a systematic manner. Using the framework, we then classify FaCT protocols and use this to provide comparisons of their characteristics.

2 Fair Content Tracing (FaCT) Protocols

A FaCT protocol is an interactive protocol that provides content distribution between a distributor and a client, in which the client who receives content can be traced in a fair manner if copies of this content are found to be illegally distributed. By *fair* we mean that a FaCT protocol fulfills the goals of fair content tracing, which we will discuss in Section 3. The majority of proposed FaCT protocols fall into the following two classes, which we now provide a very brief overview of.

BSW protocols were first proposed by Qiao and Nahrstedt [22] and later improved by Memon and Wong [15]. Later, Ju *et al.* [12] presented a protocol that also protected client privacy. Several BSW protocol variants have since been proposed, including [10,13]. In BSW protocols a trusted third party is used to generate client watermarks, instead of letting the distributor generate them. Asymmetric homomorphic encryption schemes such as Paillier [16] are deployed, together with digital watermarking schemes such as the spread spectrum watermarking scheme [4], in such a way that the distributor who embeds a watermark into content has no idea what the watermark is. This technique is termed *watermarking in the encrypted domain* [6]. Finally, digital signature schemes such as RSA [23] are used to ensure that a dishonest client cannot repudiate the fact that copies of content were illegally distributed.

AF protocols were first proposed by Pfitzmann and Schunter in [17]. This idea was extended to include client privacy in [18]. In most of these protocols, watermarking in the encrypted domain also plays a key role. Instead of introducing a trusted third party to generate watermarks for clients, the client is responsible for generating their own watermark, while the distributor is responsible for embedding this watermark into content. Homomorphic bit commitment schemes [3] are deployed in conjunction with zero-knowledge proof systems [9] to prevent the client from manipulating the watermark generation process. The client, after generating the watermark, must prove in zero-knowledge to the distributor that the generated watermark is well-formed. A watermark is said to be *well-formed* if it is a pseudo-random sequence of real numbers, otherwise it is *ill-formed*. Similar to BSW protocols, digital signature schemes are deployed to prevent a dishonest client from denying the act of illegal content distribution.

3   A Design Framework

Figure 1 illustrates our FaCT protocol design framework. It consists of two components, which we label *fundamentals* and *environment*. In the following subsections we described these two components.

3.1   Fundamentals

This part of the framework defines the players, relationships, requirements and essential phases of a FaCT protocol.

Parties Involved: The *distributor D* is a service provider who distributes (or sells) digital content. The *client C* is a user of digital content who receives (or purchases) digital content from the distributor D. There is a third party known as the *certificate authority CA*, who generates and distributes key materials. For example, a CA is required to certify the public keys of C and D. An *arbiter A* is also required, who attempts to resolve disputes between C and D. In addition, many FaCT protocols require another third party, commonly known as a *watermark certification authority WCA*, who generates client watermarks or key materials that contain the watermark information. The WCA can be either:

- *Online.* This means the WCA is always available *during* content distribution. One example protocol where an online WCA is present is the protocol proposed by Lei *et al.* [13].
- *Offline.* This means the WCA is involved *before* content distribution. In general, C (or D) contacts the WCA to request information before the actual content distribution, which means that during distribution of content, the WCA is not involved. One example where an offline WCA is present is the protocol proposed in [15].
- *Trusted Hardware.* This refers to specific hardware devices that provide the functionality of the online or offline WCA described above. Such trusted

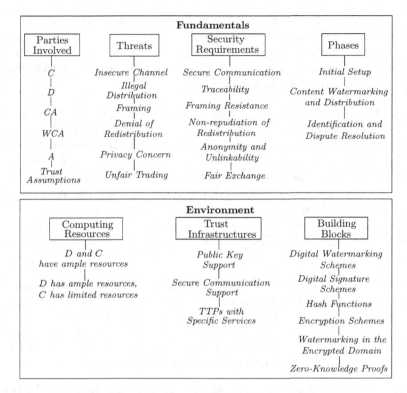

Fig. 1. A General Design Framework

hardware, which is embedded as part of the computing platform itself, allows information to be generated in a trusted environment. These means that the information can only be generated and changed by authorised computer processes. The *Trusted Platform Module (TPM)* of the trusted computing initiative [25] is one such device. Protocols proposed in this category can be found in [7,14].

The type of *WCA* depends on the underlying application. For example, one may choose to deploy a trusted hardware module if extra hardware cost is not an issue, since these are embedded into many devices and are more scalable for distributed environments. Similarly, one may choose an offline *WCA* if the underlying application dictates it most convenient for *C* to request information from the *WCA* before the actual execution of the protocol, keeping communication overheads during execution to a minimum.

Trust Assumptions. We now define the trust relationships between these parties:

- It is assumed that *C* and *D* *do not trust each other.* By this we mean that it is possible that *C* and *D* may try to gain unfair advantage against one another. For example, *C* gains advantage against *D* when he successfully redistributes a copy of content illegally without being traced by *D*.

- The arbiter A and WCA are *fully trusted*. This means that all parties trust A and WCA to behave honestly.
- The CA is *fully trusted*. This means that signatures generated by the CA are always viewed as valid when verification of these signatures based on the CA's public verification key is successful.

We remark that it is important to explicitly state the trust relationships between the parties involved since security issues may arise if these are ambiguous, as in the case of an attack known as the *conspiracy attack* [21]. Also, by definition, collusion with fully trusted parties does not occur. This reasonably reflects our common practice relationships with trusted parties, where banks and legal authorities do not typically conspire with customers. Conspiracies involving fully trusted parties would render many security applications unworkable.

Security Requirements: We now define the security requirements for a FaCT protocol:

1. *Secure Communication.* A communication channel between two parties is secure if *data secrecy (or confidentiality)* is preserved when needed, the parties involved can be *authenticated*, and *data integrity* can be checked.

This addresses the threats on the communication channel. Following this, there are three specific security requirements for FaCT protocols:

2. *Traceability.* A dishonest C who illegally distributes content can be traced to their identity by D.
3. *Framing Resistance.* An honest C cannot be falsely accused of illegal distribution by D.
4. *Non-repudiation of Redistribution.* A dishonest C who illegally distributes copies of content cannot deny such an act. This means that D is able to prove the illegal act of the client to a third party. (*Framing resistance* is a prerequisite since, without it, C can claim that it is D who redistributed the content.)

A FaCT protocol is a *weak FaCT protocol* if it fulfills only traceability and framing resistance, while it is a *strong FaCT protocol* if it fulfills all three requirements. These three requirements address the threats due to content tracing that we described in our introduction. The next two properties are optional:

5. *Anonymity and Unlinkability.* In the case where client privacy is a concern, C can obtain content anonymously from D. Furthermore, given any two contents, D cannot tell whether they are from the same client.
6. *Fair Exchange.* In the case where there is *payment* involved, either both parties (C and D) are satisfied, or no party gains advantage over the other. For example, C does not receive content if D does not receive payment.

Table 1 summarises these requirements. We note that except for the first and the last requirements, all others have been previously mentioned (in various forms and combinations) in [12,13,18].

Table 1. Security concerns and requirements for FaCT protocols

Concern	Requirement
Insecure channel	Secure communication
Illegal distribution	Traceability
	(deterrence using digital watermarking)
Framing	Framing resistance
Denial of redistribution	Non-repudiation of redistribution
Privacy concern	Anonymity and unlinkability
Fair distribution	Fair exchange
(when payment is involved)	

Protocol phases: There are three main phases in a FaCT protocol. We outline a generic structure for each phase. While not providing an instantiation, this generic structure is sufficient to identify design issues, which we later raise.

Phase 1: `Initial Setup`. The main aim of this phase is to provide key materials for C and D to support the required cryptographic services. In this phase C and D generate key materials. The CA verifies and signs the public keys of C and D. The signed public keys can then be publicly distributed to other parties who need to use them. We assume that the activities in this offline phase are carried out *before* content distribution. We also assume that prior to this WCA and A have obtained their respective authenticated public keys, which we discuss in Section 3.2. Figure 2 shows the main protocol flow, where the notation $\{\cdot\}_{AKE}$ means that the message is transmitted under secure communication support. In addition, SIG represents digital signatures on objects (such as the public keys of C) and *info* means other relevant data.

---

① `Initial Setup:`

$$C \text{ or } D \to CA : \{info\}_{AKE}$$
$$CA \to C \text{ or } D : \{info,\ \text{SIG}\}_{AKE}$$

Before
content
distribution

Fig. 2. Initial Setup

Phase 2: `Content Watermarking and Distribution`. The aim of this phase is to provide C with the requested content and at the same time fulfil the main security requirements of a FaCT protocol. It is an online process. Figure 3 shows the main protocol flow, where $f(W)$ is an object that "contains" the client watermark W. This plays a crucial role in providing framing resistance in many existing FaCT protocols. As an example $f(W)$ can be an encrypted watermark. We use $f(\widetilde{X})$ to denote an object that "contains" the marked content.

---

② Content Watermarking and Distribution:

$C \to D$: $\{info,\ f(W),\ \texttt{SIG}\}_{AKE}$

$D \to C$: $\left\{info,\ f(\widetilde{X})\right\}_{AKE}$

Content
distribution

Fig. 3. Content Watermarking and Distribution

Phase 3: **Identification and Dispute Resolution.** Figure 4 shows the main protocol flow, where $f^{WM}()$ denotes a watermark detection algorithm for a watermarking scheme [4], which returns **true** if a watermark is detected, or returns **false** otherwise. In this phase D identifies C from a found copy of content $\widehat{X}$ using $f^{WM}()$. If necessary, D proves to an arbiter A that C illegally distributed content by showing A some evidence (*info*, $\widehat{X}$ and $\texttt{SIG}$). This evidence normally consists of at least the client watermark and the client's signature on an agreement describing the content. Most FaCT protocols require that A obtains the client watermark from another party (C or a trusted third party).

---

③ Identification and Dispute Resolution:

D : $\{\texttt{true, false}\} \leftarrow f^{WM}()$

$D \to A$: $\left\{info,\ \widehat{X},\ \texttt{SIG}\right\}_{AKE}$

$A \to C$ or WCA: $\{watermark\ info?\}_{AKE}$

C or $WCA \to A$: $\{watermark\ info\}_{AKE}$

A : $\{\texttt{true, false}\} \leftarrow f^{WM}()$

After
content
distribution

Fig. 4. Identification and Dispute Resolution

3.2   Environment

The main purpose of this framework component is to provide the design "modules" (or parameters) that can be chosen and then assembled to construct a FaCT protocol.

Computing Resources: This refers to the computing power and storage available to the parties involved. The computing resources available to D and C influence the choice of building blocks for a FaCT protocol. In the scenario where C has limited resources then resource intensive mechanisms such as watermarking in the encrypted domain based on asymmetric homomorphic encryption schemes may not be suitable [20,29]. However we note that most existing FaCT protocols implicitly assume that both C and D have ample resources.

Trusted Infrastructures: A FaCT protocol may involve the following trusted infrastructures:

Public Key Support. The security properties stated in Section 3.1, notably *non-repudiation of redistribution*, requires the generation of non-repudiable proofs so that it is possible to prove the guilt of a dishonest client to a third party. A standard way of providing this proof is by deploying a digital signature scheme [23]. In addition, many existing protocols use asymmetric homomorphic encryption schemes [16] as tools for providing framing resistance. Both digital signatures and homomorphic encryption schemes require the distribution of public verification and encryption keys prior to the content distribution process. These keys must be authenticated so that a party who uses these keys knows that they belong to the legitimate parties. To achieve this, the existence of a PKI supporting the use of digital certificates is assumed.

Secure Communication Support. In a FaCT protocol, before C requests content from D, C and D must authenticate each other. The most common to provide this is by using *entity authentication and key establishment (AKE) protocols*, which are run between two parties. This is to (at a bare minimum) achieve *mutual entity authentication*, where each party gains confidence in the identity of their communication partner, and *key establishment*, where a secret "session key" is agreed between the two communicating parties, to be used for protecting data secrecy, data integrity and other security services.

There are many different AKE protocols, as reviewed in [2]. We argue that a FaCT protocol should deploy a well-established AKE protocol in order to provide secure communication, which we defined in Section 3.1.

Building Blocks: These are the technical components required to fulfill the core security services needed by a FaCT protocol. We only briefly identify the role of some typical building blocks:

- *Digital watermarking schemes* [4] are used to provide *traceability*.
- *Digital signature schemes*, such as RSA [23], which make use of *cryptographic hash functions* [11], are used to provide *non-repudiation of redistribution*. Together with public key support, these are also used to provide *anonymity and unlinkability* and *fair exchange*.
- For some FaCT protocols, *homomorphic encryption schemes*, such as Paillier [16], together with *digital watermarking schemes*, are used to provide *watermarking in the encrypted domain* [6]. This is used to provide *framing resistance*.
- For some FaCT protocols, *zero-knowledge proofs* [9] are used together with *watermarking in the encrypted domain* to provide *framing resistance*.

4   Classification

The aim of this section is to classify FaCT protocols into carefully chosen categories that facilitate design of new schemes and analysis of existing ones.

We choose to use the presence and operation of a trusted third party who provides watermark related information (normally represented by a *WCA*) as our major classification criterion. This is because the presence and role of trusted third parties significantly influences the underlying building blocks that can be deployed, and hence the subsequent process that needs to be followed during execution of a FaCT protocol. Most importantly, it raises the crucial issue of *who generates the client's watermark*, which has security ramifications for all three of the specific security requirements of a FaCT protocol. We identify four categories of FaCT protocol.

4.1   Category 1: Protocols without Trusted Third Parties

Our first category is a family of FaCT protocols that do not use a *WCA*. Their main characteristic is that C generates and possibly encrypts the watermark (for example, $f(W)_C$ in Figure 5), and this watermark is embedded into content by D in such a way that D has no knowledge of the watermark. Allowing C to generate the watermark means that extra security measures must be put in place to prevent C from generating an ill-formed watermark. AF protocols fall into this category. Figure 5 illustrates the protocol flow for the tt Content Watermarking and Distribution phase. The other two phases are similar to the general flows provided in Section 3.1.

---

② Content Watermarking and Distribution:

$C \to D$: $\{info,\ f(W)_C,\ \texttt{SIG}\}_{AKE}$ **Content**

$D \to C$: $\left\{info,\ f(\widetilde{X})\right\}_{AKE}$ **distribution**

Fig. 5. Protocols without TTPs – Content Watermarking and Distribution

4.2   Category 2: Protocols with Online Trusted Third Parties

This category includes all protocols that require an online *WCA*, in addition to the *CA*. The main characteristic of protocols in this category is that the *WCA* is tasked with generating client watermarks, thus avoiding the issue of C generating ill-formed watermarks faced in Category 1. However, the *WCA* always needs to be available for either C or D to request the client watermark. Hence requiring such an online trusted third party adds to the communication overhead. Example protocols based on this model include proposals in [13,29]. Figure 6 shows the

---

② Content Watermarking and Distribution:

$C \to D$: $\{info,\ \texttt{SIG}\}_{AKE}$ **content**

$D \to WCA$: $\{watermark\text{-}request\ info\}_{AKE}$ **distribution**

$WCA \to D$: $\{info,\ f(W)_{WCA},\ \texttt{SIG}\}_{AKE}$

$D \to C$: $\left\{info,\ f(\widetilde{X})\right\}_{AKE}$

Fig. 6. Protocols with Online TTPs – Content Watermarking and Distribution

protocol flow for the Content Watermarking and Distribution phase. As can be observed, the object that contains the watermark is generated by the WCA ($f(W)_{WCA}$), while the dashed box shows the protocol flow between D and the WCA that differs from other categories. The other two phases are similar to the general flow provided in Section 3.1.

4.3   Category 3: Protocols with Offline Trusted Third Parties

This model uses an offline WCA to generate watermark information (such as an encrypted client watermark, $f(W)_{WCA}$), which is then passed to C. The WCA is offline since it is not involved in the actual content distribution between D and C, as compared to Category 2. In other words, the WCA can be offline once C receives the watermark information. Most BSW protocols fall into this category. Other protocols in this category include [12,20]. Figure 7 shows the Initial Setup phase, the main phase that differentiates this category from the others.

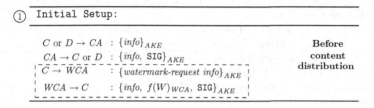

Fig. 7. Protocols with Offline TTPs – Initial Setup

4.4   Category 4: Protocols with Trusted Hardware

Protocols in this category deploy trusted hardware in D's and/or C's computing platforms. The main idea is to use this trusted hardware to generate and/or verifying client watermark information. It can also be used to securely embed watermarks into content. These devices can play the roles of either the online or offline WCA in Categories 2 and 3. For example, instead of contacting the WCA in Category 2, D may deploy trusted hardware to replace the WCA. The major advantage, especially if the device resides on C's computing platform, is that there is no single central WCA, but many different devices on each client's computing platform. This allows for scalability and so is more suitable for distributed computing environments. Such setup also allows the device to play the role of an offline WCA, albeit a distributed one. However, the extra cost of hardware implementation must be factored into the design of such protocols. Protocols proposed in this category include [7] and [14]. Figure 8 illustrates the Content Watermarking and Distribution phase with two different settings, where either the trusted hardware TH resides on C's or D's computing platform. Here $\rightleftharpoons$ denotes communication with the TH. As can be observed, if the TH is on C's computing platform then C's TH generates $f(W)_{TH}$ and sends it together with the other information to obtain content from D. Otherwise, if the TH is

② Content Watermarking and Distribution:

$C \rightleftharpoons TH$: $\{info,\ W\}_{AKE}$ content

$C \rightarrow D$: $\{info,\ f(W)_{TH},\ \mathtt{SIG}\}_{AKE}$ distribution

---

OR

$C \rightarrow D$: $\{info,\ \mathtt{SIG}\}_{AKE}$

$D \rightleftharpoons TH$: $\{info,\ f(W)_{TH}\}_{AKE}$

$D \rightarrow C$: $\left\{info,\ f(\widetilde{X})\right\}_{AKE}$

Fig. 8. Protocols with TH – Content Watermarking and Distribution

Table 2. Characteristics of FaCT Protocol Categories

Cat.	Characteristics
1	C generates watermark information. *Benefit*: No *WCA*. *Issue*: Extra measure needed to prevent C generating ill-formed watermarks.
2	*WCA* generates watermark information. D or C contacts *WCA* during content distribution. *Benefit*: Avoids the issue of ill-formed watermarks since *WCA* generates them. *Issue*: *WCA* must always be available.
3	*WCA* generates watermark information. D or C contacts *WCA* during initial setup. *Benefit*: Avoids the need for a *WCA* that must be available during content distribution. *Issue*: *WCA* required during initial setup.
4	Trusted hardware generates watermark information. *Benefit*: No *WCA*. Suitable for distributed systems. *Issue*: Extra hardware cost.

on D's computing platform then C just sends the necessary information while D obtains $f(W)_{TH}$ from the TH.

Table 2 summarises the main characteristics of FaCT protocols in the four categories. We now briefly discuss impact of the two optional requirements.

4.5 Adding Anonymity and Unlinkability

In addition to providing the three main security requirements discussed in Section 3.1, some FaCT protocols are designed to address the additional requirements of anonymity and unlinkability in order to protect client privacy. This was first introduced in [18]. Such protocols may fall into any of the four main categories discussed above. Examples of Category 3 protocols can be found in [12,13]. A typical mechanism for providing anonymity and unlinkability is, instead of establishing secure communication with D using long term public keys, C communicates with D using a set of temporary keys. Similarly to the long term keys, these temporary keys are signed by the CA to prove their validity. These keys do not contain identity information for C. Therefore, when C uses them to request content from D, D will not know the identity of C, but can verify that such keys are valid based on the signatures of the CA.

4.6   Adding Payment and Fair Exchange

Payment: One other aspect that has not been studied before in existing protocols is how to include a payment mechanism. Many protocols, such as [13] and [17], include a purchase agreement as an integral part of the protocols, which implicitly means that payment is involved, but do not provide details on how payment is conducted. Based on [26], we show in Figure 9 how this is possible by including a payment infrastructure on top of a FaCT protocol. A payment mechanism is normally agreed between C and the distributor D with their respective banks, entering into contractual relationships. This can be performed before the Initial Setup phase of a FaCT protocol in whichever category applies. With the payment infrastructure in place, a *payment token* can be included as one of the messages in the communication between the client C and distributor D. Depending on the mechanism chosen, the payment token can be, for example, *digital coins* as in an electronic cash system or credit card details of client C [24]. Although the inclusion of a payment mechanism is straightforward (at least theoretically), it raises the delicate issue of *fair exchange* between C and D.

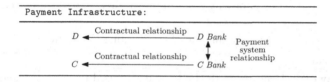

Fig. 9. Payment Infrastructure

Fair Exchange: In the context of fair content tracing, C and D *do not trust each other*. Thus when payment is included, we must also ensure that C and D will exchange the payment and content in a fair manner, in addition to the other requirements. This motivates the requirement of *fair exchange* introduced in Section 3.1. In order to fulfill this requirement, a FaCT protocol requiring payment should incorporate an existing *fair exchange scheme* such as [1].

5   Evaluation Criteria

In this section we briefly state the evaluation criteria for performance analysis of FaCT protocols based on our design framework. These can be used to compare protocols proposed within one category, or indeed to compare protocols in different categories. We suggest that FaCT protocols should be assessed based on the processes relating to the generation of the final marked content, since this represents the most important (and generally most expensive) operation, as can be observed from the general constructions discussed in Section 4. The evaluation criteria are as follows:

1. **Bandwidth:** The size of the encrypted marked content transmitted from D to C affects the bandwidth required. As an example that applies to many Category 3 protocols, if an element of a content with 32 bits is encrypted using a homomorphic encryption scheme with 1024 bit modulus, then the transmitted message is much larger than that suggested by the content.
2. **Communication:** The total communication costs of the protocol. For example, the existence of a WCA in Categories 2 and 3 adds at least two extra protocol messages to the execution of a FaCT protocol compared to protocols in Categories 1 and 4.
3. **Computation:** The degree of computation that each party needs to perform to produce the encrypted marked content. This is determined by the underlying building blocks. For example, Category 3 protocols using asymmetric homomorphic encryption schemes typically require expensive modular exponentiations.
4. **Storage:** The amount of storage required by C and D to store their respective key material and the watermark information used for generating and retrieving the encrypted marked content.

Table 3 provides a general evaluation on the four categories, where **AU/FE** denotes the addition of anonymity and unlinkability, and/or fair exchange.

Table 3. Brief Evaluation of the Existing FaCT Protocols

Cat.	Criteria
1	**Bandwidth:** Depends on the building blocks used to generate the encrypted marked content. **Comm:** No WCA hence no extra communication. **Comp:** Depends on the building blocks (e.g. asymmetric or symmetric cryptographic primitives). **Storage:** Depends on the building blocks. C stores watermark information.
2	**Bandwidth:** Depends on the building blocks as in Category 1. **Comm:** At least two extra communications with WCA during content distribution. **Comp:** Depends on the building blocks as in Category 1. **Storage:** Depends on the building blocks as in Category 1. D or WCA stores watermark information.
3	Similar to protocols in Category 2 except that the two extra communications happen during initial setup instead of during content distribution.
4	**Bandwidth:** Depends on the building blocks as in Category 1. **Comm:** At least two extra communications with TH. **Comp:** Depends on the building blocks as in Category 1. **Storage:** Depends on the building blocks as in Category 1. D or C stores watermark information.
AU/ FE	**Comm:** Extra communication with WCA to obtain pseudonym or to ensure fair exchange.

6   Applying the Framework

We have presented a framework for FaCT protocols. We then used the framework to classify FaCT protocols and compare their characteristics at a category level. There are several benefits of this framework and classification:

- *Consistency*: Many existing FaCT protocols do not clarify the model in which they are intended to operate and do not clearly define their security requirements. The framework provides a common reference point.
- *Analysis*: The framework can be used to pigeonhole deficiencies and, where applicable, quickly identify issues and flaws in the design of proposed FaCT protocols. An example of applying the framework successfully for this purpose is [21].
- *Design*: The framework can be used to identify generic issues with certain design approaches and unexplored design directions. For example, a study of existing FaCT protocols reveals no practical proposals in Category 1 that do not contain security flaws. As another example, in Category 3 many existing FaCT protocols rely on expensive homomorphic encryption, hence approaches such as [20,29] merit further exploration.
- *Formal modeling*: Our framework provides a basis for conducting formal analysis of FaCT protocols. A formal modeling approach has been initiated by Williams *et al.* [27,28], which is complementary to this work.

References

1. Asokan, N., Schunter, M., Waidner, M.: Optimistic Protocols for Fair Exchange. In: Proceedings of 4th ACM Conference on Computer and Communications Security, pp. 7–17 (1997)
2. Boyd, C., Mathuria, A.: Protocols for Authentication and Key Establishment. Information Security and Cryptography Series. Springer, Heidelberg (2003)
3. Brassard, G., Chaum, D., Crepeau, C.: Minimum Disclosure Proofs of Knowledge. Journal of Computer and System Sciences 37(1988), 156–189 (1988)
4. Cox, I.J., Miller, M.L., Bloom, J.A., Fridrich, J., Kalker, T.: Digital Watermarking and Steganography, 2nd edn. Morgan Kaufmann Publishers, San Francisco (2008)
5. Deng, M., Preneel, B.: Attacks On Two Buyer-Seller Watermarking Protocols And An Improvement For Revocable Anonymity. In: IEEE International Symposium on Electronic Commerce and Security - ISECS 2008 (2008)
6. Katzenbeisser, S. (ed.): List of potential applications interested by s.p.e.d. D3.1, Philips Research (Philips), for Signal Processing in the Encrypted Domain (SPEED) Project, IST-2006-034238, Information Society Technologies (2007), http://www.speedproject.eu
7. Fan, C.-I., Chen, M.-T., Sun, W.-Z.: Buyer-Seller Watermarking Protocols with Off-line Trusted Parties. In: Proceedings of the International Conference on Multimedia and Ubiquitous Engineering (MUE 2007), pp. 1035–1040. IEEE Computer Society Press, Los Alamitos (2007)
8. Goi, B.-M., Phan, R.C.-W., Chuah, H.-T.: Cryptanalysis of Two Non-anonymous Buyer-Seller Watermarking Protocols for Content Protection. In: Gervasi, O., Gavrilova, M.L. (eds.) ICCSA 2007, Part I. LNCS, vol. 4705, pp. 951–960. Springer, Heidelberg (2007)

9. Goldwasser, S., Micali, S., Rackoff, C.: The knowledge complexity of interactive proof-systems. In: Proceedings of the seventeenth annual ACM symposium on Theory of computing, pp. 291–304 (1985)

10. Ibrahim, I.M., Nour El-Din, S.H., Hegazy, A.F.A.: An Effective and Secure Buyer-Seller Watermarking Protocol. In: Third International Symposium on Information Assurance and Security (IAS 2007), pp. 21–26. IEEE Computer Society Press, Los Alamitos (2007)

11. Federal information processing standards (fips 180-2). Secure Hash Standard (2001), http://csrc.nist.gov/publications/fips/fips180-2/fips180-2.pdf

12. Ju, H.S., Kim, H.-J., Lee, D.-H., Lim, J.-I.: An anonymous buyer-seller watermarking protocol with anonymity control. In: Lee, P.J., Lim, C.H. (eds.) ICISC 2002. LNCS, vol. 2587, pp. 421–432. Springer, Heidelberg (2003)

13. Lei, C.-L., Yu, P.-L., Tsai, P.-L., Chan, M.-H.: An Efficient and Anonymous Buyer-Seller Watermarking Protocol. IEEE Trans. on Image Processing 13(12), 1618–1626 (2004)

14. Leung, A., Poh, G.S.: An Anonymous Watermarking Scheme for Content Distribution Protection using Trusted Computing. In: SECRYPT 2007 - International Conference on Security and Cryptography, pp. 319–326. INSTICC Press (2007)

15. Memon, N., Wong, P.W.: A Buyer-Seller Watermarking Protocol. IEEE Trans. on Image Processing 10(4), 643–649 (2001)

16. Paillier, P.: Public-key Cryptosystems Based on Composite Degree Residuosity Classes. In: Stern, J. (ed.) EUROCRYPT 1999. LNCS, vol. 1592, pp. 223–238. Springer, Heidelberg (1999)

17. Pfitzmann, B., Schunter, M.: Asymmetric Fingerprinting. In: Maurer, U.M. (ed.) EUROCRYPT 1996. LNCS, vol. 1070, pp. 84–95. Springer, Heidelberg (1996)

18. Pfitzmann, B., Waidner, M.: Anonymous Fingerprinting. In: Fumy, W. (ed.) EUROCRYPT 1997. LNCS, vol. 1233, pp. 88–102. Springer, Heidelberg (1997)

19. Poh, G.S., Martin, K.M.: A Framework for Design and Analysis of Asymmetric Fingerprinting Protocols. In: International Workshop on Data Hiding for Information and Multimedia Security attached to IAS 2007, pp. 457–461. IEEE Computer Society Press, Los Alamitos (2007)

20. Poh, G.S., Martin, K.M.: An Efficient Buyer-Seller Watermarking Scheme Based on Chameleon Encryption. In: Kim, H.J., Katzenbeisser, S., Ho, A.T.S. (eds.) IWDW 2008. LNCS, vol. 5450. Springer, Heidelberg (to appear)

21. Poh, G.S., Martin, K.M.: On the (In)security of Two Buyer-Seller Watermarking Protocols. In: SECRYPT 2008 - International Conference on Security and Cryptography, pp. 253–260 (2008)

22. Qiao, L., Nahrstedt, K.: Watermarking schemes and protocols for protecting rightful ownerships and customer's rights. Journal of Visual Communication and Image Representation 9(3), 194–210 (1998)

23. Rivest, R.L., Shamir, A., Adleman, L.: A Method for Obtaining Digital Signatures and Public-Key Cryptosystems. Commun. of the ACM 2(2), 120–126 (1978)

24. Sadeghi, A.-R., Schneider, M.: Electronic Payment Systems. In: Becker, E., Buhse, W., Günnewig, D., Rump, N. (eds.) Digital Rights Management. LNCS, vol. 2770, pp. 113–137. Springer, Heidelberg (2003)

25. Trusted Computing Group (TCG). Trusted computing group website (accessed, February 2009), http://www.trustedcomputinggroup.org

26. Tomlinson, A.: Application and Business Security: Payment and e–commerce applications. Lecture Notes IY5601, MSc. of Information Security, Information Security Group, Royal Holloway, University of London (2008)

27. Williams, D.M., Treharne, H., Ho, A.T.S.: Using a Formal Analysis Technique to Identify an Unbinding Attack on a Buyer-Seller Watermarking Protocol. In: Proceedings of the 10th ACM Workshop on Multimedia and Security (MM & Sec. 2008). ACM, New York (2008)

28. Williams, D.M., Treharne, H., Ho, A.T.S., Walker, A.: Formal Analysis of Two Buyer-Seller Watermarking Protocols. In: Anthony, T.S., Kim, H.J., Katzenbeisser, S., Ho, A.T.S. (eds.) IWDW 2008. LNCS, vol. 5450. Springer, Heidelberg (to appear)

29. Wu, Y., Pang, H.: A Lightweight Buyer-Seller Watermarking Protocol. In: Advances in Multimedia 2008, vol. 905065, 7 pages (2008) doi:10.1155/2008/905065

Fragile Watermarking Scheme with Extensive Content Restoration Capability*

Xinpeng Zhang, Shuozhong Wang, and Guorui Feng

School of Communication and Information Engineering
Shanghai University
Shanghai 200072, P.R. China
{xzhang,shuowang,grfeng}@shu.edu.cn

Abstract. This paper proposes a novel fragile watermarking scheme capable of recovering the original principal content in extensive areas. The watermark data are made up of two parts: reference-bits derived from the principal content of the host image and containing some necessary redundancy, and hash-bits matching the content of local blocks. While the reference-bits are embedded into the entire host image, the hash-bits are embedded into the local blocks. On the authentication side, after identifying the tampered areas, the watermark data extracted from the reserved regions can provide sufficient information to restore the principal content of host image even when the rate of tampered blocks is large.

Keywords: fragile watermarking, content restoration, tampering rate.

1 Introduction

The purpose of fragile watermarking is to check integrity and authenticity of digital contents [1, 2]. When a portion of the original content is replaced with fake information, it is desirable to locate the modified areas and to recover the original content.

Fragile watermarking techniques for locating modified areas can be roughly classified into two types: block-wise and pixel-wise schemes. In block-wise fragile watermarking, the host image is always divided into small blocks and the mark, e.g., a hash of the principal content of each block, is embedded into the block itself [3, 4]. If the image has been changed, the image content and the watermark corresponding to the tampered blocks cannot be matched therefore the tampered blocks can be identified. Although the block-wise fragile watermarking methods can detect a serious replacement, they can only locate tampered blocks, but not the pixels. In other words, the block-wise techniques cannot find the precise pattern of the modification. Some pixel-wise fragile watermarking schemes have been proposed to resolve this problem, in which the watermark information derived from gray values of host pixels is embedded into the host pixels themselves [5, 6, 7]. So, tampered pixels can be identified

---

* This work was supported by the Natural Science Foundation of China (60872116, 60832010, and 60773079), and the High-Tech Research and Development Program of China (2007AA01Z477).

A.T.S. Ho et al. (Eds.): IWDW 2009, LNCS 5703, pp. 268–278, 2009.

from the absence of watermark information they carry. In these methods, however, as some information derived from new pixel values may coincide with the watermark, localization of the tampered pixels is not complete, and detection of the tampering pattern is inaccurate. In [8], a statistical mechanism is introduced into fragile water-marking, and two different distributions corresponding to tampered and original pixels can be used to precisely locate the tampered pixels. If the embedded watermark data are derived both from pixels and blocks, a receiver can first identify the tampered blocks and then use the watermark hidden in the rest blocks to find the detailed modification pattern [9]. Since it takes advantages of both block-wise and pixel-wise techniques, its performance in locating tempered pixels is better than that of the method presented in [8].

Furthermore, some watermarking approaches capable of reconstructing the original content in the tampered areas have been published. Two methods are proposed in [10]. The primary DCT coefficients or a low color depth version of the original contents are embedded into the least significant bits (LSB) or the pixel differences with different positions. When malicious modification in a watermarked image is located, the information extracted from reserved regions can be exploited to recover the principal content of the tampered areas. In [11], the embedded watermark signal is exclusive-OR between a pseudo-random sequence and the polarity information of DCT coefficients. Similarly, rough retrieval of the original content in the tampered areas can be obtained by iterative projections of the polarity information on a convex set. In these methods, the main content in a region is embedded into another region of the image so that the restoration cannot be executed when certain region and the region accommodating its original information are both tampered.

In [12], the watermark data is derived from the entire original content and embedded into the host using a reversible data-hiding technique. Having located the tampered areas, one can separate the watermark data from the image and use them to restore the host image without any error. A limitation of this method is that the tampered portion must be less than 3.2% of the entire content to allow perfect image restoration. In reality, however, a pirate may replace an extensive area of the original content with fake information.

Therefore, it is desirable to develop a fragile watermarking technique that is capable of recovering the original principal content in extensive areas. In this paper, we propose such a fragile watermarking scheme, in which the embedded watermark data are made up of two parts: one derived from the principal content of host image and contains some necessary redundancy, and the other matched to the local content for tampered-area localization. Even though extensive tampering is made, the watermark data extracted from the reserved regions can still provide sufficient information to restore the principal content of the host image. Such restoration of image content is satisfactory for many applications.

2 Watermark Embedding Procedure

In the watermark embedding procedure, we first compress the principal content of each block into a number of bits, and then introduce some redundancy in them to form a series of reference-bits. While the reference-bits are embedded into the entire host image, the hash-bits for identifying the tampered blocks are embedded into the blocks themselves. Here, the 5 most significant bits (MSB) of all pixels in the host image are kept unchanged, and the 3 least significant bits (LSB) of all pixels are replaced with the reference-bits and the hash-bits.

2.1 Content Compression

Denote the numbers of rows and columns in an original image as N_1 and N_2, and the total number of pixels as N ($N = N_1 \times N_2$). Assume both N_1 and N_2 are multiples of 8, and divide the image into $N/64$ non-overlapped blocks with a same size of 8×8. We remove the 3 least significant bits (LSB) of all pixels to reduce the range of gray levels from [0, 255] to [0, 31]. Then, each block in the low gray depth version of the original image is transformed using the discrete cosine transformation (DCT). The 15 lowest frequency DCT coefficients in each block are rounded to integers, and converted to binary sequences with different lengths as shown in Figure 1. The high frequency coefficients are ignored. Figure 2 shows ranges of the 15 coefficient values. In other words, each low frequency coefficient C is represented as a K bit binary sequence in the following way.

$$b_k = \left\lfloor C_R / 2^{K-k} \right\rfloor \bmod 2, \quad k = 1, 2, \ldots, K \tag{1}$$

where K is the number corresponding to the coefficient's position in Figure 1,

$$C_R = \begin{cases} 0 & , \text{ if } C \leq R_{\min} \\ \text{round}(C) - R_{\min} & , \text{ if } R_{\min} < C < R_{\max} \\ R_{\max} - R_{\min} & , \text{ if } C \geq R_{\max} \end{cases} \tag{2}$$

and $R_{\min}/R_{\max}$ are the minimum/maximum values of the range corresponding to the coefficient's position in Figure 2. For example, if the value of coefficient at position (0, 0) is 58.32, it can be rounded and represented as (00111010) in binary notational system. At (0, 1) or (1, 0), a coefficient value of 13.73 is represented as (101101), while any value below −31 and above 32 should be clipped to (000000) and (111111). This way, we compress each block into 54 bits, named the compression-bits. So, we have obtained a total of $27 \cdot N/32$ compression-bits from all blocks.

8	6	4	3	2	0	0	0
6	4	3	2	0	0	0	0
4	3	2	0	0	0	0	0
3	2	0	0	0	0	0	0
2	0	0	0	0	0	0	0
0	0	0	0	0	0	0	0
0	0	0	0	0	0	0	0
0	0	0	0	0	0	0	0

Fig. 1. Numbers of bits used to represent the coefficients with different frequencies

[0, 255]	[−31, 32]	[−7, 8]	[−3, 4]	[−1, 2]	–	–	–
[−31, 32]	[−7, 8]	[−3, 4]	[−1, 2]	–	–	–	–
[−7, 8]	[−3, 4]	[−1, 2]	–	–	–	–	–
[−3, 4]	[−1, 2]	–	–	–	–	–	–
[−1, 2]	–	–	–	–	–	–	–
–	–	–	–	–	–	–	–
–	–	–	–	–	–	–	–
–	–	–	–	–	–	–	–

Fig. 2. Ranges of represented coefficient values with different frequencies

2.2 Reference-Bit Generation

According to a secret key, we pseudo-randomly divide the $27 \cdot N/32$ compression-bits into $N/128$ subsets, each of which contains 108 compression-bits. Denote the m-th subsets as $\mathbf{S}_m(m = 1, 2, \ldots, N/128)$, and the compression-bits in it as $c_{m,1}, c_{m,2}, \ldots, c_{m,108}$. For each subset, generate 320 reference-bits according to its 108 compression-bits,

$$\begin{bmatrix} r_{m,1} \\ r_{m,2} \\ \vdots \\ r_{m,320} \end{bmatrix} = \mathbf{A}_m \cdot \begin{bmatrix} c_{m,1} \\ c_{m,2} \\ \vdots \\ c_{m,108} \end{bmatrix}, \quad m = 1,2,\ldots,N/128 \qquad (3)$$

where $\mathbf{A}_m$ are pseudo-random binary matrixes sized 320×108, and the arithmetic in (3) is modulo-2. The matrices $\mathbf{A}_m$ are also derived from the secret key. So, we have produced a total of $5N/2$ reference-bits. In other words, redundancy is introduced to expand the $27 \cdot N/32$ compression-bits to $5N/2$ reference-bits.

2.3 Watermark Embedding

Pseudo-randomly permute the $5N/2$ reference-bits using the secret key, and divide them into $N/64$ groups, each containing 160 reference-bits. Map the groups to the $N/64$ blocks in a one-to-one manner. For each block, we collect the 320 original bits in the 5 MSB-layers, the 160 reference-bits in its corresponding group, and the block index that has a value within $[1, N/64]$ and indicates the position of the block. Then, feed them into a hash function to calculate the 32 hash-bits. Here, the hash function must have the property that any change on an input would result in a quite different output. Pseudo-randomly permute the 160 reference-bits and 32 hash-bits according to the secret key, and replace the 3 least significant bits of the block with these 192 bits to produce a watermarked image.

This way, 5 MSBs of the cover image are reserved while 3 LSBs replaced with the reference-bits and hash-bits. Assuming that the original distribution of the 3 LSBs is uniform, the average energy of distortion caused by watermarking on each pixel is

$$E_{\mathrm{D}} = \frac{1}{64} \cdot \sum_{u=0}^{7} \sum_{v=0}^{7} (u - v)^2 \qquad (4)$$

So, the approximate PSNR is

$$\text{PSNR} \approx 10 \cdot \log_{10}\left(255^2 / E_D\right) = 37.9 \text{ dB} \tag{5}$$

The entire procedure of watermark embedding is sketched in Figure 3.

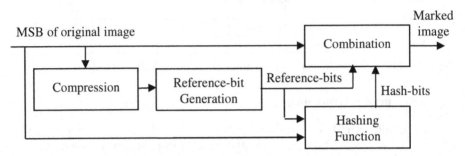

Fig. 3. Entire procedure of watermark embedding

3   Content Restoration Procedure

Assume that a pirate may have altered the content of a watermarked image without changing the image size. After receiving the suspicious image, we can first locate the blocks containing fake information according to the embedded hash-bits, and then recover the principal contents of tampered blocks by using the reference data extracted from the reserved blocks. In the following, we call the ratio between the number of blocks containing fake information and the number of all blocks as tempering rate, denoted as α.

3.1   Tampered-Block Identification

The first step in the content restoration procedure is to identify the tampered blocks. For each block sized 8×8, we extract 192 bits from the 3 LSB-layers and decompose them into 160 reference-bits and 32 hash-bits according to the same secret key. Then, feed the 320 bits in the 5 MSB-layers, the 160 extracted reference-bits, and the block index into the hash function. If the calculated hash result is different from the 32 extracted hash-bits, the block is judged as "tampered", meaning that some content in the block has been modified. Otherwise, a "not tampered" decision is made, and we call the block "reserved" for short. Here, a block without any modification must be judged as "reserved", and the probability for a block containing modified contents but being falsely judged as "reserved" is 2^{-32}, which is extremely low therefore the cases of false judgments are negligible.

As mentioned above, the $5N/2$ reference bits are embedded into the 3 LSB-layers of the host image. Then, a receiver can correctly extract the reference bits from the reserved blocks. The compression-bits of reserved blocks can also be derived from the data in the 5 MSB-layers. Our purpose is to find the compression-bits of the rest tampered blocks.

3.2 Compression-Bits Retrieving

Considering the 108 compression-bits belonging to a certain subset and the 320 reference-bits derived from them, the number of reference-bits that can be extracted from reserved blocks, denoted v, may be less than 320. Thus Equation (3) implies

$$\begin{bmatrix} r_{m,e(1)} \\ r_{m,e(2)} \\ \vdots \\ r_{m,e(v)} \end{bmatrix} = \mathbf{A}_m^{(E)} \cdot \begin{bmatrix} c_{m,1} \\ c_{m,2} \\ \vdots \\ c_{m,108} \end{bmatrix} \tag{6}$$

In (6), the left side contains all extractable reference-bits, and $\mathbf{A}_m^{(E)}$ is a matrix consisting of the rows in $\mathbf{A}_m$ corresponding to the extractable reference-bits. Furthermore, the 108 compression-bits in the subset, $c_{m,1}$, $c_{m,2}$, ..., $c_{m,108}$, can be classified into two types: the compression-bits belonging to tampered blocks, and the compression-bits belonging to reserved blocks. Actually, we may retrieve the second type of compression-bits from the MSB of reserved blocks. Even though the tampered area is extensive, the reference-bits extracted from reserved blocks can provide sufficient information to recover the first type of compression-bits.

Denote column vectors consisting of the first and second types of compression-bits as $\mathbf{B}_1$ and $\mathbf{B}_2$ respectively. Equation (6) can be reformulated as

$$\begin{bmatrix} r_{m,e(1)} \\ r_{m,e(2)} \\ \vdots \\ r_{m,e(v)} \end{bmatrix} - \mathbf{A}_m^{(E,2)} \cdot \mathbf{B}_2 = \mathbf{A}_m^{(E,1)} \cdot \mathbf{B}_1 \tag{7}$$

where $\mathbf{A}_m^{(E,1)}$ and $\mathbf{A}_m^{(E,2)}$ are matrices consisting of the columns in $\mathbf{A}_m^{(E)}$ corresponding to the first and second types of compression-bits respectively. In Equation (7), the left side and the matrix $\mathbf{A}_m^{(E,1)}$ are known, and the purpose is to find $\mathbf{B}_1$. Denoting the length of $\mathbf{B}_1$ as n_b, the size of $\mathbf{A}_m^{(E,1)}$ is $v \times n_b$. We will solve the n_b unknowns according to the v equations in a binary system. Here, if the number of unknowns, n_b, is too large, or there are too many linearly dependent equations in (7), the solution may not be unique and, in this case, we cannot find the true solution, which is exactly the original values of the first type of compression-bits, in the solution space. On the other hand, since the original values must be a solution, as long as Equation (7) for each subset has a unique solution, we can obtain the original values by using the Gaussian elimination method, leading to successful restoration of the original content.

Here is a discussion on the probability that Equation (7) has a unique solution. The sufficient and necessary condition is that the rank of $\mathbf{A}_m^{(E,1)}$ equals n_b, meaning that the n_b columns of $\mathbf{A}_m^{(E,1)}$ are linearly independent. Consider a random binary matrix containing i rows and j columns, and denote probability of its columns being linearly dependent as $q(i, j)$. We have

$$q(i,1) = \frac{1}{2^i} \tag{8}$$

$$q(i, j+1) = q(i, j) + [1 - q(i, j)] \cdot \frac{2^j}{2^i}, \quad j = 1, 2, \ldots, i-1 \tag{9}$$

$$q(i, j) = 1, \quad \text{if } j > i \tag{10}$$

Since the position for carrying a reference-bit falls into reserved bocks with a probability $(1-\alpha)$, v follows a binomial distribution

$$P_v(i) = \binom{320}{i} \cdot (1-\alpha)^i \cdot \alpha^{320-i}, \quad i = 0, 1, \ldots, 320 \tag{11}$$

n_b also follows a binomial distribution

$$P_{n_b}(j) = \binom{108}{j} \cdot \alpha^j \cdot (1-\alpha)^{108-j}, \quad j = 0, 1, \ldots, 108 \tag{12}$$

Thus, the probability of all columns in $\mathbf{A}_m^{(E,1)}$ being linearly independent is

$$P_{LI} = \sum_{i=0}^{108} \sum_{j=0}^{320} \left\{ P_v(i) \cdot P_{n_b}(j) \cdot [1 - q(i, j)] \right\} \tag{13}$$

Since there are $N/128$ subsets in total, we can recover all the compression-bits of tampered blocks with probability

$$P_S = P_{LI}^{N/128} \tag{14}$$

In summary, this probability is dependent on α and N. When the tampering is not too severe, P_S is very close to 1. The smaller the values of α and N are, the higher the probability of successful restoration. Figure 4 shows the values of P_S with different α and N. It can be seen that all the compression-bits of tampered blocks can be recovered when the rate of tampered blocks is no more than 59%.

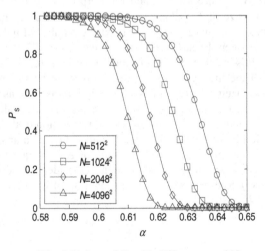

Fig. 4. Values of P_S with different α and N

3.3 Content Restoration

With the retrieved compression-bits, we can reconstruct the principal content of all tampered blocks. For a tampered block, we collect the 54 recovered compression-bits, and divide them into 15 pieces of bit string with different lengths equal to the 15 numbers shown in Figure 1. Then, for each bit string $(b_1, b_2, ..., b_K)$, calculate the corresponding DCT coefficient value

$$C = \sum_{k=1}^{K} \left(b_k \cdot 2^{K-k} \right) + R_{min} \tag{15}$$

where R_{min} is the minimum value of the range corresponding to the coefficient's position in Figure 2. After an inverse DCT and rounding operation, we can restore the 5 MSB of the tampered areas.

4 Experimental Results

Two test images Crowd and Lake sized 512×512 are used as the host, shown in Figure 5. Figure 6 gives their watermarked versions. PSNR values due to watermark embedding are respectively 37.8 dB and 37.9 dB, confirming the theoretical result in (5), and the distortion is imperceptible. We modify the watermarked images by extensively replacing the original content with fake information. The tampered images are shown in Figure 7, and the tampering rates are 45.4% and 59.1%, respectively. Figure 8 gives the result of tampered-block identification, in which the blocks judged as "reserved" and "tampered" are indicated by white and black, respectively. Here, all the tampered blocks were correctly located.

Next, we retrieve the compression-bits of tampered blocks and restore the principal content. Figure 9 shows the restored images, which consist of the watermarked content in reserved areas and the restored content in tampered areas. PSNR values in restored regions of the two images are 28.2 dB and 26.3 dB, respectively. Although the quality of restored content is lower than that of watermarked content, the restored content has reasonable quality. Experiments using other host images provide similar results.

Fig. 5. Original images Crowd and Lake

Fig. 6. Watermarked images Crowd and Lake

Fig. 7. Watermarked images Crowd and Lake

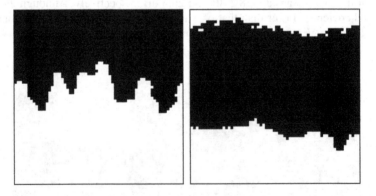

Fig. 8. Result of tampered-block identification

Fig. 9. Restored images

5 Conclusion

This paper proposes a novel fragile watermarking scheme with extensive content restoration capability. We compress the principal content of each block and introduce some redundancy to form a series of reference-bits. The reference-bits as well as the hash-bits, which match the local content, are used to replace the 3 least significant bits of all pixels. On authentication side, after identifying the tampered areas, the reference-bits extracted from the reserved regions can provide sufficient information to restore the principal content of host image even though the tampering rate is large.

Table 1 compares several fragile watermarking schemes with restoration capability. The proposed method is capable of recovering the content in the most extensive tampered areas. According to the PSNR values due to watermarking and after content restoration, it can be seen that imperceptibility of embedded watermark and the quality of restored content are also good.

Table 1. Comparison of restoration capability among fragile watermarking methods

Methods	PSNR due to watermarking	PSNR in restored area	Condition of restoration
Method 1 in [10]	43.8 dB	21.5 dB	Regions storing the original information of tampered areas must be reserved.
Method 2 in [10]	33.1 dB	28.8 dB	
Method in [11]	36.7 dB	22.8 dB	
Method in [12]	28.7 dB	$+\infty$	Tampering rate < 3.2%
Proposed method	37.9 dB	[26, 29] dB	Tampering rate < 59 %

References

1. Vleeschouwer, C., Delaigle, J.-F., Macq, B.: Invisibility and Application Functionalities in Perceptual Watermarking — An Overview. Proc. IEEE 90(1), 64–77 (2002)
2. Petitcolas, F.A.P., Anderson, R.J., Kuhn, M.G.: Information Hiding – A Survey. Proc. IEEE 87, 1062–1078 (1999)

3. Wong, P.W., Memon, N.: Secret and Public Key Image Watermarking Schemes for Image Authentication and Ownership Verification. IEEE Trans. on Image Processing 10(10), 1593–1601 (2001)
4. Suthaharan, S.: Fragile Image Watermarking Using a Gradient Image for Improved Localization and Security. Pattern Recognition Letters 25, 1893–1903 (2004)
5. Lu, H., Shen, R., Chung, F.-L.: Fragile Watermarking Scheme for Image Authentication. Electronics Letters 39(12), 898–900 (2003)
6. He, H., Zhang, J., Tai, H.-M.: A Wavelet-Based Fragile Watermarking Scheme for Secure Image Authentication. In: Shi, Y.Q., Jeon, B. (eds.) IWDW 2006. LNCS, vol. 4283, pp. 422–432. Springer, Heidelberg (2006)
7. Liu, S.-H., Yao, H.-X., Gao, W., Liu, Y.-L.: An Image Fragile Watermark Scheme Based on Chaotic Image Pattern and Pixel-Pairs. Applied Mathematics and Computation 185(2), 869–882 (2007)
8. Zhang, X., Wang, S.: Statistical Fragile Watermarking Capable of Locating Individual Tampered Pixels. IEEE Signal Processing Letters 14(10), 727–730 (2007)
9. Zhang, X., Wang, S.: Fragile Watermarking Scheme Using a Hierarchical Mechanism. Signal Processing 89(4), 675–679 (2009)
10. Fridrich, J., Goljan, M.: Images with Self-correcting Capabilities. In: Proceeding of IEEE International Conference on Image Processing, pp. 792–796 (1999)
11. Zhu, X., Hob, A., Marziliano, P.: A New Semi-Fragile Image Watermarking with Robust Tampering Restoration Using Irregular Sampling. Signal Processing: Image Communication 22(5), 515–528 (2007)
12. Zhang, X., Wang, S.: Fragile Watermarking with Error-Free Restoration Capability. IEEE Transactions on Multimedia 10(8), 1490–1499 (2008)

Improving Capability of Locating Tampered Pixels of Statistical Fragile Watermarking

Kazuya Ohkita, Maki Yoshida, Itaru Kitamura, and Toru Fujiwara

Graduate School of Information Science and Technology, Osaka University
1-5 Yamadaoka, Suita, Osaka 565-0871, Japan
{k-ohkita,maki-yos,i-kitamr,fujiwara}@ist.osaka-u.ac.jp

Abstract. A fragile watermarking scheme proposed by Zhang and Wang introduces a statistical mechanism and can accurately localize the pixels with at least one of the 5 most significant bits (MSBs) altered. However, localization of tampered 3 least significant bits (LSBs) is considered unnecessary because these bits are replaced by watermark bits. If the tampered 3 LSBs can be also localized, the pattern of tampering will be identified more correctly. This paper proposes a bit-wise scheme to localize tampered 3 LSBs using information on the tampered 5 MSBs in the statistical scheme. Experimental results show that the proposed scheme can accurately localize tampered 3 LSBs and that the combination of the previous scheme and the proposed one contributes to more exact identification of the tampering pattern. In this sense, we improve the capability of the statistical scheme.

Keywords: Image authentication, fragile watermarking, tampered-MSB localization, tampered-LSB localization.

1 Introduction

Malicious tampering of images is becoming more and more pervasive. In order to authenticate an image, many fragile watermarking schemes have been proposed [1,2,3,4,5,6,7,9,10,11,12,13]. Generally, all fragile watermarking schemes can be classified into semi-fragile schemes [2,7,10] and complete fragile schemes [1,3,4,5,6,9,11,12,13]. Semi-fragile watermarking is designed for implementing selective authentication, which allows legitimate modifications such as JPEG compression and filtering, but detects illegitimate modification. In content delivery, the server must encode original contents depending on client's needs. In this case, authentication based on semi-fragile watermarking is very useful according to its property that can allow slight modifications caused by encoding. However, in some scenarios, such as for law evidence and for military applications with high accuracy requirement, it is essential to detect any slight modifications of contents. To deal with these cases, complete fragile watermarking schemes are designed for implementing exact authentication, which cannot only detect any slight modifications but also locate the modified area. In this paper, we focus on complete fragile watermarking.

A.T.S. Ho et al. (Eds.): IWDW 2009, LNCS 5703, pp. 279–293, 2009.

The complete fragile watermarking schemes can be classified into two groups, block-wise schemes [1,4,6,12] and pixel-wise schemes [3,5,9,11,13]. The block-wise schemes identify the blocks containing tampered pixels whereas the pixel-wise schemes allow individual localization of the tampered pixels. Considering practical applications with high accuracy requirement, a pixel-wise scheme is more desirable.

The pixel-wise schemes in [3,5,9,11,13] derive a watermark from the significant bits of gray values of host pixels (7 most significant bits (MSBs) in [3,5,9] and 5 MSBs in [11,13]) and embed it into the remaining least significant bits (LSBs) so that the match between the embedded watermark in the LSBs and the watermark derived from the MSBs is destroyed by tampering. To realize effective fragility, the pixel-wise scheme in [11] embeds a tailor-made authentication data as a watermark and introduces a statistical mechanism into localization of pixels that have at least one MSB being altered. The key idea in [11] is to use two distributions corresponding to tampered and original 5 MSBs. The statistical scheme in [11] is later improved in [13] tolerant to extensive tampering. However, in [11,13], detection of alteration on the 3 LSBs is considered unnecessary because the original 3 LSBs of all pixels have been replaced with the corresponding watermark bits. To find a detailed pattern of tampering, it is also important to locate the tampered LSBs individually.

Our objective is the development of the basic statistical scheme in [11] to allow bit-wise localization of the tampered LSBs. A straightforward scheme is to use the probabilities derived or assumed in [11] without any modification. With these probabilities, we can derive two probabilities that each LSB is tampered and untampered. So, it seems that we can localize the tampered LSBs exactly by comparing the two probabilities. However, this straightforward scheme does not work fine because the two probabilities only depend on whether an LSB (i.e., an embedded watermark bit), is equal to the corresponding watermark bit or not. This means that bit-wise localization cannot be realized. To overcome this problem, we use information on the results of localizing tampered 5 MSBs. Specifically, from the two distributions corresponding to tampered and original 5 MSBs, we derive the individual probability of each LSB being tampered and untampered. The experimental results show that our proposed scheme can localize the tampered LSBs more accurately than the straightforward scheme. Take an example of alternation for which the straightforward scheme misses all tampered LSBs, the proposed scheme correctly detects almost all tampered pixels while keeping the number of falsely detected LSBs small. Moreover, we can confirm that the proposed scheme contributes to find a detailed pattern of tampering such as median filter.

The rest of this paper is organized as follows. Section 2 recalls the statistical fragile watermarking scheme in [11]. Section 3 first shows a straightforward scheme for localization of tampered LSBs and its problem. We then propose a better scheme to localize the tampered LSBs. Section 4 concludes this paper.

2 Statistical Fragile Watermarking Scheme

In [11] and this paper, it is assumed that an attacker alters the gray values of some pixels without changing the image size.[1] The scheme in [11] first generates a number of authentication bits for each host pixel according to its 5 MSBs of the gray value. It then embeds a folded version of the authentication data and some additional test data into the host image. The folding operation is performed to reduce the necessary host space for accommodating authentication data, and the test data are used to estimate the modification strength. Examination of the pixel values and the authentication data can reveal the trace of any content alteration. From this trace, a statistical judging realizes accurate localization of tampered pixels.

2.1 Watermark Embedding Procedure

Let N be the number of pixels contained in an image, and $p_i \in [0, 255]$ with $1 \leq i \leq N$ their gray values. Each p_i can be represented by 8 bits, $B(p_i, 7)$, $B(p_i, 6), \ldots, B(p_i, 0)$, where

$$B(p_i, u) = \left\lfloor \frac{p_i}{2^u} \right\rfloor \bmod 2, \ \text{for } 0 \leq u \leq 7, \tag{1}$$

or

$$p_i = \sum_{u=0}^{7} [B(p_i, u) \cdot 2^u]. \tag{2}$$

For each pixel p_i with $1 \leq i \leq N$, 31 authentication bits $b_{i,t}$ with $1 \leq t \leq 31$ are generated as follows:

$$b_{i,t} = \sum_{u=1}^{5} [B(p_i, u+3) \cdot B(t, u)]. \tag{3}$$

Here, similar to Eqs. (1) and (2), the index t is represented by 5 bits $B(t, 4), B(t, 3), \ldots, B(t, 0)$. Eq. (3) means that the 31 authentication bits of a pixel are determined by its 5 MSBs. The following property of authentication bits is used for deriving the probabilities compared in the procedure of localizing tampered pixels: any alteration on 5 MSBs of a pixel will result in the change of 16 authentication bits.

The watermark embedding procedure in [11] takes as input a host image and a secret key, and generates a watermarked image as follows.

1. For N pixels p_i of the host image, calculate all $31 \cdot N$ authentication bits and pseudo-randomly divide them into $(31 \cdot N/11)$ subsets, each of which contains 11 bits, according to the secret key. Then, calculate sums of the 11 authentication bits in each subset with modulus 2, and call the $(31 \cdot N/11)$ folding sums the sum-bits.

---

[1] This assumption means that change of the image size can be detected in some way except fragile watermarking.

2. Pseudo-randomly generate $(2 \cdot N/11)$ bits, called the test-bits, according to the secret key. The watermark bits are made up of the sum-bits and test-bits.
3. Permute the $3 \cdot N$ watermark bits in a pseudo-random way determined by the secret key, and replace the 3 LSBs of all pixels with them.

Assuming that the original distribution of the 3 LSBs is uniform, the average energy of distortion caused by watermarking on each pixel is

$$E_D = \frac{1}{64} \cdot \sum_{u=0}^{7} \sum_{v=0}^{7} (u-v)^2. \tag{4}$$

So, PSNR is approximately

$$\text{PSNR} \approx 10 \cdot \log_{10} \left(\frac{255^2}{E_D} \right) = 37.9(\text{dB}). \tag{5}$$

This PSNR value is higher than the general expectation for acceptable images, which is 35dB [8].

2.2   Effect of Tampering

Before showing the procedure of tampered pixels localization in [11], we overview the effect of tampering to the watermarked image analyzed in [11]. Denote the ratio between the number of pixels with at least one MSB altered and the image size N as r_M, and denote the ratio between the number of LSBs that have been changed and the number of all LSBs $3 \cdot N$ as r_L. Since any alteration on MSB will change 16 authentication bits, there are a total of $16 \cdot r_M \cdot N$ authentication bits being changed. For a subset, its sum-bit will be flipped if the number of changed authentication bits is odd. Denoting the event that a sum-bit is flipped as "flipped sum-bit", the probability for this event to occur is

$$e \triangleq \Pr[\text{"flipped sum-bit"}]$$
$$= \sum_{\substack{v=1,3,5, \\ 7,9,11}} \left[\binom{11}{v} \cdot \left(\frac{16 \cdot r_M}{31} \right)^v \cdot \left(1 - \frac{16 \cdot r_M}{31} \right)^{11-v} \right]. \tag{6}$$

On the other hand, since the LSBs used for storing the original sum-bits and test-bits are changed with the rate r_L, the probability of a sum-bit being different from the LSB at the corresponding position is

$$E \triangleq \Pr[\text{"LSB} \neq \text{sum-bit"}]$$
$$= e \cdot (1 - r_L) + (1 - e) \cdot r_L, \tag{7}$$

where "LSB$\neq$sum-bit" denotes the event that a sum-bit is different from the corresponding LSB. Eqs. (6) and (7) are used for estimating r_M at localization of pixels with at least one MSB altered.

Consider a pixel with 5 MSBs untampered. Its 31 authentication bits, which are also unchanged, are distributed in 31 subsets. In other words, each subset contains one authentication bit and 10 other elements. If the number of changed elements is odd, the sum-bit will be changed. Thus, denoting the event that 5 MSBs are untampered as "untampered 5MSBs", the sum-bits of this pixel are changed with probability

$$e_U \triangleq \Pr[\text{"flipped sum-bit"} \mid \text{"untampered 5MSBs"}]$$

$$= \sum_{\substack{v=1,3, \\ 5,7,9}} \left[\binom{10}{v} \cdot \left(\frac{16 \cdot r_M}{31} \right)^v \cdot \left(1 - \frac{16 \cdot r_M}{31} \right)^{10-v} \right]. \tag{8}$$

Then, the probability of the sum-bits being different from the LSBs at the corresponding positions is

$$E_U \triangleq \Pr[\text{"LSB}\neq\text{sum-bit"} \mid \text{"untampered 5MSBs"}]$$

$$= e_U \cdot (1 - r_L) + (1 - e_U) \cdot r_L. \tag{9}$$

Denoting the number of sum-bits that do not equal their corresponding LSBs as k_U, it obeys a binomial distribution

$$P(k_U = k) = \binom{31}{k} \cdot E_U{}^k \cdot (1 - E_U)^{31-k}, \text{ for } 0 \le k \le 31. \tag{10}$$

Furthermore, considering a pixel with at least one MSB altered, there must be 15 authentication bits unchanged and 16 changed. Similarly, the 15 unchanged authentication bits are distributed in 15 subsets. The 15 sum-bits of the subsets will also be changed with the probability given in Eq. (8). The probability of the 15 sum-bits being different from LSBs at their corresponding positions is the same as that in Eq. (9). The number of sum-bits that do not equal the corresponding LSBs is denoted as k_1. On the other hand, the 16 changed authentication bits correspond to 16 subsets, and their 16 sum-bits will be changed if the number of changed elements is even. Denoting the event that at least one MSB is tampered as "tampered 5MSBs", their 16 sum-bits are changed with probability

$$e_T \triangleq \Pr[\text{"flipped sum-bit"} \mid \text{"tampered 5MSBs"}]$$

$$= \sum_{\substack{v=0,2,4, \\ 6,8,10}} \left[\binom{10}{v} \cdot \left(\frac{16 \cdot r_M}{31} \right)^v \cdot \left(1 - \frac{16 \cdot r_M}{31} \right)^{10-v} \right]. \tag{11}$$

So, the probability of the 16 sum-bits being different from their corresponding LSBs is

$$E_T \triangleq \Pr[\text{"LSB}\neq\text{sum-bit"} \mid \text{"tampered 5MSBs"}]$$

$$= e_T \cdot (1 - r_L) + (1 - e_T) \cdot r_L. \tag{12}$$

The number of sum-bits that do not equal the corresponding LSBs in the 16 sum-bits is denoted as k_2. Also the number of sum-bits that do not equal the

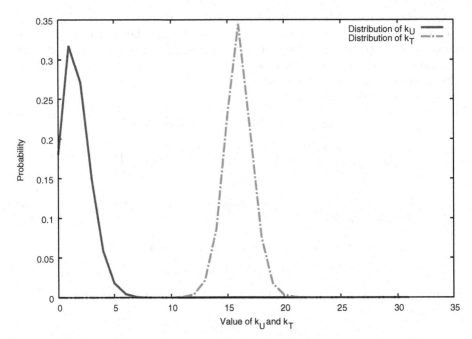

Fig. 1. Distribution of k_U and k_T with $r_M = 0.01$ and $r_L = 0.005$

corresponding LSBs in all 31 sum-bits is denoted as k_T. Here, $k_T = k_1 + k_2$, and its distribution is convolution of the following two binomial distributions:

$$P(k_T = k) = \sum_{v=max(0,k-16)}^{min(15,k)} \binom{15}{v} \cdot E_U{}^k \cdot (1 - E_U)^{15-v} \cdot$$

$$\binom{16}{k-v} \cdot E_T{}^{k-v} \cdot (1 - E_T)^{16-k+v}, \text{ for } 0 \le k \le 31. \quad (13)$$

It can be observed from Eqs. (10) and (13) that distributions of k_U and k_T are completely different. This enables identification of pixels that have at least one MSB being altered. In fact, when both r_M and r_L are small, the values of e_U and E_U are close to 0, and the values of e_T and E_T are close to 1. According to Eqs. (10) and (13), the peak of the distribution of k_U is near $k_U = 0$ while that of k_T is at $k_T = 16$. Fig. 1 gives the distributions of k_U and k_T with $r_M = 0.01$ and $r_L = 0.005$.

2.3   Procedure of Tampered-Pixel Localization

Based on the above discussion, the following localization procedure is given in [11].

1. For a given image, calculate the $(31 \cdot N/11)$ sum-bits according to its MSBs in the way as given in Step 1 of the watermark embedding procedure, and generate the same $(2 \cdot N/11)$ test-bits according to the secret key.
2. After comparing the calculated sum-bits and the generated test-bits with the LSBs at their corresponding positions, the ratio between the number of different test-bits and $(2 \cdot N/11)$ can be regarded as an estimate of r_L, and the ratio between the number of different sum-bits and $(31 \cdot N/11)$ can be regarded as an estimate of E. According to Eqs. (6) and (7), an estimate of r_M can be obtained numerically. With the estimates of r_L and r_M, the distributions of k_U and k_T can be found from Eqs. (10) and (13), respectively.
3. For each pixel, examine its 31 corresponding sum-bits, and count the number of sum-bits being different from their corresponding LSBs, k. If

$$\Pr[\text{``tampered 5MSBs''} \cap k_U = k] < \Pr[\text{``untampered 5MSBs''} \cap k_T = k], \tag{14}$$

or

$$(1 - r_M) \cdot P(k_U = k) < r_M \cdot P(k_T = k), \tag{15}$$

then this pixel is judged as a tampered pixel, indicating that there is alteration on its 5 MSBs. Note that Eq. (15) is a MAP criterion that minimizes the total number of false decisions.

There are two types of false decision: false positive and false negative. Let $N_{\text{5MSB,fp}}$ be the number of pixels falsely judged as tampered and $N_{\text{5MSB,fn}}$ be the number of pixels falsely judged as untampered. In [11], the expectations of $N_{\text{5MSB,fp}}$ and $N_{\text{5MSB,fn}}$ are analyzed as follows. The number of unaltered original pixels is $(1 - r_M) \cdot N$ and k_U obeys the distribution of Eq. (10), whereas the number of tampered pixels is $r_M \cdot N$ and k_T satisfies the distribution of Eq. (13). Let θ be a threshold of k at which the two curves $(1 - r_M) \cdot P(k_U = k)$ and $r_M \cdot P(k_T = k)$ intersect. If r_L and r_M are correctly estimated, the expectations of $N_{\text{5MSB,fp}}$ and $N_{\text{5MSB,fn}}$ are

$$E(N_{\text{5MSB,fp}}) = N \cdot (1 - r_M) \cdot \sum_{v=\lceil \theta \rceil}^{31} P(k_U = v), \tag{16}$$

$$E(N_{\text{5MSB,fn}}) = N \cdot r_M \cdot \sum_{v=0}^{\lfloor \theta \rfloor} P(k_T = v). \tag{17}$$

3 Proposed Scheme

Section 3.1 shows a straightforward scheme of localizing tampered LSBs and its problem on accuracy. In Section 3.2, we show an idea to improved accuracy and a further analysis on effect of tampering to a watermarked image. In Section 3.3, we present an improved scheme of localization. In Section 3.4, we experimentally confirm that the proposed scheme can localize tampered LSBs much more accurately than the straightforward scheme.

3.1 Straightforward Scheme and Its Problem

A straightforward scheme of localizing the tampered LSBs is to check whether the probability that an LSB is tampered is larger than the probability that the LSB is untampered. These probabilities can be derived from the rate r_L and the probability e in Eq. (6). So, the straightforward scheme seems to work fine. However, the number of false decision is large.

First consider a tampered LSB. Since "flipped sum-bit" and "tampered LSB" are independent, the conditional probability of "flipped sum-bit" on the occurrence of "tampered LSB" is

$$\Pr[\text{"flipped sum-bit"} \mid \text{"tampered LSB"}] = \Pr[\text{"flipped sum-bit"}]$$
$$= e. \tag{18}$$

Obviously, denoting the event that a sum-bit is not flipped as "unflipped sum-bit", the conditional probability of "unflipped sum-bit" on the occurrence of "tampered LSB" is

$$\Pr[\text{"unflipped sum-bit"} \mid \text{"tampered LSB"}] = 1 - e. \tag{19}$$

Furthermore, consider an untampered LSB. Similarly, denoting the event that an LSB is tampered as "untampered LSB",

$$\Pr[\text{"unflipped sum-bit"} \mid \text{"untampered LSB"}] = 1 - e, \tag{20}$$

$$\Pr[\text{"flipped sum-bit"} \mid \text{"untampered LSB"}] = e. \tag{21}$$

The straightforward procedure detects alterations on each LSB as follows.

1. In the case that an LSB is different from the corresponding sum-bit, the LSB is judged as tampered if

$$\Pr[\text{"tampered LSB"} \cap \text{"unflipped sum-bit"}]$$
$$> \Pr[\text{"untampered LSB"} \cap \text{"flipped sum-bit"}], \tag{22}$$

   or

$$r_L \cdot (1 - e) > (1 - r_L) \cdot e. \tag{23}$$

2. In the other case (i.e., an LSB is equal to the corresponding sum-bit), the LSB is judged as tampered if

$$\Pr[\text{"tampered LSB"} \cap \text{"flipped sum-bit"}]$$
$$> \Pr[\text{"untampered LSB"} \cap \text{"unflipped sum-bit"}], \tag{24}$$

   or

$$r_L \cdot e > (1 - r_L) \cdot (1 - e). \tag{25}$$

The probabilities r_L and e are common to all LSBs. This implies that the judgement only depends on whether an LSB is equal to the corresponding sum-bit or not. Specifically, any LSB that is different from the corresponding sum-bit is judged as tampered if $r_L > e$, and otherwise is judged as untampered. On the other hand, any LSB that is equal to the corresponding sum-bit is judged as tampered if $r_L > (1-e)$, and otherwise is judged as untampered. As a result, localization of the straightforward scheme is inaccurate. Note that the reason that e takes the common value to all LSBs is that the ratio r_M, which is the probability that at least one MSB is tampered $\Pr[\text{"tampered 5MSBs"}]$, is common to all pixels.

3.2 Our Idea to Improve Accuracy and Further Analysis on Effect of Tampering

Our idea to improve accuracy is to use information on localization of tampered MSBs. After localizing tampered MSBs of each pixel p_i with $1 \le i \le N$, we have known the number of sum-bits being different from the corresponding LSBs, denoted as k_i. Thus, instead of the $\Pr[\text{"tampered 5MSBs"}]$, we use the conditional probability $\Pr[\text{"tampered 5MSBs"} \mid k_i = k]$.

For each pixel p_i with $1 \le i \le N$, the conditional probability of "tampered 5MSBs" on the occurrence of $k_i = k$ is given by

$$
\begin{aligned}
P_{M,i} &\triangleq \Pr[\text{"tampered 5MSBs"} \mid k_i = k] \\
&= \frac{\Pr[\text{"tampered 5MSBs"} \cap k_i = k]}{\Pr[k_i = k]} \\
&= \frac{\Pr[\text{"tampered 5MSBs"} \cap k_i = k]}{\Pr[\text{"tampered 5MSBs"} \cap k_i = k] \cup \Pr[\text{"untampered 5MSBs"} \cap k_i = k]}.
\end{aligned}
\tag{26}
$$

From Eqs.(14) and (15),

$$
P_{M,i} = \frac{r_M \cdot P(k_T = k)}{r_M \cdot P(k_T = k) + (1 - r_M) \cdot P(k_U = k)}.
\tag{27}
$$

There are $(31 \cdot N/11)$ subsets of 11 authentication bits. For the j-th subset, let $I_j \subseteq \{1, 2, \ldots, N\}$ be the set of indices of the corresponding 11 pixels. We derive the conditional probability of its sum-bit being flipped same as e in (6) by replacing r_M by $P_{M,i}$ with $i \in I_j$ as follows: The sum-bit will be flipped if the number of changed authentication bits is odd; defining $\mathcal{I}_{j,v} = \{I' \subseteq I_j \mid |I'| = v\}$ for odd v, whose element indicates a set of changed v authentication bits, the conditional probability for the sum-bit to be flipped is

$$
e'_j = \sum_{\substack{v=1,3,5,\\7,9,11}} \sum_{I' \in \mathcal{I}_{j,v}} \left(\prod_{i \in I'} \left(\frac{16 \cdot P'_{M,i}}{31} \right) \prod_{i \in I'_j \setminus I'} \left(1 - \frac{16 \cdot P'_{M,i}}{31} \right) \right).
\tag{28}
$$

The proposed procedure of localizing tampered LSBs uses e'_j instead of e in the straightforward procedure.

3.3 Proposed Procedure of Tampered-LSBs Localization

Based on the above analysis, we propose a procedure of localizing tampered LSBs, which is executed after the procedure of localizing tampered 5 MSBs.

1. For each pixel p_i with $1 \leq i \leq N$, calculating the conditional probability $P_{M,i}$ in Eq. (27).
2. For each LSB, calculate e'_j of the corresponding sum-bit in Eq. (28). We can judge whether the LSB is tampered or not by replacing the probability e by e'_j in Eqs. (23) and (25) of the straightforward scheme. The judgement is given in the following step.
   (a) In the case that the LSB is different from the corresponding sum-bit, it is judged as tampered if

$$r_L \cdot (1 - e'_j) > (1 - r_L) \cdot e'_j. \tag{29}$$

   (b) In the other case, the LSB is judged as tampered if

$$r_L \cdot e'_j > (1 - r_L) \cdot (1 - e'_j). \tag{30}$$

3.4 Experimental Results

We first compare the number of falsely judged LSBs between the straightforward scheme and the proposed scheme for different numbers of tampered LSBs. Let $N_{\text{LSB,fp}}$ (resp. $N_{\text{LSB,fn}}$) be the number of LSBs falsely judged as tampered (resp. untampered). We use a test image Lena as the host, which is a grayscale image sized 512×512. Fig.2 shows the test image Lena and the watermarked image. We tamper an adequate number of pixels of the watermarked Lena by painting white. Denoting the number of painted pixels N_T, the expectations of r_M and r_L are given by $E(r_M) = \frac{31 \cdot N_T}{32 \cdot N}$ and $E(r_L) = \frac{N_T}{2 \cdot N}$, respectively [11]. Fig. 3 shows the experimental results of $N_{\text{LSB,fp}}$ and $N_{\text{LSB,fn}}$ of tampered-LSB

(a) Host image Lena   (b) Watermarked image

Fig. 2. Host image Lena and watermarked image

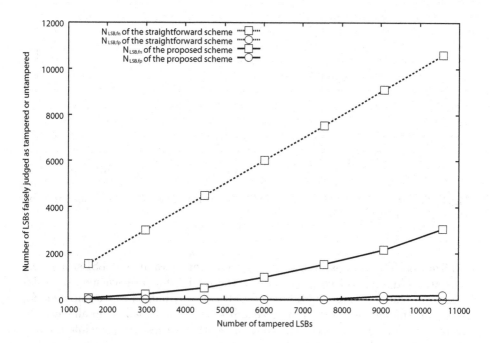

Fig. 3. Experimental results of false decision in localization of tampered LSBs

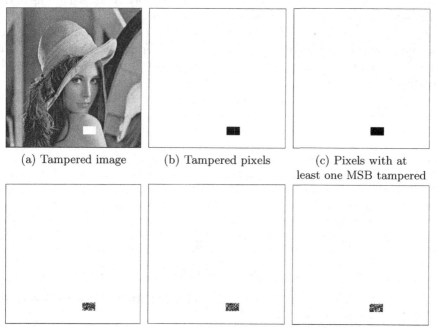

(a) Tampered image   (b) Tampered pixels   (c) Pixels with at
least one MSB tampered

(d) Tampered first LSBs (e) Tampered second LSBs (f) Tampered third LSBs

Fig. 4. Example of a tampered image

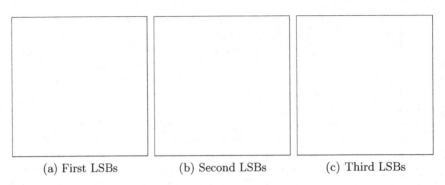

(a) First LSBs   (b) Second LSBs   (c) Third LSBs

Fig. 5. Positions of first LSBs, second LSBs, and third LSBs judged as "tampered" by using the straightforward scheme

localization. The abscissa represents the number of tampered LSBs, and the ordinate is $N_{\mathrm{LSB,fn}}$ and $N_{\mathrm{LSB,fp}}$. Because the straightforward scheme cannot localize the tampered LSBs, all tampered LSB is falsely judged as untampered. So, $N_{\mathrm{LSB,fn}}$ is the number of the tampered LSBs, but $N_{\mathrm{LSB,fp}}$ is zero in all case. On the other hand, the proposed scheme significantly reduces $N_{\mathrm{LSB,fn}}$ while keeping $N_{\mathrm{LSB,fp}}$ very small.

We then show the results of bit-wise localization of tampered LSBs for the case that the number of altered LSBs is 1543 (see Fig. 4). As shown in Fig. 5, the straightforward scheme cannot detect any tampering. That is, $N_{\mathrm{LSB,fn}}$ is 1543, but $N_{\mathrm{LSB,fp}}$ is zero. In contrast, the proposed scheme detects a total of 1468 bits correctly judged as tampered (see Fig. 6). Thus, $N_{\mathrm{LSB,fn}}$ is 75 and $N_{\mathrm{LSB,fp}}$ is zero. We can see that the proposed scheme significantly decreases $N_{\mathrm{LSB,fn}}$ while keeping $N_{\mathrm{LSB,fp}}$ small.

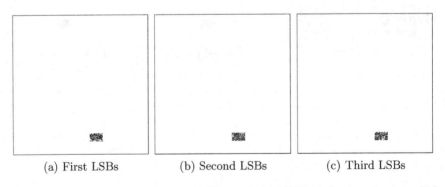

(a) First LSBs   (b) Second LSBs   (c) Third LSBs

Fig. 6. Positions of first LSBs, second LSBs, and third LSBs judged as "tampered" by using the proposed scheme

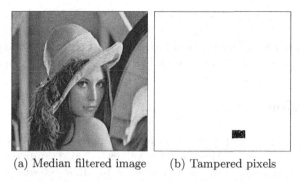

(a) Median filtered image   (b) Tampered pixels

Fig. 7. Median filtered image and tampered pixels

Fig. 8. Positions of pixels with at least one MSB judged as "tampered" by using the previous scheme

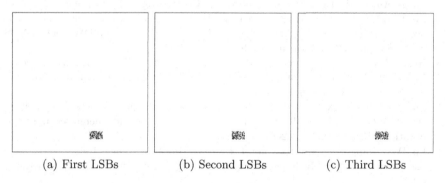

(a) First LSBs   (b) Second LSBs   (c) Third LSBs

Fig. 9. Positions of first LSBs, second LSBs, and third LSBs judged as "tampered" by using the proposed scheme

We also confirm that the proposed scheme contributes to a detailed analysis of the pattern of alteration. We apply median filter to 1000 pixels of the girl's shoulder. Fig. 7 shows the median filtered Lena and the tampered pixels. In this case, median filter mainly affects LSBs, as shown in Figs. 8 and 9. Specifically, the number of pixels with at least one MSB is altered is 167, whereas the number of altered LSBs is 1243. This pattern of alteration cannot be detected only by the previous scheme, which localizes pixels with at least one of 5 MSBs tampered. In this sense, the proposed scheme is useful for analyzing the pattern of alteration.

4   Conclusion

In this paper, we have improved the statistical pixel-wise scheme in [11] to localize not only tampered 5 MSBs of gray values but also tampered 3 LSBs. The important feature of the proposed scheme is to allow bit-wise localization of the tampered 3 LSBs. To realize accurate localization, we use information on the tampered 5 MSBs. Experimental results show that the proposed scheme can localize tampered LSBs more accurately than the straightforward scheme. One of the future work is to devise the theoretical number of 3 LSBs falsely judged. Another future work is to improve the accuracy of localizing tampered 5 MSBs by using information on the tampered 3 LSBs. We also consider to improve the other statistical scheme in [13] which is an extension of the scheme in [11]. Another possible future work is to develop the statistical schemes in [11,13] to restore tampered contents with the use of the proposed scheme.

References

1. Chana, C.S., Changb, C.C.: An Efficient Image Authentication Method Based on Hamming Code. Pattern Recognition 40(2), 681–690 (2007)
2. Hassan, M.H., Gilani, S.A.M.: A Semi-Fragile Watermarking Scheme for Color Image Authentication. Trans. Engineering, Computing and Technology 13 (2006)
3. He, H., Zhang, J., Tai, H.M.: A Wavelet-Based Fragile Watermarking Scheme for Secure Image Authentication. In: Shi, Y.Q., Jeon, B. (eds.) IWDW 2006. LNCS, vol. 4283, pp. 422–432. Springer, Heidelberg (2006)
4. Ho, A.T.S., Zhu, X., Shen, J., Marziliano, P.: Fragile Watermarking Based on Encoding of the Zeroes of the z-Transform. IEEE Trans. Information Forensics and Security 3(3), 567–569 (2008)
5. Liu, S.H., Yao, H.X., Gao, W., Liu, Y.L.: An Image Fragile Watermarking Scheme Based on Chaotic Image Pattern and Pixel-Pairs. Applied Mathematics and Computation 185(2), 869–882 (2007)
6. Lu, W., Chung, F.L., Lu, H., Choi, K.S.: Detecting Fake Images Using Watermarks and Support Vector Machines. Computer Standards and Interfaces 30(3), 132–136 (2008)
7. Sang, J., Alam, M.S.: Fragility and Robustness of Binary-Phase-Only-Filter-Based Fragile/Semifragile Digital Image Watermarking. IEEE Trans. Instrumentation and Measurement 57(3) (2008)
8. Taubman, D.S., Marcellin, M.W.: JPEG2000 Image Compression Fundamentals. Standards and Practice. Kluwer Academic Publishers, Boston (2002)
9. Wu, J., Zhu, B.B., Li, S., Lin, F.: A Secure Image Authentication Algorithm with Pixel-level Tamper Localization. In: Proc. of Int. Conf. on Image Process, vol. 3, pp. 301–306 (2004)

10. Xiao, J., Wang, Y.: A Semi-fragile Watermarking Tolerant of Laplacian Sharpening. In: Int. Conf. on Computer Science and Software Engineering, vol. 3, pp. 579–582 (2008)
11. Zhang, X., Wang, S.: Statistical Fragile Watermarking Capable of Locating Individual Tampered Pixels. IEEE Signal Process. Lett. 14(10), 727–730 (2007)
12. Zhang, X., Wang, S.: Fragile Watermarking with Error-Free Restoration Capability. IEEE Trans. Multimedia 10(8) (2008)
13. Zhang, X., Wang, S.: Fragile Watermarking Scheme Using a Hierarchical Mechanism. Signal Processing 89(4), 675–679 (2009)

Camera-Model Identification Using
Markovian Transition Probability Matrix

Guanshuo Xu[1], Shang Gao[1,2], Yun Qing Shi[1], RuiMin Hu[2], and Wei Su[3]

[1] New Jersey Institute of Technology
Newark, NJ USA 07102
{gx3,shang.gao,Shi}@njit.edu
[2] Wuhan University
Wuhan, Hubei, China 430072
hrm1964@public.wh.hb.cn
[3] US Army CERDEC
Fort Monmouth, NJ 07703
Wei.Su@us.army.mil

Abstract. Detecting the (brands and) models of digital cameras from given digital images has become a popular research topic in the field of digital forensics. As most of images are JPEG compressed before they are output from cameras, we propose to use an effective image statistical model to characterize the difference JPEG 2-D arrays of Y and Cb components from the JPEG images taken by various camera models. Specifically, the transition probability matrices derived from four different directional Markov processes applied to the image difference JPEG 2-D arrays are used to identify statistical difference caused by image formation pipelines inside different camera models. All elements of the transition probability matrices, after a thresholding technique, are directly used as features for classification purpose. Multi-class support vector machines (SVM) are used as the classification tool. The effectiveness of our proposed statistical model is demonstrated by large-scale experimental results.

Keywords: Camera Identification, Markov Process, Transition Probability Matrix.

1 Introduction

Although camera model information is stored in the EXIF header of each image during the formation of the image, our daily-use image-editing software can easily remove or modify this piece of information, thus, making the camera model identification no longer straightforward. However, finding the source camera model from the given images or matching images to their source cameras, if possible, might sometimes become significant evidence in the court. Our research reported in this paper focuses on this topic, i.e., given an image, we try to tell the source camera model of the image without using the EXIF information. To achieve this, knowledge of how the images are produced by digital cameras is a must. Fig. 1 displays a typical image formation pipeline which consists of a lens system, a group of filters, a color filter

A.T.S. Ho et al. (Eds.): IWDW 2009, LNCS 5703, pp. 294–307, 2009.

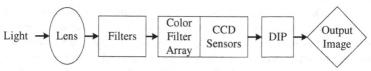

Fig. 1. A typical image formation pipeline

array (CFA), imaging sensor, and a digital image processor (DIP) inside a camera. Various researches have been (or being) conducted based on these parts of the image formation pipeline.

When light comes in, it first goes through a lens system which can cause straight lines in object space to be rendered as curved lines in images. This kind of lens aberration was used in [1] for camera classification. In [1], the three-camera classification accuracy can reach more than 91%. After light comes out from the lens system, it goes through a filter system which consists of infra-red and anti-aliasing filters and possibly other kinds of filters. The output of the filter system is then input into a charge-coupled device (CCD) sensor by which it is transferred to electric signals. Filler et al. [2] considered the photo-response nonuniformity noise (PRNU) [3] which is caused primarily by different sensitivity of pixels to light caused by the inhomogenity of silicon wafers and imperfections during the sensor manufacturing process. In [2], seventeen different camera models from eight different brands were tested. The average classification rate is about 87%. As sensors are of high cost, most digital cameras use only one sensor instead of three to record color images and a color filter array is used in front of the sensor. By doing this, each pixel only records one color component in stead of three. The other two components are recovered from nearby pixels according to some algorithm fulfilled by digital image processor (DIP) which is shown in Fig. 1. This kind of processing is called color interpolation. Inspired from the fact that different cameras use different color filter array and interpolation methods, Swaminathan et al. [4], Long et al. [5] and Bayram et al. [6] proposed their methods based on the difference of the color filter array and interpolation algorithms adopted by different camera models. In [4], the authors tested 16 different camera models from 8 brands. The average model classification accuracy is around 83%. Five cameras from five different brands were tested in [5]. The brand classification accuracy is more than 95%. The average brand classification accuracy in [6] can reach 96% by assuming a 5x5 interpolation kernel based on three different cameras. As most cameras output images in the JPEG format, besides color interpolation, the digital image processor also fulfils the task of JPEG image compression. Choi et al. [7] proposed to use the bit per pixel and the percentage of non-zero integers in each DCT coefficient as features for camera model identification. The average accuracy of classifying four camera models is about 92%. Compared with all the above mentioned methods, Kharrazi et al. [8] provided a more universal method based on the statistical difference of the output images caused by the whole image formation pipeline. Images from five cameras of different models were classified. The average accuracy is 88%.

Inspired from the fact that different camera models adopt different JPEG quantization matrices and color interpolation algorithms, which will certainly result in the statistical difference of the quantized block DCT (BDCT) coefficients, together with other different image processing algorithms inside the DIP, such as different image smoothing and sharpening algorithms, as well as possible different lens and CCD sensors, which will also give a joint effect on the quantized block DCT coefficients, we propose a new statistical model which is capable of capturing the statistical difference of the quantized block DCT coefficients of each JPEG image. Markov probability transition matrix is used here as our statistical model. Instead of directly calculating the probability transition matrix from the block DCT coefficients, we focus on the difference JPEG 2-D array consisting of the difference of the magnitude of the quantized block DCT coefficients. By taking difference, we assume that the influence caused by different image content can be reduced and the statistical difference can be enlarged, resulting in easier and hence more accurate and reliable classification of images from different camera models. For simplicity, in this paper, only one-step Markov process is considered and a thresholding technique is proposed to achieve an effective feature-size reduction. In this paper, all the images are in JPEG format. We use YCbCr as our color model as it is the most widely used color model for JPEG compression. Probability features from 4-directional (horizontal, vertical, diagonal and marginal diagonal) Markov probability transition matrix are extracted from Y component of each JPEG image and only 2-directions (horizontal, vertical) are considered for Cb component (detailed explanation of the feature selection for our statistical model will be explained in the experiment section). Those features will then be used as the input of the classifiers for classification purpose. Multiclass-SVMs are used here as the classifier. The effectiveness of our proposed statistical model is displayed by large-scale experiments.

The rest of the report is organized as follows. In Section 2, we discuss how to build the Markov statistical model and extract features for classification. In Section 3, the procedure of experiments and the results are presented. In Section 4, conclusions and some discussions are made.

2   Markovian Statistical Model

In this section, we focus on how to build our statistical model for camera model classification. In Section 2.1, we discuss the causes of the statistical difference within quantized block DCT coefficients of images from different camera models. Difference JPEG 2-D arrays are defined in Section 2.2. The complete statistical model is provided in Section 2.3. In Section 2.4, we give an intuitive show of the discrimination capability of our proposed statistical model.

2.1   Causes of Statistical Difference on Quantized Block DCT Coefficients

Quantization is one of the key steps of the JPEG compression procedure. It is accomplished by dividing 8x8 block DCT coefficients by a specific quantization table followed by a rounding process. Although there is standard quantization tables published by the Independent JPEG Group, the quantization matrices within different models of cameras are still different, resulting in the statistical difference of quantized block DCT coefficients. In [7], [9], the authors did some research regarding the difference of JPEG quantization matrices.

Color interpolation is another important cause of the statistical difference of the block DCT coefficients. In [5], the authors studied some kinds of interpolation algorithms, such as bilinear kernel interpolation and bicubic kernel interpolation algorithms. As the missing colors are calculated by their neighbors according to some algorithms, the frequency components—block DCT coefficients will definitely be affected.

Different JPEG quantization matrices and color interpolation algorithms, as shown above, are only part of the reasons to cause the statistical difference. Other parts of the image formation pipeline, such as different image smoothing and sharpening algorithm inside the DIP, different lens systems and CCD device etc. are all responsible for the statistical difference of the output image from difference camera models. In other words, the statistical difference on quantized block DCT coefficients is caused by the different image formation process with different camera brands and models.

2.2 Difference JPEG 2-D Array

In Section 2.1, we discussed some major factors that cause the statistical difference of quantized block DCT coefficients. In this section, we consider where to extract effective statistical features in order to capture the statistical difference for camera models classification purpose.

Instead of extracting statistical features directly from quantized block DCT coefficients, features are extracted from the difference JPEG 2-D array. JPEG 2-D array can be calculated by taking the absolute value of each quantized block DCT coefficient. It is defined as a 2-D array that consists of the magnitudes of quantized block DCT coefficients. In our experiment, the contents of all the images vary a lot and differ from each other, which are not desired for camera model classification. To reduce the influence of the image contents, we introduce the difference JPEG 2-D array, which is defined by finding the difference between an element and one of its neighbors in the JPEG 2-D array. By calculating difference, we should consider the direction. Here we consider calculating difference JPEG 2-D arrays along four directions--horizontal, vertical, main diagonal and minor diagonal. (shown in Fig. 2).

Fig. 2. From left to right: horizontal, vertical, main diagonal and minor diagonal

Denote the JPEG 2-D array generated from a given test image by $F(u,v)$ ($u \in [1, S_u]$, $v \in [1, S_v]$), where S_u is the size of the JPEG 2-D array in horizontal direction and S_v in vertical direction. The difference arrays in horizontal direction are generated by the following formula:

$$F_h(u,v) = F(u,v) - F(u+1,v) . \tag{1}$$

where $u \in [1, S_u-1]$, $v \in [1, S_v-1]$ and $F_h(u,v)$ denote the difference arrays in horizontal direction. $F_v(u,v)$, $F_d(u,v)$, $F_{md}(u,v)$ are denoted as the difference arrays in the other three directions, respectively. They can be calculated in the same way.

It is expected that the image content influence can be reduced largely by considering the difference between an element and one of its neighbors in the JPEG 2-D array. By taking difference, the statistical difference caused by different camera pipelines is expected to be enhanced, resulting in better discrimination ability (as will be shown in our experiments section).

Note that here those four difference arrays are not calculated directly from the quantization block DCT coefficients, but from the JPEG 2-D arrays, which consists of the magnitudes of quantized block DCT coefficients. There are three reasons that we take absolute values before calculating the difference: 1) The magnitude of the DCT coefficients decreases along the zig-zag scanning. This characteristic can be more easily maintained by taking absolute before calculating difference. 2) Taking absolute value before calculating difference can to some extent reduce the dynamic range of the resulting 2-D arrays compared with the 2-D arrays generated by calculating difference from the original block DCT coefficients directly. 3) The signs of DCT coefficients mainly carry information of the outlines and edges of the original spatial domain image [10]. As the outlines and edges are related only with the contents of images, they carry little useful information for camera model classification. Hence, by taking absolute values, almost all the information regarding camera models remains.

2.3 Markovian Transition Probability Matrix

In Section 2.2, we introduced the idea of extracting features from difference JPEG 2-D arrays. In this section, we talk about how to extract effective features from difference JPEG 2-D arrays.

It is known that the BDCT coefficients have been decorrelated effectively. However, there still exists intrablock correlation [11] within a local 8x8 block. Therefore, we propose to model difference JPEG 2-D arrays by using Markov random process which takes into consideration the correlations among the BDCT coefficients [12]. Markov process can be specified by the transition probabilities. For simplicity, here we only consider one-step Markov process, i.e., only correlations between immediate neighbors within difference JPEG 2-D arrays are considered. Fig. 3 shows a typical one-step transition probability matrix which is given in [13]. As there are four difference JPEG 2-D arrays calculated from four directions, the transition probability matrices are calculated from their corresponding difference JPEG 2-D. Thus, totally we can generate four transition probability matrices from each JPEG 2-D array. Those transition probabilities are the features for classification purpose.

$$
P = \begin{bmatrix}
p_{00} & p_{01} & p_{02} & \cdots \\
p_{10} & p_{11} & p_{12} & \cdots \\
\cdot & \cdot & \cdot & \\
p_{i0} & p_{i1} & \cdots & \\
\cdot & \cdot & \cdots &
\end{bmatrix}
$$

Fig. 3. The matrix of one-step transition probabilities P

Note that the size of a transition probability matrix depends on the number of different values within the difference JPEG 2-D array. There is certain chance that the number of different values is large, resulting in a huge number of transition probabilities, which is not desired in practice. To solve this problem, we decide to use a thresholding technique [12]. In Fig. 4, the statistical average of histograms of horizontal difference JPEG 2-D arrays generated from the Y components of 40,000 images are shown. This figure tells us the statistical distribution of the values within a JPEG 2-D array. Since it is a Laplacian-like distribution and the information are very concentrated around zero, we propose a thresholding technique that limits the range of values from –T to +T. For those values that are either smaller than –T or large than +T, instead of discarding them, we force them to –T and +T, respectively, so as to keep as much information as possible. By introducing this thresholding technique, we are able to achieve a balance between the computational complexity and classification performance. This procedure results in a transition probability matrix of dimensionality $(2T+1)\times(2T+1)$. The probabilities values in the transition probability matrix generated from a difference JPEG 2-D array in horizontal direction are given by

$$p\{F_h(u+1,v)=n \,|\, F_h(u,v)=m\} = \frac{\sum\limits_{v=1}^{S_v-1}\sum\limits_{u=1}^{S_u-1}\delta(F_h(u,v)=m, F_h(u+1,v)=n)}{\sum\limits_{v=1}^{S_v-1}\sum\limits_{u=1}^{S_u-1}\delta(F_h(u,v)=m)} . \tag{2}$$

where $m \in \{-T,-T+1,\cdots,0,\cdots,T\}, n \in \{-T,-T+1,\cdots,0,\cdots,T\}$, and

$$\delta(A=m, B=n) = \begin{cases} 1, & if \ A=m \ and \ B=n \\ 0, & Otherwise \end{cases} . \tag{3}$$

Probability values from the other three directional difference JPEG 2-D array can be calculated in the same way.

When images are JPEG compressed inside the camera, the first step is to convert images from RBG color model to YCbCr model. Therefore, it is natural to extract features from YCbCr representation. We calculated all the four directional difference JPEG 2-D arrays and transition probability matrices from Y component. As Cb and Cr are color components, there is also some useful information for classification within these two components. In our experiments, we show that features generated from Cb and Cr are highly correlated, hence we only use features from Cb component. Since we know that Cb and Cr has been downsampled during JPEG compression, only two directions are considered in Cb component, resulting in further complexity reduction. In summary, from Y component, we generate four transition probability matrices, each corresponding to one direction. There are $(2T+1)\times(2T+1) = 81$ probability features in each of these four transition probability matrices. (Here we set T=4. Detailed study of selecting the proper threshold will be shown in Section 3.2) In total, we have $4\times(2T+1)\times(2T+1)=324$ probability features from Y component of an image. As we only consider two directions for Cb component, we can generate $2\times(2T+1)\times(2T+1)=162$ probability features from Cb component. Combining all the features generated from Y and Cb component together, in total, 324+162=486 probability features are generated from each image. The block diagram of our proposed model is given in Fig. 5.

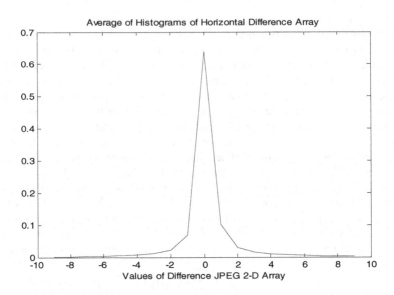

Fig. 4. The statistical average of histograms of horizontal difference arrays generated from the image set consisting of 40,000 JPEG images

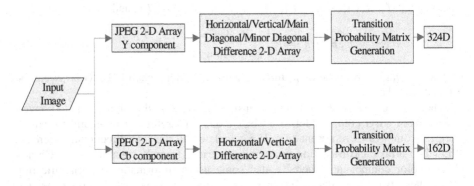

Fig. 5. Block diagram of our proposed model

2.4 Discrimination Ability of Our Proposed Model

A simple example is provided in this section to demonstrate the discrimination ability of our proposed model. Nikon Coolpix L18 and Nikon Coolpix S50 were selected as two camera models to be classified in this example. Each camera took 75 images. Each pair of the 75 images was taken from exactly the same scene by the two cameras. Transition probability matrices were calculated from Y component of each image. There are four transition probability matrices (four directions) extracted from each image. Fig. 6 gives us a comparison of the shapes of the scaled and averaged transition probability matrices calculated along horizontal and vertical directions from these two cameras. These matrices in Fig. 6 are calculated by grouping the transition probabilities in the same position of the matrices, scaling them position by position (positions of the probabilities in the transition probability matrices) together to the range [0,1] followed by taking average of those scaled probabilities from the two cameras position by position, respectively. The difference of the shapes can be easily observed in both the two directions, which shows the effectiveness of our proposed model. This kind of observation is one of the important motivations to large scale experiments.

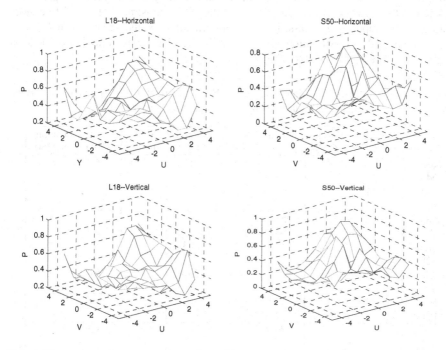

Fig. 6. Comparison of average values of transition probability matrices. U and V are values in the difference JPEG arrays. P axis is the scaled probability values.

3 Experiments

In Section 3.1, the experimental procedures, including classifier selection, data collection and experimental results are presented. Some discussions are given in Section 3.2 to Section 3.6.

3.1 Classifier Selection, Data Collection and Classification Results

The support vector machine (SVM) is used in this paper as classifier. We use the polynomial kernel [14] with degree of 2 in our experiment.

In the experimental parts of most of the previous works in this field such as in [1], [5], [6], [7], each camera model was represented by only one camera. This is not adequate for the model identification in practice. As the images produced by only one camera from each model might be too much centralized that the classifier may not be able to correctly classify images generated by different cameras of the same model. In this work, we did the experiments in a more practical and rational way. We collected 5,000 images from each camera model. For each model, 5,000 images generated from 30 to 40 different cameras are used for the test. By doing this, we can say that we have captured the characteristic of a camera model instead of a specific camera. 4,000 out of 5,000 images are used for training from each model, 1,000 for testing. We have 8 different models. Thus, totally we have 40,000 images. All these images were downloaded from www.flickr.com. We used the model illustrated in Fig. 6 to extract features as the input of the classifier. The classification results are shown in Table 1. The average model classification accuracy is 92.5%. The average brand classification accuracy reaches 98.1%, which is high.

Table 1. Confusion Matrix for using 486 features. Y—4 directions. Cb—horizontal and vertical directions. Rates less than 2% are denoted by *. Average Accuracy=92.5%.

	Kodak 6490	Kodak Z740	Nikon D40	Nikon 3200	Nikon 4600	Sony P200	Canon 350D	Canon SD750
Kodak 6490	81.5	17.2	*	*	*	*	*	*
Kodak Z740	14.4	84.6	*	*	*	*	*	*
Nikon D40	*	*	95.7	*	*	*	*	*
Nikon 3200	*	*	*	93.7	4.3	*	*	*
Nikon 4600	*	*	*	4.4	93.1	*	*	*
Sony P200	*	*	*	*	*	98.4	*	*
Canon 350D	*	*	*	*	*	*	95.7	*
Canon SD750	*	*	*	*	*	*	*	97.5

Table 2. Brand Classification Confusion Matrix Calculated from Table 1. Values less than 2% are represented by *. Average Accuracy= 98.1%.

	Kodak	Nikon	Sony	Canon
Kodak	98.9	*	*	*
Nikon	*	98.2	*	*
Sony	*	*	98.4	*
Canon	*	*	*	97.0

3.2 Experimental Study on Different Threshold Values

In this paper, a thresholding technique is used in order to reduce the dimensionality of features, hence manageable complexity. However, setting threshold is always accompanied by information loss. How to find the proper threshold value is what we are concerned. In this section, we conducted some experiments on how different threshold values affect the average model classification result together with the information loss (proportion of the values in the difference JPEG 2-D array that fall out of the thresholding range). For simplicity, here we only consider extracting features from horizontal difference JPEG 2-D array of Y component only. In this case, feature size is $(2T+1)\times(2T+1)$. In Table 3, relationship among feature dimension, average classification accuracy and information loss are shown. Note that dimension of feature vector grows very fast with the increase of the threshold value. Comparing the case when threshold =4 and Threshold =5, the difference of dimensionality of features is 40, while there is only limited difference of classification accuracy and there are only 0.5% more values of coefficients that fall out of the threshold range due to the Laplace distribution previously shown in Fig.4. Therefore, threshold=4 is a proper choice.

Table 3. Relationship among feature dimension, average classification accuracy and information loss

	Feature Dimension	Average Accuracy	Information Loss
TH=1	9	49.1%	19.1%
TH=2	25	72.1%	14.1%
TH=3	49	77.8%	11.4%
TH=4	81	80.3%	9.2%
TH=5	121	81.4%	8.7%

3.3 Feature-Correlation between Cb and Cr Component

In Section 2.3, we mentioned that features extracted from Cb component and Cr component are very much correlated so that we only need to consider one of them. Now we provide the average correlation coefficient values plus the classification accuracy of different combination of color components in Table 4. For comparison, from each component, we extract 162 features (two directions). We found that the correlation between Cb and Cr component almost doubles the correlation either between Y and Cb or between Y and Cr. Combing features from Y and Cb together, the classification accuracy is 91.1%. If features from Cr are added in, the accuracy is 91.4%, only 0.3% increase, with the cost of more dimensionality (from 324 to 486). Based on these results, we use only Y and Cb component in this paper.

Table 4. Correlation and Classification Accuracy

Color Components	Correlation Coefficients	Feature Dimension	Classification Accuracy
Y		162	85.4%
Cb		162	80.9%
Cr		162	81.0%
YCb	0.4605	324	91.1%
YCr	0.4642	324	90.7%
CbCr	0.9043	324	85.0%
YCbCr		486	91.4%

3.4 Taking Absolute Values Versus without Taking Absolute Values

In Section 2.2, we explained why we need to take absolute value of quantized DCT coefficients before calculating the difference array. In this section, we compared the classification effects between taking absolute values and without taking absolute

Table 5. Confusion Matrix for using 162 features without taking absolute values. Y—horizontal and vertical directions. Rates less than 2% are denoted by *. Average Accuracy=84.6%.

	Kodak 6490	Kodak Z740	Nikon D40	Nikon 3200	Nikon 4600	Sony P200	Canon 350D	Canon SD750
Kodak 6490	75.0	22.0	*	*	*	*	*	*
Kodak Z740	21.0	76.7	*	*	*	*	*	*
Nikon D40	*	*	90.9	2.1	*	*	2.0	*
Nikon 3200	*	*	*	75.3	20.2	*	*	*
Nikon 4600	*	*	*	20.4	75.7	*	*	*
Sony P200	*	*	*	*	*	97.1	*	*
Canon 350D	*	*	2.4	2.2	*	*	91.4	*
Canon SD750	*	*	*	*	*	*	*	95.0

Table 6. Confusion Matrix for using 162 features with taking absolute values. Y—horizontal and vertical directions. Rates less than 2% are denoted by *. Average Accuracy=85.4%.

	Kodak 6490	Kodak Z740	Nikon D40	Nikon 3200	Nikon 4600	Sony P200	Canon 350D	Canon SD750
Kodak 6490	75.3	22.8	*	*	*	*	*	*
Kodak Z740	20.2	78.5	*	*	*	*	*	*
Nikon D40	*	*	90.2	2.4	*	*	3.6	*
Nikon 3200	*	*	*	78.4	18.5	*	*	*
Nikon 4600	*	*	*	18.2	77.9	*	*	*
Sony P200	*	*	*	*	*	96.2	*	*
Canon 350D	*	*	3.2	*	*	*	91.2	*
Canon SD750	*	*	*	*	*	*	*	95.0

Table 7. Confusion Matrix for using 162 features without taking difference values of quantized BDCT array. Y—horizontal and vertical directions. Rates less than 2% are denoted by *. Average Accuracy=82.8%.

	Kodak 6490	Kodak Z740	Nikon D40	Nikon 3200	Nikon 4600	Sony P200	Canon 350D	Canon SD750
Kodak 6490	75.0	21.8	*	*	*	*	*	*
Kodak Z740	25.4	72.0	*	*	*	*	*	*
Nikon D40	*	*	88.4	*	2.0	*	2.9	3.1
Nikon 3200	*	*	*	74.4	20.5	*	*	*
Nikon 4600	*	*	*	20.6	74.8	*	*	*
Sony P200	*	*	*	*	*	95.4	*	*
Canon 350D	*	*	3.5	*	*	*	89.2	3.0
Canon SD750	*	*	3.0	*	*	*	*	92.8

values to the quantized DCT coefficients. Again for simplicity, we extract features from horizontal difference JPEG 2-D array of Y component only. The detailed confusion matrix of not taking absolute values is given in Table 5. Table 6 is the confusion matrix with taking absolute values. Comparing those two tables, we find that the average classification accuracy is higher (although not much higher) if we take absolute values before calculating difference.

3.5 Block DCT Coefficients Array Versus Difference JPEG 2-D Array

In our paper, features are only extracted from difference JPEG 2-D arrays instead of from quantized block DCT coefficient arrays because we believe that by taking difference, the statistical difference can be enhanced. We proved this assumption in our experimental work. Table 7 gives us the classification result of the features generated from block DCT coefficient arrays. To make it comparable with Table 6, we extract features from horizontal difference JPEG 2-D array of Y component only. The average classification accuracy is 82.8%, obviously lower than the result in Table 6, which proved our assumption.

3.6 Discrimination Ability by Dimensions and Color Components

In order to find out how much every transition probability matrices calculated along different directions and from different color components contribute to our statistical model. We conducted several experiments in which every part of our statistical model are tested separately. The results are shown and compared in Fig. 8. The horizontal axis in Fig. 8 represents different parts or combined parts. We use h,v,d,m to denote horizontal, vertical, main diagonal and minor diagonal, respectively. It is observed that the discrimination power of features generated along four different directions within one color component does not differ much. The performance of features calculated from Y component is generally better than features from Cb components. Hence, the number of features from Cb component in our statistical model is only half the number of features from Y component. The red bar is the final classification result of our proposed model.

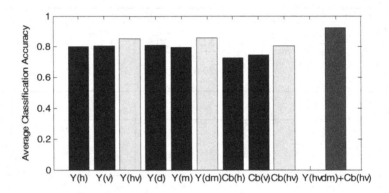

Fig. 8. Classification ability by directions and color components

4 Conclusion and Discussion

Markovian transition probability matrix is used in this paper to build a statistical model which captures statistical difference of difference JPEG 2-D arrays that caused by difference of the image formation pipelines inside different camera models such as different JPEG quantization matrix, different color interpolation algorithms. In total, 486 features are extracted from each image along four directions from Y component and along two directions from Cb component. The results of large-scale experiments have demonstrated the effectiveness of our model.

In this paper, we use YCbCr as our color image model. In fact, this model can also be implemented to other color models such as RGB. Further research will be carried on to study the effect of our proposed model on other color models. Also, we want to mention that for simplicity, in this paper, only one-step Markov transition probability matrix is considered. The m-step (m>1) Markov transition probability matrix can be calculated in the same way, which is also one of our future work.

It is noted that the proposed statistical model can also be used for identify camera models from given uncompressed images such as BMP and TIFF images. In doing so, one only needs to apply the Markov process to difference image pixel 2-D array instead of to difference JPEG 2-D array as detailed in this paper.

In our future work, some feature selection algorithms will also be implemented to further reduce the complexity of our statistical model.

References

1. Choi, K.S., Lam, E.Y., Wong, K.K.Y.: Source Camera Identification Using Footprints from Lens Aberration. In: Proc. of SPIE, pp. 172–179 (2006)
2. Filler, T., Fridrich, J., Goljan, M.: Using Sensor Pattern Noise for Camera Model Identification. In: Proc. of ICIP, pp. 1296–1299 (2008)
3. Lukas, J., Fridrich, J., Goljan, M.: Digital camera identification from sensor pattern noise. IEEE Transactions on Information Forensics and Security 1(2), 205–214 (2006)
4. Swaminathan, A., Wu, M., Ray Liu, K.J.: Non-Intrusive Forensics Analysis of Visual Sensors Using Output Images. In: Proc. of ICASSP, pp. 401–404 (2006)
5. Long, Y., Huang, Y.: Image Based Source Camera Identification Using Demosaicing. In: Proc. of IEEE MMSP, pp. 419–424 (2006)
6. Bayram, S., Sencar, H.T., Memon, N.: Improvements on Source Camera-Model Identification Based on CFA Interpolation. In: Proc. of WG 11.9 Int. Conf. on Digital Forensics (2006)
7. Choi, K.S., Lam, E.Y., Wong, K.K.Y.: Source Camera Identification by JPEG Compression Statistics for Image Forensics. In: TENCON, pp. 1–4 (2006)
8. Kharrazi, M., Sencar, H.T., Memon, N.: Blind Source Camera Identification. In: Proc. of IEEE ICIP, pp. 709–712 (2004)
9. Farid, H.: Digital image ballistics from JPEG quantization. Technical Report TR2006-583, Department of Computer Science, Dartmouth College (2006)
10. Arnia, F., Fujiyoshi, M., Kiya, H.: The use of DCT coefficient sign for content-based copy detection. In: International Symposium on Communications and Information Technologies, pp. 1476–1481 (2007)
11. Tu, C., Tran, T.D.: Context-based entropy coding of block transform coefficients for image compression. IEEE Transactions on Image Processing 11(11), 1271–1283 (2002)
12. Shi, Y.Q., Chen, C., Chen, W.: A Markov Process Based Approach to Effective Attacking JPEG Steganography. In: Camenisch, J.L., Collberg, C.S., Johnson, N.F., Sallee, P. (eds.) IH 2006. LNCS, vol. 4437, pp. 249–264. Springer, Heidelberg (2007)
13. Leon-Garcia, A.: Probability and random processes for electrical engineering, 2nd edn. Addison-Wesley Publishing Company, Reading (1994)
14. Chang, C.-C., Lin, C.-J.: LIBSVM: a library for support vector machines (2001), http://www.csie.ntu.edu.tw/unicode/~cjlin/libsvm.

A Survey of Passive Image Tampering Detection

Wei Wang, Jing Dong, and Tieniu Tan

National Laboratory of Pattern Recognition,
Institute of Automation, Chinese Academy of Sciences,
P.O. Box 2728, Beijing, P.R. China, 100190
{wwang,jdong,tnt}@nlpr.ia.ac.cn

Abstract. Digital images can be easily tampered with image editing tools. The detection of tampering operations is of great importance. Passive digital image tampering detection aims at verifying the authenticity of digital images without any a prior knowledge on the original images. There are various methods proposed in this filed in recent years. In this paper, we present an overview of these methods in three levels, that is low level, middle level, and high level in semantic sense. The main ideas of the proposed approaches at each level are described in detail, and some comments are given.

Keywords: Image Tampering, Image Tampering Detection, Imaging Process, Image Model.

1 Introduction

Traditionally, a photograph implies the truth of what has happened. However, in today's digital age, sometimes seeing is no longer believing, since our modern life is full of digital images and (maliciously) tampering these digital images is easy and simple by using digital processing tools which are widely available (*e.g.* *Photoshop*). Many tampered images emerge in news items, scientific experiments and even legal evidences. Therefore, we cannot take the authenticities of images for granted any more. The tools and techniques that can detect image tampering are highly desirable. Although digital watermarking can be used as a tool to provide authenticity to image, like [1,2], it is a fact that most of images that are captured today do not contain digital watermarks. And this situation is likely to continue for the foreseeable future [3]. Furthermore, the effectiveness and robustness of digital watermark for image tampering detection are not testified yet and the third-party is also needed to license watermarks. Hence, passive image tampering detection is more practical and more important. It aims at verifying the authenticity of digital images without any a prior knowledge, like embedding watermarks in original images. In recent years, more and more researchers focus on image tampering detection, especially on passive methods.

Image tampering detection is a branch of image forensics which aims at assessing the authenticity and the origin of images. The tasks of image forensics can be divided into the following six categories: source classification, device linking, processing history recovery, forgery detection and anomaly investigation

A.T.S. Ho et al. (Eds.): IWDW 2009, LNCS 5703, pp. 308–322, 2009.

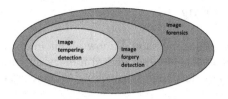

Fig. 1. The relationship among image tampering detection, forgery detection and forensics

[4]. The relationship among (image) tampering detection, forgery detection and forensics can be illustrated in Figure 1. In our opinion, tampering image only means modifying the actual image (either from digital camera, or film camera and then digitally scanned). However, apart from that, forging image also includes computer-generated realistic images.

The past few years have seen a growth of research on passive digital image tampering detection which can be categorized at three levels (similar to those mentioned in [5]):

1. **Low Level.** Methods at this level use statistical characteristics of digital image pixels or DCT coefficients. For example, demosaicing or gamma correction during the image acquiring process will bring consistent correlations of adjacent pixels, whereas tampering will break up this consistency. Investigating double JPEG compression for tampering detection is an example of using statistical characteristics of DCT coefficients. Using a model of authentic images which tampered images do not satisfy for tampering detection also belongs to this level. In short, no semantic information is employed at this level.

2. **Middle Level.** At this level, we detect the trace of tampering operation which has some simple semantic information, like splicing[1] caused sharp edges, blur operation after splicing and inconsistencies of lighting direction, etc.

3. **High Level**, i.e., semantic level. Actually, it is very hard for computer to use semantic information to do tampering detection because the aim of tampering is changing the meaning of image content it originally conveyed. But, sometimes it still works. For example, it does not make sense to have an image in which George W. Bush is shaking hands with Osama bin Laden.

As we know, at least in recent years, computers still have difficulties in high level image analysis. Nevertheless, they can be helpful in middle level and low level analysis. Actually, they are better than human at these two levels [5]. In this paper, we will give an overview of state-of-the-art passive digital image tampering detection techniques. The rest of this paper is organized as follows. In Section 2, we briefly introduce image tampering operation. It is followed by an overview of low level image tampering detection in Section 3 and middle level in Section 4. Finally, our conclusions and discussion will be given in Section 5.

---

[1] Splicing is defined as a simple cut-and-paste operation of image regions from one image onto the same or another image without performing post-processing.

2   Image Tampering

To detect image tampering, we should know about image tampering operation itself first. In [6], the author divided digital forgery operation into six different categories: compositing, morphing, re-touching, enhancing, computer generating and painting.

In fact, almost all state-of-the-art tampering detection technique aims at compositing operation. With powerful image editing tool (*e.g. Photoshop or lazy snapping* [7]), compositing tampered images is much easier and can result in much more realistic images. It always involves the selection, transformation, composition of the image fragments and the retouching of the final image [8]. Here, we want to emphasize that a tampered image means part of the content of a real image is altered. This concept does not include those wholly synthesized images, e.g. images completely rendered by computer graphics or by texture synthesis. In other words, an image is tampered implies that it must contain two parts: the authentic part and the tampered part [9]. All the algorithms introduced later focus on the tampered images defined here.

3   Low Level Digital Image Tampering Detection

Just like the roles of steganography and steganalysis, tampering creators and detectors are opponents. Since it is not hard to use digital image edit tool to make a sophisticated tampered image, which means less trace of tampering operation can be seen from content of the tampered image, many tempering detection algorithms have to focus on imaging process and image statistical characteristics.

3.1   Detection Based on Imaging Process

As we known, a consumer level digital camera consists of a lens system, sampling filters, color filter array, imaging sensor, color interpolation and post-processor as shown in Figure 2 [10]. The lens system collects and controls the light from the scene. It is essentially composed of a lens and the mechanisms to control exposure, focusing, and image stabilization. The light is then focused onto imaging sensor (CCD or CMOS). Because each imaging sensor element is essentially monochromatic, capturing color images requires separate sensors for each color component. However, due to cost considerations, in most digital cameras, only a single sensor is used along with a color filter array (CFA). The CFA arranges pixels in a pattern so that each element has a different spectral filter. Hence, each element only senses one band of wavelength, and the raw image collected from the imaging sensor is a mosaic of different colors. The missing color values for each pixel need to be obtained through color interpolation (demosaicing) operation. The last part of digital camera is post processing like white point correction, image sharpening, aperture correction, gamma correction and compression. The processing in each stage varies from one manufacturer to the other, and even in different camera models manufactured by the same company [3].

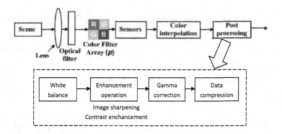

Fig. 2. CCD camera imaging pipeline

As we mentioned above, only one third of the samples in a color images are captured by the camera. The other two thirds are interpolated using color interpolation (demosaicing). This interpolation introduces specific correlations among adjacent pixels of a color image. When tampering a digital image, these correlations may be destroyed or altered. *Popescu* and *Farid* [11] proposed a method based on this judgement. Since the color filters in a CFA are arranged in a periodic pattern, these correlations are periodic. The authors first modeled this interpolated operation linearly. Then, expectation-maximization (EM) algorithm was employed to estimate the probability of pixel being linearly correlated to its neighbors. Finally, the similarity between the probability map of a whole image (or selected window) and corresponding synthetic probability map was calculated to measure the periodic correlations. If the similarity was below a specified threshold, no periodic pattern was assumed to be present in the probability map (i.e. the image region was tampered). In this paper, the authors did some experiments on well-designed images and images acquired from three commercially digital cameras. All the results were promising for non-CFA interpolation detection. The detection method was robust to some operations, like JPEG compression, additive noise, or luminance nonlinearities, to some extent. However, there are some problems such as those listed as follows:

1. Tampered images composed by images from different digital cameras are not tested in their experiment. They have different CFA interpolated regions instead of some CFA interpolated and some non-CFA interpolated regions. Maybe we can expect that the windows including different regions using different interpolation algorithms are lack of the period.
2. If a tampered image is resampled onto a CFA and then reinterpolated, this method will fail. This was also mentioned in the paper, but the authors argued that it required knowledge of the camera's CFA pattern and interpolation algorithm which may be beyond the reach of a novice forger. However, in our opinion, it is harder for detector to achieve it.

To make tampered image more imperceptible, resizing, rotating and stretching are often involved. Although these resampling operations are often imperceptible, they introduce specific correlations into the image. They can be used for tampering detection. Hence, the same authors proposed another approach to detect image tampering based on detecting traces of resampling [12,13]. They used the similar method as that mentioned above to detect the periodic correlations in resampled regions of a tampered image. However, there is a problem. If an authentic image is globally resized with no image content changing, this method will also detect it as tampered image. Besides, other un-resampled parts of the tampered image still have periodic correlations coming from CFA interpolation. Why this method did not detect these regions as having periodic correlations? We think it is because the periodic correlations introduced by resampling and those caused by CFA interpolating are different. In other words, the similarities between a set of synthetic probability maps, which are generated by different resampling parameters, and these CFA interpolated (un-resampled) regions should be quite low so that they can not be detected as resampling regions. Comparing these two techniques, we can find that they seem to be contradictory. One is detect the periodic correlations in resampled regions of a tampered image and the other is detect the lack of periodic correlations in tampered image. Actually, as we just said, the periodic patterns of these two kinds of correlations are different. This may be testified by the similarity between the synthetic probability maps used in these two methods. The similarity score should be very low, if we calculate.

Mahdian and *Saic* [14] also used periodic properties of interpolation caused by resampling for tampering detection. The periodic property of nth derivative (or its variance) of the interpolated signal was demonstrated in this paper. The tampering detection method proposed in this paper was based on a few main steps: ROI selection, signal derivative computation, radon transformation, and searching for periodicity. The detection performance decreased as the order of interpolation polynomial increased, hence, CFA interpolation (most are high order interpolation) were hardly detected by this method. In [15], the authors mentioned that this method was more difficult to detect as each interpolated sample value was obtained as a function of more samples. Furthermore, it also had weak results when the interpolated images were altered by further operations like noise addition, linear or median filtering. In fact, this method has the same problem as [12] has. Noise inconsistency was also used as a clue of tampering occurring [15]. Technique for estimating the variance of the noise on a wavelet component was employed.

Johnson and *Farid* [16] proposed another new approach by inspecting inconsistencies in lateral chromatic aberration as a sign of tampering. Lateral chromatic aberration results from the failure of an optical system to perfectly focus light of different wavelengths. Suppose the positions of short wavelength and long wavelength lighting on the sensor are (x_r, y_r) and (x_b, y_b). Image tampering will lead to inconsistencies in the lateral chromatic aberration, i.e. $(x_r - x_b, y_r - y_b)$. Hence, given an image, the aberration can be estimated from the entire image first, then compare it with estimates from small blocks. Any block that deviates significantly from the global estimate is suspected of having been tampered. The reported experiment results were promising, but for the forensics experiment in their paper, they did not test authentic images. Hence, we do not know about the false alarm rate (the probability of authentic image being detected as tampered image). Besides, this experiment is based on two assumption: only a small portion of an image can be tampered and tampering operation will not significantly affect a global estimate [16].

Inconsistencies of the response function of the camera are used in [5] for tampering detection. *Lin et al.* proposed an approach that computed the response function of the camera by (manual) selecting appropriate patches in different ways. The camera response function is the mapping relationship between the pixel irradiance and the pixel value. The irradiance of the pixel on the edge should be a linear combination of those of the pixels clear off the edges [5]. The linear relationship beaks up among the pixel values because of nonlinear response of the camera. Usually, the camera response function is monotonically increasing with no more than one inflexion point. The response functions of R, G, and B channels are close to each other. Hence, the inverse camera response function, which can recover the linear relationship around edges, is also obey this rules. The features that can reflect these three rules were calculated from each normal or abnormal patch (from tampered part of image) and SVM classifier was used to train to get an effective model in [5]. If the image is tampered, some inverse response functions of the patches along the synthesis edges will become abnormal. However, the author also mentioned that their approach might fail if the component images were captured by the same camera and these components were not synthesized along object edges.

Besides inconsistencies, the absence of some camera intrinsic characteristics can also be used for tampering detection. *Lukáš et al.* [17] used sensor pattern noise to detect digital image forgeries. This method was based on detecting the presence of the camera pattern noise in individual regions in the image. It is a unique stochastic characteristic of imaging sensors. The tampered region was the one that lacks of the pattern noise. This method is only applicable when the tampered image is claimed to have been taken by a known camera or at least, we have other images taken by the camera. In this method, first the camera reference pattern noise was obtained. Then, for a given image, noise residuals and the correlations between noise residuals and camera reference pattern were calculated. Finally, hypothesis testing was used to determining whether the selected regions were tampered or not. Two approaches were proposed in their paper: the user selecting a suspicious area for detecting and automatically searching the tampering area. Lossy compression or filtering can influence the accuracy. *Chen et al* [18] detailed and improved this approach with rigorous mathematical derivation. The detection results are very good. Actually, this approach is device identification mentioned in Section 1. Similarly, *Swaminathan et al.* thought the absence of camera-imposed fingerprints (in-camera and postcamera fingerprints) from a test image indicated that the test image was not a camera output and was possibly generated by other image production processes. Any change or inconsistencies among the estimated in-camera fingerprints, or the presence of new types of postcamera fingerprints suggested that the image has undergone some kinds of processing after the initial capture, such as tampering or steganographic embedding [10]. In-camera fingerprints were estimated using the method mentioned in

[19]. All manipulation operations were considered as filtering. The coefficients of this manipulation filter served as postcamera fingerprints were estimated using blind deconvolution. For a given image, the manipulation filter coefficients were first obtain, and then similarity score between these coefficients and reference pattern was calculated. Finally, threshold was employed to give a decision. This was for global manipulation detection. To locate tampered regions, the authors suggested to divide a test image into several overlapping blocks and estimate the color interpolation coefficients [20] in each block. The k-means clustering algorithm was then employed to cluster these features into two classes. The detection result was satisfying. However, if the test image is composed of more than two kind of camera captured authentic images, clustering two classes will be not reasonable.

Due to JPEG compression is the last step of most digital image devices, both the original and tampered images are possibly stored in this format. Therefore, checking wether a given image having undergone double JPEG compression will be a good method for tampering detection [13]. *Popescu* and *Farid* found that Fourier transforms of DCT histograms of tampered image (with double JPEG compression) had high frequency peaks. *Fu et al.* [21] presented a novel statistical model based on the generalized Benford's to detect double compressed JPEG image. *Luo et al.* [22] designed a blocking artifact characteristics matrix (BACM) and showed that the original JPEG images's BACM exhibited regular symmetrical shape, but for images that were cropped from another JPEG image and resaved as JPEG images, the regular symmetrical property of the BACM was destroyed. Experiments using real tampered images are needed in this method.

However, We should note that the evidence of double JPEG compression does mean tampering occurring. For example, it is possible for a user to simply resave a high quality JPEG image with a lower quality [13]. But if we check the inconsistencies of double JPEG compression image, in other worlds, some regions in the image undergoing twice JPEG compressing and the others undergoing only once or twice compressing with different quality factor, the tampering operation may be detected. Some algorithms checking these inconsistencies are introduced as follows.

Ye et al. believed that when creating a tampered digital image, the resulted image might inherit different kind of compression artifacts from different sources. Hence, these inconsistencies could be used to check image integrity [23]. In their method, suspicious area was selected for evaluation, the other areas were used to estimate the quantization table, and then block artifact measure (BAM) of the image was calculated based on the estimated table. So if blocking inconsistencies are detected, the image will be deemed as suspicious. The block artifact of each block was used to tell where the tampered areas are (high value means high suspicion). *Farid* proposed a technique to detect whether a part of an image was initially compressed at a lower quality than the rest of the image [24]. In his paper, a test image's central region was recompressed at JPEG quality Q_1 lower than its original JPEG quality Q_0. Then it was resaved at various qualities Q_2.

The normalized difference image was calculated as a function of Q_2. The K-S statistic was used to compute the statistical difference between the testing image's central region and the rest of the image. If the K-S statistic for any quality Q_2 exceeded a specified threshold, the image would be classified as manipulated. For an actual tampered image, we can divide the image into several blocks. If the K-S statistic for any quality in any block exceeds the threshold, the image will be classified as tampered image, and the block whose K-S statistic exceeds the threshold will be classified as tampered block.

He et al. [9] proposed a method under an assumption that both tampered and authentic part of a tampered image undergo double JPEG compression. They found that the DCT coefficient histograms of the authentic part had double quantization (DQ) effect (periodic pattern of peaks and valleys), but the histograms of tampered part did not have DQ effects. They thought there were several reasons: the first was that the tampered part might cut from other lossless images; the second was that the DCT grid of the tampered part might mismatch with that of the authentic part; and the third was that $8 * 8$ blocks along the boundary of the tampered part consisted of pixels both from tampered part authentic part. In their paper, for a given image, the periods of the DCT coefficient histograms were firstly calculated. Next, the posteriori probability of a given bin being a tampered block or an authentic block was calculated. And then, a normality map of blocks of image was obtained. Finally, features were extracted from this map using clustering result, and SVM classifier was employed to train and predict. If a test image is detected as tampered one, those blocks whose normalities are below threshold should be considered as tampered ones. The examples shown in the paper were all successfully detected. This method is an excellent working method.

3.2   Detection Based on Image Model

As we know, natural scene images should occupy a highly regularized subspace in the entire image space, and random pixel images take up the rest of the space [8]. If the distribution of the natural scene images is deterministic and fully known, the tampered image is easy to find. However, tampered image creators can also know this distribution, and then they will make a tampered image obeying it so that disable the tampering detection methods using this distribution. Luckily, it is difficult to achieve such perfect distribution. Without a complete model for the natural scene images, the knowledge of the opponent's technique would become a great advantage [8]. Instead of preventing image tampering creators from having a full knowledge of the detection algorithms, the image tampering detectors should make an effort to master image tampering creation process and find some clues to design detection algorithms. In this approach, we need to design a set of features that are sensitive to image tampering and use it to train a model with machine learning algorithms, and then employ this model for predicting the category of a testing image.

Farid and *Lyu* [25] described a statistical model for natural images that is built upon a multi-scale wavelet decomposition. The model consists of first-and higher-order statistics that capture certain statistical regularities of natural images. The image decomposition was based on separable quadrature mirror filters (QMFs). The statistical moments, mean, variance, skewness and kurtosis, of the subband coefficients at each orientation and scale and those of the log error between the actual coefficients and predicted coefficients were combined to form a feature vector of "natural image". In their paper, this image model's effectiveness in steganalysis, distinguishing computer graphics and photograph and classifying live and re-broadcast images were testified by high detection accuracies. However, it was not proofed in tampering detection. In our opinion, it may still work to detection tampering, but only can tell whether a given image is tampered or not. Tampered areas cannot be located with this method. *Bayra et al.* [26] developed several single tools to detect the tampering operation first, and then fused these "weak" detectors together to detect tampering. The feature vectors BSM [27], IQM [28], and HOW [29], which were initially proposed for steganalysis, were used in this paper. In the feature selection process, sequential forward floating search (SFFS) was employed to create a core feature set. *Shi et al.* [30] believed that on one hand, steganography and splicing had different goals and strategies causing different statistical artifacts on images, on the other hand, both of them made the touched (stego and spliced) image different from corresponding original ones. Therefore, they built a natural image model using the features including statistical moments of characteristic functions and Markov transition probabilities from image 2-D array and multi-size block discrete cosine transform 2-D array. A similar approach was proposed in [31]. All the ideas of the methods mentioned above are borrowed from steganalysis. However, how to use such models to distinguish tampered images from stego ones may be a problem.

In the frequency domain, a "natural" signal has weak higher-order statistical correlations. Some "un-natural" correlations will be introduced if this signal is passed through a non-linearity (which would almost surely occur in tampering) [32]. Based on this, *Ng et al.* [33] studied the effects of image splicing on magnitude and phase characteristics of bicoherence (the normalized bispectrum). The difference between means of magnitudes of a test image's bicoherence and its estimating authentic vision's bicoherence and the difference between negative phase entropy of those two were used as features. The classification accuracy was about 63%. The best performance was 71% when these features and edge pixel percentage feature were combined. Theoretical justification for this approach was proposed in [34].

3.3   Other Low Level Image Tampering Detection Algorithms

Although duplicated regions of tampered image can be detected by some of the algorithms mentioned above, there are several targeted techniques for detecting them. Copy-move is a specific type of image tampering, where a part of the image is copied and pasted on another part of the same image. A correlation between the original image part and the pasted one were introduced by copy-move. This correlation can be used as a clue for a detection of this type of tampering [35].

Fridrich et al. [35] chose a block with $B * B$ pixels first, and then slid it by one pixel along row and column. Arriving at each new position, the block values were turned into row vector and stored it into the row of matrix A. The rows of the matrix A were lexicographically ordered. The matching rows were easily searched by going through all rows of the ordered matrix A. For robust matching, quantized DCT coefficients of image were used. *Popescu* and *Farid* [36] applied a principal component analysis (PCA) on small fixed-size image blocks to yield a reduced dimension representation. This representation was robust to minor variations in the image due to additive noise or lossy compression. Similar to [35], duplicated regions were then detected by lexicographically sorting all of the image blocks. The detection accuracy was very good except for the situation that the block sizes are small and the image undergos low JPEG qualities after tampering. *Bayram et al.* [37] proposed to extract features from the image blocks by using Fourier-Mellin Transform. The authors thought these features were not only robust to lossy JPEG compression, blurring, or noise addition, but also to scaling and translation invariant. Both lexicographic sorting method and counting bloom filters were implemented in their paper. Actually, because of using hash function, counting bloom filters can only detected the duplicated blocks which are exactly same.

In fact, using these methods to detect duplicate regions, some flat, uniform areas, such as the sky, may lead to false matches. Furthermore, the more robust the algorithm is, the higher probability of this false matching is.

4   Middle Level Digital Image Tampering Detection

As we know, some image tampering operation will leave some semantic cues that can be used for us to detect tampering, such as splicing caused edges which are sharper and less smooth than other original edges in image. And sometimes there are inconsistencies of lighting direction in the composited image. In this section, we will introduce some techniques that utilize these semantic clues to detect tampering.

Chen et al. [38] thought that spliced image may introduce a number of sharp transitions such as lines, edges and corners. Phase congruency, which had been known as a sensitive measure of these sharp transitions, were used as features for splicing detection. In addition, statistical moments of characteristic functions of wavelet subbands were also employed. Consequently, the proposed scheme extracted image features from 2-D phase congruency and wavelet characteristic functions of image and its predict-error image. Though the experiment results are not bad, feature extraction is time consuming. Actually, both low level and middle level features are used in this method.

Blurring is a very common process in digital image tampering. It could be used to conceal the influence caused by splicing or to remove unwanted defects. Hence, if a suspectable blurring operation is detected in a image, we may say that it may undergo tampering operation. *Hsiao et al.* [39] proposed local blur estimation method. Firstly, a quality factor of blur percentage of whole image was quantified, and then a mapping function between it and threshold (which will be used for determine which parts of image are blurry) was estimated. Therefore, given an image, we can estimate its quality factor first, and then use the mapping function to calculate the threshold. Finally with this threshold we can tell which part of the image is blurry. We should note that there are also blurry parts of authentic image, hence this method cannot provide direct answer to the tampered area. However, if there are blurred regions appearing oddly in focused regions, we should highly doubt these regions [39].

In [40], *Johnson* and *Farid* considered the use of light source direction inconsistencies across an image to detect image tampering. The light source direction was estimated from a given image. Surfaces of known geometry (e.g., plane, sphere, cylinder, etc.) in the image were manually partitioned into approximately eight small patches first, and next three points near the occluding boundary were selected for each patch and fitted with a quadratic curve. And then, the surface normals of each patch were estimated from these curves. Finally, the infinite light source (local and multiple light source can be considered as a single virtual light source) direction was estimated from the surface normals. Hence, if there is inconsistencies of light direction in an image, it will be regard as tampered image. However, there is a restriction in this method, i.e., we should select the patches manually. Another problem is when pictures of both the original and tampered objects were taken under similar lighting or non-directional lighting conditions, the method does not work. The authors proposed another approach [41] which was appropriate in more complex lighting environments containing multiple light sources or non-directional lighting (e.g., the sky on a cloudy day). An arbitrary lighting environment was expressed as a non-negative function on the sphere to make the estimation of the coefficients of lighting environment easy. For tampering detection, an error measure between estimated lighting environments of two different objects in an image was computed. If the error is larger than the threshold, the image will be detected as tampered one. Similarly, they proposed a method to detect tampering through specular highlights on the eye because they were a powerful cue to the shape, color and location of the light source [42]. The known geometry of the eye was exploited to estimate the camera calibration parameters. Then the surface normal of eye and camera view direction were calculated so that the light source direction was worked out.

5   Discussions and Conclusions

There is a growing need for digital image tampering detection. Many techniques, some of which were introduced in this paper, have been proposed to address various aspects of digital image tampering detection. From this survey, we can find that most proposed tampering detection methods aim at detecting inconsistencies in an image, and the majority of them belong to the low level category. Although many of these techniques are very promising and innovative, they have limitations and none of them by itself offers a definitive solution [43].

Actually, with growing attention, image tampering detection encounters some attacks. A targeted attack is a method that avoids traces detectable with one particular forensic technique which the developer of the attack usually knows. *Kirchner* and *Bohme* [44] aimed at attacking against a specific technique to detect trace of resampling in uncompressed images proposed by *Popescu* and *Farid* [12]. They proposed three types of attacks in their paper. Conversely, universal attacks try to maintain or correct as many statistical properties of the image as possible to conceal manipulation even when presented to unknown forensic tools. In this sense, a low quality JPEG compression of tampered images can be interpreted as universal attack [44]. Forensic and counter-forensic techniques play a cat-and-mouse role. Thereby we can believe that such competition is mutually beneficial.

Therefore, we can hope that as more detection tools are developed it will become increasingly more difficult to create convincing tampered digital images. Besides, as the suit of detection tools expands we believe that it will become increasingly harder to target attack each of the detection schemes [13]. However, there are several issues requiring attention when we want to propose new approaches.

1. **Public Image Database and Performance Evaluation.** With more and more tampering detection algorithms being proposed, performance comparison cannot be ignored. Consequently, public image database is urgently needed and it should cover as many kinds of authentic images and diverse tampering manners as possible. The only one public image set [45] is for splicing detection and is a little bit simple. In addition, criteria are required when we compare performances of different algorithms, like ROC curves and location accuracy of tampered region.

2. **Usability.** Many proposed approaches can only detect some kinds of tampering operations. Furthermore, some of them are tested on well-designed tampered images. If we expect image tampering detection techniques to be of practical importance, usability can not be ignored.

3. **Detection Strategy.** There are several techniques based on checking whether some parts of an image undergo some operations that may occur in image tampering. But it will cause some problems. For example, if an authentic image undergoes global scaling or blurring, but image content does not change, these techniques will also consider the authentic image as tampered. Hence, checking inconsistencies of some statistical characteristics of an image for tampering detection is a wise choice.

As image tampering detection is just at its infancy stage, there is still much work to be done and some ideas can be borrowed from other research areas, like techniques developed for camera identification. Also, knowledges from computer vision, signal processing, computer graphics, pattern recognition and imaging process will be needed for further analysis [8].

Acknowledgments. The work presented in this paper was supported by Nature Science Foundation of China (Grant No.60603011).

References

1. Kundur, D., Hatzinakos, D.: Digital watermarking for telltale tamper proofing andauthentication. Proceedings of the IEEE 87(7), 1167–1180 (1999)
2. Rey, C., Dugelay, J.: A survey of watermarking algorithms for image authentication. EURASIP Journal on Applied Signal Processing 2002(6), 613–621 (2002)
3. Sencar, H.T., Memon, N.: Overview of state-of-the-art in digital image forensics, part of indian statistical institute platinum jubilee monograph series titled 'statistical science and interdisciplinary research (2008)
4. Chen, M., Fridrich, J., Goljan, M., Lukas, J.: Determining image origin and integrity using sensor noise. IEEE Transactions on Information Forensics and Security 3(1), 74–90 (2008)
5. Lin, Z., Wang, R., Tang, X., Shum, H.Y.: Detecting doctored images using camera response normality and consistency. In: IEEE Computer Society Conference on Computer Vision and Pattern Recognition, vol. 1, pp. 1087–1092 (2005)
6. Farid, H.: Creating and detecting doctored and virtual images: Implications to the child pornography prevention act. Technical Report TR2004-518, Department of Computer Science, Dartmouth College (2004)
7. Li, Y., Sun, J., Tang, C., Shum, H.: Lazy snapping. In: International Conference on Computer Graphics and Interactive Techniques, pp. 303–308. ACM, New York (2004)
8. Ng, T.T., Chang, S.F., Lin, C.Y., Sun, Q.: Passive-blind image forensics. In: Multimedia Security Technologies for Digital Rights Management. Elsevier, Amsterdam (2006)
9. He, J., Lin, Z., Wang, L., Tang, X.: Detecting doctored JPEG images via DCT coefficient analysis. In: Leonardis, A., Bischof, H., Pinz, A. (eds.) ECCV 2006. LNCS, vol. 3953, pp. 423–435. Springer, Heidelberg (2006)
10. Swaminathan, A., Wu, M., Liu, K.: Digital image forensics via intrinsic fingerprints. IEEE Trans. Info. Forensics and Security 3(1), 101–117 (2008)
11. Popescu, A., Farid, H.: Exposing digital forgeries in color filter array interpolated images. IEEE Transactions on Signal Processing 53(10), 3948–3959 (2005)
12. Popescu, A., Farid, H.: Exposing digital forgeries by detecting traces of resampling. IEEE Transactions on Signal Processing 53(2), 758–767 (2005)
13. Popescu, A., Farid, H.: Statistical tools for digital forensics. In: 6th International Workshop on Information Hiding, pp. 128–147. Springer, Heidelberg (2004)
14. Mahdian, B., Saic, S.: Blind authentication using periodic properties of interpolation. IEEE Transactions on Information Forensics and Security 3(3), 529–538 (2008)
15. Mahdian, B., Saic, S.: Detection and description of geometrically transformed digital images. In: Proc. SPIE, Media Forensics and Security, vol. 7254, pp. 72540J–72548J (2009)
16. Johnson, M., Farid, H.: Exposing digital forgeries through chromatic aberration. In: Proceedings of the 8th workshop on Multimedia and security, pp. 48–55. ACM, New York (2006)
17. Lukáš, J., Fridrich, J., Goljan, M.: Detecting digital image forgeries using sensor pattern noise. In: Society of Photo-Optical Instrumentation Engineers (SPIE) Conference Series, vol. 6072, pp. 362–372 (2006)
18. Chen, M., Fridrich, J., Goljan, M., Lukas, J.: Determining image origin and integrity using sensor noise. IEEE Transactions on Information Forensics and Security 3(1), 74–90 (2008)

19. Swaminathan, A., Wu, M., Liu, K.: Non-intrusive component forensics of visual sensors using output images. IEEE Transactions on Information Forensics and Security 2(1), 91–106 (2007)

20. Swaminathan, A., Wu, M., Liu, K.: Component forensics of digital cameras: A non-intrusive approach. In: Annual Conference on Information Sciences and Systems, pp. 1194–1199 (2006)

21. Fu, D., Shi, Y., Su, W., et al.: A generalized Benford's law for JPEG coefficients and its applications in image forensics. In: Proc. of SPIE Security, Steganography, and Watermarking of Multimedia Contents., vol. 6505, pp. 47–58 (2007)

22. Luo, W., Qu, Z., Huang, J., Qiu, G.: A novel method for detecting cropped and recompressed image block. In: IEEE International Conference on Acoustics, Speech and Signal Processing (ICASSP), vol. 2, pp. 217–220 (2007)

23. Ye, S., Sun, Q., Chang, E.: Detecting digital image forgeries by measuring inconsistencies of blocking artifact. In: IEEE International Conference on Multimedia and Expo, pp. 12–15 (2007)

24. Farid, H.: Exposing digital forgeries form jpeg ghosts. IEEE transactions on information forensics and security 4(1), 154–160 (2009)

25. Farid, H., Lyu, S.: Higher-order wavelet statistics and their application to digital forensics. In: IEEE Conference on Computer Vision and Pattern Recognition Workshop (2003)

26. Bayram, S., Avcıbaş, İ., Sankur, B., Memon, N.: Image manipulation detection. Journal of Electronic Imaging 15(4), 1–17 (2006)

27. Avcibas, I., Memon, N., Sankur, B.: Steganalysis using image quality metrics. IEEE transactions on Image Processing 12(2), 221–229 (2003)

28. Avcibas, I.: Image steganalysis with binary similarity measures. EURASIP Journal on Applied Signal Processing 2005(17), 2749–2757 (2005)

29. Lyu, S., Farid, H.: Steganalysis using higher-order image statistics. IEEE Transactions on Information Forensics and Security 1(1), 111–119 (2006)

30. Shi, Y.Q., Chen, C.-H., Xuan, G., Su, W.: Steganalysis versus splicing detection. In: Shi, Y.Q., Kim, H.-J., Katzenbeisser, S. (eds.) IWDW 2007. LNCS, vol. 5041, pp. 158–172. Springer, Heidelberg (2008)

31. Shi, Y., Chen, C., Chen, W.: A natural image model approach to splicing detection. In: Proceedings of the 9th workshop on Multimedia & security, pp. 51–62. ACM Press, New York (2007)

32. Farid, H.: Detecting digital forgeries using bispectral analysis. Technical report, MIT AI Memo AIM-1657, MIT (1999)

33. Ng, T.T., Chang, S.F., Sun, Q.: Blind detection of photomontage using higher order statistics. In: IEEE International Symposium on Circuits and Systems, vol. 5, pp. 688–691 (2004)

34. Ng, T.T., Chang, S.F.: A model for image splicing. In: IEEE International Conference on Image Processing, vol. 2, pp. 1169–1172 (2004)

35. Fridrich, J., Soukal, D., Lukas, J.: Detection of copy-move forgery in digital images. In: Digital Forensic Research Workshop (2003)

36. Popescu, A., Farid, H.: Exposing digital forgeries by detecting duplicated image regions. Technical report, Department of Computer Science, Dartmouth College

37. Bayram, S., Sencar, H.T., Memon, N.: An efficient and robust method for detecting copy-move forgery. In: IEEE International Conference on Acoustics, Speech, and Signal Processing. (2009)

38. Chen, W., Shi, Y., Su, W.: Image splicing detection using 2-d phase congruency and statistical moments of characteristic function. In: Security, Steganography and Watermarking of Multimedia Contents IX, Proceeding. of SPIE, San Jose, CA, USA (2007)
39. Hsiao, D., Pei, S.: Detecting digital tampering by blur estimation. In: International Workshop on Systematic Approaches to Digital Forensic Engineering, pp. 264–278 (2005)
40. Johnson, M., Farid, H.: Exposing digital forgeries by detecting inconsistencies in lighting. In: Proceedings of the workshop on Multimedia and security, pp. 1–10 (2005)
41. Johnson, M., Farid, H.: Exposing digital forgeries in complex lighting environments. IEEE Transactions on Information Forensics and Security 2(3), 450–461 (2007)
42. Johnson, M., Farid, H.: Exposing digital forgeries through specular highlights on the eye. In: International Workshop on Information Hiding (2007)
43. Gloe, T., Kirchner, M., Winkler, A., Böhme, R.: Can we trust digital image forensics? In: Proceedings of the 15th international conference on Multimedia, pp. 78–86. ACM, New York (2007)
44. Kirchner, M., Bohme, R.: Tamper hiding: Defeating image forensics. In: Furon, T., Cayre, F., Doërr, G., Bas, P. (eds.) IH 2007. LNCS, vol. 4567, pp. 326–341. Springer, Heidelberg (2008)
45. Ng, T., Chang, S., Sun, Q.: A data set of authentic and spliced image blocks. Technical report, DVMM, Columbia University (2004), http://www.ee.columbia.edu/ln/dvmm/downloads/AuthSplicedDataSet/photographers.htm

An Enhanced Statistical Approach to Identifying Photorealistic Images

Patchara Sutthiwan, Jingyu Ye, and Yun Q. Shi

Dept. of ECE, New Jersey Institute of Technology, Newark, New Jersey, USA
ps249@njit.edu, jy58@njit.edu, shi@njit.edu

Abstract. Computer graphics identification has gained importance in digital era as it relates to image forgery detection and enhancement of high photorealistic rendering software. In this paper, statistical moments of 1-D and 2-D characteristic functions are employed to derive image features that can well capture the statistical differences between computer graphics and photographic images. YCbCr color system is selected because it has shown better performance in computer graphics classification than RGB color system and it has been adopted by the most popularly used JPEG images. Furthermore, only Y and Cb color channels are used in feature extraction due to our study showing features derived from Cb and Cr are so highly correlated that no need to use features extracted from both Cb and Cr components, which substantially reduces computational complexity. Concretely, in each selected color component, features are extracted from each image in both image pixel 2-D array and JPEG 2-D array (an 2-D array consisting of the magnitude of JPEG coefficients), their prediction-error 2-D arrays, and all of their three-level wavelet subbands, referred to as various 2-D arrays generated from a given image in this paper. The rationale behind using prediction-error image is to reduce the influence caused by image content. To generate image features from 1-D characteristic functions, the various 2-D arrays of a given image are the inputs, yielding 156 features in total. For the feature generated from 2-D characteristic functions, only JPEG 2-D array and its prediction-error 2-D array are the inputs, one-unit-apart 2-D histograms of the JPEG 2-D array along the horizontal, vertical and diagonal directions are utilized to generate 2-D characteristic functions, from which the marginal moments are generated to form 234 features. Together, the process then results in 390 features per color channel, and 780 features in total Finally, Boosting Feature Selection (BFS) is used to greatly reduce the dimensionality of features while boosts the machine learning based classification performance to fairly high.

Keywords: Moments of Characteristic Functions, Computer graphics classification, boosting.

1 Introduction

Computer graphics (CG) have become more and more photorealistic due to the advancement made in rendering software. As a result, it has become very much

A.T.S. Ho et al. (Eds.): IWDW 2009, LNCS 5703, pp. 323–335, 2009.

difficult for people to visually differentiate them from photographic images (PG). Therefore, high photorealistic CG may be exploited as either a convincing form of image forgery or a replacement of hard-oriented scene in movie production; consequently, identifying CG appears to be an important task in both image forgery detection and a benchmark for rendering software. From a practical point of view, an automatic classification system is certainly more suitable and realizable to deal with this issue than human inspection which is hard to reach high accuracy, confidence and reliability in identifying high photorealistic CG.

The objective of this research is to develop a statistical model-based approach to automatically discriminate CG from PG. The effectiveness of the image feature vector is then evaluated by the classifier in the machine learning (ML) framework, such as Support Vector Machines (SVM) classifier.

In the literatures, several classification systems based on different types of image features have been reported. In [1], modeling characteristics of cartoon plays a crucial role in classifying cartoons, a particular type of CG. The features are extracted from the color saturation, color histogram, edge histogram, compression ratio, pattern spectrum and the ratio of image pixels with brightness greater than a threshold, resulting in the image feature vector of size 108. In [2] image decomposition based on separable quadrature mirror filters (QMFs) was employed to capture regularities inherent to photographic images. Half of features, of size 36, are derived from the first four order statistics of horizontal, vertical and diagonal high-frequency subbands. The other half of features is collected from the same four statistics of the linear prediction error for the high-frequency coefficients. The total number of features is 72 per RGB color channel, yielding a grand total of 216 features. In [3] 192 geometry features are extracted by analyzing the differences existing between the physical generative process of computer graphics and photographic images and characterized by differential geometry and local patch statistics. In [4] and [5], moments of characteristic functions of wavelet subbands are used with HSV and YCbCr color models, respectively. Each color component image is decomposed into three levels using Haar wavelet. At each level $i, i = 1, 2, 3$, there are four subbands (LL_i, HL_i, LH_i, HH_i). Totally, there are 13 subbands involved in the feature extraction if the component image itself is deemed to be a subband at level 0. For each subband, the first three moments are computed, resulting in 39 features. In addition to the component image, its prediction error image is applied to the same process to reduce the influence of image content, so a total of 78 features are the output of a color component. Both two and three color component images are used and reported in [4] and [5], which correspond to 156 and 234 features, respectively.

In this paper, all features were constructed in YCbCr color system using statistical image model based on moment of 1-D and 2-D characteristic functions to separate CG from PG. There are differences between CG and PG. For examples, CG are smoother in color than PG in texture area, but the changes in color intensities from one region to another can be abrupt. Edge and shade of computer graphics hold different characteristics from photographic images. Fewer colors are contained in computer graphics. Scrutinizing how CG and PG generally differ from each other, we are certain that their different nature causes the statistical difference which can be well captured by statistical moments. Therefore, statistical moments of 1-D and 2-D characteristic functions are employed to formulate the statistical model for classification. Per each color component, the moments of 1-D characteristics are partially calculated from the given image pixel 2-D array and all subbands resulted from three-level discrete wavelet decomposition applied to the images. The same process is later applied to the JPEG 2-D array containing the magnitude of all of the quantized block DCT coefficients of the given image, thus producing the other half of moments of 1-D characteristic functions. In addition, one-unit-apart 2-D histogram of the JPEG 2-D array along the horizontal, vertical and diagonal directions are utilized to generate 2-D characteristic functions, from which the marginal moments are generated to from the third part of features. After all, the process will then result in 390 features per one color channel. Here we use only Y and Cb channels in feature formulation to keep computational complexity manageable, resulting in 780 features in total. These moment features together formulate a statistical model for CG and PG. Further, we apply Boosting Feature Selection (BFS) to reduce feature dimensionality, nevertheless, turning in a fairly enhanced classification performance.

The rest of the paper is organized as follows. In Section 2, we discuss the statistical model formation. Next in Section 3, experimental results are shown. Later in Section 4, we detail about Boosting. Finally in section 5, conclusion will be drawn together with the direction for our future work.

2   Image Statistical Model

In this section, the feature formation procedure based on moments of 1-D and 2-D characteristic functions are presented.

2.1   Moments from Image Pixel 2-D Array

The histogram of a digital image is essentially the probability mass function, the characteristic function of which can be calculated by taking the Fourier transform of the histogram. The absolute moments of characteristic function used in our method is defined as [6]

$$M_n = \frac{\sum_{i=1}^{\frac{N}{2}} x_i^n |H(x_i)|}{\sum_{i=1}^{\frac{N}{2}} |H(x_i)|} \qquad (1)$$

where $H(x_i)$ is the characteristic function component at discrete Fourier transform (DFT) frequency x_i, N is the total number of different pixel values in the image. The magnitude of its DFT is symmetric because the histogram is real-valued. Therefore, we can just take half of the points into consideration which much simplifies calculation. Note that here we do not concern $H(x_0)$ due to the fact that $H(x_0)$ indeed represents the total number of pixels in an image, which should not be considered as a distinguishing feature because two different images may have the same resolutions.

Apart from the image itself, the prediction-error image is proposed here to greatly eliminate any domination caused by image content over the statistical differences of CG and PG. In that, we estimate each pixel grayscale value in the original image and form a prediction-error image by subtracting the predicted image from the original image. By doing so, most of the image content can be eliminated by a large degree. Therefore, we believe that the prediction-error image is effective in detecting CG and PG.

For a 2×2 block in image pixel 2-D array, the prediction [7] is given in (2) and Fig. 1.

$$\hat{x} = \begin{cases} \max(a,b) & c \leq min(a,b) \\ \min(a,b) & c \geq max(a,b) \\ a+b-c & \text{otherwise} \end{cases} \tag{2}$$

where a,b are the neighbors of the pixel x. c is at the diagonal position of x,and $\hat{x}$ is the prediction value of x.

Fig. 1. The context of prediction error

Discrete wavelet transform has image decorrelation capability, so features generated from different subbands in the same level are uncorrelated with each other, which is a desired property for classification. In our approach, three-level Haar wavelet transform is used to decompose an image into four subbands for each level, resulting in 12 subbands in total. Adding the original image itself with these 12 subbands, we have totally 13 subbands. For each subband, the first three moments of characteristic functions are computed, resulting in 39 features. We go through the same process for the prediction-error image, which gives us another set of 39 features. Thus, a total of 78 features are formulated from the given image and its three-level DWT decomposition.

2.2 Moments from Image JPEG 2-D Array

JPEG images have been in widely use and the most available format nowadays. In our experiment, all the images are in JPEG format. As the difference in the characteristics between CG and PG may induce the statistical difference on the JPEG coefficients, extracting features in the JPEG domain along with the features generated from the spatial domain would certainly be beneficial. In this paper, JPEG 2-D array is defined as a 2-D array consisting of the magnitude of JPEG coefficients. That is, for a given JPEG image, we apply Huffman decoding, resulting in quantized block discrete cosine transform coefficients arranged in non-overlap and consecutive 8×8 blocks. For each of these coefficients we take magnitude, producing the so-called JPEG 2-D array.

1-D Histogram and Moments of 1-D Characteristic Function. Here only the JPEG 2-D array of a given image is considered. The same fashion as done with the image pixel 2-D array described in Section 1 is done with the JPEG 2-D array, thus generating another set of 78 features.

2-D Histogram and Marginal Moments of 2-D Characteristic Function. As show generally in random signal processing [8] and specifically in steganalysis [7] that 1-D histogram does not carry sufficient information about the correlations among pixels nearby to one another so the usage of the 2-D histogram [9] has been introduced to capture more statistical properties of an image.

The 2-D histogram [9], so-called dependency matrix or co-occurrence matrix, measures the joint occurrence of pairs of pixels separated by a specific distance and orientation and is defined in (3).

$$h_d(j_1, j_2; \rho, \theta) = \frac{N(j_1, j_2; \rho, \theta)}{N_T(\rho, \theta)} \tag{3}$$

where $N(j_1, j_2; \rho, \theta)$ is the number of pixel pairs (j_1, j_2) separated by the distance ρ and angle θ with respect to the horizontal axis and $N_T(\rho, \theta)$ is the total number of pixel pairs in the image separated by (ρ, θ).

Fig. 2. From left to right: horizontal, vertical, diagonal orientation

This joint occurrence implies correlation of the pixels or JPEG coefficients of an image. Therefore, it can be used to differentiate CG from PG on the correlations of JPEG coefficients caused by color distribution and edge information in a given image. We believe that features derived from the 2-D histogram can substantially enhance the discriminative capability of the classifier. In 2-D histogram calculation, the geometric relation between pixels does matter. In this work, horizontal, vertical and diagonal directions with unit distance(shown in Fig. 2) are concerned;in other words, the pairs $(x, a), (x, b)$ and (x, c) in Fig. 1 are separated by $(1, 0), (1, \frac{-\pi}{2})$ and $(1, \frac{-\pi}{4})$.

In our work, we only consider calculating 2-D histograms from the magnitude of the JEPG 2-D array and its three-level wavelets transforms. We then apply the 2-D DFT to 2-D histograms and obtain the 2-D characteristic functions. For each of the three different orientations, we can generate two marginal moments from a 2-D array (one moment for each axis), which can be calculated along the u (horizontal) and v (vertical) axis. The marginal moments [7] of the 2-D characteristic functions are given by

$$M_{u,v} = \frac{\sum_{j=1}^{\frac{N}{2}} \sum_{i=1}^{\frac{N}{2}} u_i^n |H(u_i, v_j)|}{\sum_{j=1}^{\frac{N}{2}} \sum_{i=1}^{\frac{N}{2}} |H(u_i, v_j)|} \tag{4}$$

where $H(u_i, v_j)$ is the 2-D characteristic function component at frequency (u_i, v_j). N is the total number of different absolute values of coefficients in a subband of interest.

In summary, the JPEG 2-D array and its all of three level wavelet decomposition result in 13 2-D arrays. For each 2-D array, we use three different orders, i.e., 1st, 2nd, and 3rd order of two marginal moments. With three orientations, i.e., three 2-D histograms along horizontal, vertical and diagonal direction, we can generate $3 \times 2 \times 13 \times 3 = 234$ marginal moment features from the JPEG 2-D array.

2.3 Block Diagram

Blending the 234 features generated in Section 2.2 with the features generated in the previous sections, we attain $78+78+234 = 390$ features in total from one component image. The comprehensive representation of the whole feature extraction procedure is shown in Fig 3 and detailed whole statistical model is in Fig 4.

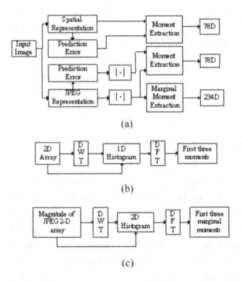

Fig. 3. The comprehensive block diagram of our image statistical model:(a) block diagram, (b) sub-block diagram for moment extraction, (c) sub-block diagram for marginal moment extraction

2.4 Correlation Analysis among Color Components

In this subsection, we reveal an interesting phenomenon from our study on the correlation among the features derived from our proposed method from different color components. In our work, the correlation level is measured by the correlation coefficient $\rho_{X,Y}$ between two random vectors, X and Y, whose expected values are respectively represented by μ_X and μ_Y and standard deviations are by σ_X and σ_Y, and from [8]

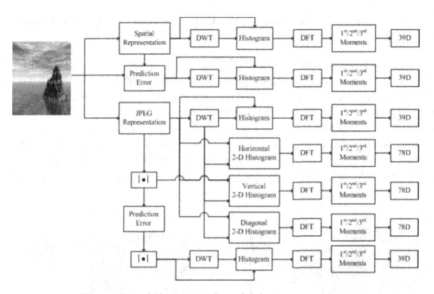

Fig. 4. Detailed statistical model for one component

$$\mu_{X,Y} = \frac{cov(X,Y)}{\sigma_X \sigma_Y} = \frac{E((X - \mu_X)(Y - \mu_Y))}{\sigma_X \sigma_Y} \tag{5}$$

The 390 features per color component were extracted from 3 color components, Y, Cb and Cr, from 4,000 CGs and 4,000 PGs, and then were used as inputs to (5). Therefore, for each class and each combination of two color components, there were 4,000 correlation coefficients which would later be arithmetically averaged and tabulated in Table 1.

Table 1. The arithmetic average of the correlation coefficients of feature vectors from any two color components in YCbCr color system

Color components	ρ_{avg} computed from 4,000 CGs	ρ_{avg} computed from 4,000 PGs
YCb	0.5853	0.6498
YCr	0.5453	0.6095
CbCr	0.9033	0.9239

The resultant statistics has obviously shown that the features generated from Cb and Cr components are much more highly correlated than any other combinations of two components, YCb and YCr. Since the correlation of features from YCb and YCr combination are very close, we can select either of them without significant difference in detection rate. This fact led us to select only Y and Cb components in feature formation process, resulting in 780 features, which can dramatically reduce the computational complexity.

2.5 An Example to Demonstrate Effectiveness of Proposed Image Statistical Model

The scaled 780-feature values derived from two different sets of 100 randomly selected CGs are depicted in comparison with those of PGs in Fig. 5 and in Fig. 6, in which the graphs for CG category are on the left and that of PG on the right, where the horizontal axis defines the index of the 780 features and the vertical axis represents the scaled features values ranging from 0 to 1.

Even though the image contents in those sets of images are totally different, the two feature patterns in the same category displayed in Figs. 5 and 6 closely resemble each other whereas those in different category differ apparently,

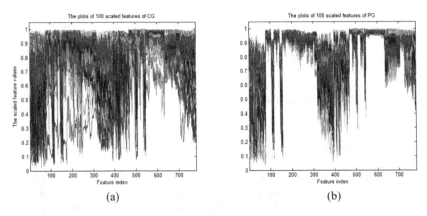

(a)   (b)

Fig. 5. The comparison of CG and PG features from the first sets of 100 images randomly selected from large image datasets of CG and PG: (a) the plots of 100 scaled features of CG and (b) the plots of 100 scaled features of PG

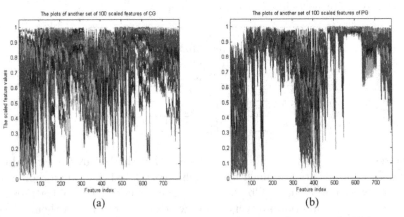

(a)   (b)

Fig. 6. The comparison of CG and PG features from another sets of 100 images randomly selected from large image datasets of CG and PG: (a) the plots of another set of 100 scaled features of CG and (b) the plots of another set of 100 scaled features of PG

which demonstrate that our statistical model can capture the unique statistical pattern of images in each category with less influence on the contents of the images.

3   Experiment

In our simulation, CGs are collected from [10] and [11] where more than 50 redering softwares, for examples 3D Studio Max, After Effects and AutoCad, are used to generate photorealistic images. For PG, a small portion of our image sets are also from [10] while the majority is gathered by our group. We also impose two restrictions on the size of image sets in the experiment: 1) the ratio of the number of PG over that of CG be approximately 2:1 in order to draw a fair comparison with [4] and [5]; 2) the ratio of the total number of images over the dimensionality of features be about or greater than 10. Both constraints imply sufficient statistics. In our experiments, 15,200 PGs and 7,492 CGs are used in simulations.

In order to compare our results with [4], SVM classifier with Radial Basis Function (RBF) kernel is employed as it is used in [4]. The RBF kernel is described in [12].

$$H(x, x') = exp(-\gamma \|x - x'\|^2), \gamma > 0 \qquad (6)$$

where γ is a kernel parameter and here is determined by default calculation of Matlab SVM toolbox. Throughout 20 runs of experiments, we train classifier by randomly selecting 5/6 of images in the sets, and the rest 1/6 of images in the sets are used for testing. The arithmetic average of detection rates is shown in Table 2 where TP (true positive) stands for the correct detection rate of CG, TN (true negative) defines the detection rate of PG, and the accuracy is the arithmetic weighted average of TP and TN. The classification performances of our method are also compared with the best performance reported in [2], [3], and [4]. It is obvious that our proposed 780 features outperform those reported in [2], [3] and [4].

Table 2. Detection rates in percentage (The numbers are shown as reported in [2], [3] and [4] and the mark "-" stands for no information available)

Method	[2]	[3]	[4]	Proposed	BFS
TP	68.6	-	71.9	67.8	85.9
TN	92.9	-	92.3	97.3	96.0
Accuracy	80.8	83.5	82.1	87.6	92.7
Feature size	216	192	243	780	450

4   Performance Boosting

Although the proposed scheme with 780 feature perform well in CG classification, the large number of features leads to high computational complexity, in particular in feature extraction from large number of images. Therefore, we utilize boosting algorithm for feature selection in our work, which is reported in this section.

4.1   Boosting

It is well known that Discrete AdaBoost [13],a learning algorithm, enhances binary classification performance. The logic behind this algorithm is to combine a set of weak classifiers (weak learners) to form a strong classifier in a weighted manner. Given a set of training data $(x_1, y_1), \ldots, (x_m, y_m)$ with a variable of the feature vector x_m and its corresponding label $y_m \in \{-1, 1\}$, where $m = 1, \ldots, M$. (Here +1 denotes the positive samples and -1 the negative ones), one can define:

$$F(x) = \sum_{i=1}^{M} c_m f_m(x) \tag{7}$$

The outline of discrete AdaBoost algorithm is as follows:

1. Start with weights $\omega_i = \frac{1}{N}, i = 1, \ldots, N$,
2. Repeat for $m = 1, \ldots, M$,
   2.1 Fit the classifier $f_m(x) \in \{-1, 1\}$ using weights ω_i on the training data.
   2.2 Compute $err_m = E_\omega[1_{(y \neq f_m(x))}]$, and then $c_m = \log(\frac{1-err_m}{err_m})$
   2.3 Set $\omega_i \leftarrow \omega_i \exp[c_m \cdot 1_{(y_i \neq f_m(x_i))}, i = 1, \ldots, N$, and re-normalize it so that $\sum_i \omega_i = 1$.
3. Output the classifier $sign[\sum_{m=1} M c_m f_m(x)]$.

4.2   Boosting Feature Selection

In [14] BFS algorithm combines AdaBoost and ensemble feature selection together. The effective features for classification are distinctively selected on the basis of lowest weighted error err_m for the given weighted ω_i. As the weight changes, different input variables are selected for the current classifier $f_m(x)$. Mathematically, one can denote:

$$f_m(x) = \beta_m b(x, \gamma_m) \tag{8}$$

where β_m is a multiplier and γ_m is the order of dimensionality of x in the whole input vector, and $b(.)$ denotes the mth column of the input feature vector. In [14], it is stated that one can solve for an optimal set of parameters through a "greedy" forward stepwise approach with updates:

$$\{\beta_m, \gamma_m\} \leftarrow \underset{\beta, \gamma}{\arg \min} E[y - F_{m-1}(x) - \beta b(x; y)]^2 \tag{9}$$

for $m = 1, 2, \ldots, M$ in cycles until convergence, where $\{\beta_m, \gamma_m\}_1^{M-1}$ are fixed at their corresponding solution values at earlier iterations in the algorithm. After several iterations, a powerful classifier could be produced using only a portion of all input variable.

Applying BFS in our work has resulted in 450 features out off 780 features and it is turned out that the classification performance based on our feature selection is even higher than that achieved by the original 780 features, which is shown in the right-most column of Table 2. Specifically, the classification rate with 450 features reaches 92.7%, 5.1% higher than using 780 features.

In Table 3, the SVM classification performances with different numbers of effective features are detailedly shown. It is observed that the maximum detection rate is achieved as 450 features are selected.

Table 3. The SVM classification rates in percentage based on the numbers of selected features (M)

TP	40.12	76.58	80.98	83.68	84.78	86.82	86.22	85.94	84.04	83.04	79.70	74.33
TN	90.07	93.14	93.57	94.35	94.79	95.50	95.78	95.99	96.02	96.03	96.01	96.87
Accuracy	73.58	87.67	89.41	90.83	91.48	92.63	92.62	92.67	92.06	91.74	90.62	89.43
M	10	100	200	300	350	400	425	450	475	500	600	700

Table 4 shows the distribution of 450 selected features from each category in percentage. The statistics in this table can basically tell us the level of contribution of features in each category to classification system.

Table 4. The distribution of 450 selected features from each category in percentage

Spatial 1D CF of Y	JPEG 1D CF of Y	JPEG 2D CF of Y	Spatial 1D CF of Cb	JPEG 1D CF of Cb	JPEG 2D CF of Cb
2.67	12.44	37.78	5.33	12.22	29.56

5 Conclusions and Future Works

Moments of 1-D and 2-D characteristic functions are used in this paper to build a statistical model that captures statistical difference between computer graphic (CG) and photographic image (PG). Feature formation process is conducted in the YCbCr color domain because the report in [5] reveals its superior efficiency to those on several other color systems and the YCbCr color model has been adapted in JPEG.

Based on our correlation analysis in which the features generated from Cb and Cr are strongly correlated, we choose only Y and Cb components as inputs to feature formation, yielding $2 \times 390 = 780$ features in total, which brings out a great reduction in computational complexity.

The time required for feature extracting depends on resolution. For HP Pavilion dv6930us, Core 2 Duo T5750 2GHz, the time ranges from 7.2 to 19.6 seconds and the average feature extraction time on one image over the dataset is about 10 seconds.

For each image, aside from the image itself, i.e., image pixel 2-D array and image JPEG 2-D array, their prediction-error 2-D arrays in both domains are also employed in feature extraction in order to reduce the influence caused by image content. All of them are afterward decomposed into three-level wavelet subbands. Thus, a total number of 156 features are generated from each color component. With Y and Cb two components, a total number of 312 features are derived. The discrete wavelet transform (DWT) is adopted because of its superior decorrelation capability. The coefficients of different subbands at the same level are uncorrelated to each other, so the features extracted at the same level but from different subbands are also uncorrelated.

Next, we add features from 2-D histogram since it has been represented in [7] and [9] that 1-D histogram does not provide enough statistical information of an image and the usage of 2-D histogram together with 1-D histogram in feature formation can reinforce such information. For 2-D histogram feature generation, only JPEG 2-D array and its prediction error 2-D array are exploited to form 234 features from the marginal moments of one-unit-apart 2-D histograms of the JPEG 2-D array along the horizontal, vertical and diagonal directions. With two color components, 468 features are generated from the marginal moments of 2-D characteristic functions. In this way, for each color image, we have totally 312+468=780 features in our CG classification scheme.

Because some features possibly do not statistically represent the image well, i.e., there is some redundancy among 780 features, we need feature selection to way-out this problem. Therefore, we apply boosting feature selection (BFS) technique to select some effective features to distinguish between computer graphic images and photo graphic images. Specifically, we applied well-known Discrete AdaBoost for feature selection. Our experimental results have shown that with 450 selected features the system outperforms the original 780 features by 5.1% in classification rate. In this way, the boosting feature selection technique has shed light to our further work. One of our work in progress is to combine different types of features before applying Boosting Feature Selection to reduce the dimensionality of the heterogeneous features, while increasing the detection rate substantially.

In a nutshell, our proposed statistical model can well capture the statistical different between CG and PG. With the boosting feature selection, the classification performance achieved by the original 780 features, 87.6%, is increased to 92.7% with only using 450 features to characterize an image. The final result, 92.7%, is much higher than prior arts, indicating a significant advancement we have achieved.

Acknowledgement

Authors would like to express their sincere gratitude to Mr. Xiao Cai and Mr. Guanshuo Xu for their kind support for running feature extraction algorithm partially over the image database and to Ms. Jing Dong for her time and effort for introducing Boosting Feature Selection algorithm to us.

References

[1] Ianeva, T., de Vries, A., Rohrig, H.: Detecting cartoons: a case study in automatic video-genre classification. In: Proceeding of IEEE International Conference on Multimedia and Expro (ICME 2003), vol. 1, pp. 449–452 (2003)

[2] Lyu, S., Farid, H.: How realistic is photorealistic? IEEE Transactions on Signal Processing 53, 845–850 (2005)

[3] Ng, T.-T., Chang, S.-F., Hsu, J., Xie, L., Tsui, M.-P.: Physics-motivated features for distinguishing photographic images and computer graphics. In: Proceeding of ACM Multimedia, Singapore (November 2005)

[4] Chen, W., Shi, Y.Q., Xuan, G.: Identifying computer graphics using HSV color model and statistical moments of characteristic functions. In: Proceeding of IEEE International Conference on Multimedia and Expo. (ICME 2007), Beijing, China, July 2-5 (2007)

[5] Chen, W.: Detection of Digital Image and Video Forgeries, Ph.D. Dissertation, Department of Electrical and Computer Engineering, New Jersey Institute of Technology (2008)

[6] Shi, Y.Q., Xuan, G., Zou, D., Gao, J., Yang, C., Zhang, Z., Chai, P., Chen, W., Chen, C.: Steganalysis based on moments of characteristic functions using wavelet decomposition, prediction-error image, and neural network. In: Proceeding of International Conference on Multimedia and Expo. (ICME 2005), Amsterdam, Netherlands (2005)

[7] Chen, C., Shi, Y.Q., Chen, W., Xuan, G.: Statistical moments based universal steganalysis using JPEG-2D array and 2-D characteristic function. In: Proceeding of Proceeding of IEEE International Conference on Image Processing (ICIP 2006), Atlanta, Georgia (2006)

[8] Leon-Garcia, A.: Probability and Random Processes for Electrical Engineering, 2nd edn. Addison-Wesley Publishing Company, Reading (1994)

[9] Pratt, W.K.: Digital Image Processing, 3rd edn. John Wiley & Sons, Inc., Chichester (2001)

[10] Columbia University DVMM Research Lab: Columbia Photographic Images and Photorealistic Computer Graphics Dataset

[11] http://www.creative-3d.net, http://www.creative-3d.net and

[12] Abe, S.: Support Vector Machines for Pattern Classification, 1st edn. Springer, Heidelberg (2005)

[13] Friedma, F., Hastie, T.: Additive logistic regression: a statistical view of boosting. An Official Journal of the Institute of Mathematical Statistics (2002)

[14] Tieu, K., Viola, P.: Boosting image retrieval. In: Proceeding of IEEE Conference on Computer Vision and Pattern Recognition (2002)

Author Index